# Remembering Histories of Trauma

# Remembering Histories of Trauma

## North American Genocide and the Holocaust in Public Memory

GIDEON MAILER

BLOOMSBURY ACADEMIC
LONDON • NEW YORK • OXFORD • NEW DELHI • SYDNEY

BLOOMSBURY ACADEMIC
Bloomsbury Publishing Plc
50 Bedford Square, London, WC1B 3DP, UK
1385 Broadway, New York, NY 10018, USA
29 Earlsfort Terrace, Dublin 2, Ireland

BLOOMSBURY, BLOOMSBURY ACADEMIC and the Diana logo are trademarks of Bloomsbury Publishing Plc

First published in Great Britain 2022



Cover image: The Holocaust Memorial, Miami Beach. Detail of *A sculpture of Love and Anguish* by Kenneth Treister, Miami, USA. Godong / Bridgeman Images



A catalogue record for this book is available from the British Library.
A catalog record for this book is available from the Library of Congress.

ISBN: HB: 978-1-3502-4062-9
PB: 978-1-3502-4063-6
ePDF: 978-1-3502-4065-0
eBook: 978-1-3502-4064-3

Typeset by RefineCatch Ltd, Bungay, Suffolk NR35 1EF, UK

To find out more about our authors and books, visit www.bloomsbury.com and sign up for our newsletters.

# CONTENTS

*List of Figures* vii
*Preface* ix

Introduction: Indigenous and Jewish Worlds of Trauma 1

**PART ONE** Theory

1 "Humanitarian feelings . . . crystallized in formulae of international law."
Biological Determinism and the Problem of Perpetrator Intent 17

2 "Metaphysical Jew Hatred" and the "Metaphysics of Indian-hating."
Public Memory and the Problem of Imperial Power 45

**PART TWO** North America

3 "We are waiting for the construction of our museum."
Indigenous People, Jews, and the North Americanization of the Holocaust 61

4 "The shrines of the soul of a nation."
Traumatic Memory, Assimilation, and Vanishing in North America 89

**PART THREE** Europe

5 "A permanent statement of our values."
Indigenous Genocide, the Holocaust, and European Public Memory 111

6 "The void has made itself apparent as such."
Placing Group Memory in Public History 137

Conclusion 157

*Notes* 167
*Select Bibliography* 237
*Index* 271

# FIGURES


0.1 "Keep America Beautiful," (ad campaign poster), Iron Eyes Cody, *c.* early 1970s. 4
0.2 Brazilian street artist Eduardo Kobra and his assistant work on a large graffiti artwork of Anne Frank at the shipyard at Amsterdam's NDSM shipyards, September 2016. 4
1.1 National Day of Remembrance of the Greek Jewish Witnesses and Holocaust Heroes, in Thessaloniki, Greece, January 2020. 24
1.2 Mike Bear Comesout, of the Northern Cheyenne, ties a wight flag under the American flag during the dedication of the Sand Creek Massacre National Historic Site. 29
1.3 Chaplain Samuel Blinder examines one of hundreds of "Saphor Torahs" (Sacred Scrolls) in the cellar of the Race Institute in Frankfurt, Germany, July 1945. 39
1.4 People watch as a convoy of truckers and other vehicles travel in front of the former Kamloops Indian Residential School in support of the Tk'emlups te Secwepemc people, June 5, 2021. 43
3.1 Replica of Massasoit by Cyrus E. Dallin in Front of the Utah State Capitol. 72
3.2 Teepees at the National Museum of the American Indian, Washington, D.C. 80
3.3 National Holocaust Monument, Ottawa, Canada. Aerial view with Sky Void and Stairs of Hope. 83
3.4 US President Barack Obama and Elie Wiesel, Holocaust survivor and Founding Chairman of the United States Holocaust Memorial Council, are reflected in a wall in the Hall of Remembrance at the United States Holocaust Memorial Museum, April 2012, Washington, D.C. 86
5.1 The atrium of the Royal Museum of Ethnology in Berlin, Germany, 1887. 112
5.2 Karl May Museum, "Villa Shatterhand," in Radebeul bei Dresden, Germany, 1995. 115
5.3 Prince Charles, Prince of Wales, Camilla, Duchess of Cornwall, German President Frank-Walter Steinmeier, and First Lady Elke Buedenbender visit the Neue Wache Memorial to Victims of War and Tyranny in Berlin, November 2020. 119

5.4 A boy hops from one to another of the 2,711 stellae at the Memorial to the Murdered Jews of Europe, also called the Holocaust Memorial, Berlin, October 2013. 120
5.5 French President Jacques Chirac gives a speech at the inauguration of the Musée du quai Branly, Paris, June 2006. 122
5.6 Dr. Fritz Klein, camp "doctor" at Bergen-Belsen concentration camp, makes a statement into a microphone set up by the BBC's Richard Dimbleby, in front of a mass grave of primarily Jewish victims, after the camp had been turned over to the Allied 21st Army Group, April 1945. 125
5.7 Soviet-built memorial to Holocaust victims adjacent to the IX fort (out of thirteen), where thousands of Jewish people were executed, Kaunas, Lithuania. January, 2017. 131
6.1 Visitors at the entrance to the underground Information Centre at the Memorial to The Murdered Jews of Europe, Berlin, Germany, 2005. 139
6.2 Interior architecture of the Memory Void room at the Jewish Museum in Kreuzberg, Berlin, Germany, 2001. 141
6.3 The monument commemorating the victims of racist and anti-Semitic persecutions in Paris, during a ceremony marking the anniversary of infamous 1942 Vél'd'Hiv' round-up of 13,000 French Jews. 143
6.4 Richard LeBeau from South Dakota looks at a Ghost Dance Shirt that had been held in the Kelvingrove Art Gallery in Glasgow since 1882, November 1998. 146
6.5 Interior gallery, Pitt Rivers Museum, Oxford. 149
6.6 The Ziibiwing Center of Anishinabe Culture & Lifeways, a museum operated by the Saginaw Chippewa Indian Tribe of Michigan, 2019. 151
6.7 Stolpersteine (stumbling blocks) erected in memory of the Jewish Marcuse family, in Gipsstrasse, Mitte, Berlin. 155

# PREFACE

I began thinking about this project nearly two decades ago, after flying from London to Denver, Colorado, to intern on public history projects with the Colorado Historical Society (now known as History Colorado). I spent time considering the treatment of people as objects and the subsequent treatment of their remains, including clothes retrieved from their corpses by museums and memorials. Some of those thoughts were inspired by discussions about the 1864 Sand Creek Massacre, when members of Colorado Cavalry units exterminated more than 150 (some estimate up to 500) Cheyenne and Arapaho people. A few members of the cavalry units are thought to have refused orders. A diverse team of researchers, curators, and public historians educated me about the tricky role of public history and public memory in the area. Near the Colorado Capitol Building, where I often sat eating my lunch, a large statue erected in the first decade of the twentieth century honored the Colorado soldiers who fought and died for the Union in the US Civil War, in part to prevent the expansion of slavery in the United States. But as I learned, a few also took part in the Sand Creek Massacre, including Colonel John M. Chivington, who infamously stated "Damn any man who sympathizes with Indians . . . Kill and scalp all, big and little; nits make lice." The year before the massacre, the Rocky Mountain News had called for "extermination against the red devils."[1] I arrived in Denver a year after the Colorado Historical Society and the Colorado General Assembly authorized an explanatory plaque on the existing monument in Denver that "mischaracterized" the massacre as a battle during the Civil War era.

Several years later, I would read a poem by Tiffany Midge, who is an enrolled member of the Standing Rock Sioux. The poem described viewing the "Holocaust Museum's Room of Shoes and a Gallery of Plains' Indian Moccasins," in Washington D.C., in which the latter was displayed as "artifact" in contrast to the former as "atrocity." Though associated with Indigenous histories of trauma, the poem suggests, the retrieval and display of moccasins is used to define hazy cultural ideals rather than to represent the specific murder of populations. The poem contrasts that status with the display of shoes from murdered Jews in other Washington D.C. exhibitions. Yet I had recently viewed displays of Holocaust materials in European and North American institutions that reduced their specific meanings and even their association with Jewish loss, in a structural parallel with the evasion of Indigenous suffering identified by Tiffany Midge. Given that many members of my own family were exterminated during the Holocaust, I have given considerable thought to such questions and allusions while making my way through the material that now forms this book, which has contributed to one of two parallel research tracks in my career as a Title A Fellow at St. John's College, University of Cambridge, and as a member of the history department at the University of Minnesota, Duluth. My work in both tracks highlights how painful historical events such as the American Revolutionary wars, the consolidation of transatlantic slavery, or the murder of Jews and Indigenous people have impacted the way moral, religious, and philosophical ideas are subsequently understood and represented.[2]

Since 2016, the scope and content of this book has benefited from my ongoing engagement with public history and museum studies as chair of the History Program at the University of Minnesota, Duluth, a position which I am due to conclude as this work is published. I have learned from other department members as we have spearheaded a new public history and museum studies track for undergraduates, helping them to negotiate the tension between group history and public memory to enter full time employment in cultural, civic, and educational institutions. I have also learned much from the pioneering work of my colleagues in the Department of American Indian Studies, led by Jill Doerfler (White Earth Anishinaabe) as well as the cutting-edge work in Indigenous studies of those such as Jennifer Gómez Menjívar who are homed in other departments; not least the need to ground our efforts in public history and museum studies in light of the university's Land Acknowledgment, which reminds us that our place of work and research is "located on the traditional, ancestral, and contemporary lands of Indigenous people . . . land that was cared for and called home by the Ojibwe people, before them the Dakota and Northern Cheyenne people, and other Native peoples from time immemorial." I live only a Greyhound Bus ride away from neighboring South Dakota, where on December 29, 1890, a massacre at Wounded Knee occurred—a bloodbath that Tiffany Midge references in her poem.

American Indian people in northern Minnesota join other Indigenous communities across North America in encountering public institutions that overlook, de-specify, or universalize their histories of trauma as well as occluding the resulting importance of tribal sovereignty as a parallel form of cultural and jurisdictional autonomy. As I have learned more about these tensions and ambiguities in the memory work of my adopted home state, and thanks to advice and critiques from readers and reviewers of the material in this book, I have tried to avoid using my understanding of the representation of the Holocaust to make normative claims about the public representation of Indigenous histories, and to foreground Indigenous methodologies and authors alongside parallel insights from Holocaust studies without identifying either as a definitive category for the other.

While writing this book, I have become more aware how far European civilizational rhetoric is confounded by the experience of Indigenous people in North America. The legacy of interventions by French, British, Dutch, Spanish, Russian, and other Europeans can be traced in Indigenous memories of trauma—all despite the aloofness, even smugness, that is often apparent in European conceptions of Indigenous dispossession as somehow an "American" issue. While visiting Glasgow, Scotland, for example, I became aware of historical controversies at the city's Kelvingrove Art Gallery and Museum. Through the 1990s, the display of a Lakota Sioux Ghost Dance Shirt demonstrated the tendency of British institutions to overlook their historical role in Indigenous cultural genocide. The shirt is thought to have been obtained by a US soldier from the body of a deceased Native American man during the massacre at Wounded Knee. The Glasgow museum initially claimed to offer a site of neutral protection for the shirt, without realizing how such a justification overlooked the fraught legacy of the British imperial interventions that underlay Indigenous death, including at Wounded Knee.

Through this project I have asked myself how, if at all, we can compare the memory of the removal of shirts from dead Indigenous bodies in settler-colonial contexts to that of stolen clothes from murdered Jews in towns like Vilnius in Lithuania, where much of my family was exterminated, likely some of the 80,000 Jews who were shot dead by Nazis and Lithuanian allies near a railway station. As Kazimierz Sakowicz, a Polish witness, noted in July 1941, "Since July 14 [Jewish victims] have been stripped to their underwear. Brisk business in clothing." An August 1–2 entry suggested, "For the Germans 300 Jews are 300 enemies of humanity; for the Lithuanians they are 300 pairs of shoes, trousers, and the like." On August 22 he concluded, "the Germans have been taking the valuables, leaving the Lithuanians with the clothes and the like." On November 21, a "Shaulist" [a Lithuanian volunteer allied with Nazis] responded to another local Lithuanian who asked him if he could buy a coat for his wife with "Let them wait," so that he could "choose" a woman the same size as the man's wife at one of the line-ups of soon-to-be-dead Jews.[3]

Further research has revealed Rachela Auerbach's description of the site around the Treblinka extermination camp as "a Polish Colorado"—a site where non-Jewish villagers near the camp bartered and traded with Nazis and their local allies who sold and bought objects and services from the camp workers, as well as objects from dead or doomed Jewish arrivals. They excavated mass graves for anything of worth from Jewish bodies, making "the former Jewish dustbin of things, which is turned into Polish Colorado, dug up, a carefully-searched golden field."[4] Writing in 2013, Sławomir Buryła drew similar allusions while discussing the phenomenon in which local villagers dug for gold from the teeth of Jewish corpses buried around Nazi Death Camps. "Jewish gold—as it did for the Spanish Conquistadors," according to Buryla, possessed "the magical power. . . . the gold fever . . . as raging and impossible to control as in the times of Cortez and of the nineteenth-century American pioneers in the wild West . . ."[5] The dispossession, dehumanization, and murder of Indigenous people followed the Gold Rush in nineteenth-century America, particularly in California but also in Colorado, as settlers destroyed communities who were in the way of material riches. In the case of dead Jews outside the Treblinka site, gold was mined from their teeth. And so, I have asked what a phrase like "Polish Colorado" might mean to Indigenous people, Jews, and anybody else concerned with public memory. Is such a phrase too metaphorical, too relativistic, too likely to superimpose one history of trauma onto another? Or are such comparisons useful and even vital? Do comparisons contribute to the relativization, abstraction, and universalization of memory in problematic ways? Or are they in fact necessary to critique those approaches?

I would like to thank Maddie Holder at Bloomsbury for all her support and her expert advice on this project. It has been more than a privilege to work under the editorial expertise of a historian and professional publisher like Maddie. I am also grateful to Abigail Lane for all her editorial assistance at Bloomsbury. The comments and advice from the four anonymous reviewers in the two stages of review has been indispensable, challenging my unthinking assumptions and raising new concepts and ideas. At UMD, Natalie Belksy's early reading of material came at a pivotal moment. Dr. Belsky's work with Deborah Peterson-Perlman and the rest of the Baeumler Kaplan Holocaust Commemoration Committee at UMD has continued to inspire this project. I am indebted to Steve Matthews for leading the committee that hired me, in part, because of my interests in public history, and for his work alongside David Woodward in creating the public history and museum studies program in our department. Cynthia Rugeley has offered immense support and guidance along with the Dean of the College of Liberal Arts, Jeremy Youde. I also thank other colleagues in my department, including Geraldine Hughes, Rosemary Stanfield-Johnson, Steffan Spencer, Scott Laderman, Jeffrey Rop, and Qiang Fang.

I owe a debt of gratitude to Modupe Labode, then Chief Historian at the Colorado Historical Society and now curator at the National Museum of American History, who allowed me to work that summer in Denver, as well as Brian Shaw, who inspired me in his work as manager of the Historic Marker Program and who has since become a close friend. I thank Martin Woolf for having read portions of this work at another important stage in its development, as well as the editorial assistance I have received from Heather Dubnick and Lisa Carden. As ever, I thank the historians who have also become mentors, such as Betty Wood, Mary Beth Norton, Sylvia Frey, Hillary Stroh, and Sylvana Tomaselli. During the final months of writing this book, it has been devastating to lose Betty and Sylvia.

And of course, there are my parents, who escorted me on trips to Auschwitz and to former ghettos and museums and archival centers in Warsaw, Prague, Krakow, Berlin, and Budapest. My mother also accompanied me to the infamous *Irving versus Penguin* trial in early 2000, where she practically had to restrain me from asking Richard J. Evans, Anthony Julius, and Deborah Lipstadt for their autographs. And I must thank my grandmother, whose husband's family were wiped out in the Holocaust, but who herself turned 100 in quarantine on the other side of the Atlantic during the final months of writing this book.

With my grandmother and others, I share a group memory of trauma that has stimulated further research, reading, site visits, and discussions with survivors—all the stuff of objective historical scholarship, countering those who suggest that group memory is too subjective and emotional to be connected to the neutral work of historiography. As well as my grandmother, I learn from those such as Halina Birenbaum, who was born in Warsaw in 1929 and is still alive today as a survivor. The titles of Birenbaum's books are relevant to the following chapters of this study, which consider the despair that sometimes follows the realization that traumatic memories are not matched or recognized in public sites. But the titles are also germane to the continuation of hope despite the public tendency to occlude those histories of trauma; what Indigenous scholars such as Gerald Vizenor describe as "survivance"—the ability to remember and represent historical suffering while avoiding the assumption that communities are prone to vanish or suffer the irrevocable loss of cultural vitality. The titles by Birenbaum include: *Hope Is the Last to Die* (Nadzieja umiera ostatnia), *Scream for Remembrance* (Wołanie o pamięć), *Far and near echoes* (Echa dalekie i bliskie), *Life Is Dear to Everyone* (Życie każdemu drogie), *My Life Began from the End* (Moje życie zaczęło się od końca), *They Still Ask* (Wciąż pytają), *Return to Ancestors' Land*, (Każdy odzyskany dzień: Wspomnienia), *Every Recovered Day: Memories*, and finally, *I Am Looking for Life in the Dead* (Szukam życia u umarłych).

Those are the words—the memory work—of Halina Birenbaum. Thanks to the work of organizations such as the United States Holocaust Memorial Museum (USHMM) and their collection of testimonies, I am also reminded of the survival of women like Agi Geva. Their words can, perhaps, speak to Indigenous conceptions of survivance, and vice versa. In testimony delivered to the USHMM in 2019, Agi remembers waking up after a dream thinking she was still in a concentration camp, only then to discern that there was in fact "music coming from somewhere, mixed with the chirping of birds . . ."

*September 2021, Duluth, Minnesota.*

# Introduction

# Indigenous and Jewish Worlds of Trauma

Hidden behind large bushes of tropical pink flowers, Sephardic Jews once covered the floors of their Caribbean synagogues with white beach sand to muffle their prayers. They fled Iberian inquisitions that continued to hound and murder them as they tried to escape Europe for Recife in Brazil, Cartagena in Colombia, and islands such as Curaçao in the present-day Dutch Antilles and what is now St. Thomas in the US Virgin Islands.[1] Making their way to and from precarious South American, Central American, and Caribbean entrepôts through the 1600s, some eventually settled in New Amsterdam and later New York, as well as Rhode Island, Savannah, Charleston, and Philadelphia.[2] Others may even have escaped to the Spanish borderlands of "Vast Early America," which stretched into present-day Colorado and New Mexico, and where to this day, some ostensibly Catholic women light candles every Friday night, and have begun to ask: *Why*?[3]

The obsession with purity of blood (*limpieza de sangre*) in Iberian pogroms against Jews preceded and then coincided with the development of violent racism in European imperialism—a separate phenomenon that directly led to the death of millions of the first people of what Europeans came to describe as the Americas.[4] In the paranoid fantasies of a few sixteenth-century Spanish imperial agents, some of those people were suspected to be secret Jews, either descended from the lost tribes of Israel or from more recent Iberian communities.[5] But in their fervent desire for land and resources, most Europeans were not required to think of indigenous nations as Jews to motivate their murder or dispossession. That they were not members of their own nations and religions was more than enough to contribute to the disruptive and sometimes murderous interventions of Spanish, Portuguese, English, Scottish, French, Dutch, Swedish, Danish,

Russian, and other European colonial states from the 1500s through the 1800s. The actions and attitudes of those European colonizers, according to new scholarship, influenced the later approach of independent white settlers and their supporters in state and federal governments during the western expansion of the United States from the American Revolution through the final decades of the nineteenth century, as well as during the consolidation of Canadian independence from Britain and in Canadian land disputes with the United States. Whether under colonial European jurisdiction or during the later period of American and Canadian independence, European-descended perpetrators disrupted and sometimes destroyed Indigenous communities in what came to be known as continental North America.[6] Scholars have begun to group those cases from the 1500s to the 1900s under the broader historical category of North American genocide.[7] Though often focused on intentional massacres by colonial European, American, or Canadian settlers, that category also includes the disruptive human intent that led to slavery, dispossession, and the degradation of Indigenous health and immunity—structural, systemic, and settler-colonial interventions that contributed to the demographic nadir that Native American, First Nations, Inuit, and Métis people experienced at the end of the nineteenth century.[8]

The late-nineteenth-century population nadir of Indigenous people in North America coincided with the mass migration of Ashkenazi Jews to the same continental region. Near the harbor of what the Lenape first called *Manahatta*, American Sephardi communities and surviving Indigenous nations witnessed the newer arrival of Ashkenazim who fled Eastern European pogroms. A *New York Times* report from a 1903 pogrom in Kishinev, Bessarabia, in present day Moldova, described the "well laid-out plan for the general massacre of Jews on the day following the Orthodox Easter . . . the general cry, 'Kill the Jews', was taken up all over the city. The Jews were taken wholly unaware and were slaughtered like sheep . . . The scenes of horror attending this massacre are beyond description. Babies were literally torn to pieces by the frenzied and bloodthirsty mob. The local police made no attempt to check the reign of terror. At sunset the streets were piled with corpses and wounded. Those who could make their escape fled in terror, and the city is now practically deserted of Jews."[9] Such massacres motivated hundreds of thousands of Jews to migrate to North America between 1880 and 1924, when immigration was restricted in the United States and Canada.[10]

Those Jews who remained in Eastern Europe, as well as their co-religionists in other parts of the continent, would soon experience a catastrophic and irrevocable population collapse that included the murder of 1.5 million children. Merely two decades after the final boats of Jewish migrants arrived in North America, most Jews in Germany, Hungary, the Netherlands, Poland, Lithuania, Latvia, Yugoslavia, Czechoslovakia, and in the ancient Sephardi community of Salonika had been murdered. Many were tortured or treated with unimaginable sadism by Nazis and some of their non-German allies.

Huge portions of the Jews of France, Greece, Romania, Scandinavia, and Italy had suffered the same fate. Three Jewish women (Marianne Grunfeld, Auguste Spitz, and Therese Steiner) were even deported to Auschwitz from the irenic Channel Island of Guernsey, so close yet so far from the relative safety of mainland Britain.[11] A massive Nazi German bureaucratic push—allied with the murderous, chaotic, and often opportunistic blood lust of German and non-German local perpetrators—had tried to ensure that no single Jew could be allowed to live on Earth; the necessary biological elimination of a diabolical and even metaphysical force—*Jewishness*—that Nazis defined as the only power that could truly undermine their ideological goals.[12] The descendants of those who fled European pogroms for North America thus found themselves in a global Jewish community that had suddenly entered its demographic nadir. They became aware of that terrible milestone only a half-century after the surviving Indigenous peoples of North America met their own horrible statistic.

*Remembering Histories of Trauma* examines and compares how the events leading to those separate nadirs have been represented in European and North American public spaces from the nineteenth century to the present day. It considers what Alain Finkielkraut has identified as the contradiction "between Memory and Metaphors that gradually replace the event of which they are the reminder."[13] Though Finkielkraut published his maxim in a discussion of the ambiguous trajectory of Holocaust remembrance among Jewish and non-Jewish Europeans, it is also useful to approach the distinction between Indigenous histories of population loss—including genocide—and their representation by non-Indigenous people in the broader public sphere in Europe and North America. Indigenous people and Jews are frequently described by people outside their communities using tribal terminology, yet they also often find their traumatic histories shorn of specificity and either universalized, appropriated, overlooked, or superseded in the same public contexts. Abstract terms like "biological immunity" or "man's inhumanity to man" are common in public allusions to North American genocide and the Holocaust, as are images such as the "Crying Indian" or the smiling Anne Frank. This book compares the effects of such representations on debates about the link between group history, public memory, and cultural assimilation.[14]

These discussions will engage three chronological contexts. The first encompasses the experiences of genocide and population loss among Indigenous people in North America from 1500 through the first half of the twentieth century. The second encompasses the attempted extermination of Jews during the Holocaust. The third comprises the period from the nineteenth century to the present day, in which public representations of Indigenous death preceded and then accompanied separate representations of the Holocaust in North America and Europe. Within these chronological trajectories the book tracks the geographic movement of memory from local contexts around perpetrator sites to other public sites and media on both

**Figure 0.1** *"Keep America Beautiful" (ad campaign poster), Iron Eyes Cody, c. early 1970s. Courtesy: CSU Archives / Everett Collection © Alamy.*

**Figure 0.2** *Brazilian street artist Eduardo Kobra and his assistant work on a large graffiti artwork of Anne Frank at the shipyard at Amsterdam's NDSM shipyards on September 27, 2016. © Getty Images.*

sides of the Atlantic. It traces the move from local and group archives of memory to national and supra-national frameworks that were less detailed and more abstract in their representation of genocide. It examines the differing motivations for abstract and universalistic depictions: In some cases, the specific histories of Jewish or Indigenous victims are universalized on behalf of other experiences or ideological agendas. In other cases, those histories are de-specified by civic and cultural institutions without necessarily being universalized. They are described in abstract terms that occlude their specific nature and scale and thus avoid contradicting the narratives of tolerance and freedom that those institutions often emphasize through their memory work. The following chapters compare how these phenomena have affected internal Jewish and Indigenous debates about the link between traumatic memory and assimilation. And they demonstrate how these comparative discussions can contribute to a useful critical template for memory studies, museum studies, and public history.

This book departs from scholarship that has tended to focus on the direct comparison between the histories of the Holocaust and Indigenous genocide, and which has sometimes stimulated tensions between Indigenous people, Jews, and their allied scholars. The potential for empathy between descendants of different communities, according to A. Dirk Moses, has too often been undermined by "the Terror of History." Even the memory of death, in these anxious contexts, is perceived to be threatened by competing memories and definitions from other groups.[15] Heated scholarly and popular controversies have been connected to debates over the tricky chronological comparison between centuries of Indigenous population decline and the concentrated scale of death during the few years of the Holocaust, as well as qualitative and quantitative distinctions regarding the "biocentric intentionality" of genocidal intent against Jews during the Holocaust.[16] Such tensions have prevented Jews and Indigenous people from acknowledging how their separate histories have been represented by cultural and civic bodies in structurally similar ways as well as the comparable ideological agendas underlying those representations.[17]

This book seeks what Peter Carrier defines as "a shift in causality, from a quest to explain the event to a quest to explain the meaning and effects of the event for those who look back on it."[18] Indeed, the similar public treatment of their histories of genocide goes some way towards explaining why many Jews and Indigenous people have come to fear comparing those histories in scholarly and other realms. As members of both communities have found their memories of trauma displaced from their origin sites and reduced in specificity, they have become likelier to dread further displacement through the act of historical comparison in academic or popular contexts. By comparing the divergence between group histories of trauma and their subsequent public representation, this book challenges the civilizational narratives that have contributed to that discrepancy and the resulting tensions over comparative history. It shows how comparing the universalization and abstraction of the Holocaust and North American genocide—rather than examining their representation separately—provides a critique that is powerful enough to stimulate a broader sea change among public historians, cultural agents, political bodies, and educators.[19]

The insights of Finkielkraut and other scholars of Holocaust memory should not be employed to make normative claims about the public representation of Indigenous histories. Rather, this book foregrounds

Indigenous methodologies and authors alongside those parallel insights without identifying either critique of public memory work as a definitive category for the other. While often welcoming non-Indigenous historians and comparative genocide theorists into their field, Indigenous scholars have shown how important it is to avoid paying mere lip service to Indigenous methodologies and archives of memory, or as Mi'kmaw scholar Bonita Lawrence has noted, demanding that "indigenous scholars attempting to write about their histories conform to academic discourses that have already staked a claim to expertise about our past."[20] Scott Richard Lyons has outlined the importance of "rhetorical sovereignty" as "the inherent right of [Indigenous] peoples to determine their own communicative needs and desires in this pursuit, to decide for themselves the goals, modes, styles, and languages of public discourse."[21] Thus, we must consider the interventions of Gerald Vizenor, enrolled member of the Minnesota Chippewa Tribe, White Earth Reservation. Euro-American representations of Indigenous history, according to Vizenor, have too often turned "The Indian" into "a misnomer, a simulation with no referent and with the absence of natives; Indians are the other, the names of sacrifice and victimry . . . The indigene is the noble savage, the stoical warrior, evermore the metaphor, of the native at the littoral, the passive native in the treeline. The history of the Indian is an aesthetic sacrifice, an absence of natives that has become a perverse presence of the other, the modernist manner of a counter simulation, and that absence is a commodity." By transforming histories of trauma into shorthand "metaphor" the absence of specificity becomes its own comforting commodity and allows public bodies to forget uncomfortable aspects of their past. Demonstrating the utility of absence, metaphors make the "dead Indian" represent "the wants or desires of the dominant discourse . . . a series of functioning and ever present stereotypes and clichés with little, if any, actual Indigenous content." As best they can, the following chapters approach these and other Indigenous critiques of public memory, and their common connection to land and place, on their own terms. They examine differences and similarities in public representations of historical trauma by placing Indigenous voices front and center alongside those of Jews and allied scholars.[22]

This book examines public representations of the Holocaust as what James E. Young defines as "memorial texts" that interact between their subjects, their viewers, and the broader national context in which they appear.[23] It considers their interaction with broader media such as educational curricula, books, films, and political statements to create what Oren Baruch Stier has described as "Holocaust icons"—the "certain symbols that have come to represent the Holocaust in encapsulated form—those that summarize complex narratives of the Shoah, simplifying, condensing, and distilling these narratives and producing meanings for cultural consumption . . . [stripping] out much of the historical context and specificity of each icon" so that "the more we see and hear about the Holocaust in the twenty-first century, the less we seem to actually know."[24] Many scholars have noted the tendency for Europeans and Euro-Americans to abstract the Holocaust as an aberrant "perversion" of otherwise universal human rights discourse in their cultural development.[25] In examining such representations this book adapts what Harold Marcuse has described as a "synchronic approach" to show how "knowledge about the scope and nature of the Holocaust spread only gradually to a wider public, which then struggled to find proper expressions of its understandings of the events." Such an approach, as Marcuse reminds us, "allows us to discern how crucial the agents behind Holocaust memorials and their intended audiences were to the forms those projects ultimately attained." It will help us to consider how Holocaust memory has been marshaled as an abstract counterpoint to delineate contemporary narratives rather than to represent the specificity and scale of Jewish suffering on its own terms.[26]

But this book moves beyond these more familiar critiques of Holocaust universalization to show how they have often been preceded—and even influenced—by structurally similar Indigenous responses to the public representation of their histories. Understanding those precedents is necessary to comprehend the complicated reactions of Jewish and Indigenous commentators to the foundation of North American institutions such as the United States Holocaust Memorial Museum (USHMM) and the National Museum of the American Indian (NMAI) in Washington, D.C. and the Canadian Museum for Human Rights (CMHR) in Winnipeg, as well as European institutions such as the Karl May Museum in Germany and the Kelvingrove Museum in Glasgow, Scotland. The despecification of Indigenous population loss in North American public sites and in European ethnographic displays has often preceded or coincided with operationally similar depictions of the Holocaust as a generalized phenomenon without due attention to perpetrator intent. Indigenous commentators have been primed to critique the abstraction of historical suffering on behalf of unrelated agendas.[27]

This book will reveal two related reasons that civic and cultural institutions on both sides of the Atlantic have preferentially used metaphors or shorthand terminology to memorialize Indigenous genocide and the Holocaust: First, to circumvent accountability in tangible terms (such as reparations); and second, to underscore positive national or supra-national identities. By overlooking the connection between the imperial European dispossession of Indigenous people and the subsequent era of North American state-building, it becomes easier for American and Canadian public bodies to distinguish the special trajectory of rights-based pluralism on the western side of the Atlantic from its inevitable repudiation in the European Holocaust. Conversely, European museums, educational curricula, and civic bodies often describe Indigenous mass death as an inevitable result of hazily defined American rather than European cultural chauvinism. By obscuring their historical role in Indigenous genocide, they are then able to siphon the memory of the Holocaust as an aberrant counterpoint to the otherwise positive historical trajectory of their civilizational identity. Though the Holocaust and North American genocide are historically distinct and should not be relativized, therefore, they threaten the same narratives of Euro-American progress. Structural aspects of their subsequent public representation have become more likely to converge as cultural and political bodies have sought to prevent such an unsettling phenomenon.[28]

*Remembering Histories of Trauma* interrogates the convergence introduced above by integrating hitherto separate scholarship on the imperial dimension of the Holocaust and the settler-colonial dynamic of Indigenous genocide. There are high stakes for public history in comparing the imperial frameworks that contributed to the Holocaust and North American genocide. Omer Bartov has differentiated the motivations and effects of pre-twentieth century European colonialism from ontologically distinct Nazi anti-Semitism. But even if we follow Bartov's division between "colonization-fueled genocides" and "totalitarian ideologies," we do not have to dismiss the potential of broader comparisons of imperially structured frameworks of authority. Such frameworks contributed to the destruction of Native American and First Nations populations from the sixteenth century through the nineteenth century and could also be detected in the supra-national assertion of power that the Nazis used to liquidate the Jews of Europe.[29]

By examining how representations of the Holocaust and North American genocide have occluded structurally similar historical frameworks of imperial power, this book provides a template to stimulate alternative approaches among public historians and cultural agents outside the narrow scholarly sphere. The first part of the template repudiates the common notion that group memories of trauma depart from the attention to specificity and causation of neutral archival research. The production of group memory has often required closer engagement with historical records than among the lay community and their chosen public historians—whether in private collections that are curated by private individuals and families or in more formal archival sites and scholarly narratives. Survivors and their descendants have often been the first to be informed by local archives, testimonies, artifacts, and written records. Those sources were often initially rejected by public agents outside their communities who had no wish to contradict opaque and idealized narratives of past events. The cultural and spatial distance of those who have often written the first accounts of genocide has contributed to the distillation of specific cases into shorthand terminology and abstract metaphors that undermine more accurate accounts in group archives of memory.[30]

In reasserting those more accurate accounts this book will underline the utility of the United Nations definition of genocide, which focuses in part on the strict intent of states to destroy groups, as well as more recent settler-colonial and structural paradigms that are more common in Indigenous studies. Doing so will illuminate the divergence between traumatic histories and their subsequent public representation.[31] Recent definitions of "cultural genocide" will also be helpful to comprehend that divergence. Discussions of cultural genocide have occasionally stimulated scholarly critiques from Jewish studies and Holocaust scholars, who have suggested that the concept broadens the definition of genocide at the expense of the nature and scale of the Nazi intent to eliminate global Jewry. But there are other ways that emphases on cultural destruction in Indigenous Studies and Holocaust Studies can jointly inform critiques of present practices in public history. The response of First Nations people to the public memory of Canadian Residential Schools, for example, can be considered alongside the pioneering work of Jewish genocide theorists such as Raphael Lemkin. While directing the formulation, drafting, and reception of the UN Genocide Convention from the 1940s through the 1950s, Lemkin also highlighted the biological and demographic legacy of the destruction of unifying cultural media such as languages and art. More recently, a 2015 summary document of the Indigenous-supported Truth and Reconciliation Commission, which responded to the memory of cultural genocide in Canadian Residential Schools, stated that for "members of the Jewish community, their experience of the Holocaust is a source of empathy in approaching the topic of residential schools."[32] Indigenous people and Jews can both speak to the unifying role of historical commemoration as a cultural medium. However benevolent their intentions may be, abstract or universalistic public representations of Indigenous genocide and the Holocaust risk unsettling that unifying medium—an affront to surviving communities whose ancestors once experienced the attempted destruction of other aspects of their cultures.[33]

The second part of this book's template identifies and compares positive recent developments in the incorporation of Indigenous and Jewish archives of memory in public institutions and sites where they were once evaded. Some of those initiatives have been influenced by Indigenous definitions of "survivance," offering a potential model for Jewish groups. Others deliberately expose the subjective and fragile nature of public Holocaust memory and provide a potential paradigm for cultural institutions that strive to acknowledge similar problems in the representation of Indigenous genocide. This part of the template also emphasizes the role of group memory among Indigenous people and Jews as an ongoing educational process rather than a static entity that is automatically transferred from one generation to another. Public cultural bodies are less likely to universalize the historical experiences of populations when survivors show that they have not simply vanished and that they can provide living testimony through the preservation of oral lore, commemorative rituals, and other educational materials. Collaborative initiatives between public institutions and survivor groups underscore the role of incremental and ongoing historical education from books, cultural rituals, and site visits. As a form of commemoration, they counter the tendency to supplant specific historical knowledge with abstract motifs.

Both parts of the template will account for ongoing distinctions among survivor communities and their descendants and the degree of heterogeneity among those who distinguish their attachment to group memory from public memory. It will show how some trends relate more explicitly to European Jews than North American Jews, and vice versa, the nuanced differences within each of those subgroups, and the distinctions between first and later generations of survivors.[34] It will delineate discussions that relate more explicitly to definitions of memory among Native Americans in the United States than among First Nations people in Canada, as well as the myriad nuances among various Indigenous subgroups throughout North America. It will also note key differences in the way sites, regions, and contemporary structures of power affect Indigenous people and Jews. There may be asymmetries between their experiences in the realm of public representation, making some of the tangible and symbolic benefits of this book's critical template different for Indigenous people than for Jews.

It will also be necessary to consider where the distinction between specificity and generality does not always match the divide between group memory and public memory. Some Indigenous people and Jews have come to fear the effect of public representations of their histories of trauma *within* their communities. Internal debates over the link between assimilation and memory are best understood in relation to contiguous anxieties about the universalization of historical suffering in external media and its potential effect on younger generations within each group. Those debates hinge on the shifting association between the commemoration of historical loss and the prevention or encouragement of the assimilation of younger generations into broader society, as defined by out-marriage or by more nebulous measures such as the knowledge and practice of spiritual and cultural rituals. By overlooking centuries of positive historical memories, some Indigenous and Jewish thinkers have argued, ubiquitous public representation of historical trauma may impact younger group members and prevent their contribution to pride, unity, and cohesion.[35] Others, conversely, warn that emphases on survival, agency, and cultural renewal have diminished general public knowledge about the total and systemic destruction wrought on global Jewry and Indigenous people, including certain aspects of demography that are unrecoverable. The hazy and overly positive focus of public memory, they suggest, will likely influence their own group members. Only greater awareness of inescapable historical horror, they argue, will galvanize younger generations in surviving populations and prevent their outward assimilation.[36]

Highlighting tensions between group history and public memory will help us to understand related anxieties in both communities about the link between population loss and cultural destruction. Ellen Fine has described the paradoxically unifying aspect of "absent memory" among generations of French Jews after the Holocaust. On the one hand, according to Fine, they fear their inability to adhere to the same cultural, spiritual, and linguistic traditions as those that were shattered during the 1930s and 1940s. Recognizing such a dissonance, on the other hand, becomes an ironic cultural medium to maintain group cohesion.[37] It is worth considering similar thought processes among other Jewish communities as well as among Indigenous nations in the United States and Canada. It is also worth assessing other approaches to cultural loss, particularly those that are concerned with the outward dissemination of languages, art, ecological knowledge, and spiritual rituals. The purveyance of cultural and spiritual practices outside Native American, First Nations, and Jewish worlds risks diluting and limiting the galvanizing capacity of those practices among survivor communities, mirroring the failure to safeguard the unifying cultural memory of historical trauma itself.[38]

With these important qualifications in mind, *Remembering Histories of Trauma* sets out to compare structural similarities in the dissonance between Indigenous and Jewish group histories and their public representation. Just as Holocaust memory has often been adapted as an intangible icon to delineate the progression of American, Canadian, European, or Western civic identity, the following chapters will show how the ubiquitous role of Euro-American perpetrators in Indigenous genocide has habitually been overlooked to distinguish later ideological agendas. In a discussion of the Holocaust, slavery, and colonization, Kitty Millet has asked: "How does one talk about the human in the face of so much loss, so many dead bodies?" Responding to that question, this book provides a way for Indigenous people, Jews, and allied scholars to forge a joint critique of the public representation of their historical trauma. It offers a template for public historians and cultural bodies to understand how the tendency towards universalism and abstraction in public memory has often been rooted in similar civilizational assumptions, and how they might do better. It shows what can be learned from Indigenous and Jewish archives of memory and their integration in public sites outside their immediate communities.[39]

To fulfill this brief, Chapter 1 explores the controversies that have stemmed from the comparison between Indigenous histories of population loss since the sixteenth century and the murder of Jews during the Holocaust. The former has often been represented as a tragic process that stemmed from differing biological immunity, without explaining the contributing role of settler colonial interventions. Tensions over such definitions have prevented Indigenous people, Jews, and allied scholars from considering structural similarities in the way the Holocaust has often been treated in public sites. To transcend those tensions, the chapter examines and compares recent discussions of perpetrator intent and the contingency of genocide in their respective scholarly worlds. Those comparative discussions provide a template to critique abstract or universalistic depictions of causation such as those that employ the notions of innate biological immunity or generalized human intolerance.

Chapter 2 examines the imperial turn in the historiography of genocide, which has been influenced by techniques and concepts in the separate fields of comparative genocide studies and settler-colonial studies. Imperial frameworks unsettle the common distinction between Euro-American humanitarianism and the horror of the Holocaust, which has often led public representations to universalize the Jewish experience while overlooking the history of Indigenous genocide altogether. Alongside other comparative insights, the imperial turn in genocide studies ought to align public memory more closely with the group memory of Indigenous people and Jews, providing a useful baseline to consider divergent approaches in public sites and media on both sides of the Atlantic.

Chapter 3 compares how Native Americans, Jews, and First Nations people have approached the dissonance between their histories of trauma and the subsequent public representation of those histories in the United States and Canada. Critiques of the universalization of Holocaust memory since the 1970s have been preceded and even influenced by structurally similar Indigenous responses to the representation of their history in public spaces. Understanding those similarities is necessary to comprehend the complicated reactions of Jewish and Indigenous commentators to the foundation of institutions such as the United States Holocaust Memorial Museum (USHMM) and the National Museum of the American Indian (NMAI) in Washington, D.C. and the Canadian Museum for Human Rights (CMHR) in Winnipeg.

Chapter 4 compares the ambiguous ways that Native Americans, First Nations people, and North American Jews have connected traumatic memory to cultural renewal and the prevention of assimilation. Within both communities, the commemoration of historical loss has come to be defined as a discrete cultural medium with a strong unifying capacity. But there is not yet a consensus in either community about the nature of the connection between traumatic memory and cultural assimilation. Debates about that connection are best understood in relation to the perceived universalization of historical suffering in public media. The representation of historical trauma has become associated with fears over the outward dissemination of cultural and spiritual practices by surviving community members. The outward flow of cultural media may dilute and limit their galvanizing capacity at just the point when the ritual of historical commemoration suffers the same limitations thanks to its appropriation in public sites.

Chapter 5 shows how European memory work has often obscured the Jewish experience during the Holocaust while overlooking European involvement in the massive loss of Indigenous life over four centuries. As in North America, abstract ethnographic representations of Indigenous history have often prefigured structurally similar depictions of the Holocaust in public spaces as well as in the supra-national cultural institutions of the European Union. Though North American acts such as the Native American Graves Protection and Repatriation Act (NAGPRA) tacitly recognize the European colonial roots of Indigenous dispossession, they do not apply any jurisdictional force to the curation of Indigenous objects in European nations. The resulting lacunae in the representation of Indigenous historical artifacts speaks to ongoing European controversies over the erroneous display of materials associated with the Holocaust as well as the question of reparations and restitution for objects that were looted from Jewish families.

Chapter 6 compares recent positive developments in the integration of Indigenous and Jewish archives of memory in European public sites and shows how they can inform museums, memorials, and public officials on both sides of the Atlantic. Collaborative initiatives between cultural institutions and survivor groups underscore the role of ongoing historical education as a form of commemoration and counter the tendency to supplant specific historical knowledge with abstract motifs. Some of those collaborative cultural programs have been inspired by Indigenous definitions of survivance, offering a potential template for Jewish groups. Other initiatives intentionally represent the opacity of public Holocaust memory to stimulate alternative approaches, providing a useful model for Indigenous "counter-memory" efforts.

PART ONE

# Theory

# CHAPTER ONE

# "Humanitarian feelings . . . crystallized in formulae of international law."

## Biological Determinism and the Problem of Perpetrator Intent

In the commemoration and representation of their traumatic histories, Indigenous people and Jews share much in common as they try to balance the will to survive against the totality of loss. But these commonalities have been obscured by an unfortunate set of conflicts over the definition of genocide in relation to the intent to destroy groups. This chapter interrogates those conflicts, which relate to the representation of biological determinism and disease by scholars of the Holocaust and scholars of Indigenous population loss. It considers how the post-World War II legal definition of genocide has influenced the power imbalances that some Indigenous commentators have detected in the normative use of Holocaust memory to represent other histories of genocide.[1]

But this chapter also explores new ways that Indigenous people, Jews, and allied scholars can compare the Holocaust and North American genocide without requiring one case to provide a normative benchmark for the other. By integrating hitherto separate methodological literatures from Holocaust Studies, First Nations Studies, and Native American Studies, as well as related insights from scholarship on settler-colonialism in regions such as Australia and New Zealand, it identifies simple, pertinent, and unexplored comparisons between aspects of Indigenous history and Holocaust history. Those comparisons are helpful to transcend competitive strains over the nature of mortality statistics or the relative merit of strict versus loose or structural definitions of genocidal intent.[2] They clarify rather than obscure the separate histories of Indigenous population loss and the Holocaust, including as they are represented in public spaces. As what Michael Rothberg has described as "lines of historical insight," they illuminate the powerful role of societal interventions in the destruction of populations and in the prevention of their demographic recovery. They provide a useful conceptual vocabulary to critique abstract or universalistic depictions of causation such as those that employ the notions of innate biological immunity or generalized human intolerance. They offer necessary grounding for the chapters that follow, which consider structural similarities in the dissonance between Indigenous and Jewish memories of trauma and their public representation.[3]

## Biological determinism and the breakdown of the Indigenous–Jewish alliance

Until surprisingly recently, civic memorials and public education efforts in the United States, Canada, and many European nations have often followed mainstream scholarship in claiming that Native Americans in a "virgin land" were unable to cope with the pathogens inadvertently introduced by Europeans after the arrival of Christopher Columbus. The high death rate among post-contact communities has been invoked to support the notion that invisible biological agents, rather than the activities and choices of colonial settlers, contributed to demographic collapse. Indigenous death has thus been linked to immediate pandemics rather than gradual societal collapse in the context of colonization. Only a disease pandemic, according to this emphasis, could have been so deadly and efficient in the pre-industrial era: Europeans inadvertently introduced diseases, which their populations apparently survived due to their superior inherited or innate immunity.[4]

Over the last few decades, however, scholarship of global infectious disease has shown that societies have often been able to recover demographically from near collapse following massive outbreaks, usually in around 150 years. Disturbances such as epidemics have tended to result in only short-term demographic decline, with populations returning to pre-disease levels of growth, decline, or stability. The history of European disease pandemics, and the possibility for recovery in a few generations, underscores the facile nature of any suggestion that disease determines demographic outcomes irrespective of context or human interventions. Even massive population losses are recoverable, provided contextual circumstances improve. Though they often relate to Eurasian historical contexts, these insights refocus our understanding on the ways in which human interventions exacerbate demographic decline in the face of disease; whether in terms of reduced immunity before infection, reduced ability to fight pathogenic invasion, or compromised health among subsequent generations of survivors in affected populations.[5]

A later generation of scholars, activists, and public memorial specialists have therefore modified the claim that Native American, First Nations, Métis, and Inuit communities were decimated after European contact because their immunity was distinct from populations in the "Old World." These newer and more accurate perspectives are necessarily grounded in Indigenous understandings of ancestral loss and are verified by Indigenous and non-Indigenous scholarship in the fields of biology and epidemiology. They caution against assuming certain communities are more prone to syndromes and infectious diseases, whether due to genetic differences or a comparative lack of exposure to specific pathogens. The biological determinism of many Euro-American accounts, they point out, rests on several problematic assumptions from the perspective of biological science and epidemiology. Indigenous communities and Europeans may have retained different immunities during the period of contact. But suggesting that many Indigenous nations in North America were predisposed to *near-total* demographic collapse solely due to their relative lack of immunity overlooks the disruption of their health by contingencies of colonization. The notion of a "biological exchange" of infectious disease incorporates an overly deterministic account of health outcomes, eschewing the unsettling role of human interventions either in exacerbating Native American susceptibility to infectious disease and/or metabolic syndromes, or even as a primary factor in their increasing mortality and declining fertility after European contact.[6]

Structural forces—sometimes described as "structural intent"—made diseases likely to proliferate, reduced the ability to maintain sound immunity, and impeded the recovery of communities during subsequent decades. Without these forces, the mere presence of new microbes would not have translated to the final population nadir among Indigenous sub-groups during the nineteenth century. For example, interventions that altered the living circumstances necessary to avoid disease, or the nutrient-density and metabolic profile necessary for optimal immune function, often took place at just the point when disease epidemics became more likely due to the arrival of Europeans. During the seventeenth century, indeed, epidemics tended to follow decades-long delays after first European contact. This relatively new insight from the historiography of Indigenous demographic collapse further demonstrates the importance of societal disruption in the ensuing years, rather than immutable biological differences—a key point that ought to influence public memorials for Indigenous death without raising anxiety among Holocaust scholars and museum professionals.[7]

Yet these recent developments have sometimes also accompanied tensions between Holocaust scholars and those concerned with the representation of the history of Indigenous population loss and Indigenous genocide. Those tensions have most often been stimulated by the definitive trajectory of the concept of "genocide" as it has moved from legal terminology to public discourse. As Christian Gerlach has shown, the term originated as "a normative, action-oriented concept that has historically and essentially been created for the political struggle, not for scholarly analysis, . . . a *politischer Kampfbegriff* [political rallying cry]." Having entered the scholarly realm, however, the term has often carried the same political energy, encouraging competition among different groups for public recognition of historical suffering and linking the ostensibly sober academic sphere to highly charged political questions about structural inequality, power imbalances, and the necessity of reparations from states and institutions.[8]

During the 1990s and early 2000s, for example, several scholars in Holocaust Studies and Jewish Studies exhibited a strong reaction to representations of Native American and First Nation population loss that incorporated references to the Holocaust, or which used terminology that had hitherto been reserved for discussions of the destruction of Jews by the Nazis. Several of those representations were indeed polemical in tone. Others sought instead to draw attention to the ways that public memorials and educational texts have failed to portray the role of perpetrator intent and the scale of destruction in the decimation of several Native American nations. Whatever the nature or intent of these scholarly interventions, which differed in degree, a few Holocaust researchers categorized all of them as mischievous attempts to dilute, relativize, or even replace the Jewish aspect of Holocaust memory. Such a perception may have been understandable considering the broader polemical context for the representation of Holocaust memory, which became more apparent outside the Indigenous world during the same period. Scholars may continue to find merit in Stephen Katz's suggestion that the Nazi Holocaust was "phenomenologically" unique due to the "merciless, exceptionless, biocentric intentionality of Hitler's 'war against the Jews.'" But unfortunately, Katz and several others have sometimes minimized the massive human contribution to Indigenous population loss by employing models of disease mortality that stressed the biologically deterministic role of differing immunity.[9] In response, the understandable indignation of several Indigenous and allied scholars and commentators has led them to describe the "exclusivism" of Holocaust scholarship with a far broader brush, including the problematic claim that Jewish interest groups maintain an outsized control over public historical commemoration in the United States.[10]

Such tensions have prevented members of both groups from acknowledging the similar ways their separate histories of trauma have often been misrepresented in public spaces. The impasse in Indigenous–Jewish discussions of genocide and civic memory can be reduced by comparing instances of strict, loose, and structural genocidal intent in Holocaust history and Indigenous history. These fresh comparisons are helpful to illuminate how the histories of Indigenous population loss and the Holocaust have been appropriated, universalized, or misrepresented in similar ways.

## The local and oral context for comparative genocide

Notwithstanding the ongoing repudiation of biological determinism, there remains a degree of ambiguity in the use of genocide terminology to describe Indigenous history. Some scholars describe the entire period following the arrival of Europeans in North America as a genocide, potentially overlooking demographic, regional, and temporal distinctions between different sub-groups or nations. Other scholars and commentators, conversely, fail to employ genocide terminology to describe specific cases where it seems appropriate.[11] This lack of consensus has led some researchers to question the viability of the comparison between Indigenous mass death and the Holocaust, as well as any attempt to extrapolate broader historical definitions, legal norms, or standards of commemoration from such a comparison. Several historians have distinguished the overall Jewish experience in the Holocaust as genocidal by pointing to factors such as the inability to adapt or recover demography in any way, the intent of Nazis to destroy all Jewish sub-groups irrespective of regional context, and the potential for the "Final Solution" to divert energy and resources from other supposedly primary Nazi strategic aims. The most predominant distinguishing factor of the Holocaust, according to these assessments, relates to its concentrated time frame over a vast region that encompassed many nations. Given the lengthy period of European colonization in Indigenous North America, and the tendency to measure Indigenous demographic loss in decades or even centuries, the same notion is trickier to apply.[12]

The reaction of commentators outside Indigenous Studies should not be the primary concern of those within its scholarly community. But it is likely that "splitting" different Indigenous experiences in regionally and temporally specific case studies of genocide, rather than "lumping" them together, would receive more support from Holocaust scholars, facilitating their greater engagement alongside scholars of Native American and First Nations history and allied scholars in comparative genocide studies.[13] Discrete subgroups within European Jewry and Indigenous North America have always been distinguished by history, language, culture, and spiritual heritage: in Europe, for example, Dutch Jews, the Jews of Salonika, and Lithuanian Jews; or in North America, for example, the Passamaquoddy, the Penobscot, and the Maliseet. Each of those relatively discrete ethnocultural populations also suffered high death rates, at up to 90 percent, without later demographic recovery. But their experiences, which certainly conform to modern numerical standards for "genocide," are often subsumed within overall percentage rates that may be slightly lower. Aside from comparing strict and loose definitions of genocidal intent in the histories of the Holocaust and Indigenous population collapse, then, it is worth identifying other comparisons that might stimulate public bodies to incorporate more nuanced ethnocultural and demographic distinctions in their acts of commemoration.

Consider the mortality rates of specific Indigenous nations such as the Abenaki. They and other groups, according to David Stannard, ought to be examined more discretely to categorize and memorialize them according to accepted scholarly and legal definitions of genocide. If Jews were classed as "European" or "white" in the way that Indigenous nations are cast as one monolithic entity, they would become a "small and invisible . . . undifferentiated collectivity whose loss of life under the Third Reich reduced the population of Europe by hardly more than 1% between 1939 and 1945."[14] Inadvertently, Stannard's statements offer a useful warning to Holocaust scholars and memorial specialists. In 1992, it may have seemed far-fetched or even perverse to dilute Jewish mortality by including it as a broader portion of European demographic history. Such a conception in fact underlay Stannard's rhetorical use of the example to show how Indigenous nations *had* been lumped together in problematic ways. But since Stannard's rhetorical maneuver, several interpretative trends have come close to realizing such a phenomenon in their approach to Jewish loss. In Eastern Europe, non-Jewish groups have increasingly asserted their dual victimhood as one of many groups who suffered during the 1940s. On the western side of the Atlantic, a few activists have recently described the Holocaust as a "white on white" European crime, causing a furor among Jewish commentators.[15]

Moving away from these polemical contexts, we can note how discussions of the Abenaki and other Indigenous groups ought to complement work being carried out by a new generation of Holocaust scholars. Those scholars have begun to refine our understanding of cultural and demographic distinctions among different Jewish populations in Europe during the Holocaust, without overlooking the ways that Nazis sought to erase Jews in their entirety.[16] Until their near-annihilation by the Nazi advance through the Greek-speaking world, for example, Salonikan Jews represented a cohesive and culturally unique community among European Jewry. They were a cohesive sub-group within Greek Sephardim, rather than the Ashkenazi Jews we usually associate with population collapse during the Holocaust. Unlike Jews in mainland Bulgaria, some of whom were Sephardi, Salonika's community were nearly all murdered in Auschwitz Birkenau. Unfamiliar with the Yiddish spoken by other inmates, they could hardly be defined in the same ethnocultural terms as Jews, say, from Germany. In his memoir of his time in Auschwitz, Primo Levi described the Salonikans he met as "the most coherent national nucleus in the Lager, and in this respect, the most civilized"—an insight shown more recently by Paris Papamichos Chronakis in a discussion of the special connection between the Jewishness and Greekness of Salonikan Jews.[17] Continued memory wars over the representation of Salonikan Jewish victimhood show how their ethnocultural identity was distinct even from other Greek Jews, as was the context for their treatment by collaborators with Nazis. Culturally specific business interests, economic opportunism, and racialized discourses in Salonika help to explain why the experience of its Jewish community was so markedly dire in comparison to other communities in Greece—one of the highest per-capita loss of any discrete sub-group of Jews during the Holocaust. Current disputes about the representation of the Salonika Jewish cemetery, Liberty Square, the Baron Hirsch ghetto area, and the train station where deportations to camps began have often overlooked local complicity in the destruction of Jews that can even be distinguished from elsewhere in Greece.[18] Distinct from Ashkenazi victims of the Holocaust, moreover, their former homeland has in their absence become a unifying (though ambiguous) symbol for other global Sephardi communities.[19] These examples remind us that the demography of some European Jewish communities were affected to a greater extent than others, even while *all* Jews were targeted for annihilation across Europe, with massive percentage losses all round. Specifying demographic loss in these and many other examples counters the problematic notion that the percentage of overall Jewish survivors after the Holocaust somehow reduces its scope and scale. That the per-capita loss among smaller subsets of European Jewry could be so high—so unrecoverable—reminds us of the overall intention of the Nazis, notwithstanding their failure to carry out that intention in some communities due to contingent circumstances.

Distinguishing the mortality rates of sub-groups reminds us that however useful and appropriate they may be in many contexts, collective nouns such as "European Jewry" or "Native America" or "First Nation" risk erasing differences in the historical experience of mass death. Splitting rather than lumping the mortality rates of sub-groups is not dichotomous with their contiguous placement in more broadly defined categories such as "Jewish" or "Indigenous." Nor does such an emphasis diminish the flow of empathy, trauma, or collective memory from one sub-group to another. We are simply reminded of the need for greater attention to detail, specificity, and internal cultural differences when we talk about, write about, and commemorate the horrific experiences of victim groups. That Euro-American settlers or Nazis often defined Indigenous people and Jews as one monolithic group does not mean that our account of their persecution ought to overlook demographic nuances and distinctions in the subsequent impact of their interventions.

Splitting rather than lumping, moreover, underscores the role of contingent and specific human interventions even where death was widespread, further unsettling the way that invisible biological forces such as differing immunity or abstract human tendencies such as "intolerance" have come to characterize public accounts of demographic collapse in both communities. This is even more apparent when we identify exceptional cases at the other end of the scale of mortality during the Holocaust and in the "shatter zones" of the Euro-American–Indigenous encounter. New work in Holocaust Studies, for example, has emphasized the possibility of non-Jewish resistance to Nazi anti-Semitism in countries such as Bulgaria and Albania, adding to earlier studies on the Danish example. These cases remind us that intolerance was not an amorphous agent that swallowed up all in its path. It was possible for non-Jewish agency to support the contiguous Jewish will to survive. The Bulgarian and Albanian "exceptions" remind us that mortality could be contingent on human choices, even under the shadow of the Nazis.[20] Indeed, the distinction between the Jews of Salonika and those elsewhere in Greece and neighboring Bulgaria is more complex than scholars once assumed. In Eastern Macedonia and Thrace, for example, animosity toward Greeks led Bulgarian occupiers in the region to support German attempts to liquidate Greek Jews from the region.[21] And in other parts of Greece, greater survival depended on the contingent interests of local civic institutions and their chillingly pragmatic evaluation of how those interests related to Greek national power versus what could be gained by collaborating more closely with Nazis.[22]

In early American Studies and Indigenous Studies, scholars have emphasized their own set of exceptions to the overall story of Indigenous mortality to show that death was never an inevitable result of abstract or nebulous forces. The example of the Comanche illustrates that strict or loose forms of intent were often required to counteract the Indigenous will to survive. Comanche community members were able to achieve greater access to nutrient-dense foods, such as bison, through greater physical mobility. Their adaption of European technologies and horsepower complemented their ability to remain isolated from the "shatter zones" of Euro-American colonization. Physical distance from colonial interventions and adaptation of European technologies enabled an initial period of survival and even

**Figure 1.1** *National Day of Remembrance of the Greek Jewish Witnesses and Holocaust Heroes, in Thessaloniki, Greece, on January 26, 2020. © Getty Images.*

growth. The relative demographic success of the Comanche and a few other Indigenous groups shows that despite their immunological distinction, far more prosaic and contingent factors allowed their population numbers to grow in the medium term. Similar arguments could be made distinguishing the initial fate of Choctaw communities from Cherokee nations during the second half of the eighteenth century. Unlike the Cherokee, Choctaw groups harnessed geographical and subsistence strategies to remain apart from European colonizers, notwithstanding their initial exposure to European diseases. The dissolution of those contingent advantages, conversely, accompanied the destruction of Choctaw communities during later generations. The contingency of mortality is also demonstrated in David J. Silverman's recent work on the role of firearms in resistance to colonial disruption through the nineteenth century.[23]

In all these historical examples, the will to survive required the right external context: those who might become potential perpetrators choosing instead to act against prevailing power structures, or the availability of time and space for potential victims to assert their agency to survive. The few cases where either or both requirements were met unsettle the narrative of inevitability in most of the cases where they were *not* achieved. Comparing instances of survival thus provides a framework to understand and represent the role of external interventions in the many other cases with more negative outcomes.[24]

Simple comparisons between the Holocaust and regional Indigenous case studies also remind us of the specifically local spatial and temporal contexts in which their subjects often suffered, the role of bystander intent in those contexts, and the importance of including oral testimony from survivors. Until relatively recently historians, politicians, museum curators, and national archivists tended to draw rigid qualitative distinctions between oral and written records, as well as between the role of states and the role of local bystanders and collaborators—sometimes to the detriment of their representation of Indigenous and Jewish histories of trauma. Different methodological approaches in Holocaust Studies and Indigenous Studies, which often derive from Indigenous and Jewish archives of memory, have unsettled such qualitative distinctions. They are worth comparing, not least because they provide a useful benchmark to critique public sites of memory in subsequent chapters.

From the 1970s through the early 1980s, Claude Lanzmann's seminal use of oral interviews among Holocaust survivors in European towns began to alter public understanding about the role of bystanders in the destruction of Jews. In his *Shoah* documentary work, Lanzmann underscored how the oral records of surviving Jews in Eastern European communities often provided more insightful and accurate accounts about the local contexts for genocide than available written records.[25] Since Lanzmann's interventions, much more emphasis on oral testimony, memory, and place has appeared in the work of scholars such as Hannah Pollin-Galay, in the important work of institutions such as the United States Holocaust Memorial Museum (USHMM), and in the microhistories pioneered by historians such as Omer Bartov.[26] The public memory of the Holocaust in nations such as the Netherlands and Belgium often suggests the tolerance and even heroism of non-Jewish occupied people. Yet the overlooked role of bystander intent is helpful to understand the dissonance between those public narrative and the remarkably high percentage of exterminated Jews in those same nations. Jan Grabowski and others have drawn similar insights about the role of bystander intent in Eastern European contexts. These discussions are germane to new emphases on the role of bullets and ad hoc massacres in the destruction of Jews, as distinct from traditional emphases on Death Camps. The actions and choices of local non-Jewish occupied communities in Eastern European "bloodlands" remind us that the density and scale of Jewish loss during the Holocaust was not derived solely from industrialized and bureaucratized processes that shielded mass murder from most non-Jewish people.[27]

These developments speak to separate insights in early American Studies and Indigenous Studies. Consider the early work of the Smithsonian scholar James Mooney, who engaged in ethnographic assessments of the Wounded Knee Massacre and published *The Ghost Dance Religion and the Sioux Outbreak of 1890* in 1896. Through an analysis of the continuing mourning rituals of the Lakota in their specific regional contexts, Mooney identified where members of the community died, contradicting erroneous accounts by state and federal officials during the same period. More than a century later, Ari Kelman's account of the "misplacement" of the memory of the Sand Creek Massacre in Colorado has identified a similar set of tensions between written archival methods and Indigenous rituals that approach the history of the event in their local context.[28] Most recently, Christine M. DeLucia and Lisa Brooks have highlighted the importance of place-based and linguistically diverse material in Indigenous oral, written, and material archives, which are often more rewarding than written records produced by non-Indigenous agents who were far removed from the genocidal events and regional spaces that they purported to explain.[29] Given their connection to contexts and places where surviving subjects have continued to live, oral and other non-traditional records are also likely to repudiate approaches that employ the histories of Indigenous trauma and the Holocaust to serve broader civic aims. It is more difficult, after all, to universalize the experiences of populations when survivors show that they have not simply vanished from their ancestral lands or local regions, and that they can provide living testimony through the preservation of oral lore, commemorative rituals, and other materials.[30]

## Representing strict genocidal intent

The notion of "strict" genocidal intent would fit more neatly into assessments and representations that split rather than lump regional case studies of Indigenous history in comparison to the Holocaust. Strict intent defines the premeditated intervention of perpetrators among discrete populations who suffered massive per-capita population loss as a result. Many Indigenous groups, in their regional context, experienced targeted elimination. The traditional UN definition of genocide can be applied in such instances, without requiring the claim that *all* Indigenous people in North America were always subject to similar acts of perpetrator intent in the period between 1500 and the 1900.[31]

Consider, most infamously, Lord Jeffrey Amherst's 1763 letter to Colonel Henry Bouquet, which suggested that smallpox-infected blankets be distributed to the Ottawa and Lenape people: "You will do well to [infect] the Indians by means of blankets as well as to try every other method that can serve to extirpate this [execrable] race." Such a statement is particularly meaningful because it may demonstrate the intent of a broader colonial system of governance, rather than the independent actions of settlers in their local context, in the weaponization of disease to destroy a discrete "race." In addition to the Amherst case, we can find evidence of the attempted distribution of smallpox blankets by members of the US Army, and some fur traders, during the nineteenth century, particularly on the upper Missouri River in 1837.[32]

Yet there is not yet a scholarly consensus that the intentional infliction of disease in these cases was common enough to suggest a broader genocidal policy that characterized Euro-American engagement with Indigenous people throughout North America.[33] Rather than restricting discussions of genocidal intent to the weaponization of disease, therefore, other methods of intentional population destruction can be compared with aspects of the Jewish experience during the Holocaust. In 1782, for example, members of the Ohio militia took part in a chilling "vote" to destroy around 100 (Christianized) Indians at Gnadenhütten in eastern Ohio—a clear case of top-down driven genocidal intent. Historians have often treated such episodes as isolated expressions of genocidal intent. But as comparative genocide theorists have pointed out, isolated actions may still have been rooted in ubiquitous exterminatory "discourses" that circulated more widely among settlers, soldiers, and politicians, and which were "periodically activated" in what can be described as "genocidal moments." Within the North American context, such moments likely included the 1863 Bear River Massacre of around 400 Shoshoni men, women, and children, and the infamous December 28, 1890, Wounded Knee Massacre of often unarmed Cheyenne women and children as well as Miniconjou and Hunkpapa Lakota women and children at Wounded Knee Creek. Given what Jeffrey Ostler has summarized as "a disposition to regard all Indians" in Sand Creek "as deserving of extermination," and Army officer statements such as "the only good Indians I ever saw were dead," several scholars have described the 1864 Sand Creek Massacre of up to 500 Southern Cheyenne and Arapaho people, mostly women and children, as genocidal. Similarly, official white written records that relate to the 1890 Wounded Knee massacre show how terms such as "treachery" and "fanaticism" were increasingly and deliberately linked to definitions of supposedly innate racial characteristics among Cheyenne, Miniconjou and Hunkpapa Lakota people.[34]

The massive population decline of California's Indigenous community between around 1848 and 1860 (particularly between 1851 and 1852) is perhaps the clearest example of the combination of factors that define genocidal experience according to the legal definition in the United Nations Genocide Convention. Racist and exterminatory rhetoric bound state intent, as represented by Governor Weller, to the localized intent of settlers and militia members. In merely ten years, the Indigenous population in California declined from 150,000 to 30,000. Settlers enslaved Indigenous children, confiscated food-producing lands, and massacred them through militia shootings. These destructive acts, particularly among the Yuki people in northern California, were not merely the manifestation of settler–Indigenous warfare and reprisals. Governor Weller, the state legislature, and even the US Congress set aside money to support militia efforts, in full knowledge of their activities and their intent to engage in "direct killing" of nations such as the Yukis and Yanas. In 1851, Governor Burnett infamously suggested his support for a "war of extermination . . . until the Indian race becomes extinct." The next Governor, McDougal, warned that failed negotiations with resident Indigenous people would lead to the inevitable "extermination [of] many of the tribes." Yuki Indians in Northern California lost up to 90 percent of their population over the following years, suggesting that failed treaties were indeed accompanied by premeditated subjugation, deliberate societal dislocation, and murder. Jack Norton has thus described "the genocide committed against the aboriginal peoples of Northwestern California" who "were annihilated as a people and a culture in the 'final solution' to the Indian problem." In a case of splitting rather than lumping, Norton uses terminology associated with the Holocaust to define the genocidal intent to destroy the Yuki nation, without necessarily applying it to the broader geographical and temporal scope of Indigenous history in the whole of North America.[35]

Some scholars and public history practitioners remain wary of using the genocide moniker alongside the Holocaust in public spaces, even in relation to the specific regional and temporal case studies detailed above. Such comparative terminology, they suggest, risks relativizing the "Final Solution" in public memory as one of many global instances of mass death. Thus, they would likely support the cohort of scholars who define cases such as the Sand Creek massacre as closer to "ethnic cleansing" rather than genocide, due to the perceived distinction between the intent of militia men and state and federal politicians.[36]

Yet the possibility and utility of comparing examples such as the Sand Creek Massacre with episodes in the history of the Holocaust need not even be contingent on their prior assessment as genocidal. Whether or not public historians use the genocide moniker to describe cases such as Sand Creek or Wounded Knee, the extensive literature on the lethal mobilization of racial chauvinism against Jews can speak to their representation in public spaces.

The stimulation of perpetrator intent in Sand Creek, for example, can be clarified by comparison with dehumanizing statements made about Jews in the Jelgava massacres in Latvia, the Bucharest Pogrom, or the Dzyatlava massacres in Belarus, just as the mobilizing power of those statements can be illuminated by comparing them with statements made about Native Americans by those who became perpetrators in Sand Creek. The description of Jews as lice or bacteria allowed Nazi leaders and their proxies to frame their murderous intent, and its violent manifestation, in passive and even biologically deterministic terms: as a natural cleansing of non-human threats, helping to prime local perpetrators in Latvia, Romania, Belarus, and elsewhere to engage in brutal acts of extermination. Those acts are often overlooked in public descriptions of the Holocaust, which tend to focus on the industrialized horrors of Auschwitz or the formal constraints of ghettos.[37] Before they attacked unarmed and often sleeping men, women, and children among Chief Black Kettle's Cheyenne and Arapaho at Sand Creek, Colonel John M. Chivington's Colorado Cavalry had been exposed to similar dehumanizing motifs among their political leadership. Colorado Governor John Evans instructed Chivington in his duty to "kill and destroy, as enemies of the country, wherever they may be found . . . hostile Indians." Chivington responded to Evans's instruction by highlighting his duty to "kill and scalp all, little and big; that nits made lice."[38]

**Figure 1.2** *Mike Bear Comesout, of the Northern Cheyenne, ties a white flag under the American flag before raising it above the crowd during the dedication of the Sand Creek Massacre National Historic Site, fifteen miles west of Eads, Colorado. © Getty Images.*

Methods, models, and techniques from Holocaust historiography can thus be used to understand and represent these cases, without having to suggest that all Indigenous history was bound by the same nature and scale of perpetrator intent. The imposition of the vanishing euphemism on Indigenous communities, as another example, can be compared to the Nazi perversion of the naturalistic analogy to describe the destruction of European Jewry. Nazi ideology infamously avoided defining Jews on a human continuum, refusing even to place them at the bottom of a racist pecking order. They were rarely even compared to mammals. Instead, they were regularly described as microbes, bacteria, parasites, or at best vermin. Giorgio Agamben has suggested that "Jews were exterminated not in a mad and giant holocaust but exactly as Hitler had announced, 'as lice,' which is to say as bare life."[39] Scholars have noted the similarities between these depictions of Jews and the dehumanizing rhetoric of some Euro-American settlers as they expanded into Indian country. Specific definitions of genocide are not required to compare these similar discourses, nor their motivating effects. Jews and Indigenous people were both commonly described as "lice" by political authorities, before being targeted for murder by local militia groups and lay persons. These simple comparisons provide important insight about the power of parasitic terminology to mobilize local perpetrators and militias in alliance with central directives.[40]

Some scholars, such as Carroll P. Kakel, have moved beyond the mode of comparative assessment to suggest the direct causal association between the Euro-American notion of the "Vanishing Indian" and the euphemistic Nazi discussion of Jewish "extinction." Thomas Kühne has provided a convincing critique of such accounts of *direct* causation.[41] Nonetheless, it remains useful to compare how, in their separate contexts, most Nazis and some Euro-American settlers were primed to describe acts of mass murder as natural and providential, having already described victim populations in less than human terms. Nineteenth-century Euro-American descriptions of Indigenous vanishing, to be sure, were more likely than Nazi statements to express a degree of wistful regret, however disingenuous such an expression may have been. But both definitions shared a tendency to describe the destruction of groups as an inevitable matter of historical and environmental evolution, obfuscating the role of perpetrator intent in the process. In both cases, the same racial chauvinism that stimulated perpetrator intent also underlay its subsequent misrepresentation or wholesale erasure in public memory.

## Towards consensus on structural intent, disease, and contingency

The careful identification of regional occurrences of strict genocidal intent in the destruction of Indigenous nations is important on its own terms, as well as in comparison with episodes from the history of the Holocaust. But such an approach does not tell the whole story of Indigenous demographic loss, nor indeed aspects of the Holocaust. Drawn from Indigenous experiences in settler-colonies in North America as well as Australia, "structural," "loose," and "general" notions of intent are often necessary to understand—and commemorate—the contingency of population loss. As broader criteria for intent, they are not dependent on isolating state directives. In relation to Indigenous history, for example, they emphasize structural and societal determinants for population destruction, including those that made disease mortality more profound or demographic recovery after epidemics less likely, or when perpetrators knew that unsettling actions would cause later demographic destruction.[42]

Eschewing looser definitions of genocidal intent makes it all too easy to privilege isolated episodes of strict intent, such as the use of smallpox-infested blankets, to distinguish those episodes from the supposedly broader and more inadvertent effects of abstract biological phenomena. That distinction once governed the consensus among mostly non-Indigenous historians and demographers and has continued to expose tensions between Holocaust scholars and Indigenous Studies experts. But rather than retreating to rejoinders or counterarguments, the utility of looser and structural definitions of intent can be shown by considering the congruence between discussions of disease and enslaved labor in Holocaust Studies and Indigenous Studies, without relativizing, de-specifying, or minimizing the nature and scale of loss in either context.[43]

Many centuries after the medieval plagues, infectious disease contributed to the scale of European Jewish death during the Holocaust. But only the most extreme Holocaust denier would suggest that the role of infection in those instances diminishes the agency or culpability of Nazis and their enablers in determining the fate of Jews.[44] Though Anne Frank likely died of typhus, no serious scholar would suggest that her death derived from an inevitable biological process, without requiring human intervention to manifest in the way that it did.[45] Starved and physically overworked by slave labor, Anne Frank and others concentrated in dense camps suffered vastly compromised immunity, within a societal context that already allowed disease to flourish. Holocaust Studies thus provides a simple and well-accepted model of the contingent nature of disease mortality and the common requirement of external intent. Susceptibility to disease was increased by the combination of malnourishment and extreme physical labor, which is known to compromise working immunity. Nazi leaders knew very well that grueling forced labor made Jews much more likely to die from malnutrition and disease before more direct forms of murder even became necessary. In ghettos and camps, the Nazis knowingly implemented labor patterns that greatly increased the potential for imminent death, blurring the distinction between loose and strict genocidal intent.[46]

These seemingly axiomatic observations from the realm of Holocaust Studies, which have drawn from examinations of the process of "annihilation through work," are germane to the historiography of Indigenous mass death. Despite the many problematic aspects of Anne Frank's post-War representation—such as universalization, instrumentalization, and de-Judaization—most would find it egregious to suggest that Anne's death resulted from abstract biological forces, without perpetrator intent; even if Holocaust deniers gain a frisson of misplaced excitement from just such a claim when they point out that she died of typhus rather than in a gas chamber or in front of a firing squad. Yet biological abstraction continues to characterize public representations of Indigenous population loss, on both sides of the Atlantic. Native Americanists and First Nations scholars, after all, are still often required to counter popular assumptions regarding the deterministic role of disease, irrespective of the contingent choices made by Euro-American perpetrators. We do not have to draw direct parallels between Nazi camps, ghettos, and sites of Indigenous population loss to suggest broader insights from these and similar discussions of loose or structural intent. They provide conceptual vocabularies to understand—and memorialize—the effects of disease in Indigenous "shatter zones" after the arrival of Europeans in North America.[47]

Loose definitions of genocidal intent often require a critical mass of settlers to have distinguished their human worth—even the nature and scale of their humanity—from Indigenous populations. Only then could they knowingly implement or perpetuate societal frameworks that made death from disease more likely. In early North America, such a distinction manifested in a ubiquitous form of "cultural chauvinism" that privileged the sanctity of European life over Indigenous people. For example, new work on the wars between English Puritan settlers and Pequots (1636–8) has shown a startling degree of settler knowledge about the connection between land use, forced migration, servitude, and massive Pequot population collapse. Even if the erasure of the Pequot as a biological group had not been the specific intent of the English population at the outset, their eventual "legal declaration of national extinction" of the Pequot reflected their failure to value life in equal ways long before that statement. Their chauvinism allowed destructive societal frameworks to be created and reduced the likelihood of their removal as their effect on Pequot death became apparent.[48]

Many other examples from early America suggest a similar link between cultural chauvinism and loose genocidal intent. Consider, for example, how public memorials and civic statements might approach Spanish *entradas* into the Southwest and Southeast during the sixteenth century. New work has emphasized the long delay between the first arrival of Spanish settlers and subsequent Indigenous demographic decline. That delay unsettles the notion that virgin soil epidemics due to immunological differences immediately sparked pandemics with high mortality. Rather, it suggests the imposition of societal disruptions and constraints that reduced mortality over the longer term—"genocide under a looser interpretation of intent."[49] Or consider Paul Kelton's pioneering work on the spread of smallpox, which has shown the contingent effects of slavery, nutritional degradation, and forced relocation in determining high mortality rates in regions such as Virginia after 1696. Despite the disease having appeared more than a century earlier, mass death and an inability to recover demography among survivors only became apparent following the consolidation of European colonial power in the region. In these cases, as in the Pequot example, colonizers rarely described their direct intent to cause mass demographic collapse. But their failure to mitigate the well-known effects of their interventions demonstrated a willful lack of concern for Indigenous life. These and other similar examples underline the interpretative importance of the notion of loose and structural intent, which can be placed on a continuum leading to stricter forms of intent in understanding the destructive forces that led to the massive loss of Indigenous lives—of Indigenous forms of nationhood—in what came to be known as Virginia.[50]

These insights from early American historiography support the ongoing repudiation of biological determinism in the allied field of settler-colonial studies. Certain "genocidal moments" in present-day Canada and the United States conform to traditional notions of strict perpetrator intent. But the steep population loss that preceded and followed them over a longer period can be described as a structural framework that required ongoing interventions and conscious choices by states and settlers.[51] As Whitt and Clarke summarize, settler colonialism's potential "eliminatory dynamic is a product of its unrelenting commitment to land resource acquisition and the attendant conviction that the colonized, Indigenous population—regarded as inferior in multiple respects—presents a primary obstacle to such acquisition"; a definition that draws on separate discussions of "structural" and "systemic" genocide rather than relying solely on strict definitions of perpetrator intent drawn from the UN Convention.[52]

The perceived inability to gain liberty through landholding in England made white settlers eager to gain it at the expense of Indigenous communities in seventeenth-century Virginia. Those who did enjoy landed wealth in England, conversely, expanded their worth by investing in the land and labor that poorer settlers consolidated in the colonial world through institutions such as the Virginia Company. An alliance between those two interests required the disruption of Indigenous conceptions of treaty negotiation among the Powhatan Tsenacommacah. That ongoing disruption, to be sure, could also quickly descend into what Alfred A. Cave describes as "racial warfare and episodes of genocide" that correspond with stricter definitions of perpetrator intent according to the UN Convention. Those deadly moments, then, cannot so easily be distinguished from structural disruptions to Indigenous life over longer periods. Both were necessary to buttress ongoing occupation techniques that generated the same result over time, in the "systemic genocide" that led to the overall population nadir of communities such as the Powhatan.[53]

By unsettling the binary distinction between structural and strict approaches to genocidal intent, settler colonial frameworks complement separate Indigenous ways of understanding the historical destruction of their populations and the ongoing importance of national autonomy.[54] Consider, for example, how Leanne Simpson describes "Kina Gchi Nishnaabegogamig"—the name rooted in the territory of the northern shore of Lake Ontario that "emphasizes the relational aspect of our conceptualization of nationhood" to define "the place where all live and work together." The distinction between structural and strict conceptions of genocide breaks down when viewed from such a perspective of nationhood, where any threat to ways of being in a specific territorial context destroys how *being* is defined more generally.[55] Glenn Coulthard (Dene) has therefore defined "a way of knowing, of experiencing and relating to the world and with others . . . a system of reciprocal relations and obligations" that are part of the land, rather than seeking to dominate or extract expanding wealth from it.[56] Similar insights can be gained from other regional histories, such as the destruction of cultural and societal patterns in Newfoundland from the eighteenth century through the mid-nineteenth century. An 1836 British House of Commons Select Committee Report elucidated structural disruptions to Indigenous life and land-based forms of identity, interspersed with accounts of more overt eliminationism such as captivity and murder, and then concluded: "In the colony of Newfoundland, it may therefore be stated that we have exterminated the natives."[57] Indigenous conceptions of population loss are not identical to discussions of the structural or "relational" context for genocide in the work of scholars such as Patrick Wolfe and Lorenzo Veracini.[58] But both show how Indigenous conceptions of agency, as represented in early attempts to negotiate treaties, were rejected in favor of structural forms of dispossession that destroyed their attachment to land and threatened their core definition of Being.[59]

In what came to be known as Canada and the United States, acknowledging the deadly effects of structural intent in Indigenous history, including through often-overlooked Indigenous ways of approaching community, identity, and loss, is in fact congruent with the pioneering efforts of early Jewish theorists of genocide such as Raphael Lemkin. As a foreign affairs adviser in the American War Department, Lemkin combined the Greek word for race with the Latin word for killing through murder to define the liquidation of European Jewry, as well as the 1915 Armenian massacre by Turkish forces.[60] His exact definition of "genocide" was as follows: "Any co-ordinated, methodical plan aimed at destroying the life and culture of a people, and threatening their biological and spiritual unity."[61] Periodically used during the 1945–6 Nuremberg Trials, the term was more officially adopted two years later as a framework for legal judgment by the General Assembly of the United Nations in the Convention on the Prevention and Punishment of the Crime of Genocide. The 1948 UN Convention definition suggested that genocide was determined by "any of the following acts committed with intent to destroy, in whole or in part, a national, ethnical, racial or religious group, as such: (a) Killing members of the group; (b) Causing serious bodily or mental harm to members of the group; (c) Deliberately inflicting on the group conditions of life calculated to bring about its physical destruction in whole or in part; (d) Imposing measures intended to prevent births within the group; (e) Forcibly transferring children of the group to another group."[62] It has become common to marshal Lemkin to support the notion that modern genocide terminology begins with the yardstick provided by the Holocaust, rather than the comparison between historical cases from various periods and contexts. Such a claim has often been drafted in response to the perceived universalization or relativization of the Holocaust in cultural institutions and in broader public discourse. Yet new work has demonstrated Lemkin's influence by events that preceded the Holocaust in his definition of the term genocide. He did not eschew what he described in *Axis Rule* (1944) as the "classical examples of wars of extermination in which nations and groups of the population were completely or almost completely destroyed." Those examples included "the destruction of Carthage in 146 B.C.; the destruction of Jerusalem by Titus in 72 A.D.; the religion wars of Islam and the Crusades; the massacres of the Albigenses and the Waldenses; and the siege of Magdeburg in the Thirty Years War [May 1631]." He also highlighted those "[s]pecial wholesale massacres [that] occurred in the wars waged by Genghis Khan and by Tamerlane." When he stated in his *Memorandum,* written at some point in the early to mid-1940s, that "All cases of genocide, although their background and conditions vary, follow, for the most part, the same pattern," Lemkin developed a relatively broad definition of what the "object of destruction" of "a specific human group" might entail. He included examples of cultural destruction, even in cases where individuals remained alive, as well as examples where the premeditated intent of biological or cultural elimination was more ambiguous. The destruction of a human group, according to Lemkin, need not have been solely biological—a high percentage of a discretely defined group marked out for murder to prevent its demographic viability—to have been categorized according to a "'common element' that required criminalization" as a form of genocide.[63]

Some have suggested that Lemkin's elucidation of the category for genocide is too loose to be able to do full justice to the scope of Nazi efforts against Jews and is thus problematic in allowing the Holocaust to be placed alongside other non-Jewish cases as one of many comparative genocides. It has also been posited that during World War II, and in its immediate aftermath, Lemkin did not realize the extent of Jewish annihilation during the Holocaust and thus continued to define his concept of genocide in a broader, comparative way.[64]

Yet there remains a good deal of evidence from Lemkin's personal correspondence, stored at New York Public Library, that he registered the horror of the Holocaust, at least to the extent that any other Jewish observer was able to do so in the immediate aftermath of World War II. Notwithstanding this knowledge, gained in part through direct familial associations, Lemkin maintained his broader definition of genocide and its association with multiple examples, including the Holocaust. He remained open to the formation and definition of genocide terminology through comparisons between the Jewish experience under the Nazis and the experiences of non-Jews in other contexts—including Indigenous people in the Americas.[65]

Lemkin often entered his discussions of demographic collapse among Indigenous populations in the western hemisphere through reference to Bartolomé de las Casas, the sixteenth-century Spanish friar and fierce critic of the Spanish imperial destruction of "Indian" communities. Las Casas, who joined Francisco de Vitoria (1483-1546) in defining the inborn rights of Indigenous people subjugated by the Spanish Empire, provided an important model for Lemkin, who suggested that his "name has lived on through the centuries as one of the most admirable and courageous crusaders for humanity the world has ever known." The "history of genocide," Lemkin summarized in his unpublished *Proposal for Introduction to the Study of Genocide*, "provides examples of the awakening of humanitarian feelings which gradually have been crystallized in formulae of international law. The awakening of the world conscience is traced to the times when the world community took an affirmative stand to protect human groups from extinction. Bartolomé de las Casas, Vitoria, and humanitarian interventions, are all links in one chain leading to the proclamation of genocide as an international crime by the United Nations."[66]

According to one assessment, "Lemkin's reliance on Las Casas blinded him to one of the most significant findings emerging in the 1930s and 1940s—that the population of Indians in the Americas declined precipitously after contact with Europeans because of newly introduced diseases." But this purported weakness in Lemkin's account of "biological genocide" in fact reveals its conceptual strength from the standpoint of modern historiography. Lemkin dismissed prevailing Euro-American assessments of Indigenous disease mortality in the research that preceded his pioneering definition of genocide during the 1940s and 1950s. He chided other scholars for their tendency to ignore insights first provided by Las Casas during the sixteenth century. Too many scholars, in his view, accounted for indigenous population loss in the Americas as an inevitable occurrence within the ebb and flow of human civilization—as a set of cultures that vanished in the way of other historical civilizations. Lemkin insisted that the contingent effects of perpetrator intent, rather than nebulously defined environmental or societal phenomena, ought to frame the assessment and commemoration of historical instances of mass-death. His use of Las Casas's narrative of destruction, which centered on "exhausted slave mothers not able to nurse their children, and the separation of families by slavehunters," thus anticipated the later critiques of biological determinism detailed above. Those critiques, we have noted, highlight the structural effects of colonial interventions and the resulting contingency of disease mortality. The same intrusive processes that heightened disease mortality, moreover, prevented reproduction and motherhood. Through this insight, Lemkin's reading of Las Casas prefigured later work that has highlighted the importance of recovery, including through the fertility of maternal survivors, in assessing demographic loss and genocide. The "father" of genocide studies provided an account of structural genocidal intent, and a more holistic understanding of population loss, long before these interpretative approaches were elucidated more formally in historical scholarship, sociology, and legal theory. These new ways of understanding Lemkin's legacy can complement the use of structural or even loose genocidal intent in public representations of historical Indigenous population loss, rather than suggesting its problematic relativization of stricter definitions drawn from the Holocaust.[67]

## Toward consensus on the representation of cultural genocide

The congruence between Indigenous notions of land-based nationhood and Raphael Lemkin's "descriptions of the cultural relationship between a group of people and the physical space that they occupied" is germane to recent discussions of cultural genocide in Holocaust Studies and Indigenous Studies. Lemkin, according to Thomas M. Butcher, "held that techniques of genocide that attack the relationship between a people and their physical space are extraordinarily effective, because they affect multiple 'aspects of life' simultaneously."[68] Referencing Lemkin, Ward Churchill has thus reasserted the definitive importance of "Cultural Genocide, by which is meant the destruction of the specific character of the targeted group(s) through destruction or expropriation of its means of economic perpetuation; prohibition or curtailment of its language; suppression of its religious, social or political practices; destruction or denial of access to its religious or other sites, shrines, or institutions; destruction or denial of use and access to objects of sacred or sociocultural significance; forced dislocation, expulsion or dispersal of its members; forced transfer or removal of its children, or any other means."[69] Unfortunately, Churchill's polemical remarks on Jewish "exclusivism" in Holocaust commemoration have prevented scholars from taking his separate discussion of cultural genocide more seriously—it is often dismissed as a rhetorical sleight of hand, designed to supersede the scale of Jewish loss with Native American suffering, a competitive attempt to dilute the importance of strict intent and coordinated physical and biological elimination by widening the definitive scope of ethnocultural loss. Churchill's critics have thus often suggested that the notion of cultural genocide crudely compares the destruction of physical bodies with the curtailment of ethnocentric rituals and ideas. During the last few decades, therefore, the potential to collapse the legal and scholarly definition of cultural genocide into more traditional accounts of biological destruction has often divided Holocaust scholars from their counterparts in Indigenous Studies.[70]

Yet Lemkin did not indeed always restrict his definition of modern genocide terminology to the destruction of physical bodies. In *Axis Rule*, Lemkin suggested that "[g]enocide has two phases: one, destruction of the national pattern of the oppressed group; the other, the imposition of the national pattern of the oppressor. This imposition, in turn, may be made upon the oppressed population which is allowed to remain, or upon the territory alone, after removal of the population and the colonization of the area by the oppressor's own nationals." Lemkin, according to Moses, tended to "associate 'destruction'—a word he preferred to 'extermination'—with what he called 'crippling' a group: genocide, he wrote in 1946, is 'the criminal intent to destroy or cripple permanently a human group.'" This broader definitive scope underscored Lemkin's attachment to a conception of cultural genocide, which he often elucidated through reference to Spanish interventions among Indigenous people in the Caribbean and South America, as well as those of Euro-American settlers among Indigenous people in North America. In these discussions, as McDonnell and Moses have pointed out, Lemkin "regarded the extinction of the culture as genocide. It did not require the entire physical extermination of the victims, only the elimination of the culture-bearing strata." In a 1947 article in the *American Journal of International Law*, Lemkin described the "permanent crippling" of a people as "tantamount to genocide." In his *Thoughts on Nazi Genocide*, which was likely a chapter in a general history of genocide that he never published, Lemkin wrote: "Side by side with the extermination of 'undesirables' went a systematic looting of artworks, books, the closing of universities and other places of learning, the destruction of national monuments." These and other statements have led theorists to suggest that Lemkin's reading of European interventions in the Americas was "reminiscent of his observations about the Nazi attacks on the culture of the victims during the Second World War."[71]

Lemkin's autobiographical reminiscences are too often overlooked in our understanding of his approach to genocide during the debate and drafting of the UN Genocide Convention. There, as John Docker has shown, Lemkin outlined his conception of "cultural genocide." According to Lemkin, the deliberate destruction of languages, social frameworks, inter-generational rituals, and binding ideologies was likely to affect "the biological and physical structure of the oppressed group." In an autobiography he wrote less than a year before his death in 1959, Lemkin recalled his work on the concept of "cultural genocide" at a UN committee meeting convened immediately after World War II. The concept, which he defended through two drafts before it was rejected by other committee members, "meant the destruction of the cultural pattern of a group, such as the language, the traditions, the monuments, archives, libraries, churches. In brief: the shrines of the soul of a nation . . ."[72]

Scholars and commentators can certainly debate whether the Holocaust *ought* to assume the role as an ultimate definitive touchstone, given the

Figure 1.3 *In the cellar of the Race Institute in Frankfurt, Germany, Chaplain Samuel Blinder examines one of hundreds of "Saphor Torahs" (Sacred Scrolls), among the books stolen from every occupied country in Europe, July 6, 1945. © Getty Images.*

horrific and extreme experience of Jews under the Nazis and the nature of the Nazi obsession with their biological extermination above all other strategic concerns during the war. They are free to differ in their view of the tense association between general genocide terminology and the memorialization of the Holocaust as a definitive genocide. But such discussions should not require us to overlook Lemkin's contribution to the intellectual history of comparative genocide studies.[73]

Lemkin's insights on cultural genocide have been corroborated by much recent work on the construction of ethnicity among nations, tribes, and groups. Using their own archives of memory as well as settler colonial frameworks for understanding dispossession and death, Indigenous and allied scholars have produced similar definitions. They have underscored how the unifying impetus of cultural media are sometimes difficult to separate from the biological aspects of human demography. The destruction of linguistic, religious, and intellectual systems prevents survivors from maintaining the cultural cohesion that those systems once generated and as a result may curtail biological reproduction and demographic renewal. Shared cultural norms often cement existing ethnic distinctions or even create those distinctions *de novo*. In either case they are often necessary to delineate potential reproductive mates or to incorporate the offspring of inter-cultural unions. The UN Genocide Convention (UNGC) links the imposition of "measures intended to prevent births" within a particular ethnocultural "group" to a definition of genocide. The definition is usually marshaled to describe deliberate attempts to destroy the ability of group members to isolate each other as reproductive partners, including through forced relocation, enslavement, sterilization, or gender separation. But the repudiation of cultural practices has often achieved the same ends. The Holocaust destroyed myriad aspects of Jewish culture as well as Jewish subcultures—some of which were renewed by survivors, albeit in new diasporic contexts. But this was not necessarily the case for other cohesive groups who provided few or no survivors, such as the Jews of Salonika or discrete Hasidic sects in Hungary and Poland. They once maintained constantly evolving linguistic and cultural systems. During the Holocaust, their idiosyncratic languages, idiolects, and cultural frameworks were lost forever as means of delineating members of their reproductive communities. We can make similar observations regarding Indigenous communities. While many have been able to recover their cultural heritage alongside demographic renewal, others have not. If cultural destruction is intended to prevent living descendants of a particular group from maintaining any sort of cohesion, their likelihood to reproduce becomes strongly reduced.[74]

The biological and demographic legacy of cultural destruction highlights the particular importance of linguistic loss in both communities. Language has long been defined as a form of "fossil poetry"—a framework for communication that contiguously transmits cultural ideas and values across generations, while also marking a reproductive community. The linguistic medium carries a message of historical and cultural continuity, contributing to the biological reproduction of its speakers and its own continued future transmission.[75] Consider, for example, the way the poetry of Bouena Sarfatty (1916–97) has been documented by Renée Melammed in *An Ode to Salonika*. The poems, as Melammed notes, "sketches the life and demise of the Sephardi Jewish community" using 500 "coplas" written in Salonican Ladino to provide "a rare entrée into a once vibrant world now lost." By destroying a cultural medium, Melammed's work suggests, we are left only with a wistful ode to a lost community: demographic and cultural vitality were intertwined, leading the destruction of each to impact the other.[76]

Melammed's insights are supported by a separate body of work among Indigenous communities in North America. In the Salonikan case, a few surviving Jews found themselves sheared of their linguistic and cultural heritage, dispersed in small disparate diasporas, unable to connect with each other in cultural ways, and thus prevented from reproducing any sort of demographic cohesion. There have been many similar Indigenous cases where biological destruction was contiguous with the loss of discrete culture. Some communities, therefore, have outlined the importance of renewing cultural systems—particularly languages—to avoid the demographic legacy of their earlier destruction. William A. Geiger, for example, has described a "Decolonial Theory of Tlingit Language Revitalization" that links linguistic preservation to the resistance of Alaska Native communities to assimilation and demographic decline. A 2016 Tlingit language textbook was even titled *Haa Wsineix̱ Haa Yoo X̱'atángi, Our Language Saved Us: A Guidebook for Learning the Tlingit Language*.[77] Identifying the often-overlooked link between linguistic resurgence and biological reproduction should allow a useful degree of cooperation—as well as empathy—between Jews and Indigenous people in scholarly and public commemorative realms.[78]

Scholars interested in the definition of cultural genocide in North America, including the role of Indigenous languages, have also begun to consider templates from Australian Aboriginal Studies alongside those drawn from Holocaust history. Australia's "stolen generation" of Aboriginal people experienced "forced assimilation" through their removal from biological parents and their placement in boarding schools or among white families (up to 25,000 children between 1910 and 1970). Those acts can be described as genocide according to prevailing international legal definitions, even though most of the individual children did not lose their physical lives. The UN Genocide Convention (UNGC) prohibits "forcibly transferring children of the group to another group." This definition has become central to discussions of cultural restriction and forced assimilation as a barrier to biological reproduction in American and Canadian residential schools. Richard Henry Pratt, the founder of the Pennsylvania Carlisle Indian School, delivered the following infamous rationale for removing children from their parents and communities: "Kill the Indian, Save the Man." Removing children from Indigenous parents prevented births within their communities by shearing them of all cultural reference points and then placing them in dispersed families after graduation. These activities highlight the place of cultural destruction within broader biological definitions of genocide—what has been described as "education for extinction" in the United States and Canada.[79]

Canada's Indian Residential Schools (IRS) system lasted between 1834 and 1996. From the 1880s, Catholic and Protestant churches in Canada managed more than 150,000 children in 125 schools for over a century, with federal government support. Removed from their parents and deliberately sheared of their cultural heritage, Indigenous children were nutritionally deprived while living in cramped circumstances, making disease even more likely to affect them. In 1991, a Royal Commission on Aboriginal Peoples (RCAP) was set up to deal with historical complaints about the IRS, which stimulated the formation of a Canadian Truth and Reconciliation Commission (TRC) with top-down involvement from Indigenous people and institutions. From 2009 to 2015, the TRC examined the historical nature and contemporary legacy of genocide in the IRS system and elsewhere in Canadian and colonial settings.[80]

No official statement from the TRC invoked the specific term genocide. Nonetheless, its exposure of the activities of Canadian Residential schools moves us more closely to traditional biological definitions of genocide in the UN Convention, particularly the intent to "destroy, in whole or part, an identifiable group of persons." That definition is further supported by a discussion that was buried in the references to the TRC summary statement, which was issued in 2015 and noted: "It is difficult to understand why the forced assimilation of children through removal from their families and communities—to be placed with people of another race for the purpose of destroying the race and culture from which the children come—can be deemed an act of genocide under Article 2 (e) of the UN's Convention on Genocide, but is not a civil wrong." But the TRC commission did eventually adopt the term "cultural genocide" in its 2015 summary report:

> For over a century, the central goals of Canada's Aboriginal policy were to eliminate Aboriginal governments; ignore Aboriginal rights; terminate the Treaties; and, through a process of assimilation, cause Aboriginal peoples to cease to exist as distinct legal, social, cultural, religious, and racial entities in Canada. The establishment and operation of residential schools were a central element of this policy, which can best be described as "cultural genocide."[81]

Settler-colonial dynamics help to explain how residential schools exerted such destructive effects on Indigenous children so long after Canada became a nation-state. As ongoing structural forms of power rather than singular events their "shift-shaping" following the colonial era became evident in Canadian IRS models. The ostensibly progressive agenda of the IRS system ("protecting" children from "vanishing") rejected Indigenous ways of knowing and being just as European colonial interventions once counteracted land-based definitions of identity and sovereignty. Both acts of cultural destruction were deadly for many Indigenous people in Canada.[82]

The potential for settler-colonial dynamics to shape-shift and reconfigure in the cultural genocide of Canadian IRS institutions can be elucidated through comparison with the Nazi use of bureaucratic metaphors and euphemisms to describe the destruction of Jews. According to Dean Neu and Richard Therrien, the rupture of Indigenous life and culture during the colonial era was later "filtered through and managed through a complex field of bureaucratized manipulations, controlled by soft technologies such as strategic planning, law and accounting . . . a continuance, no less painful, of the more overt forms of violence that have always driven colonization." Influenced by Zygmunt Bauman's seminal discussion of the role of bureaucratic vocabulary during the Holocaust, Neu and Therrien's assessment of forced assimilation in Canadian Residential Schools has uncovered examples where Indigenous nations were described as "weeds" to be extracted from an "ideal garden."[83] Even if we discount direct

**Figure 1.4** *People watch as a convoy of truckers and other vehicles travel in front of the former Kamloops Indian Residential School in support of the Tk'emlups te Secwepemc people after the remains of 215 children were discovered buried near the facility, in Kamloops, Canada, on June 5, 2021. © Getty Images.*

equivalence or causal association between residential schools and Nazi ideology, their broader comparison illuminates the power of disease and weed metaphors to combine with bureaucratic terminology to obscure cultural eradication. Bernie Farber, the former head of the Canadian Jewish Congress, thus called for concerted recognition of Indigenous genocide in Canada in statements that were sparked by revelations about medical experiments in Indian Residential Schools: "The time has come for Canada to formally recognize a sixth genocide, the genocide of its own aboriginal communities; a genocide that began at the time of first contact and that was still very active in our own lifetimes; a genocide currently in search of a name but no longer in search of historical facts."[84]

Other forms of empathetic engagement have followed the work of Canadian tribunals on residential schools. One of the most poignant recent examples involves Nate Leipciger, a Canadian Holocaust survivor from Poland who has begun to elucidate the sexual assaults he experienced at Fünfteichen, a "subcamp" of Gross-Rosen. Leipciger did not speak publicly about this aspect of his Holocaust experience until a 2010 visit to Auschwitz with his family. As Dorota Glowacka has shown, his "decision to finally open up about the abuse was inspired by the example of former youth athletes and male survivors of Indian residential schools in Canada who in the 1990s began coming forward with their stories." Leipciger had become a close friend with Theodor Fontaine, former chief of the Sagkeeng Ojibway First Nation in Manitoba, who had survived sexual abuse while attending two Indian Residential Schools between 1948 and 1960.[85]

To be sure, the complicated connection between cultural genocide and conventions of biological genocide in Canada's TRC also raises a key difference with the way Holocaust memory has traditionally been approached in national and international commissions. The mandate of the TRC, as MacDonald reminds us, was "deliberately antithetical to the principles of Nuremberg Tribunal. This was not to be a retributive commission focused on finding and punishing perpetrators but rather was driven by survivor priorities, given that it was funded by survivors and was designed to promote healing from over a century of trauma."[86] That impetus, indeed, might provide a model for the descendants of Holocaust survivors as new information becomes available about the destruction of Jewish life and culture. Rather than looking to the Nuremberg priorities, which were relevant to the immediate aftermath of the Holocaust when perpetrators were alive, survivor-centric models might be used in parts of the world, such as Eastern Europe, where Jewish narratives continue to be occluded by communities who fear the consequences of formal legal tribunals. Instead, Jewish culture and survival could be supported by commissions and tribunals that allow external acknowledgement of their historical trauma to aid their commemorative efforts.

However simple they may seem, the comparisons identified in this chapter can contribute to a powerful interpretative alliance between Holocaust scholars, Native Americanists, and experts in First Nations Studies. They do not require any group to eschew the specific and distinct contexts that encompassed the agency to survive but also the likelihood of mass death. Rather, comparisons generate useful conceptual models that illuminate the powerful role of societal interventions in the destruction of populations and in the prevention of their demographic recovery. They can contribute to a joint critique of commemorative approaches that define supposedly transhistorical determinants of mortality such as biological immunity or human intolerance. Rather than resurrecting older competitive comparisons regarding the relative per-capita losses experienced by Jews and Indigenous people or the distinction between strict and loose notions of genocide, new approaches in Holocaust history can be informed by critiques of monocultural representation within Indigenous Studies, and vice versa.

# CHAPTER TWO

# "Metaphysical Jew Hatred" and the "Metaphysics of Indian-hating."

## Public Memory and the Problem of Imperial Power

This chapter examines the recent imperial turn in the history of genocide, which has been influenced by techniques and concepts in the separate fields of comparative genocide studies and settler-colonial studies. Understanding the imperial frameworks of power that contributed to the murder of Jews during the Holocaust and the genocides of Indigenous people in North America is important to interrogate the chief concern of this book: the subsequent tendency to universalize, de-specify, or overlook those histories in North American and European public memory. Acknowledging imperial frameworks of genocide unsettles the way Americans and Canadians have so often represented Indigenous histories of trauma as aberrations in the unfolding trajectory of North American freedom. It provides a way to critique the common distinction between North American freedom and the horror of the European Holocaust, which has often universalized or de-specified the Jewish experience while overlooking Indigenous genocide altogether. It disturbs the way Europeans have often represented it as an "American" rather than also a European event and helps us to understand why such distinctions have commonly accompanied the definition of the Holocaust as an aberrant archetype. Greater attention to the ubiquity of Indigenous death in imperial frameworks challenges the definition and commemoration of the "Final Solution" as an anomalous perversion of otherwise contiguous civilized values, whether European, American, or

"Western"—a definition that, as we will see, has also contributed to the de-Judaization of the Holocaust in public memory.[1]

It is legitimate to distinguish between the effects of European colonialism, including among Indigenous people in North America, and the ways that anti-Semitism was deployed against Jews during the Holocaust. But more nuanced insights from comparative genocide studies and the imperial historiographical turn avoid drawing analogies or causal links between the Nazi East and the American West, or between Adolf Hitler and Christopher Columbus, which have the potential to collapse all historical knowledge, including that of the Holocaust or Indigenous genocide, into a relativistic narrative. Whatever our view of the possible association between colonial European interventions and later Nazi policies, acknowledging how those interventions destroyed Indigenous lives reduces the claim that transcendent European or even "Western" values were somehow undermined by the anomalous occurrence of Nazi persecution.

Indigenous people, Jews, and their allied scholars are thus well positioned to formulate a joint critique of the way their separate histories have been used to delineate civilizational ideologies by universalizing or de-specifying their suffering and loss. But before we can consider the power of that critique in relation to Euro-American museums, monuments, political declarations, civic statements, and public media, it is necessary to outline broader theoretical insights that can be gained by considering Indigenous genocide and the Holocaust within an imperial framework. It is pertinent to examine how the imperial turn in genocide studies *ought* to align public representations more closely with the group memory of Indigenous people and Jews. Alongside comparative insights from the previous chapter, that assessment will provide a useful baseline to consider divergent approaches in public sites of memory on both sides of the Atlantic in the chapters that follow.

## The Nazi East and the American West

Consider the possible impact on European and North American public memory of three related scholarly claims, each of which is more controversial than the other: that colonial European interventions stimulated Indigenous genocides; that Nazis used structurally similar forms of imperial authority in their attempt to liquidate global Jewry; and most contentiously, that the colonial framework of nineteenth-century American westward expansion was linked to the imperial model that Nazis used to occupy Europe and eliminate its Jews. These claims derive in part from the imperial turn in the historiography of the Holocaust and in the separate field of comparative genocide studies over the last few decades. They have also been stimulated by the relatively recent advancement of settler-colonial paradigms to understand the histories of Indigenous genocide in colonial North America, the United States, and Canada.[2]

For more than a century, Indigenous people in North America have noted the parallels, continuities, and links between the destruction wrought by European colonial settlement from the sixteenth century and the westward movement of the United States during the nineteenth century. Their assessment has been corroborated by a recent consensus in the historiographies of early America and Canada, formulated by Indigenous and non-Indigenous scholars, which emphasizes the ways that the actions of white citizens in the nineteenth century were often rooted in acts of dispossession—and even genocide—perpetrated by European settlers in North America during previous centuries.[3] These insights provide a critical template to examine public memory work in North America and Europe. Abstract or hazy representations of the history of Indigenous genocide in the colonial era are likely to overlook the specific imperial European power dynamics that enabled the subsequent formation and geographical expansion of the United States and Canada as independent states.

It is worth considering the possible comparative effects of two more contentious scholarly trends, which may also unsettle the tendency towards universalism and abstraction in the representation of the Holocaust and Indigenous genocide in European and North American public memory. A separate and relatively recent historiographical controversy has centered on the possible link between the nineteenth-century expansion of American settlers into Indigenous lands and the later attempt by Nazis to exterminate Jews. The link is more controversial than that between European colonialism in North America and the later actions of white American and Canadian settlers through the nineteenth century. Rather than looking to the clear association between the settler-colonial ideology of nineteenth-century white citizens and the European colonizers who preceded them, Carrol P. Kakel, James Q. Whitman, and several other scholars treat the nineteenth-century actions of American settlers as a *sui generis* influence on the later actions of Nazis.[4]

The underlying approach of those who propose a US–Nazi link is comparable to the way nineteenth-century German expansion in Africa has often been treated by a separate school of historians and genocide theorists. There exists a far more well-developed, though still contested, historiographical link between nineteenth-century European colonialism in Africa and Nazi persecution. Several scholars have suggested that the structures of violence and dispossession that governed European interventions in Africa provided a precursor, or even a partial model, for later Nazi efforts to eradicate Jews. Discussions of the colonial origins of Nazi activity during the last few decades recall an earlier generation of European anti-colonial writers and theorists, including Aimé Césaire and Hannah Arendt. Nazi horrors, they suggested, brought hitherto extra-European colonial frameworks of violence into the European heartland. Having exported face-to-face murder to colonial frontiers, in their critique, European media, philosophers, legal theorists, politicians, and lay people had been able to maintain a notion of civility within their continental borders. In the ascent of Nazism, including the

Holocaust, they eventually experienced the effects of violence within those borders, which Césaire depicted as a "boomerang" from the colonial sphere, where it had previously been exported (notwithstanding the problematic nature of the term "boomerang" in this instance). Others have questioned direct causal associations between Nazi ideology and nineteenth-century European colonization in Africa and have warned against situating the Holocaust as one of many genocides on a colonial continuum. Such an approach, they point out, minimizes the singular nature of anti-Semitism as a causal effect of Nazi policies toward Jews. Only exterminationist anti-Semitism, they suggest, could unite competing factions within Nazism, bring it to the boil, and remain a priority even after the Nazi apparatus had begun to lose strategic control of European lands.[5]

These scholarly trends may expose interpretative tensions among Indigenous people, Jews, and allied scholars as they confront the treatment of the Holocaust and Indigenous genocide in public memory on both sides of the Atlantic. The recently proposed link between the Holocaust and nineteenth-century US settler expansion is likely to face an even greater critical response than that which has followed the connection between Nazism and European colonialism in nineteenth-century Africa. Some Jewish commentators and allied scholars are sure to question any perceived attempt to locate the origins of the "Final Solution" in non-Jewish imperial contexts, including in North America during the 1800s, not least because the proposed ontological status of anti-Semitism may then be diminished in representations of the Holocaust in museums, public sites of memory, and educational curricula.[6]

Aside from referencing the ontological status of anti-Semitism in Nazi ideology and strategy (common in critiques of the link between African colonialism and Nazism) several historians have highlighted the surprising lack of interest in the American West among the Nazi architects of the Holocaust.[7] Claiming a direct causal association between American settler history and Nazi state-building, others point out, overlooks the ideological and strategic rupture between nineteenth-century liberal expansionism—whether American or German—and later Nazi ideology. White US settlers were often valorized as independent and individualistic, a description that remains in popular discourse. During the World War II era, conversely, German settlers in Eastern European frontiers were rarely treated as emblems of individual self-reliance, lest such a doctrine reduce the overarching power and authority of the Nazi state and the Führer himself. Nazi plans for the East, therefore, differed from the Republican ideology of expansion into the American West a century earlier.[8]

But there are less ambiguous ways for comparative imperial frameworks to unsettle common representations of the Holocaust and Indigenous population loss. Notwithstanding the difference between Nazi state control and the American Republican emphasis on self-reliance, American expansion into the West followed earlier colonial European approaches by depriving Indigenous people of power, land, and life to make *them* more reliant on the US state. It denied their sovereignty, including through the eventual construction of the Reservation system. American Free-Soil liberalism and Nazi expansionism may have been antithetical in their definition of the state's role in the lives of settlers. But the destruction of Native American independence, partially rooted in earlier European settler-colonial frameworks, was rather closer to the structural and ideological control imposed by Nazis than some of the critiques above imply.[9]

Even if we follow Omer Bartov's measured division between "colonization-fueled genocides" and "totalitarian ideologies," therefore, we do not have to dismiss the potential insights that can be gained from broader comparisons between imperially structured frameworks of authority. Imperial agendas contributed to the destruction of Indigenous populations by European colonists and US settlers. They could also be detected in the supranational assertion of power that Nazis used to liquidate the Jews of Europe. It was, as Dirk A. Moses reminds us, through "empire and its structures that the Nazis sought to round up the Jews . . . pursued across an entire empire, deploying all the varying regional and subordinate structures of power that existed in the different regions under Nazi rule" to eliminate the Jewish people. Comparing the structural frameworks that governed these different cases does not necessarily require any suggestion of their direct interaction or causal association, nor any equivalence of outcomes within them. In adopting such an approach, moreover, we do not have to eschew separate ontological roots for the lethal deployment of anti-Semitism against Jews or settler-colonial ideology against Indigenous people.[10]

Holocaust scholars have often dismissed broad links between discursive models from different periods and contexts as a problematic manifestation of postmodern or poststructuralist influences. Those scholarly trends are said to play fast and loose with meaning and context in their tendency to link multiple narratives and discourses without apparent concern for their objective or empirical association. Such critiques have made important points about the potential to collapse all historical knowledge, including that of the Holocaust or Native American genocide, into one relativistic morass.[11] But in heeding these warnings, it has become all too easy to dismiss more subtle forms of discourse analysis, which provide a bridge between classic discussions of rhetorical theory and more recent work in comparative genocide studies.

In a seminal statement, published in 1964, the philosopher and sociologist Marshall McLuhan suggested that "the medium is the message." Though the outward form of languages, concepts, and models may be conceived in specific regional and temporal contexts, according to McLuhan, they are then able to shape "the scale and form of human association and action" in other contexts and periods. The medium used to transmit ideas, rather than the ideas themselves, may become the most important stimulant for perceptions and actions, whether in their primary context or in later periods.

The nature of a medium, defined as the channel through which a message "introduces into human affairs," may become as influential in its ability to determine actions as the specific content of the message it originally encompassed.[12]

Comparative genocide theorists have built on these insights to define the potential movement of discursive concepts from one context to another, including from imperial settings to Nazi Europe. Nazi outreach to non-Jewish European subjects outside Germany was indebted to nineteenth-century models and vocabularies, notwithstanding Nazi opposition to the *message* of liberal expansionism that those models had often sought to communicate. Colonial frameworks contributed to the determination of subsequent modes of thought in new historical contexts, including in the structural ways that Nazi totalitarianism approached the elimination of European Jewry. The contexts that preceded Nazi imperial expansion, including the experience of Indigenous populations in the Americas, bequeathed conceptual frameworks that helped to steer the direction of anti-Semitism, which was of course already part of Nazi ideology. The medium of the terminology Nazis inherited influenced their conception that Jews somehow unsettled the imperial structure of power that they suddenly administered—even if their general obsession with Jews above other minority groups derived from anti-Semitic influences with separate genealogies.[13] Nineteenth-century white American settlers may have been unaware of colonial precedents for their acts of dispossession and their racially charged thought patterns. Nazi strategists may have consciously sought to repudiate colonial history due to their disdain for nineteenth-century liberal imperial expansionism, whether German or American. But their understandings of identity and power relations could still have been determined in part by conceptual languages that they inherited from earlier contexts that they ignored or repudiated. The medium of communicating ideas and concepts, derived in part from imperial ways of defining power structures, may have determined particular messages or outcomes among perpetrator populations.[14]

The possibility of discursive links between pre-twentieth-century European imperialism and Nazism, to be sure, will always divide scholars. The validity of such an interpretative approach will depend on their view of the power of conceptual media to determine human actions outside their immediate regional and temporal contexts; how historical precedents may bequeath linguistic terms and models to future populations without their realizing those precedents; whether the status of anti-Semitism or colonial chauvinism ought to be considered as causal agents in and of themselves; and even more generally, the extent that information has ebbed and flowed between different civilizations.

But even if we discount the notion that conceptual frameworks from one context will necessarily influence behavior in another, we can still gain much from comparing media and modes of expression from within each of them. We can work out whether and why their separate contexts may have generated structurally similar ways of describing the relationship between majorities and minorities; or the association between central ruling authorities, the outlying national communities they governed, and minority third parties. Broad similarities between different historical contexts may have made certain conceptual frameworks more likely to manifest. It is not necessary to draw direct or even discursive links between two case studies to consider and compare how particular sorts of power structures in each of them may have produced potentially genocidal aspirations or outcomes. Genocidal aspirations, moreover, may have required the subsequent construction of imperial power structures to produce particularly lethal results. Irrespective of any direct causal link between contexts, or any association between inherited interpretative media, it remains valuable to consider whether broad organizational similarities between European and Nazi imperialism may have allowed, or even required, minority groups to be defined in threatening ways.[15]

These insights provide further material for any template that critiques public memory work in North America and Europe. The identification of imperially structured power dynamics through comparative history ought to influence the representation of the separate cases of the Holocaust and Indigenous genocide. Whether we focus on specific structural links or simple conceptual comparisons, imperial frameworks provide a useful set of terms and concepts to counter abstract or universalistic approaches to memory that overlook key aspects of perpetrator intent across historical periods and contexts—including the Nazi destruction of European Jewry and the colonial European roots of Indigenous dispossession from the sixteenth century through the twentieth century.

## Subaltern genocide, Indigenous history, and Holocaust memory

The helpful interpretative model of "subaltern genocide" is revealed by comparing the separate experiences of Jews and Indigenous people under imperial frameworks of power. The model provides a powerful way of representing the nature of perpetrator intent without overlooking contextually specific stimuli such as anti-Semitism or settler-colonial ideology in their separate cases. Genocides are usually described as having been perpetrated by dominant host cultures, or dominant invaders, against weaker or minority groups. But in late eighteenth-century Haiti, for example, white French settler elites feared their domination by subaltern people of color. The fears of colonizer elites in the 1780–2 Andean Great Rebellion have been described in similar ways. In these and other imperial examples, exhibiting the fear of subaltern genocide offered a quick way to encourage popular violence against minorities. But it also reflected real and deep-seated paranoia about the potential for dominant settler populations to be targeted for biological elimination by those whom they colonized or had once colonized.[16] Such an interpretative framework is useful to approach conceptual similarities between Indigenous dispossession by Euro-American settlers and common Nazi descriptions of the "Jewish problem." Let us turn to the North American context before examining how those discussions might inform the history and commemoration of Nazi anti-Semitism.

Consider the history and legacy of the Pequot Wars, which took place during the late 1630s in New England. Comparative discussions of Pequot population decline have often been characterized by divisions over the notion of the Holocaust's uniqueness as a category of genocide, leading to a conceptual *impasse* over its place in comparative genocide studies. Yet the interpretative framework of subaltern genocide offers a particularly useful way to approach the Pequot example. Though ostensibly deferential to English imperial authority, Puritan leaders exerted a degree of autonomy in their declaration of the requirement to "punish" surviving Indigenous communities for their suspected role in attacking English traders. English militiamen duly set fire to a Pequot village on the Mystic River, murdered any civilians who tried to escape, and carefully tracked down surviving Pequots over the following two years. They imposed a treaty that explicitly declared the abolition of "the Pequot nation"—an intent to destroy at least a large portion of particular group that is close to modern definitions of genocide that "include cases of an intention to destroy a group by physically eliminating a substantial portion of its numbers."[17] According to Laurence M. Hauptman, the Pequot War thus "laid a foundation of white-Native relations that included the possibility and actualization of genocide"—not only through direct perpetrator intent, but also due to broader structural forces that prevented demographic recovery in the longer term. For more than a century, moreover, the mere survival of Pequot communities led non-Indigenous populations to fear retribution from the now subaltern Pequot population and to justify further Indigenous death as necessary to prevent the destruction of their own people.[18]

Through the nineteenth century, many white American politicians and settlers demonstrated a similar degree of paranoia in their paradoxical synthesis between anti-colonial ideology and imperial expansionism. By 1800, it was common for US settlers to describe their Western movement into Indian country using a vocabulary of anti-colonization, which they had inherited from the Revolutionary era. Having thrown off the shackles of British imperial rule during the 1770s and 1780s, they were finally allowed to expand into Western frontiers. Yet they claimed to fear hostile minorities within that same expansive realm. By the second decade of the nineteenth century, influential "War Hawks" recommended that President James Madison lead a "Second War of Independence" against Britain. Though British garrisons were few and far between, War Hawks became obsessed with the possibility that a numerical minority threatened to re-colonize and even eliminate the majority population of free white Americans. The determination to vanquish colonizers within their realm ironically reinforced what scholars of the resulting War of 1812 have increasingly described as its most potent motivation: the consolidation of federal structures of state expansion into hitherto autonomous Indigenous "nations." Those nations were accused of allying with former British colonial rulers. Informed by earlier European imperial models of Indigenous dispossession, therefore, the war against Britain was motivated by the attendant desire to diminish the sovereignty of subaltern yet dangerous Indigenous nations and even to eliminate those who resisted such a development.[19]

The imperial framework of power in the expanding American state required discipline from local white settler communities and a degree of deference to federal authority in Washington D.C. Yet that same authority was not guaranteed and required a *quid pro quo*: settlers in the American West were granted a degree of independence, particularly in their organization of armed militias against Native Americans. Indigenous people were considered as a security threat to imperial structures of American Western expansion and the local settler communities who helped to consolidate those structures. Conflicts with them helped to reduce tensions between white settlers and overarching federal power. The civic discipline necessary to defer to centralized power could give way, allowing repressed emotions and violent passions to be expressed in local acts of bloody slaughter. The repression of emotional passions among white settlers was regulated in part by sudden outbursts of rage vented against Indigenous or other minority populations.[20]

Such encounters bore similarity to those that had preceded them in colonial North America, such as in the Pequot examples. That comparative insight becomes more meaningful if we consider the association that historians have recently drawn between Indigenous dispossession by European imperial powers in the colonial era and the later expansion of the independent United States during the nineteenth century. Indigenous people maintained different ethnocultural and linguistic identities while also being defined as a discrete group that transcended the various occupied settlements in both periods. Non-Indigenous people in those settlements were ostensibly bound by centralized authority, whether in the form of colonial governance or under the later federal power of the independent US government. But they also cherished their autonomy to control, curtail, or dispossess Indigenous people in the same settlements.[21]

Definitions of subaltern genocide, including those drawn from comparing or linking the actions of Europeans in colonial North America with those of nineteenth-century US settlers, provide a useful conceptual framework to examine and represent Nazi structures of power. Richard T. Drinnon has highlighted a "national metaphysics of Indian-hating" rooted in the earliest colonial European encounters with Indigenous people, which became "central to the formation of national identity and political policy in the United States" during the nineteenth century. In the *Origins of Totalitarianism,* Hannah

Arendt used similar terminology to suggest that "metaphysical Jew hatred" in the "subterranean stream of Western history" provided an impetus for Nazi anti-Semitism. Rather than divorcing anti-Semitism from its more specific structural context, as has sometimes been the case in subsequent readings of such statements, it is worth considering how pre-existing genealogies of anti-Semitism were incorporated in imperial frameworks of understanding. We can compare those frameworks with similar conceptions of Indigenous dispossession within the expanding American state. It is not necessary to identify direct qualitative or quantitative parallels between Indigenous mass death and the "Final Solution" to note broad structural similarities between Euro-American conceptions of Indigenous dispossession and the Nazi vision of a *judenrein* Europe.[22]

Nazis regularly accused Jews of having captured control of nineteenth-century European and American imperial expansionist efforts, and of having beckoned those efforts towards a form of liberal commercialism that led to the degradation of the German people. But Nazis rarely connected so-called Jewish influences to the initial stimulus for imperial structures of power. As recent work has suggested, Hitler and many of those around him sought to emulate—and eventually replace—"Anglo-Saxon" imperial models that they detected in the British Empire and in the expansion of North American states. They certainly did not repudiate the basic structural form of those models. The Nazi state comfortably maintained an imperial formulation by occupying and subsuming the authority of previous national regimes. A simple reading of the subaltern genocide paradigm would suggest that within that new formulation, Nazi leaders were preoccupied with the potential for indigenous Hungarians, Ukrainians, Lithuanians, Croatians, and other nations to target Germans for elimination. Yet Nazi leaders suddenly found themselves administering a multi-national imperial framework with minority Jewish communities in each of its constituent parts. Like earlier European imperial strategists, and even the nineteenth-century United States, they balanced central authority with the devolution of autonomy to other allied populations or settler communities. Jews, and not those other allied populations, were thus defined as the ultimate subaltern danger, which threatened to destroy the German *Volk* as well as its non-Jewish occupied communities. Anti-Semitic fears led Nazis to perceive Jews as a paramount "security threat" to their imperial structure of fascist rule in Europe. Hungarian Jews, Danish Jews, and Croatian Jews, rather than non-Jewish Hungarians, Danes, or Croats, were defined as the only truly hostile entity with trans-national powers—above and beyond any threat from non-Jewish resistance efforts.[23]

Some Nazi-occupied populations were thus given a degree of autonomy to persecute, dispossess, and murder Jews. They achieved greater unity with their occupiers through these activities. And even in those cases where Nazi authorities took care to direct the liquidation of Jews, often clandestinely, anti-Semitic propaganda was still regularly deployed to bind non-Jewish occupied populations to Nazi power. The Nazi imperial framework balanced secondary national cultures alongside the primary national identity of the German *Volk* at the center of the "New Order." The violent interventions of groups such as the Hungarian Arrow Cross and the Croatian Ustaša demonstrated how existing ethno-national identities could coexist alongside Nazi imperial authority, united by a desire to eliminate Jews as well as by paranoia regarding other minorities in their ethnocultural spheres.[24] We do not have to settle the debate on the "ontological" or "redemptive" status of anti-Semitism to note the utility of an imperial perspective in these examples. It helps us to understand the conceptual terminology that allowed Germans, but also the non-German nations they administered, to be defined as biological victims of colonization by a minority group of Jews. Just as the strongest person could become colonized by deadly bacteria, Nazis suggested that Aryan Germans and the non-German nations they administered risked becoming victims of colonization by a minority group. German blood and soil, as well as other European national cultures, was said to have been infiltrated by an entity that transcended regular cultural and ethno-national boundaries. Nazi ideology thus described Germans as an "indigenous people" who had suffered "under foreign occupation" by global Jewry.[25] Its anti-colonial terminology described the elimination of Jews as a defensive move to regain the freedom of Germans as well as other non-Jewish Europeans under the imperial umbrella of the Third Reich. German imperial occupation, paradoxically, was said to free and protect other nations from the subaltern danger posed by Jews. By opposing the existence of Jews in Europe, Nazi leaders deployed the terminology of an anti-colonization movement precisely to reinforce their imperial structure of authority over other non-Jewish European groups.

The incorporation of Germans and other non-Jewish subjects into the imperial Nazi state apparently required their self-discipline, their repression of individual emotions, and their regularization of movement. Yet the imperial structure of the Nazi state also granted a degree of agency to its settlers in regions such as Romania, Ukraine, and Belarus, as well as to the local non-Jewish populations they occupied, allowing large numbers in *both* those groups to vent otherwise repressed emotions and passions in orgies of violence and murder.[26] Historians once emphasized the Nazi fear that ordinary Germans and their allies would become fraught with emotion if they were exposed to the bloody scale of the murder of Jews. In response, an "industrialized" form of murder is said to have been characterized by bureaucratic procedures, the use of euphemisms, and the geographic isolation of closed sites such as Auschwitz. But as new scholarship is beginning to show, the association between industrialized murder and the repression of individual passions overlooks the bloody fervor that accompanied the expansion of Nazi jurisdiction into Eastern Europe. The manifestation of hitherto repressed sensual urges in chaotic instances of bloody violence, and their expression by more than a minority of Nazi subjects, is only now being documented as a precedent for the "Final Solution" and as a phenomenon that continued in Eastern Europe and elsewhere long after the construction of Auschwitz. The repression of emotions required by Nazi ideology accompanied envy and resentment of Jews, who were seen as somehow freer in their purported cultural distinction from the disciplined majority in the expanding Third Reich.[27]

These insights, which rely on an imperial understanding of German supranational power, support Dan Michman's recent call to move beyond "the intentionalism–functionalism debate" and to ask instead how non-German European communities contributed to the Nazi German goal to eliminate all Jews from Europe. A "broad wave of research on grassroots activities by both Germans and locals," Michman notes, makes it clear "that the Holocaust—the comprehensive Nazi anti-Jewish enterprise—though German-initiated and led by Hitler, was in fact a Europe-wide project and has to be researched as such, and not just as a German one. And thus, the demarcation line between the perpetrator and bystander categories often blur." Michman has been critical of the imperial turn in Holocaust Studies, joining other scholars in warning against the potential for superficial comparison, relativism, and even de-Judaization. But imperial frameworks in fact complement his assertion that the Holocaust cannot solely be defined as a purely bureaucratic "event" given the leeway that Nazi leadership offered to local communities in the destruction of Jews in non-German lands—a degree of autonomy and individual choice that is not characteristic of bureaucracies and which enabled the liquidation of Jewish communities in a horrifyingly short period of time.[28]

The synergy between centralized Nazi directives and improvised local violence by non-Germans recalls the way imperial European powers balanced metropolitan directives with the autonomy of local occupied communities or settlers who had moved to those regions. From the early modern era through the nineteenth century, European imperial agents in London, Paris, Amsterdam, and Madrid were fully aware that their colonial aims were most efficiently met by offering leeway to local strategic allies or settler populations who would facilitate the appropriation of land and the dispossession of Indigenous people. By granting outlying communities the power to dispossess other groups, or by cementing divisions between one outlying group and another, their colonial aims would be met and tensions between the metropole and periphery would be reduced.[29] During the nineteenth century, we have noted, the American federal government employed a similar balance between its central authority and outlying white settler communities. American settlers synthesized anti-colonial ideology with the assertion of imperial structures of power through western expansion. They often defined their movement into Indigenous lands using the anti-colonial rhetoric of the earlier Revolutionary era. The suggestion that Native Americans had allied with British colonial adversaries offered a pretext for their dispossession as a dangerous subaltern threat to Euro-American territorial consolidation.

In demonstrating the ubiquitous association between imperial frameworks of power and mass slaughter, comparative historical insights from the discussion of subaltern genocide return us to the pioneering work of Raphael Lemkin. Having examined the horrors of mass population loss in Hispaniola and elsewhere in the Spanish Empire, Lemkin made extensive notes on the infamous intervention of Jeffery Amherst, in which the British representative is thought to have directed his military units to infiltrate Indigenous communities with smallpox infused blankets. But Lemkin also emphasized the broader structural effects of colonization on indigenous mass death, whether in South, Central, or North America, even after the departure of colonizers. In emphasizing the contingent association between Native American demographic collapse and European interventions, Lemkin prefigured later historiographical trends that link the disregard for Indigenous life in the Spanish Universal Monarchy to later theories of Native American dispossession in British North America.[30]

Rather than merely examining the potential for "genocide in colonial contexts," Lemkin "defined the concept as a technique of occupation" that was "intrinsically colonial"—a definition of genocide that emerged as "the culmination of a long tradition of European legal and political critique of colonization and empire." Many imperial unions, Lemkin pointed out, eventually lost the regional and strategic outposts that they had sought to occupy. But the near-total destruction of ethnocultural groups within those outposts remained as their legacy. Lemkin thus described a model of "genocide" that was rooted in acts of "occupation." Though Spanish and Nazi occupiers eventually departed their imperial realms, certain groups and cultures were irrevocably damaged, demonstrating how perpetrators could win "the peace even though the war itself is lost." In *Axis Rule*, Lemkin noted "two phases" in his definition: "one, destruction of the national pattern of the oppressed group: the other, the imposition of the national pattern of the oppressor. This imposition, in turn, may be made upon the oppressed population which is allowed to remain, or upon the territory alone, after removal of the population and the colonization of the area by the oppressor's own nationals."[31]

Lemkin's model does not require either the Jewish experience during the Holocaust or the Indigenous experience of mass death to be de-specified or universalized. From his earliest readings of Las Casas to his writings after World War II, after all, Lemkin avoided assigning direct causal links between the various imperial models he examined. He did not fixate on understanding why certain groups were targeted in their differing imperial contexts. Nor did he minimize the contiguous and deep-seated effects of anti-Semitism or its ontological status. Rather, Lemkin simply sought to explain the structural contexts that have often facilitated genocidal thinking or actions. His approach is relevant to our broader suggestion that the model of power-sharing adopted by the expanding American and Canadian states was partially rooted in earlier European colonial contexts; and that the association between European colonialism, North American state-building, and Indigenous dispossession can at least inform discussions of the relationship between Nazi expansion and anti-Semitism.[32]

An imperial framework, rooted in European expansionism, helps to explain the ubiquity of the notion that minority populations might erase culturally or numerically superior groups—a notion deployed lethally against Indigenous people and Jews.[33] The suggestion that European and American settlers sought to control myriad Indigenous nations through imperial frameworks of power does not diminish the unique Indigenous histories and memories of mass death within those settings. Comparing those frameworks to the way Nazis conceived their administration of a multi-national European sphere does not diminish the unique Jewish histories and memories of the Holocaust within that administration, in all their horror and specificity. Nor does it prevent our consideration of differences in the nature, scale, and outcome of the Holocaust versus historical case studies in other imperial settings.[34]

Rather, by comparing European imperialism with the supra-national consolidation of Nazi power over European Jews, we are better positioned to examine why concepts such as subaltern genocide have been overlooked in North American and European public sites of memory. Imperial histories of genocide and dispossession preceded and even contributed to the foundation of the various states that now make up Europe, Canada, and the United States. Their identification allows us to avoid superficial distinctions that laud the trajectory of American or European civic ideology: whether between American liberty and European horror or between European humanitarianism and the nineteenth-century doctrine of US settlement. Such distinctions, we will see, have often relied on universalistic representations of the Holocaust and the abstraction or occlusion or Indigenous genocide altogether. They overlook the common thread of imperially structured power over space and time: in early modern European colonization; in the influence of colonial European frameworks on the later mode of nineteenth-century North American western expansion; and in the strategic formula that Nazis used to consolidate their power over European nations and liquidate Jews within those nations as a highest priority. The power for these associations to unsettle common conceptions of European civilization and North American exceptionalism will help to explain why they have been overlooked in public memory on both sides of the Atlantic, to the detriment of an accurate portrayal of Indigenous history and the Holocaust.

PART TWO

# North America

# CHAPTER THREE

# "We are waiting for the construction of our museum." Indigenous People, Jews, and the North Americanization of the Holocaust

In 1993, the United States Holocaust Memorial Museum (USHMM) opened in Washington, DC, to memorialize the mass murder and attempted elimination of all Jews, as well as other groups such as the Roma, who were targeted for murder under the Nazis during World War II. The museum stands in a region once inhabited by the Nacotchtank people, before their population collapsed due to murder, starvation, constrained immunity, disease, nutritional degradation, slavery, and forced relocation over the two centuries after the arrival of European settlers in the Native American trading center.[1] Three years after the opening of the USHMM, the Spokane Native American poet Sherman Alexie published a long poem in the prestigious *Beloit Poetry Journal*. The Native American narrator of the poem travels with his wife to Germany, to visit Dachau, the death site of a different people. "Once there," according to the narrator, "I expected to feel simple emotions: hate, anger, sorrow. That was my Plan / I would write poetry about how the season / of winter found a perfect home in cold Dachau. / I would be a Jewish man who died in the camp. / I would be the ideal metaphor." But the apparently "simple" act of empathy is unsettled when the Indigenous narrator is reminded of sites of suffering in his North American home. The poet is hosted and guided by non-Jewish Germans who "are truly ashamed of Dachau" but who also ask the Native American: "what about all the Dachaus / in the United States? What about the death camps / in your country?" "Yes, Mikael and Veronika, you ask simple/ questions which are ignored, season after season," the poem continues, before then asking: "What do we indigenous people want from our country?" The poem issues the following response: "We stand over mass graves. Our collective grief makes us numb / We are waiting for the construction of our museum." The Native American tourist immediately perceived the historical centrality of the Holocaust, having presumably encountered its memorialization in North America. But the questions from his hosts interrupt the act of empathy by disturbing the narrator's ability to experience a site of Jewish suffering and to use it as a metaphor for his own people. As one literary critic asks of the poem's link between Jewish and Native American historical suffering: "who is whose metaphor?"[2]

When Alexie published the poem, no national museum for Native Americans yet existed in Washington, DC. The USHMM was already three years old. By going to sites of Jewish mass death in Europe, the Native American narrator thought he might find a metaphorical framework for his own people's losses, and that Jews might be able to find a similar framework in Native American sites of destruction. But once in Europe, he is reminded that no such interpretative site exists for "him" in North America. Native Americans "too," the poem suggests, "could stack the shoes of our dead and fill a city to its thirteenth floor." Having used the controversial phrase "American Holocaust," the narrator reminds readers and listeners, "[w]e are waiting for the construction of our museum," as "[w]e stand over mass graves." "After we are free," in a union such as the United States, the narrator asks, "how would I mourn the dead?"[3]

Alexie's poem invoked tensions that had been expressed more explicitly by some Indigenous activists in response to the recent founding of the USHMM. Those critiques contributed to a broader tendency to question the effects of the "Americanization of the Holocaust" on public approaches to Native American memory. It became more common to suggest that Holocaust memory has been "Americanized" around the time that Alexie published his poem, though by no means solely within Indigenous circles. The term describes the ways that American civic institutions are said to have commemorated European Jewish suffering to distinguish it from the more exceptional trajectory of tolerance and pluralism in the United States. Native American writers, scholars, and activists have sometimes juxtaposed the developing historical understanding of the Holocaust among ordinary Americans with the contiguous civic failure to commemorate Indigenous loss.[4]

The public successes of many Jews in post-War America has contributed to the common liberal narrative of a land of opportunity in contrast to the darkness of the Old World. In comparison to other groups with European ancestry, the disproportionate involvement of Jews in movements for African-American rights, Indigenous rights, workers' rights, gay and lesbian rights, and women's rights has often underscored rather than contradicted such a narrative. A common definition of American liberalism since the

1960s has historicized the expansion of individual liberty on the western side of the Atlantic by including the civil rights movements of the 1960s and 1970s as a key final impetus. Purified by the abolition of slavery during the Civil War and culminating in the protection of pluralism through twentieth-century activism, the progression of liberal ideology is said to have prevented instances of genocide as extreme as the Holocaust from manifesting in America. Arriving at Ellis Island and pushing westwards through St. Louis, Jews are often said to have formed communities that eventually worked with figureheads like Martin Luther King to rescue the exceptional potential of America's founding union, which they contrasted with European horror.[5]

Yet among other lacunae, the distinction between European horror and modern American freedom has always overlooked the specific hardships faced by Indigenous people as well as the continued legacies of those hardships in structural inequalities through the twentieth century. Since Sherman Alexie composed his poem, to be sure, a National Museum of the American Indian (NMAI) opened in Washington, D.C., in 2004. But scholars and commentators continue to highlight the marginalization of Indigenous suffering, mass death, and genocide in North American public commemoration.[6] Several commentaries, in fact, have explicitly distinguished the portrayal of Indigenous history in the NMAI from the depiction of Jewish population collapse in the USHMM. The NMAI, they claim, has portrayed Indigenous death in abstract and universalistic ways, distinct from approaches to Holocaust commemoration in Washington, D.C. and elsewhere in the United States.[7]

Conceptually similar critiques have been applied to the Canadian context for public memory. First Nations and allied scholars have suggested that institutions have instrumentalized Holocaust memory to distinguish the trajectory of Canadian pluralism while overlooking the foundation of the state in the dispossession of Indigenous people. Such critiques have manifested most prominently in response to the opening of the Canadian Museum for Human Rights (CMHR) in Winnipeg in 2014. They have drawn similar distinctions between the representation of Indigenous history and the Holocaust at the museum.[8]

Yet this chapter modifies the binary distinction between the particularism of Holocaust memory and the universalistic representation of Indigenous trauma at sites such as the NMAI and the CMHR. Such a distinction overlooks early criticisms of the USHMM and other North American institutions from *within* the Jewish community. Since the 1980s, many Jews and Holocaust scholars have become convinced that the specific nature of Jewish loss under the Nazis has itself been minimized and even "de-Judaized" to generate universal tenets of American and Canadian liberalism—the same tenets questioned in Indigenous critiques of public memory work.[9] The similarity—even the connection—between Indigenous and Jewish critiques of universalism has hitherto been overlooked in the literature on the Americanization and Canadianization of Holocaust memory. So too has their precedent in earlier Indigenous responses to public memory work since the late nineteenth century. Rather than reflecting a desire to compete for public recognition of genocide (as is often suggested), Indigenous responses to the universalization of Holocaust memory are often grounded in the experience of structurally similar public representations of Indigenous mass death for more than a century.

In examining how Native Americans, Jews, and First Nations people have approached the dissonance between their memories of ancestral trauma and their representation in public sites, the discussions that follow avoid using Holocaust memory as a normative category to define the appropriation, abstraction, and universalization of traumatic Indigenous history. Comparing structural similarities in the way their histories have been represented, rather, endeavors to avert what Michael Rothberg has described as "collective memory as competitive memory—a zero-sum struggle over scarce resources." Such a template ought to prevent the migration of tensions from comparative genocide studies to the fields of public history and memory studies. It should also allow us to examine broader similarities in related debates that have taken place in each community. Those debates seek to determine the best way to commemorate survival versus loss and the individual agency of victims versus the overriding effect of perpetrator intent. These discussions add a new dimension to the growing critical literature in museum studies and memory studies on the cultural trajectory of institutions such as the NMAI, the CMHR, and the USHMM. Later chapters will examine the positive models offered by Indigenous-led tribal museums in North America and new forms of Indigenous collaboration with public institutions in Europe. They will consider how those models can inform separate debates about Jewish engagement with Holocaust sites and museums on both sides of the Atlantic. This chapter precedes those discussions by examining the common departure from Jewish and Indigenous archives of memory in North American public sites and cultural institutions.[10]

## The foundation of the USHMM and the problem of universalism

President Jimmy Carter's formation of the President's Commission on the Holocaust in 1978 laid the statutory groundwork for the eventual founding of the USHMM in Washington, D.C. On US television during the same year, the NBC series titled *Holocaust* was watched by millions, establishing the ubiquity of the term in broader American culture.[11] Yet several American Jewish commentators became uneasy with the rhetorical distinction between Old World horror and American pluralism during the formative period of the USHMM. Such a distinction, they suggested, relied on a universalized representation of the Holocaust. In 1979, while proposing federal support for the construction of the USHMM, President Carter described the "eleven million innocent victims exterminated—six million of them Jews" during the Holocaust. Carter's statement, according to Yehuda Bauer, was stimulated by the desire of some Jewish museum proponents "to make non-Jews feel like they are part of us" and thus "create sympathy for the Jews." According to Walter Reich, the second director of the museum, whatever the exact nature of Carter's motivation, it "set a legacy for those who for any reason would wish to universalize the Holocaust into platitude."[12] Rather than facilitating greater sympathy with Jews, Carter's stance has been described as symptomatic of the "de-Judaization" of the Holocaust since the 1970s.[13] According to Mark Weitzman, a director at the Simon Wiesenthal Center, the eleven million motif has subsequently been used as a "tool to minimize the Jewish aspect [of the Holocaust], to write it out of history, or to maximize other victims' suffering to make them the prime victims and claim a place of honor in the role of victims." Commemoration, in such an assessment, "becomes a competitive game, especially for political purposes."[14]

Immediate concerns with the eleven million motif among some Jewish critics were compounded by subsequent statements made by Michael Berenbaum, the Deputy Director of the President's Commission on the Holocaust. Berenbaum outlined the institution's movement "beyond the boundaries of ethnic memory" to correspond with "American values" that repudiated Nazi fascism. Commentators questioned why Jews were asked to transcend their historical suffering to provide a unifying message against hatred and injustice. Early statements also universalized Jewish liturgy, particularly the Exodus story, to frame the USHMM's broader mission. These formulations, according to Avril Alba, defined "the modern narrative of Jewish suffering" in a "redemptive end beyond the Jewish world." Individuals in any global community might become victims of that which Jews *happened* to suffer in Europe. The Holocaust served to stimulate eternal vigilance among all potential victim communities, helping to maintain the course of liberal freedom.[15]

Jewish responses to the foundational rhetoric of the USHMM drew from a broader critique of the role of Holocaust memory in American cultural media, as evident in the ubiquity of Anne Frank imagery or the use of Holocaust terminology to describe myriad non-Jewish concerns from the 1970s through the 1980s. The early statements of USHMM founders were linked to the broader tendency among Jews and non-Jews alike to allude to the memory of the Holocaust as a signal of "man's inhumanity to man" and the ability of all groups to survive and counter such a phenomenon. According to Bauer's influential assessment, "to view the Holocaust as just another case of man's inhumanity to man, to equate it with every and any injustice committed on this earth—and, God knows, the number is endless—to say that the Holocaust is the total of all the crimes committed by Nazism in Europe, to do any or all of this is an inexcusable abomination based on the mystification of the event."[16]

Responding to these perceived trends in 1984, Saul Friedländer's *Reflections of Nazism* offered the earliest sustained attempt to interrogate the ubiquity and banality of Holocaust terminology in statements spanning different political ideologies and media. Friedländer warned of the constant use of the term "Holocaust" as reference point for other case studies and cultural phenomena. The phenomenon risked reducing the effect—and the affect—of the very memories the term sought to evoke. The increasingly common allusion to the Holocaust in cultural media outside the museum space, according to Friedländer, masked or even diminished specific understandings of the Holocaust as a historical event that affected Jews disproportionately.[17]

The perception that Jewish victimhood had become universalized during the foundational period of the USHMM was compounded by the growing popularity of literary works such as *Sophie's Choice*. Like Sophie, according to William Styron's novel, many non-Jews "suffered as much as any Jew." Styron's bestselling depiction of the life and death of a Polish Catholic in Auschwitz, popular through the 1980s and 1990s, was immediately criticized by many commentators for its attempt to broaden the memory of the Holocaust as an event with multiple victim groups. Styron's statements publicizing the book were particularly controversial in their use of purported numerical evidence to describe Auschwitz as a site where non-Jews were targeted in the same manner as Jews. These and similar statements, according to D. G. Myers, represented an "Ideology of Liberal Anti-Judaism" through their deployment of "tragic universalism" to situate "Jews Without Memory." In Alan L. Berger's 1985 assessment, Styron's work legitimized Holocaust denial closer to home: it "may well be the case that Styron accomplishes in the literary world what the so-called revisionists—the falsifiers and deniers of history—are trying to achieve among academics and the gullible public, de-Judaizing the Holocaust." One year after the opening of the USHMM in 1993, Styron was accused by another scholar of "stealing the Holocaust from the Jews who were its victims."[18]

The fear of facile universalism induced by the popularity of *Sophie's Choice* is relatively well known. But another context for the novel's difficult reception among Jews and Holocaust researchers in North America since the 1980s is far less reported. The rise of *Sophie's Choice* to become an American bestseller coincided with the increasing tendency for commemorative institutions, scholars, and polemical commentators in Poland and other Eastern European nations to claim that non-Jewish citizens ought to be included equally alongside Jews as victims of Nazism. Since the 1980s, a few Eastern European politicians and writers have veered toward Holocaust denial in their desire to portray their own national populations as the genuine victims of Nazism.[19] But more commonly, a vision of multiple victimhood has been promoted in that region's commemorative strategies. A growing scholarly literature on contemporary Eastern European Holocaust memory has described the tendency for some non-Jewish Lithuanians, Ukrainians, Belarussians, Latvians, Hungarians, and Poles to supplement the memory of Jewish suffering under the Nazis with an account of their own equal victimhood, to describe the Holocaust as an event with multiple Eastern European victims rather than as a primarily Jewish experience, or to overlook those in their nations who had tacitly or explicitly supported Nazi efforts against Jews. These approaches belie the proportion of Jews murdered relative to other segments of Eastern European society, the nature and logistics of their persecution, and the reasons leading to their murder. They also overlook the potential involvement of indigenous forms of nationalism in supporting Nazi anti-Semitism.[20] Other writers and activists have placed primarily non-Jewish Eastern European victims of Soviet occupation on par with Jewish victims of Nazism. Some have even sought to supersede discussions of Jewish victimhood through reference to the era of Soviet occupation that followed Nazism.[21]

These Eastern European phenomena, and their most recent iterations, will be explored in greater depth in Chapter 5. But at this point, it is pertinent to note the Christological understandings of redemption and suffering that have motivated some Eastern Europeans in their usurpation of Jewish victimhood. Immediately after World War II, as the plans for the never-built memorial at Treblinka demonstrate, many Poles assumed a Christian interpretation of Jewish suffering by defining a redemptive and universal meaning to martyrdom at sites in which Jews had been murdered by Nazis.[22] More recently, Polish political statements and media representations about Auschwitz have often collapsed the suffering of Catholic Poles (particularly nuns) at the institution with the experiences of Jews on the same site. They have defined the suffering of both groups as redemptive in relation to that of all humans. Their departure from Jewish understandings of victimhood reflects the universal vision of Christ's torment in the New Testament, which sought to replace the covenanted suffering of Jews as represented in the Torah.[23]

It would be a stretch to claim that these Eastern European frameworks of memory—including in their Christological form—are directly correlated with the tendency to universalize the Holocaust in North American liberalism during the last four decades. Nonetheless, they share certain structural similarities in their broader definition of victimhood and suffering at the expense of specific memories of Jewish population loss. And they provide another lens to understand the anxious response to Styron's popular narrative of Polish victimhood on the western side of the Atlantic, including its definition as a literary equivalent to "the falsifiers and deniers of history" who engage in "de-Judaizing the Holocaust." More recent commentaries, indeed, have warned of the translation of egregious developments from Eastern European historiography to North America, where they risk being synthesized with universalistic or relativistic approaches already prevalent in the region.[24]

Whether or not it was directly influenced by a specifically Polish Christological framework, the popularity of *Sophie's Choice* raises broader questions about the reception of Jewish victimhood among North Americans, many of whom shared the novel's redemptive vision of suffering. That vision, after all, had already begun to govern the reception of another text about a girl who was sent to Auschwitz. Though deriving from a Western European context, the subsequent trajectory of *The Diary of Anne Frank* led it to assume what Judith Goldstein describes as a "redemptive myth" that derived "much of its force from a deeply ingrained Christian template. Anne's story converges on elements of Christian belief and symbolism: a hidden child, a virgin, a betrayal, the Holocaust as Hell, a form of resurrection through words." The reception of *The Diary of Anne Frank*, like *Sophie's Choice*, demonstrated what Oren Baruch Stier describes as a keenness for non-Jewish North Americans to find "a kind of martyr . . . [who] despite not having chosen her fate . . . out of millions of nearly anonymous others . . . has become the recognizable face of Nazi victimization with whom millions identify, thus bearing witness not so much to the truth of Judaism as to the falsity and absolute evil—the negative transcendence—of Nazi ideology."[25]

As these redemptive icons have become increasingly prevalent, and since Friedländer and Bauer issued their warnings, a rich literature has continued to respond to the problematic trajectory of Holocaust terminology in North American public discourse. The use of the Holocaust term as a stylized shorthand, Andreas Huyssen noted in 1995, promotes "the ubiquitousness, the excess of Holocaust imagery everywhere in our culture . . . [from] the fascination with fascism in film and fiction . . . to the proliferation of an often-facile Holocaust victimology in a whole variety of political discourses." As a result, "the Holocaust has indeed become dispersed and fractured through the very different ways of memorializing it." In films such as *Schindler's List*, in the rise of Anne Frank as a moral reference point, and in commemorative statements by politicians, as Alvin H. Rosenfeld and others point out, the Holocaust has been memorialized as a symbol of a generalized form of intolerance. Though retaining the capacity to appear in any temporal or geographical context, human intolerance is said to have been kept in check by the exceptional trajectory of American liberalism in contrast to Europe. Such representative frameworks, according to commentaries at the time, influenced the early curatorial decisions of the USHMM after it finally opened in 1993. Its curation of European horrors on Washington, D.C.'s Mall, in an assessment by Rosenfeld, initially served to re-establish "museum visitors in the familiar and consoling realities of American space, and in doing so they can also have the effect of telling them that the exhibits they just saw, for all of their horror, signify an essentially European event." Philip Gourevitch has described the USHMM's early exhibitions as a framework providing a "sense of the 'Holocaust' being the 'Other' and thus being portrayed as the great antithesis to all-American values."[26]

## Indigenous memory and the problem of universalism

During the foundational era of the USHMM, then, the distinction between the history of the Holocaust and the ongoing trajectory of American freedom contributed to the universalization of Jewish historical trauma in public media. A conceptually similar distinction led to the misrepresentation and universalization of Indigenous history in North American public spaces long before the 1970s. Erroneous representations of Indigenous trauma from the late nineteenth century through the Cold War era help to explain why Indigenous commentators were primed for an ambiguous response to the foundation of the USHMM, as documented by Rachel Rubinstein and Edward T. Linenthal.[27] They also help to explain similar responses to the foundation of Canadian institutions such as the Canadian Museum for Human Rights (CMHR) during the twenty-first century. Indigenous critiques of sites in Washington, D.C., Ottawa, or Winnipeg have rarely questioned the importance of representing the full horror of the Jewish experience during the Holocaust.[28] Their proponents, rather, have been primed to notice how *any* historical representation valorizes the ongoing progression of American or Canadian rights. Such representations have often governed the way their own histories have been universalized, abstracted, or de-specified by non-Indigenous people since the late nineteenth century.

Consider, for example, what Jean M. O'Brien has described as the tendency for nineteenth-century white American historians to write "Indians out of existence in New England" by "Firsting and Lasting." Influenced by Michel-Rolph Trouillot's *Silencing the Past: Power and the Production of History,* O'Brien has shown how self-proclaimed historians of New England re-wrote Indigenous histories of population loss to describe them as mournful examples of "vanishing" that preceded white settlement. Historical Indigenous communities, in their representations, were subject to the ebb and flow of abstract environmental phenomena such as natural extinction. Those representations provided a counterpoint to the progressive establishment of English settlement, which was said to promote civilized control *over* nature rather than allowing degeneration by environmental phenomena *within* nature.[29]

O'Brien's discussion of naturalistic imagery in the representation of Indigenous population loss echoes seminal insights from Philip J. Deloria and Richard Drinnon, who have traced the long genealogy of Euro-American depictions of Indigenous death as a natural phenomenon. From the sixteenth century through the nineteenth century, those depictions regularly described Indigenous population loss as an inevitable form of "vanishing" due to the variability of environmental phenomena. They described their subjects as *of* the environment, rather than as humans with agency within the environment. "By playing Indian," for example, Deloria notes how late-eighteenth-century white settlers often rioted against elite white landowners by evoking and inventing "local understandings about the freedom, naturalness, and individualism of native custom." They conflated "the Indians and land" by suggesting "that these qualities lay embedded in the American continent itself and that the environment reshaped settlers' personalities, [so that] freedom and liberty made their way into the psychic makeup of white Europeans." The few Indigenous people who were represented as individuals still assumed the form of natural archetypes in Euro-American historical narratives from the late-eighteenth century through the nineteenth century. They signified positive traits that the North American environment was said to have bestowed on its inhabitants, sooner than offering any specific representation of Indigenous agency. Facing the risk of degradation by environmental phenomena, those traits were said to be protected by the advanced civilization of white settlement. From the nineteenth century through the first half of the twentieth century, therefore, historians continued to chart the unfolding history of a "vanishing race" as an unavoidable process of nature. The "crucial issue at stake" in such vanishing motifs, according to Drinnon, centered on the "collective refusal to conceive of Native Americans as persons."[30]

Coinciding with the proliferation of vanishing motifs during the nineteenth century, American federal and state governments used their bureaucratic apparatuses to dispossess Indigenous communities and to disguise the role of perpetrator intent in cases of genocide.[31] Settler colonial perspectives have connected those nineteenth-century activities to earlier European imperial contexts for Indigenous trauma as well as later twentieth-century state-building.[32] Unsurprisingly, therefore, vanishing and Firsting/Lasting archetypes continued to influence the historical commemoration of events such as the December 29, 1890, massacre of more than 100 mostly unarmed women and children by the U.S. Seventh Cavalry near Wounded Knee Creek. One white correspondent immediately called the incursion among the Miniconjou Lakota Big Foot's band a "war of extermination" due to the tendency for soldiers to fire at close range "until not a live Indian was in sight." Over the following decades, Lakota people underlined how state and federal powers had supported the incursions of the Seventh Cavalry against defenseless women and children, and how those powers had continued to dispossess Indigenous lands after the massacre. Five thousand soldiers (around one-quarter of the U.S. Army at the time) contributed to the occupation and consolidation of Lakota territories in 1890–1. But outside Lakota spaces, the public commemoration of the Wounded Knee Massacre came to be shaped by those with a vested interest in remembering it as the *last* time that a harsh "frontier" environment would threaten chaos for Indigenous and white people; and thus also the *first* moment of their civilized protection by the United States. In lengthy and erroneous accounts of the Lakota "Ghost Dance" ceremony, white soldiers, politicians, and eager journalists described the "savage" descent of local Indigenous communities in their harsh environment. The subsequent settlement of state and federal authority, in their descriptions, returned Indigenous people to their passive archetype and counteracted the effects of that environment. Soldiers who took part in the massacre were later rewarded with Medals of Honor and promotions and commemorated with monuments in South Dakota, Kansas, and elsewhere. Proponents of an objective account of the events at Wounded Knee, according to David W. Grua, "lost the struggle over memory" in the broader context of American state-building during the first half of the twentieth century. Instead, the event was integrated into accounts that distinguished contemporary American pluralism from a hazily defined frontier past.[33]

The archetypal models identified by O'Brien, Drinnon, Deloria, and Grua can be detected in other regional and temporal contexts, all of which underline how common the misrepresentation and universalization of Indigenous history had become well before the founding era of the USHMM. Consider, for example, the development of the "Thanksgiving" motif in Plymouth Rock, New England, and eventually the United States. The motif became popular in part because of the work of the Improved Order of Red Men (IORM), a fraternal organization founded by white settlers in 1834 in the context of Jacksonian Indian Removal. The IORM called for a memorial to the seventeenth-century Pokanoket Wampanoag leader *8sâmeeqan*, the Sachem, that highlighted the civilized protection offered by his English interlocutors.[34] Reflecting the historical approach of their nineteenth-century predecessors, white community leaders marked the tercentenary of the Plymouth Rock settlement in 1921 by universalizing Indigenous historical experiences to distinguish their own civic identity. A bronze statue erected in 1921 on Cole Hill, near Plymouth Rock, represented *8sâmeeqan*. Its "Massasoit" moniker was applied by its non-Indigenous sculptor, Cyrus Edwin Dallin, who was born in the mid-nineteenth century. As the Supreme Sachem of the Wampanoag people, the statue's subject oversaw the 1621 treaty with English settlers at Plymouth, which was central to white accounts of the "first Thanksgiving" meal shared between English and Indigenous people. Contributing to the broader trajectory of the Thanksgiving motif as an "American" tradition, the erection of the Massasoit statue was stimulated by the desire of civic and educational leaders to represent the benign inclusivity and civilized protection offered by white settlement in New England. The statue's Massasoit subject was constructed as an archetype of abstract qualities rather than as a specific representation of his historical role in Indigenous culture. Dallin, who sculpted the memorial to the seventeenth-century Supreme Sachem, even used a live model who was not Indigenous. The model was an African-American man named Thomas E. McKeller, who was marshaled in a bare-chested representation of the Massasoit.[35]

That the Massasoit sculpture represented a non-Indigenous archetype became even clearer in its unveiling and dedication during the Pilgrim tercentenary activities between 1921 and 1922. A placard described Massasoit as a "protector and preserver of the Pilgrims" and linked those activities to "1621" and presumably the treaty of the same year. By placing the statue near to where white pilgrims landed, the Sachem was represented as a bridge towards consensual association with the civilized community, suggesting a land transfer from a community who did not conceive of property as private to colonists who did. Thus it contributed to the Thanksgiving motif rather than signaling the era of dispossession and mass death that followed the arrival of pilgrims. The subsequent movement of the

**Figure 3.1** *Replica of Massasoit by Cyrus E. Dallin in front of the Utah State Capitol. © Getty Images.*

statue's plaster mold to the capitol rotunda in Utah, followed by similar replicas in Kansas City, Spokane, Washington, and Chicago, highlighted its increasingly universalized meaning, which could be appropriated by myriad white communities throughout the United States—irrespective of any connection to its Indigenous historical subject.[36]

In the decades after the Plymouth tercentenary, during the early Cold War era, white Americans continued to represent Indigenous history to define the civilized protection that the United States offered its citizens. Terminology associated with the state protection of pluralism and individual rights gradually replaced the civilizational motifs that had governed nineteenth-century New England historiography and the commemorative movement around the Massasoit statue. From the 1950s through the 1980s, civic memory work rarely represented the causal effect of Euro-American interventions on Indigenous population loss. More often, Indigenous figures were presented as archetypes of tragic loss, which was distinguished from the modern American experience of tolerance and individual freedom. The distinction between traumatic Indigenous history and contemporary American liberty also assumed a geopolitical dimension by positioning the United States as a beacon of freedom in contrast to the Soviet Union.[37]

These Cold War contexts are illustrated by the historical representation of Cherokee removal in Georgia. During the presidency of Andrew Jackson, federal authorities largely supported the state of Georgia in subjugating the Cherokee, culminating in the 1835 treaty at New Echota in which the Cherokee people were required to give up their land east of the Mississippi and to transfer to western territories within two years. From 1835 to 1840, between 4,000 and 10,000 Cherokee people died in the westward movement. Through the late 1950s and early 1960s, the Georgia state government restored the old Cherokee capital, New Echota, largely from a non-Indigenous impetus. Chambers of Commerce and politicians in southern Appalachia popularized performances of the outdoor drama about Cherokee removal, *Unto These Hills*. But rather than acknowledging the roots of state-building in Cherokee removal, and its continued legacy among surviving Indigenous communities inside and outside Georgia, these and other civic, educational, and tourism initiatives provided white Georgians with a satisfying synthesis between the specific and the universal: On the one hand, they drew on Indigenous history to display their empathetic attachment to universal ethical ideals. On the other hand, they lauded the specific constitutional context that allowed such moral universalism to flourish. In displaying their empathy for the victims of abstractly defined historical trauma, they underlined the advanced civic framework in which they believed individual rights had come to be protected. Such acts of historical commemoration also allowed their proponents to display their moral introspection without having to attend to the ongoing and separate denial of African-American civil rights. Their representation of Indigenous suffering was "safe" because it allowed white Georgians to display their capacity for moral universalism even while they often ignored the separate and contiguous struggle for black freedom.[38]

The commemoration of Cherokee removal, including the establishment of the Trail of Tears National Historic Trail by Congress in 1987, was designed to appeal to tourists. In some circumstances, Cherokees in the region found ways to turn that fact to their advantage. Wilma Mankiller, one-time principal chief of the Cherokee Nation, promoted the trails as sites to educate non-Indigenous people about the role of perpetrator intent. They used them to raise money for autonomous tribal communities, even as non-Indigenous people ignored those concerns in their reading of Cherokee history. Similar processes accompanied the commemoration of massacres in other regions. In Oregon, on the one hand, Indigenous communities did their best to raise awareness of their histories of trauma as well as funding for autonomous initiatives through alliances with public memory work. On the other hand, the "violence and ethnic cleansing" of the 1873 Modoc War in southern Oregon, as Boyd Cochran has shown, was subsequently transformed by Cold War era Chambers of Commerce, educational initiatives, and civic memorials into "a redemptive narrative of American innocence." As in Georgia, they described Indigenous population losses in abstract ways while lauding their ability to display humanitarian empathy with past subjects.[39]

During the Cold War era, in contrast, Indigenous activists rarely supported the delineation of rights-based pluralism through the representation of historical injustice. Contrary to other prominent narratives of the Civil Rights movement, they avoided the notion that color-blind equal protection resurrected the founding principles of the United States from historical aberrations. Instead, they sought to reassert the continuity of tribal sovereignty. That form of sovereignty, as Kevin Bruyneel has argued, was formulated as a "third space" between the ostensibly progressive doctrine of equal protection and the institutional persecution that preceded its development. Unsurprisingly, such a vision of parallel autonomy was often overlooked by those who used Indigenous history to valorize and distinguish the protection of rights by the modern state.[40]

Having segued from Cold War ideology into newer expressions of multiculturalism during the 1990s, distinctions between American liberty and aberrant historical contexts continued to overlook the move to tribal sovereignty as an ongoing process of decolonization from settler-colonial authority. By focusing on Indigenous people as victims of pre-twentieth-century contexts, according to Margaret S. Jacobs, "the dispossession of Indigenous peoples through many phases of settler colonialism" *since then* have been overlooked. By distinguishing Indigenous memories of trauma from the present trajectory of multiculturalism, civic memorials and educational media perpetuated a settler-colonial model by valorizing external control over autonomous communities under the guise of color-blind civil protection.[41] Consider, for example, the "misplacement" of the 1864 Sand Creek massacre in public memory during the 1990s. On November 29,

1864, led by Colonel John Chivington, Colorado militia attacked 700 Cheyennes and Arapahos who had settled along Sand Creek, near the border with Kansas. They had received reports of "hostile" Cheyennes but fired into a "friendly" camp and killed more than 150 people, mostly women, children, and the elderly. They also scalped and mutilated some of the bodies. During the twentieth century, white educational and commemorative media incorporated the massacre alongside Wounded Knee, the Cherokee Removal, and the Trail of Tears as one of a few tragic aberrations that the modern era of Civil Rights would prevent from reoccurring. Yet even as the National Park Service (NPS) adopted a more regretful tone from the 1990s through the early 2000s, its efforts to create the Sand Creek National Historic Site demonstrated continuing tensions with Indigenous understandings of white perpetrator intent. Many Cheyennes and Arapahos saw the benefits of the site in raising revenue for their communities while providing an opportunity to redress imbalances in the received historical narrative. But NPS officials retained a commitment to cultural pluralism that countered Cheyenne and Arapaho conceptions of tribal sovereignty. Rather than engaging Indigenous communities as parallel constituents, NPS representatives framed the initiative as a sign that all minorities were now acknowledged, protected, and incorporated in the multicultural American state.[42]

The NPS's attachment to liberal pluralism rather than tribal sovereignty helps to explain its decision to avoid representing the Sand Creek Massacre in the context of the US Civil War, despite Chivington having been well known as a Union war hero. The Civil War has subsequently come to be defined as a pivotal event in which the United States regained its trajectory towards freedom and pluralism. But just as in Minnesota's Dakota wars, the involvement of Union troops in the massacre of Indigenous people unsettles such a narrative. By removing early plaques and memorials that defined the massacre in the context of the Civil War, the NPS activities reinforced the notion that it was somehow aberrant to the ongoing process of American state-building. In justifying their decision, ironically, they described the importance of public history in promoting multicultural citizenship, which they feared undermining by representing the Union effort as contiguous with Indigenous dispossession. Far better to remember violence against Indigenous people as part of the atypical "Indian Wars."[43]

Moving from the 1990s to the 2000s, civic memorials have continued to distinguish histories of Indigenous dispossession from the protection of rights by the modern American state. Consider, for example, the 2004 public debate that was sparked by a series of unofficial legal tribunals on the death of Chief Leschi in the Puget Sound War of 1855–8. Leschi was a Nisqually leader at a time when several tribal nations opposed the implementation of narrow reservation boundaries by Washington Territory authorities. In 1857, Leschi was convicted of murdering a soldier, Abram Benton Moses, as well as another militiaman, and hanged in Washington Territory's first execution. Over the following decades, white depictions either described Leschi as a collaborative interlocutor or as a tragic figure whose demise reflected the inevitable chaos of frontier environments rather than perpetrator intent.[44]

Over the following century, however, members of the Nisqually community rejected white representations of Leschi's execution. They continually questioned his specific role in the deaths of the militiamen, as well as the jurisdiction of the Washington Territory that decided his fate. Their activism over more than a century eventually led to the establishment of a *Committee to Exonerate Chief Leschi* and the formation of the Washington State Historical Court of Inquiry. Convened in 2004, the unofficial Historical Court included judges from Washington state courts, the Washington Supreme Court, and a Lummi Tribal Court. By redefining Leschi as an enemy combatant due to the "state of war" that prevailed at the time, the tribunal's non-binding verdict concluded that Leschi "should not, as a matter of law, [have] been tried for the crime of murder" as a civilian. Yet by focusing on Leschi's jurisdictional status above all other factors, the tribunal tacitly endorsed the Washington Territorial Government's supposition that he murdered militiamen and overlooked evidence from Euro-American and Indigenous archives that cast doubt on Leschi's role in their deaths. In suggesting that the territorial governments of Washington were at war with Indigenous people, and that its decisions in the Leschi affair ought to have accounted for that jurisdictional state, the tribunal also inadvertently supported the broader legal status of Euro-American settler wars that had dispossessed thousands of Indigenous people and destroyed their tribal sovereignty. Those who had opposed Leschi's trial as a civilian, after all, had often been territorial expansionists. They were keen to define Indigenous people as warring enemies rather than as sovereign nations whose land had been invaded.[45]

The Leschi case is emblematic of the way Indigenous history has been presented by civic bodies from the twentieth century through the present era. On the one hand, the 2004 tribunal used legal frameworks from settler-colonial contexts to reach its decision. On the other hand, politicians and public media joined tribunal members in defining the colonial and territorial experience of war and dispossession as somehow aberrant to their contemporary civic context. These contradictions are further revealed by the failure of the tribunal and Washington public media to consider the memory of Leschi's brother Chief Quiemuth, who was murdered by white settlers in territorial violence. Lisa Blee thus asks a pertinent question: "How could law vindicate both Leschi and itself if Quiemuth's story revealed it is a tool of colonialism?" These and other contradictions revealed the tribunal's focus on equal protection and "individual equality" and its own quasi-legal foundation in ideas that were drawn from settler-colonial contexts. Those contexts had also occluded parallel Indigenous sovereignty in their claim to encompass Indigenous people under territorial protection.[46]

As Canada has grappled with the legacy of its Indian Residential Schools (IRS) system, which lasted between 1834 and 1996, initiatives such as the

Canadian Truth and Reconciliation Commission (TRC) have responded with a little more sensitivity to Indigenous histories and memories of trauma than the Leschi tribunals. Having already noted its connection to the memory of cultural genocide in Chapter 1, it is now pertinent to consider several other aspects of the legacy of the IRS system that relate to Canadian memory work.

Since the 1950s, Canadian cultural sites have often mirrored the problematic assumptions that led to the removal of children from their First Nations parents and their placement in Indian Residential Schools. As Paulette Regan has shown, the initial tendency to portray the removal of children using ostensibly "benevolent" reasoning can be connected to the broader way in which Canadians have described themselves as "peacemakers" at home and abroad, including in the museums, civic sites, and educational curricula that accompanied the Residential School era and have continued thereafter. These rhetorical tendencies can be compared with those adopted in the US sites examined above. Canadian cultural institutions have often used their memory work to suggest that historical white populations attempted peaceful negotiations with Indigenous people, or that a failure to adopt such an approach was an aberration that underscores the later inclusivity of Canadian state-building.[47]

Through the 1950s and 1960s, therefore, as Residential Schools continued to expand in Canada, First Nations people questioned depictions of inclusivity and benevolence in museums and public sites. Their critiques crystallized in the formation of a separate "Indians of Canada Pavilion" at Expo 67. Spearheaded by Indigenous people who worked within the Canadian federal civil service, the display represented what Ruth B. Phillips has described as a "palace coup that enabled them to take curatorial control of its exhibitions and messages." Remarkable for its time, the exhibition displayed scenes that suggested what has now been defined more formally as cultural genocide, including depictions of Christian missionizing as a front for the political destruction of Indigenous communities and culture. The displays also suggested the ongoing legacy of colonial and Canadian interventions in the socio-economic marginalization of Indigenous people and the importance of parallel forms of land sovereignty to mitigate those legacies.[48]

Such radical critiques were perhaps made possible by the temporary nature of the exhibitions at Expo 67. It is unlikely they would have been permitted in more static displays at state funded sites such as the Canadian Museum of Civilization in Ottawa. Nonetheless, Indigenous critiques of Canadian public memory continued through the following decades and culminated in the boycott by First Nations and allied groups of a 1988 exhibition of Aboriginal art that was designed to coincide with the Calgary Winter Olympic Games during that same year. Opponents of *The Spirit Sings* exhibition suggested that it was cynical in its attempt to show the inclusivity of Canadian culture through the display of Indigenous cultural objects without recognizing their provenance in colonial contexts that included dispossession and death.[49]

The fallout of *The Spirit Sings* boycott led officials in Canadian public museums to call for greater sensitivity in their curatorial approach to the history and culture of First Nations, Inuit, and Métis people. The Assembly of First Nations collaborated with the Canadian Museums Association in advising the Task Force on Museums and First Peoples, which worked between 1989 and 1992 to produce a final report and recommendation that some objects be repatriated to Indigenous communities while others remain in Canadian institutions under the proviso that those institutions work with local Indigenous populations and refrain from suggesting their protection of the objects from vanishing. The Task Force's recommendations were strengthened by the 1996 Report of the Royal Commission on Aboriginal People (RCAP).[50]

These collaborative developments reflected similarly positive agendas in the United States, such as the Native American Graves Protection and Repatriation Act (NAGPRA), which will be explored in Chapter 5. With Indigenous consultation, RCAP sought greater uniformity in the return of human remains and other Indigenous cultural objects and complemented contiguous Indigenous land claims as parallel to the Canadian state. It also encouraged museums to work with Indigenous communities even when they held on to cultural artifacts, mitigating their initial removal under colonial and neo-colonial regimes by integrating them in Indigenous rituals and memory work on site or by loaning them to Indigenous communities. But the preservation of Indigenous material by institutions has also often supported the claim by many representatives of the Canadian state that they protect Indigenous values *alongside* those of other citizens, rather than recognizing parallel forms of Indigenous sovereignty.[51] Unsurprisingly, therefore, no permanent memorial to the IRS system exists in Canada, despite a series of temporary Indigenous-led exhibitions on the system, which appeared between 2000 and 2010 under the auspices of the Aboriginal Healing Foundation (AHF) and the Legacy of Hope Foundation (LHF).[52] Within Canada's national museum system, moreover, there is still no concerted account of the connection between settler-colonial interventions and Indigenous population loss.[53]

The construction and proliferation of Massasoit statues, the civic commemoration of Cherokee removal, and the universalized representation of the Modoc War all preceded the founding era of the USHMM. Similarly, the critiques of Indigenous people in Canada from the 1950s through the 1990s preceded their response to the National Holocaust Monument (NHM) in Ottawa and the Canadian Museum of Human Rights (CMHR) in Winnipeg. They primed Indigenous and allied commentators to question the Americanization and the Canadianization of the Holocaust. They were also conceptually similar to critical Jewish responses that accompanied the public treatment of Holocaust memory in North America from the 1970s through the 1990s. Indigenous and Jewish critiques of public history have questioned the use of historical memory to define the triumph of individual rights on the western side of the Atlantic and the resulting tendency to universalize or occlude their respective histories of trauma, dispossession, and death.

## The Problem of Multicultural Memory in Canada and the United States

The unsettling of American liberalism by Indigenous histories of dispossession helps to explain why no national museum attended to those histories during the foundational period of the USHMM. With the erection of the National Museum of the American Indian (NMAI) in 2004, therefore, greater public understanding of Indigenous mass death, Euro-American perpetrator intent, and Indigenous survival became a possibility. These possibilities were signaled, for example, by NMAI promotional literature that suggested that it would be situated on "host tribes" lands—a relatively radical statement for most non-Indigenous people at that time, given the status of the institution under public legal statutes and federal agencies. Thanks to the work of its Indigenous collaborators, the museum indicated its intent to "honor the host tribes on whose land the museum was being built." The planning literature also nodded to the institution's desire to represent Indigenous life in North America in order to transcend arbitrary Euro-American boundaries, both geographically and spiritually. Such assertions, according to Amanda Cobb, led NMAI planners to promote a "practice of cultural sovereignty" despite the institution's role in American civic identity. These rhetorical agendas would not have been possible without the efforts of Indigenous activists, including through the Red Power movement, during previous decades.[54]

Yet according to the critical literature on the early curatorial offerings of the NMAI, its exhibitions framed Indigenous death using abstract and deterministic environmental metaphors and motifs, belying the institution's ostensible determination to emphasize Indigenous agency rather than older vanishing tropes. In a prominent critique that bore similarity to discussions of the Americanization of the Holocaust, Amy Lonetree showed how the representation of Indigenous suffering sought to unify all museum visitors as potential victims of intolerance. Even when the museum emphasized Indigenous stories of agency, survival, and regeneration, according to several similar critiques, those narratives strengthened post-war American liberal notions of individual opportunity rather than focusing on histories of Indigenous loss and their continued legacy in structural inequalities. Museum curators, according to Lonetree, highlighted survival and the ethnographic display of cultures rather than narrating the ubiquitous historical contexts

Figure 3.2 *Teepees at the National Museum of the American Indian, SW, Washington, D.C. © Getty Images.*

for dispossession and genocide. The impact of European settler-colonialism, including its contribution to independent American state-building, became what Myla Vicenti Carpio describes as an "absent presence" in the first NMAI offerings. Those offerings allowed the NMAI to become a symbol of "conflict resolution" in the United States rather than highlighting the ongoing importance of parallel forms of Indigenous autonomy.[55]

Repudiating the assimilationist legacies of settler-colonialism through tribal sovereignty provides another way to approach critical discussions of universalism and multiculturalism at the NMAI, civic memorials, and in educational curricula. Indigenous theorists rarely laud the establishing of the NMAI or other similar institutions as a sign that Indigenous people can join other minorities under the banner of pluralism. Lonetree has thus registered her agreement "with the American Indian Movement activists who criticized the museum [NMAI] for not telling the story of the American Indian holocaust along with our stories of survival." Those activists are cited as having claimed that the "museum falls short in that it does not characterize or does not display the sordid and tragic history of America's holocaust against the Native Nations and peoples of the Americas." The use of the word "holocaust" in these critiques of the NMAI would likely raise anxieties among many Jews and Holocaust scholars, who have defined similar statements in other contexts as a form of appropriation, relativization, or even deliberate supersession of victimhood. Yet Lonetree's statements rarely reflect such phenomena. Rather than fixating on Jewish motivations or the nature and scale of the Holocaust itself—a problematic and potentially anti-Semitic tendency—Lonetree's response to initial NMAI displays reflected the critical Indigenous response during the founding era of the USHMM. It was primed by earlier Euro-American attempts to universalize, abstract, and distort the historical representation of Indigenous mass death and to distinguish it from present trajectories of American liberal freedom.[56]

Since the founding of the NMAI, indeed, Indigenous references to the USHMM have often sought to emulate what they perceive as its successful model. This emulative approach became particularly common after the controversial public statement issued by J. Richard West, an early director of the NMAI: "We do not want to make the National Museum of the American Indian into an Indian Holocaust Museum." With positive intentions, which reflected new trends in the portrayal of agency and "survivance," West sought to avoid framing Native American history through a primarily doleful lens, "only about 5 percent" of thousands of years of civilization. But although Jews also enjoyed agency and civilizational achievement before the Holocaust, Lonetree points out, "in comparison" to the NMAI "the U.S. Holocaust Memorial Museum did not sacrifice the specifics of the difficult and painful history of the Jewish holocaust." Neither did it "obscure the specifics of the Jewish people's past or try to frame the violence they suffered at the hands of the Nazis as a force of nature—a story."[57]

The commemoration of total and systemic murder in the USHMM, in Lonetree's estimation, ought to have influenced institutions such as the NMAI, qualifying their positive message of agency and survival and questioning their focus on abstract and environmental determinants of mortality. The USHMM, apparently, was not required to intervene in contemporary discussions of agency, nor to adopt their "post-modern" methodological approach. Rather than trying "to make a larger theoretical argument about how history is constructed," the curators were said to "present the specifics in a moving narrative that does not surrender coherency to make some sort of relativistic argument in the service of postmodernism." A facile message of inspiration and hope, according to Lonetree's critique, came at the expense of visitors understanding the depressing facts of Indigenous dispossession and genocide. At the USHMM, conversely, the specific contexts of horrific loss and perpetrator intent are said to have been fully acknowledged rather than abstracted, universalized, or overlooked—a model that the NMAI and other memorials to Indigenous loss would do well to follow.[58]

A similar critical framework has responded to the representation of First Nations, Inuit, and Métis histories in state-funded Canadian museums, particularly the Canadian Museum of History in Ottawa (previously known as the Canadian Museum of Civilization) and the Canadian Museum of Human Rights (CMHR) in Winnipeg. Critiques of those Canadian institutions have often distinguished their representation of the Holocaust from hazier and more circumscribed discussions of Indigenous history. Since 2014, for example, the CMHR has incorporated one gallery dealing with the Holocaust and Jewish genocide in Europe and another that engages the definition of human rights from the perspective of Indigenous history and culture. It also includes exhibitions about Indigenous case studies in other galleries. But according to Tricia Logan, who initially curated exhibitions at the CMHR, European contexts for mass death—mostly the Holocaust, as well as the Ukrainian famine under Soviet rule between 1932 and 1933—are used as normative templates to define genocide. Canada has the world's third-largest Ukrainian-descended population after Ukraine and Russia, making it less surprising that the museum includes the *Holodomor* (Terror-Famine) as a definitive template alongside the experiences of Jewish Europeans during the Holocaust. But although Ukrainian-Canadians are an important intended audience for the museum's memory work, the inclusion of the Holodomor alongside the Holocaust underscores the broader intent of the institution to distinguish Canadian civic identity from the definitive horror experienced by Europeans in the Old World.[59]

A similar distillation of ideals appeared in the statements that many Canadian politicians delivered during the founding era of the National Holocaust Monument (NHM) in Ottawa, Canada. Beginning as a federal statute that was proposed by the Parliament of Canada in 2008, the National Holocaust Monument Act (NHMA) received "royal assent" in March 2011. The memorial, designed as a Star of David through which visitors can "journey," required further legislative work and fund-raising before Canadian Prime Minister Justin Trudeau finally opened it in September 2017. Before that point, Canadian politicians made the case for its inclusion at the heart of the Canadian capitol. The Holocaust, according to Senator Joan Fraser, followed "the apparatus of one of the world's most civilized countries . . . [becoming] devoted to the extermination of an entire people." Like many of her political counterparts in the United States and Europe, Fraser represented the Holocaust as a perversion of the tools of Western civilization towards savagery and underlined her nation's present commitment to using them for the advancement of humanity. Fraser thus continued: "Today's Canada is a nation of hope and opportunity, a beacon to those around the world seeking to find a new home and brighter future for themselves and their families . . . Our society is the dream for many around the world." MP Dennis Bevington suggested that the monument spoke "to the conclusion of the Second World War; to the role Canada played in the victory over the Axis to ensure that the Holocaust came to an end and that it would not occur again in that area of the world." The MP used the founding of the memorial to highlight Canada's role in rescuing Europeans and reasserting their values.[60]

Team Lord's design for the National Holocaust Monument symbolized the distinction between aberrant European horror and the uninterrupted civilization of Canadian state-building. A series of subterranean paths was built under a three-dimensional Star of David, the face of which ran parallel to the ground. Most of the paths were closed off to light at the surface of the monument to represent the inability of victims to escape the "Final Solution." But eventually visitors *can* find a predetermined path back up to the light, literally ascending into the freedom of Canadian soil. On the stairway up, wall murals represent Canadian diplomatic attempts to rescue Jewish individuals during the era of World War II, before a view of the Canadian Parliament becomes visible in the light at the end of the stairway tunnel. Reflecting the political statements that preceded its opening, the monument design distinguished Canadian pluralism and multiculturalism from past horror. In an op-ed which she published in 2015, sociologist Nadine Blumer thus suggested that "the redemptive narrative" of the design "could not be clearer: from Nazi fascism in Europe to salvation in Canada."[61]

Through no fault of Canadian Jews or advocates of Holocaust memory, the redemptive narrative of Canadian pluralism overlooked the histories of First Nations, Inuit, and Métis dispossession that contributed to Canadian state-building, including settler-colonial frameworks for genocide. During the foundational era of the memorial, politicians and planners described the importance of the Canadian state donating "its" land to the memorial committee, though the land was never in fact officially ceded by its Indigenous inhabitants. According to a 2010 statement from MP Joseph Volpe, the land donation was necessary because "we need the Government of Canada to speak for all Canadians—every single one of the 32 million who have subscribed to the census and have identified themselves as legitimate inhabitants in this place."[62] Similar problems can be detected in the situation of the Canadian Museum of Human Rights (CMHR) in Winnipeg, in the

**Figure 3.3** *National Holocaust Monument, Ottawa, Canada. Aerial view with Sky Void and Stairs of Hope. © Getty Images.*

province of Manitoba. The province incorporates the largest Indigenous population in Canada, while the actual museum sits at the confluence of the Red and Assiniboine Rivers in Treaty One territory that is sacred to First Nations and Métis people, exposing many Indigenous artifacts and objects during its excavation.[63]

The "Culture of Redress" in these Canadian sites has mirrored early techniques at the NMAI by underling the inclusive and open-minded civic context that allows national introspection about aberrant historical events. Their displays have circumvented discussions of reparations and elided the contribution of settler colonial frameworks to the construction of the Canadian state in its present constitutional capacity. Yellowknives Dene scholar Glen Coulthard has defined such Canadian displays of "reconciliation" as a form of "neocolonial politics" that reduces Indigenous cultural autonomy in favor of state-sanctioned definitions of multiculturalism.[64]

By drawing constitutional boundaries that overlooked Indigenous claims to land autonomy, and by subsuming Indigenous people through contemporary pluralism, the statements and actions surrounding the CMHR and the NHM can be contrasted with the situational description of a different monument that has stood in Ottawa since 1990, but which has benefited from collaboration with local Indigenous communities. In English, French, and Algonquin, the Canadian Tribute to Human Rights (CTHR) describes its situation in the following way:

> The land on which this structure stands is part of the traditional territories of the Algonquin Anishnabe people. We have occupied these lands since time immemorial. It is fitting that this symbol should stand here as a reminder of the suffering of oppressed people everywhere and of our faith in the wisdom of the Great Spirit and the promise of Life, Dignity, Freedom, and Equality for all living beings. We welcome all who come here to share in our hope.

Though adopting the language of universal human rights, which also appears in the National Holocaust Monument that was founded three decades later, the CTHR represents the *departure* from those values in the history of Canadian state-building—including, even, in the Canadian state's constitutional claim to the land upon which the Tribute is erected.[65]

Yet the binary distinction between particularism at the USHMM and universalism at the NMAI and CMHR overlooks early criticisms of North American Holocaust memory from *within* Jewish communities. As we noted earlier, Jews, Holocaust scholars, and allied commentators were far from convinced that the foundational statements and early offerings of the USHMM promoted a specific and particularistic understanding of the Jewish experience under the "Final Solution." In Canada, similar fears were initially evident among Jewish commentators in controversies over the foundation of the CMHR, when various statements in public media were seen to relativize or even diminish the Jewish experience during the Holocaust.[66] These early critiques were structurally similar to those that subsequently accompanied the founding of the NMAI and the Indigenous displays at the CMHR.

Indeed, early USHMM founders have since issued interpretative clarifications and even strong critiques of relativism and universalism on both sides of the Atlantic. During the last decade, the USHMM has addressed and countered Eastern European developments such as Double Genocide theory, as well as the separate tendency to universalize the Holocaust in North American public discourse.[67] In July 2019, the USHMM even faced public criticism from some Jewish Studies scholars, comparative genocide theorists, and Holocaust researchers for adopting what was described as an overly strong stance against the use of Holocaust terminology in analogies or motifs. The many signatories to the July 2019 open letter noted the rich and nuanced output disseminated by the USHMM during its evolution over the last few decades. Its curatorial approach, the signatories pointed out, has grown to offer a globally recognized program of research in Holocaust and Genocide Studies, as well as many important exhibitions and research agendas. The signatories claimed to be "well aware of the many distortions and inaccuracies, intentional or not, that frame contemporary discussions of the Holocaust." Nonetheless, they warned against drawing a false dichotomy between the specificity of Holocaust history and careful comparisons or analogies between different contexts and case studies. The open statement underscored the USHMM's nuanced output over the last decades, countering the notion that it had promoted an uncompromising stance against humanitarian analogies. But it also highlighted ongoing tensions over the relative balance between specificity and universalism at a time when Holocaust analogies have become common in public discourse.[68]

Indigenous and allied critiques of the NMAI and the CMHR preceded these developments and are now most comparable to ongoing Jewish responses to museums and civic institutions *other than* the USHMM, such as the San Francisco Contemporary Jewish Museum, the Skirball Cultural Center in Los Angeles, and even the Jüdisches Museum Berlin.[69] To cast their activities as pluralistic and non-particularistic, twenty-first-century Holocaust memorials and museums across North America and Western Europe often display what Sybil Milton describes as a "universal willingness to commemorate suffering experienced rather than suffering caused"—encouraging an empathetic sense that the events commemorated might affect any person in the present or future. In what has been pronounced as "contemporary memory culture," mutual feeling is valorized to a greater extent than specific causal accounts. Perpetrators, as Dan Stone notes, "often do not occupy the space one would expect . . . [and] the victims of Nazi genocide can appear to be the victims of an invisible agent, people to whom terrible things just happen." Sheared of their specific context and causation, those "things" arouse emotion and empathy only when framed as threatening to *any* individual in the present or future.[70]

Figure 3.4 *US President Barack Obama and Elie Wiesel, Holocaust survivor and Founding Chairman of the United States Holocaust Memorial Council, are reflected in a wall in the Hall of Remembrance at the United States Holocaust Memorial Museum, April 23, 2012, in Washington, D.C. President Obama toured the Museum before speaking about the Atrocities Prevention Board, the Holocaust, and contemporary conflicts. © Getty Images.*

At the San Francisco Contemporary Jewish Museum, for example, the Hebrew word for orchard, "pardes," is carved into the walls as a central motif. Museum-goers are informed that the word signifies "an environment for exploring multiple perspectives, encouraging open-mindedness," and "acknowledging diverse backgrounds." A 2016 exhibition on Passover at the Skirball Center framed the Jewish festival's importance in relation to Jews "taking active roles in civic life and supporting the global struggle for human rights" on behalf of other groups. Jewish organizations in Canada have adopted similar frameworks. Bernie Farber, chair of the Canadian Jewish Congress, delivered an address to the standing senate committee during the 2008 Canadian parliamentary proceedings on the National Holocaust Monument (NHM) in Ottawa, in which he defined the Holocaust as an important historical moment: "The Holocaust represents a watershed in human history, a period of horror that redefined the limits of the depravity of human nature, and expanded humanity's consciousness of evil. The Holocaust has become the seminal point of departure for understanding the general potential of humankind for such inhumanity."[71] North American Jews have sometimes brought these agendas to European museums:

W. Michael Blumenthal, former US Treasury Secretary and early director of the Jüdisches Museum Berlin, suggested that the museum catalog "far transcends" the history of German Jewry, demonstrating "a widely shared determination" to apply its lessons "to societal problems of today and tomorrow" and to promote "tolerance toward minorities in a globalized world."[72]

Early USHMM director Walter Reich has recently asked why so many Jews remain at the "forefront of efforts to protect human rights universally" yet are also "uncomfortable advocating for their own group?" "Do they fear," Reich continues, "that, if they focus on Jews . . . they'll be seen by their colleagues as parochial and, therefore, not fit to join the universalist club?"[73] Several writers have questioned whether "liberal" Jews will ever even gain external credit for universalizing their spiritual heritage and their ancestral suffering. In their desire to avoid the charge of clannishness or group-orientation, their engagement with broader social justice initiatives may overlook problems facing Jewish communities closer to home. A key problem, according to some commentators, centers on the use of Holocaust analogies to describe myriad non-Jewish national and global contexts, minimizing the Jewish experience in the collective memory of the Holocaust and even castigating Jews for their perceived moral failing, or at least their parochialism, in opposing such a phenomenon. Responding to Reich's question, several recent critiques of the universalization of Holocaust memory have contrasted contemporary Jewish institutions with non-Jewish "identity museums" in North America, including those that incorporate exhibitions on Native American history and culture. There "are peculiarities in interpretation and advocacy," Edward Rothstein notes in the "Problem with Jewish Museums," because in "no other setting . . . is group identity defined by the abnegation of one's own group identity."[74]

Yet Rothstein's claim overlooks the similar ways that Indigenous histories of trauma have been universalized in civic memorials and museums since the nineteenth century, culminating in the critiques of the NMAI and Canadian institutions examined in this chapter.[75] It also eschews more recent settler-colonial paradigms that help us to examine the tension between Indigenous history and public memory. Those paradigms, we have seen, highlight multiple contexts for the universalization of Indigenous memory and identify their legacy in multicultural approaches to public history during the twenty-first century. They return us to an important insight developed by Philip J. Deloria in his discussion of *Indians in Unexpected Places*: Even the desire to avoid stereotype, according to Deloria, will inadvertently buttress the power of the state. Shifting "from the simplifying tendencies" of the easy distinction between authenticity and stereotype, Deloria reminds us of the "more complex terms of discourse and ideology" that govern even the most progressive advocates of cultural pluralism who are untrained in the meaning of tribal sovereignty.[76] Twenty-first-century North American Jews and Indigenous people continue to face the translation of their memories into what Erika Doss describes as "the social and political agendas of a diffuse body of rights-bearing citizens."[77] Maintaining continued vigilance against facile universalism, abstraction, or egregious relativization, members of both communities and their allied scholars share much in common as they critique historical representations in North American public spaces.

# CHAPTER FOUR

# "The shrines of the soul of a nation."

# Traumatic Memory, Assimilation, and Vanishing in North America

More than eighty years ago, Lewis Mumford suggested that "[l]ayer upon layer, past times preserve themselves in the city until life itself is finally threatened with suffocation: then, in sheer defense, modern man invents the museum."[1] The foundation of museums in global cities may siphon off memories—including those of the Holocaust and Indigenous genocide—to prevent their intrusion in everyday public life. Outside museums, references to Indigenous and Jewish suffering in metaphors, analogies, and shorthand terminology have rarely required more detailed public knowledge of the historical frameworks from which they are drawn. Yet it is also necessary to interrogate what Alain Finkielkraut has described as a "lapse of memory disguised as devotion" among survivor populations themselves rather than merely in public narratives. Over the last half-century, Native Americans, First Nations people, and North American Jews have spent a signification proportion of their lives in the broader public sphere, exposed to the same public proclamations and media representations as those outside their communities. Commentators from both groups thus worry that public memory has become too closely aligned with group memory; and that too many of their associates have become unable to anchor generalized depictions of their ancestral loss in deeper historical context. By diminishing the palpable emotional effect of ancestral trauma, public platitudes are said to encourage assimilation among group members by reducing the power of historical commemoration as an impetus for group cohesion.[2]

Yet a separate set of critiques reject the claim that the commemoration of historical trauma will act as a bulwark against outward assimilation among Indigenous people and North American Jews. The evolving representation of traumatic memory as a unifying cultural ritual, they suggest, risks inspiring assimilation by discouraging the renewal of other cohesive linguistic, religious, and intellectual traditions. "An appropriate memorial design," J. E. Young suggests, "will acknowledge the void left behind and not concentrate on the memory of terror and destruction alone." That balance has not always been achieved. Without recourse to more positive cultural frameworks, younger generations may become *more* likely to assimilate into the broader public realm to escape negative emotional stimuli.[3]

Understanding the connection between historical commemoration, cultural renewal, and demographic assimilation is thus a tricky endeavor. This chapter tries to make sense of these connections. It compares how Indigenous people and Jews have defined the commemoration of their historical trauma as a cohesive cultural medium of its own and how those definitions can inform our understanding of the connection between cultural and demographic vitality. It addresses the fear of assimilation among North American Jews and Indigenous people from the late nineteenth century through the first half of the twentieth century before tracing its trajectory in the contemporary era. It relates those fears to recent debates about the effect of public representations of historical trauma on internal group identity.

## The Vanishing American Jew

The deep-rooted association between cultural and biological loss makes it easier to understand why terminology around vanishing has made its way into Indigenous and Jewish discussions of assimilation and survival, having once been restricted to external representations of their histories of trauma. By employing euphemistic, deterministic, or abstract terminology, vanishing motifs have often minimized the role of perpetrator intent against Jewish and Indigenous victims in subsequent public representations. Yet members of both communities have also employed vanishing terminology to describe the problem of cultural and demographic assimilation following periods of genocide.[4]

An internal reformulation of the vanishing motif among North American Jews began in the late nineteenth century and ironically incorporated language and imagery from Euro-American descriptions of Indigenous loss. The ubiquity of euphemistic descriptions of Indigenous dispossession by the end of the nineteenth century makes it unsurprising that they were appropriated by Yiddish-speaking Jewish writers who had recently migrated to North America. They used the vanishing theme, as it had been applied to Native Americans, to describe the new danger faced by Yiddish-speaking transplants to a land of ostensible safety and opportunity. *Tsvishn Indianer* (*Among the Indians*), for example, was a Yiddish playlet that was first published in 1895 by Khanan-Yakov. Its protagonist, Tenenboym, encounters Seminole nations in what is described as a "shtetl." The play explores the Jewish fear of assimilation as a form of cultural and biological loss. Though they lived in a land far away from the pogroms that threatened Jewish bodies, Tenenboym and his circle were also darkly aware that persecution had inadvertently prevented their assimilation and maintained their group cohesion in the Old World. The story suggests that Yiddish and Indian culture had already become defined through remnant historical artifacts rather than fully functioning communities. Along with several other similar late nineteenth-century texts, *Tsvishn Indianer* recalled the motif of Indigenous vanishing in James Fenimore Cooper's *Last of the Mohicans*—including in its problematic tendency to use the motif as a metaphor to address non-Indigenous concerns rather than to interrogate the nature of loss from the perspective of Native Americans themselves.[5]

Where Yiddish-American writers and community activists once yearned for the cultural cohesion of the nineteenth-century *shtetl*, many of their descendants during the 1950s eschewed vanishing motifs in favor of championing the importance of assimilation into the broader cultural sphere. Many American Jews came to experience the aftermath of the Holocaust as a specifically familial tragedy. But they may have been constrained by the language and terminology associated with dominant non-Jewish commentaries in the post-war context, making them more likely to frame discussions of the Holocaust in the pluralistic ways that broader media had already adopted. To suggest otherwise would apply potentially inaccurate or anachronistic expectations on the approach to historical representation among post-war Jewish communities.[6] Several studies have shown the contextually driven and relatively recent ways that historical suffering and victimhood has been valorized to distinguish group identity. But there is a danger in allowing these later developments to imply that earlier generations of Jews were similarly motivated. As well as being limited by broader media representations of Nazi murder, American Jews sometimes conceived of their victimhood, or that of their families, as something of a problem in an era that did not value group victim status to the same extent as in the present era.[7]

Though the full nature and demographic scale of the Holocaust became more apparent during the 1950s, many American Jewish leaders thus distinguished between the horror of the European experience and the positive opportunities offered by American freedom. As they struggled to comprehend the magnitude and shocking nature of the Nazi destruction of European Jewry, many did not initially recommend the maintenance of Jewish cultural cohesion through the ritualization of Holocaust memory. Neither did they call for the renewal of other culturally cohesive media such as the Yiddish language to secure their demographic stability and counteract the effects of the "Final Solution." Rather, many North American Jews were concerned about the potential for Holocaust commemoration to become a public spectacle that distinguished their community members as mournful survivors rather than as hopeful American citizens. Assimilation was a goal and not something to be avoided through the renewal of cultural heritage and the commemoration of ancestral trauma. The pain of Holocaust commemoration, some worried, would inspire a fatalistic identity as victims and prevent Jewish integration into the broader public sphere as optimistic Americans.[8]

As the Holocaust became more widely known outside their community, however, Jewish writers and leaders grew to be less concerned with the encouragement of assimilation and began to stress the importance of its prevention. From the 1960s through the 1980s, many recommended the bold confrontation of Holocaust memory to galvanize Jewish identity without having to jettison any attachment to American liberalism.[9] Yet a familiar worry began to accompany such recommendations. The commemoration of historical trauma, some wondered, might not provide sufficient impetus to preserve the cultural systems that had been destroyed by the Holocaust, nor the demographic cohesion that those systems had once helped to maintain. American Jews had suddenly become the largest surviving Jewish community in the world. By failing to preserve and renew cultural heritage, some feared, the mere memory of the Holocaust would not be strong enough to stimulate population growth on the western side of the Atlantic and counteract the destructive demographic legacy of the "Final Solution."[10]

Following the example of their late-nineteenth-century forebears, some Jewish writers used Native American analogies to express their fears about the connection between mournfulness and cultural assimilation. Consider, for example, the writings of Ukrainian-born Shmuel Dayksel. His 1959 collection of fiction, memoir, and ethnographic observation charted his experience traveling among Native American nations and was titled *Indianishe dertseylungen*, translated from Yiddish as *Indian Tales*. In the acknowledgments to his book, Dayksel suggested that it is "very dear to me in the sad fact that in a large number of particulars, Indian history is so similar in its fate with our own people. In each story there are interwoven historical, true chapters in the bloody history of the 'Red Men,' sad facts of a history of a people, who have been brutally robbed not only of their immense, grand, rich, and beautiful land which now bears the proud name 'America,' but who, along with their culture and beliefs, have been the targets of an effort to annihilate." Dayksel collapsed the Nazi attempt to destroy Jewish bodies with the destruction of their "culture and beliefs," particularly their ancient languages. Writing in Yiddish, he acknowledged the attempted "holocaust of our language and literature" and yearned "that our dear, heart-felt mother-tongue, with our literature, just like our people and our culture, will continue to flourish" after its near destruction. He hoped for a similar outcome among Native Americans to "help build a brotherly future for humankind in a peaceful world."[11] Dayksel did not require Jews or Native Americans to relativize or universalize their respective cultural and physical losses. Rather, he highlighted their common perception of the binding cultural force of language and their shared fear that assimilation would rupture surviving communities.

As during the late nineteenth century, other Yiddish-speaking writers used Mohican motifs to highlight the dilemma faced by seemingly ascendant North American Jewish communities. Their use of the Mohican analogy would likely be described as problematic from a modern vantage point, given its tendency to allow Jewish memories and fears to supplant those experienced by Indigenous people themselves. Unsurprisingly, writers at the time were far less aware of such a critique. Having escaped the fate of their co-religionists in Europe, they were more concerned with evaluating the association between Holocaust memory and the prevention of assimilation. Dovid Katz's seminal *Origins of the Yiddish Language*, published in 1987, described the few remaining Yiddish-speaking Holocaust survivors in Europe as "Mohicans." Several decades earlier, in Bernard Malamud's *The Last Mohican* (1958), an American Jew could only conceive of a European Jewish Holocaust survivor in otherly terms, as akin to a different ethnicity: "the last Mohican" is a "dark" protagonist who hides in Rome's Jewish ghetto. The American Jew meets a father grieving for the son he lost in the war, a figure like Fenimore Cooper's Chingachgook. The Europe of *The Last Mohican*, as Rachel Rubinstein notes, is represented as a "national landscape haunted by a vanishing people." Their decline is already distinguished from the positive experience of the North American Jew. But that is not the full message of the text. Rather, the danger posed by the "vanishing" of Europe's last Yiddish Mohicans becomes bound up with the trajectory of historical memory and the future role of commemoration on the western side of the Atlantic. When the Jewish tourist returns to his home in North America, he becomes geographically distanced from vanishing reminders of mass death, threatening his own Jewish community with a different sort of disappearance, namely assimilation.[12]

Similar anxious observations could be detected in other Yiddish-American writings over the following decades. The renewal of Yiddish culture became prominent among writers and artists, such as Shia Tenenboym, who suddenly perceived their central role in counteracting the demographic catastrophe of the Holocaust. They were required to resist assimilation at a time of growing societal integration. They had become guardians of cultural media that had been eviscerated on the eastern side of the Atlantic. But as a medium of communal identity in and of itself, the commemoration of the Holocaust risked becoming less effective due to their geographical and temporal distance from the event and the translation of its memory into general public consciousness. Both factors threatened to dilute its role as an impetus for Jewish communal solidarity and as a stimulus for the renewal of other cultural media such as the Yiddish language. In a fictional memoir, first published in Yiddish in 1977 and later translated in a 1995 collection as

"Among the Indians in Oklahoma," Shia Tenenboym drew analogies between North American Jews and Indigenous people to make these points.[13]

Since the 1980s, the fear of assimilation among American Jews has been compounded by their immersion in the broader public sphere and their perceived influence by what Alain Finkielkraut has described as the "symbols to these few majestic words, Auschwitz, Holocaust, the Six Million, which, while claiming to sum it all up, lead to amnesia by way of celebration. Three or four words for a whole genocide—what economy!" What might be mistaken as "an allegiance to memory," according to a warning Finkielkraut has repeated since the 1980s, "is really only laziness, a growing lapse of memory disguised as devotion. If a contradiction exists, it is not between Memory and History; it is between Memory and Metaphors that gradually replace the event of which they are the reminder." Such an observation applies to Jews as well as non-Jews on both sides of the Atlantic, helping to explain North American Jewish fears about the effect of public platitudes on their cultural identity and demographic vitality.[14]

Since the 1990s, anxieties regarding the replacement of group memory with generalized metaphors has contributed to the reemergence of vanishing motifs in the Jewish American world. Consider, most prominently, Alan Dershowitz's bestselling *Vanishing American Jew*, first published in 1997, and still extremely popular. The book distinguishes the experience of Jews during and immediately after the Holocaust from the present experience in North America and begins with the following statement: "THE GOOD NEWS is that American Jews—as individuals—have never been more secure, more accepted, more affluent, and less victimized by discrimination or anti-Semitism. The bad news is that American Jews—as a people—have never been in greater danger of disappearing through assimilation, intermarriage, and low birthrates. The even worse news is that our very success as individuals contributes to our vulnerability as a people." The implication here was made clear in the rest of Dershowitz's book: greater acceptance led Jews to minimize the importance of group cohesion because the traumatic memory of the Holocaust had subsided in favor of accommodation into American public life. There are references to low birth rates throughout the volume. They suggested that American Jews had once felt implored by Holocaust memory to increase, or at least preserve, their demographic strength. But with the memory of extermination becoming less salient than the feeling of acceptance, according to Dershowitz, Jews were less likely to define the necessity of cohesive communal growth. The Holocaust had become too distant from American lives in temporal terms yet also too ubiquitously present as a generalized cultural motif. Rather than highlighting the specific horrors experienced under the Nazis, according to these readings, the representation of the Holocaust served a broader purpose: it became a generalized metaphor for the dangers of intolerance as distinct from the acceptance of Jews in broader American society. The Americanization of Holocaust memory made American Jews less likely to conceive their specific community as a key site of cultural cohesion and demographic renewal.[15]

Yet other commentaries have connected American Jewish assimilation and the ritualization of Holocaust memory in a different way. They highlight the *push* of negative memories rather than stressing the *pull* of societal acceptance as a primary motor for the assimilation of Jews into American society. In his 1981 *Stranger at Home*, for example, the sociologist Jacob Neusner described the myth of "Holocaust redemption" among American Jews: "the Holocaust is that ethnic identity which is available to a group of people so far removed from culturally and socially distinctive characteristics as to be otherwise wholly 'assimilated.' 'The Holocaust' is the Jews' special thing: it is what sets them apart from others . . ." The role of Holocaust commemoration as cultural identifier, according to Neusner, crowded out other Jewish cultural media as unifying influences. During the same year that Neusner published *Stranger at Home*, literary scholar and biblical translator Robert Alter described the central American Jewish focus on the Holocaust as "the epidemic excess of a necessity . . .[that] may be more than anything else an appeal to Jewish masochism, an attempt to base collective identity on a sense of dread or—if we are utterly honest about these matters, on the special frisson of vicariously experiencing the unspeakable, in the material comfort and security of our American lives." The commemoration of loss, according to Neusner and Alter, had transformed into an ascetic and dominant cultural form at the expense of other cultural media.[16]

Through the 1980s, Neusner continued to caution against the ubiquitous contrast between bleak Jewish history and the "redemption" of Jewish demography in the second half of the twentieth century. He extrapolated a cultural warning from an ongoing historiographical critique within Jewish Studies. In 1963, Salo Baron's seminal discussion of the "lachrymose" approach to Jewish historiography defined "the notion that gentile persecution and Jewish suffering have been the shaping forces of Jewish history." Influenced by Baron's paradigm, Neusner joined other critics in questioning those who viewed the Jewish historical experience solely through the prism of the Holocaust, the Medieval Crusades, the Spanish Inquisition, and Eastern European pogroms. Such an approach, they argued, privileged periods and contexts of suffering over those that encompassed agency, survival, and rich cultural development.[17]

Neusner often used the writings of philosopher and Reform Rabbi Emil Fackenheim as a foil to critique the prevailing link between lachrymose memory and cultural cohesion. Fackenheim famously proposed that the desire to deny Hitler "a posthumous victory" was a primary impetus for the renewal of Jewish spirituality and the prevention of assimilation among the Jewish Diaspora. As a Holocaust survivor, he asserted the "614th Commandment" that "Jews are forbidden to hand Hitler posthumous victories." Fackenheim imbued the command with a divine presence and claimed its axiomatic connection to the strengthening of Jewish cultural cohesion. Neusner, conversely, recommended more positive incentives for Jewish communal identity and demographic growth than the ritualization of traumatic memory. Linguistic, spiritual, intellectual, and artistic systems were to become the primary fulcrum around which communal identity was formed, rather than contingent on their stimulation by the dominant cultural role of traumatic memory.[18]

Edna Friedberg, JTS Fellow and Historian at the United States Holocaust Memorial Museum (USHMM), has traced the continuing legacy of the tension between Fackenheim's edict and Neusner's call for a more positive approach to cultural renewal. Friedberg's 2019 assessment cites a 2013 Pew Research Survey of Jews in the United States, in which 73 percent of respondents said that "remembering the Holocaust" was essential to being Jewish. This was "the highest ranked response to the question of what made them feel Jewish, outstripping values such as 'leading an ethical and moral life,' 'observing Jewish law,' or 'caring about Israel.'" As a result, Friedberg notes, "many people have expressed concern" about the "overemphasis on Holocaust memory in our communal life today." Neusner distinguished between the positive pull of cultural practices and the negative push of traumatic memory. Yet even such a distinction, according to Friedberg, has become blurred as the "importance of the Holocaust to American Judaism is also reflected in both quasi-religious and explicitly religious ways." Examples include the Yizkor memorial service in Conservative prayer books centering around Holocaust memory; bat or bar mitzvah children often being "paired" with a boy or girl who was murdered during the Holocaust; and b'nai mitzvah rituals sometimes incorporating Torah readings from scrolls removed from destroyed European Jewish communities. The increasing importance of the annual March of the Living as a Jewish American ritual could also be included in such a list. Over a quarter of a million teens and adults have participated in the march, where the traumatic memory of the Holocaust is consciously marshaled as a bulwark against cultural assimilation. These and other rituals, in Friedberg's assessment, are in line with "Fackenheim's admonition to be vigilant Jews, lest the goals of the Nazis be fulfilled decades later through assimilation or other gradual forces." Such an approach, Friedberg continues, is now "typical of the way many American Jews relate to the Holocaust, as individuals and in group settings like classrooms, summer camps, and synagogues."[19]

But despite being a daughter of a Holocaust survivor and a historian at the USHMM, Friedberg also acknowledges the problematic aspect of these approaches in contemporary Jewish America. Though defining "remembrance in perpetuity to be a moral imperative," Friedberg does not ignore the tension between cultural renewal and the ritualization of Holocaust memory, asking the following set of questions: "should it be a feature of a Jewish milestone based on religious learning and celebrating a maturing young person? Should we choose a trauma of unprecedented proportions to be the preeminent thing that defines or unites us as American Jews? Or should we focus instead on . . . the rich Jewish textual tradition, or on Jews as creators, as artists, scientists, or philosophers over the millennia? What about God and our place as a covenantal people? Is it healthy—or even sustainable—to define ourselves primarily in terms of a legacy of victimization?" The Holocaust, as Friedberg notes, has become "one of the pillars of our civil religion—a way to keep history alive and spur new generations to act in Jewish ways." But the "paradox of the dominant American Jewish approach to the Holocaust is that it is both the vehicle to define our distinct identity, our separateness, and it simultaneously works to draw us closer to the non-Jewish majority. Are Holocaust education and memorialization different from or consistent with a Jewish tradition that has always made a ritual out of remembering tragedies from the past? How do we achieve balance between painful memory, and literacy in Judaism and other Jewish historical events and culture?"[20] That Friedberg leaves these questions unanswered speaks to the ongoing lack of consensus in the American Jewish world regarding the connection between historical commemoration, demographic assimilation, and the renewal of other cultural media. Most commentators and community leaders define the moral imperative of remembrance for all Jews. But the commemoration of the Holocaust as a dominant cultural ritual, many also warn, may encourage outward assimilation by preventing other cultural systems from providing a significant inward pull.

## Traumatic history as cultural form in Indigenous America

Indigenous trauma theorists have engaged similar debates about the perceived connection between historical suffering and group cohesion, and the relative balance between rituals of commemoration and other cultural media. Some have warned that the facile transmission of Indigenous history in public motifs, metaphors, and allusions will exert undue influence on younger community members and encourage their outward assimilation. Other theorists, conversely, caution that constant engagement with traumatic memory only serves to expand the emotional burden experienced by Indigenous people. That burden, they suggest, risks leading them to minimize their exposure to cortisol-raising stimuli, including by distancing themselves from cultural manifestations of historical commemoration in their own communities.[21]

Let us return, for example, to the ambiguous legacy of the Massasoit statue in the decades following the Plymouth Rock tercentenary. The Eurocentric sculpture stimulated a Plymouth "counter-memorial" by local Indigenous activists and the United American Indians of New England. The establishment of an annual "National Day of Mourning" near Cole's Hill in 1970 demonstrated Indigenous agency and repudiated the sculpture's attempt to valorize the pluralistic protection offered by the modern American state. The move towards a National Day of Mourning in Plymouth coincided with the growth and consolidation of the Red Power and American Indian movements elsewhere in North America. Responding in part to the attempted enforcement of cultural assimilation during the first half of the twentieth century, those movements encouraged Indigenous pride by commemorating the will to survive without overlooking the crimes and catastrophes perpetrated against Indigenous people over previous centuries. The Day of Mourning continues through the present day. Yet a question, best expressed by Lisa Blee and Jean O'Brien, has always remained pertinent: "Can a public history [such as the Day of Mourning] that embraces discomfort as an educational aim produce a deeper engagement with a complex history . . . .?"[22]

Some Native Americanists have echoed Ellen S. Fine's expression of the uneasy role of "absent memory" among Jews during the post-Holocaust era. Indigenous people, according to Jennifer Lemberg, may face the similar anxiety that their "thoughts and emotions" could become "dominated by the very memory they lack." Commemorating the absence of cultural languages and linguistic systems might come at the expense of other Indigenous cultural media, potentially encouraging outward assimilation rather than group cohesion.[23] Consider the following statements by the Traditional Hunkpapa Lakota Elders' Council, first delivered in 1990, which sought to navigate between hopeful emphases on historical survival and lachrymose accounts of death, perpetrator intent, and mourning: "We have followed tradition in our mourning," the Elders Council pointed out, but:

> . . . [w]e have not been happy, have not enjoyed life's beauty, have not danced or sung as a proud nation. We have suffered remembering our great Chief and have given away much of what was ours. . . . blackness has been around us for a hundred years. During this time the heartbeat of our people has been weak, and our lifestyle has deteriorated to a devastating degree. Our people now suffer from the highest rates of unemployment, poverty, alcoholism, and suicide in the country.

The Council statements highlighted the cultural authenticity of their mourning rituals, which reminded surviving generations of their specific histories of trauma. But the "heartbeat" of their people—passion, verve, and a spiritual zest for life—is said to have suffered due to the continuous and contiguous nature of those rituals. The unprecedented scale of Indigenous death following the Euro-American encounter required continuous mourning rituals that were once reserved as a response to isolated events. Lasting centuries rather than years or decades, the rituals continue in the present day. The resulting socioeconomic and psychological difficulties identified by the Council support the later assessment by the Indigenous psychologist, Maria Yellow Horse Brave Heart, of a "a legacy of chronic trauma and unresolved grief across generations."[24]

Or consider the work of the Takini (Survivor) Network, which was formed in 1992 to "address healing from historical trauma and historical unresolved grief among the Lakota as well as other Native people through therapeutic work, prevention, research, publication and community education." Their findings have corroborated the assessments of Indigenous and non-Indigenous psychologists and tribal historians, which have noted the tension between the commemoration of traumatic history and the desire to avoid mournful paralysis. Yellow Horse Brave Heart has issued a useful summary of the negative implications of these assessments: "Death identity—fantasies of reunification with the deceased; cheated death . . . Preoccupation with trauma, with death . . . Dreams of massacres, historical trauma content . . . Loyalty to ancestral suffering & the deceased . . . Internalization of ancestral suffering . . . Vitality in own life seen as a betrayal to ancestors who suffered so much."[25]

Indigenous discussions of the ambiguous association between historical memory and cultural assimilation are thus strikingly similar to those that have manifested among Jews and Holocaust scholars over the last several decades.[26] It is unsurprising, therefore, that work on intergenerational trauma in Indigenous communities has been influenced by clinical studies of Holocaust survivors conducted during the 1960s, particularly the notion of "survivor syndrome" in second and third generation decedents. To be sure, some Indigenous commentators share a converse fear with Jews: that focusing on positivity and survival rather than mournfulness may encourage public bodies to ignore the role of loss and perpetrator intent in their histories of trauma and influence similar lacunae among younger generations within their own communities.[27]

Yet, for more than a century, Indigenous memory work has found ways to transcend the tension between mournfulness and hopefulness by emphasizing the historical capacity for Indigenous survival without overlooking the external role of perpetrator intent in fomenting population loss. Consider, for example, the Lakota experience during the 1890 Wounded Knee massacre and their response to its depiction in white civic memorials and history books. From as early as 1903, Lakota Wounded Knee survivors linked the chauvinistic language of white written records to the assimilationist terminology of subsequent memorials. They highlighted the role of perpetrator intent in the 1903 monument they erected in response to the memorial that was built to celebrate the Seventh Cavalry. In the century after Wounded Knee, they have redefined white memorials as cultural reference points to measure the power of error and erasure in historical representation and to delineate their own alternative archives of memory and commemorative rituals. Similarly, the proliferation of vanishing terminology and assimilationist assumptions at the 1921 Massasoit statue unveiling at Plymouth was disrupted by Wootonekanuske, a Wampanoag woman and descendent of 8sâmeeqan, who was also known as Charlotte L. Mitchell. Wootonekanuske laid flowers at the monument to represent the deaths that followed the arrival of the settlers rather than supporting the erroneous notion of their friendly cooperation. Mitchell joined other Indigenous people in using the statue unveiling to publicize Wampanoag land rights in the Watuppa and Fall River regions and stimulated further responses such as petitions to the Indian Department to seek reparations and greater autonomy on ancestral lands.[28]

Nearly a century later, Indigenous rituals were employed to counteract other erroneous aspects of Massachusetts public memory. In 2010, a Sacred Run and Paddle ceremony commemorated the forced transfer of Indigenous people to Deer Island in Boston Harbor, in the freezing winter of 1675–6. *Mishoonash*, which were Wampanoag wooden dugout canoes used during the seventeenth century, were re-crafted and paddled along the Charles River and several tributaries. The extended historical ceremony highlighted the ancestral losses suffered by the Wampanoags. But it also stimulated the renewal of *other* cultural traditions, including boat building, which were connected to a specific place. The paddle ceremonies, moreover, used historical memory to highlight the ongoing importance of tribal sovereignty. Demanding an alternative spatial and constitutional association with Massachusetts, they became what Christine M. DeLucia describes as "politically charged agents of decolonization, making a provocative statement to Boston in reaffirming the city's urban heart as Native space." The Sacred Run and Paddle ceremony displayed three key aspects of memorializing Indigenous history: "recognizing and redeeming survivor accounts from the colonial archive," "acknowledging injustices and blunting the pressures of assimilationist policy," and then collapsing "the imagined distance between the past and present and foreground living Indigenous people and their perspectives." As a place-based ritual, the ceremony corresponds with other acts of Indigenous counter-memory, such as that which Kent Blansett has noted at the Alcatraz site in San Francisco. These and other examples return us to Gerald Vizenor's seminal definition of "survivance" as an "active sense of presence, the continuance of native stories, not a mere reaction, or a survivable name." In emphasizing the historical capacity for Indigenous survival without overlooking the external role of perpetrator intent in fomenting population loss they show "how memories of devastation exist relationally alongside those of regeneration." The rituals employed in mournful commemoration also demonstrate the positive survival of cultural forms, including Indigenous archives of memory.[29]

By reviving Indigenous rituals of belonging, ostensibly mournful memory work also repudiates the assimilationist tendencies of "blood quantum" and DNA analysis as a measure of Indigenous group identity. In the United States, the concept of "blood quantum" became especially prevalent between 1887 and 1934 as a mean to isolate Indigenous people by categorizing them in purportedly binary ways. Those people of mixed descent, rather than "pure" Native American blood quantum, were deemed as undeserving of tribal status and benefits, notwithstanding their given status as defined by their own communities over decades and centuries. Notions of blood quantum dispossessed many Native Americans of their legal standing at just the point when they might have gained greater status and access to land-based approaches to nationhood and belonging, including through their own commemorative rituals and archives of memory. In Canada as well as the US, as Elspeth Martini notes, "on both sides of the forty-ninth parallel" these processes continued settler-colonial dynamics by having "superimposed racial notions of belonging and exclusion over Indigenous political systems."[30] Given their potential to unsettle the connection between group belonging, cultural ritual, and historical memory, it is unsurprising that such measures have more recently been described using vanishing motifs. In 2017, for example, the editors of *The Great Vanishing Act* published a collection of essays that highlighted the deleterious role of blood quantum and DNA analysis in defining the membership of Indigenous tribes and nations in North America. Having worked with the Oneida Nation Trust and Enrollment Committee, the editors follow many other Indigenous commentators in chastising non-Indigenous individuals and institutions for enforcing assimilation—"vanishing"—through genetic profiling and blood calibration. In an age of DNA testing and identity appropriation, Henrietta Mann reminds us in a preface to the volume, "using blood quantum as a measurement for tribal membership could continue to dilute our *ma'e*, our blood, until the tribes cease to exist. A matter of life or death." From the nineteenth century to the mid-twentieth century, Indigenous people faced external agents who described their "vanishing" as inevitable, and as a euphemism that obscured non-Indigenous intent in "removal, genocide, forced assimilation, and boarding schools." But in the twenty-first century, as Mann continues, the myth of vanishing "has shape-shifted into more subtle and insidious forms. Blood quantum, the concept that being Native required a quantifiable attribute—in other words, blood—has become the new 'vanishing Indian.' Drop below a certain arbitrary fraction and—poof!—the Indian has disappeared."[31]

Dershowitz used the vanishing motif to issue a complex warning to North American Jews: fading historical consciousness prevented trauma from galvanizing their group identity in the way it once did, making non-Jewish citizens more likely to "kill us with kindness" in a context of societal acceptance. The discussions in *The Great Vanishing Act* use the motif rather differently. Indigenous archives of memory, the various authors remind us, remain strong and vibrant, offering an authentic way to define community and tribal membership in line with Vizenor's definition of survivance. A statement by the late John C. Mohawk, a Seneca, elucidates this point: "one does not belong to a nation based on one's blood quantum. Belonging to an indigenous nation is a way of being in the world." But the continued role of blood quantum measures and the growing popularity of DNA ancestry kits allow non-Indigenous individuals to claim Indigenous identity, thanks to whatever small measure of Indigenous DNA can be located, thereby supplanting more authentic measures of communal membership. DNA analysis follows earlier blood quantum measures by denigrating or simply ignoring Indigenous archives of knowledge that define community membership through lived practice—including through commemorative rituals that remind Indigenous people of their histories of trauma while underscoring the survival of their cultural media.[32]

## Plastic shamans and lucky Jews

The tense association between group history, public memory, and assimilation is also necessary to understand related debates in both communities about the dissemination of cultural heritage. The outward purveyance of cultural and spiritual practices is often said to dilute and limit the galvanizing capacity of those practices *within* their groups; just as a failure to safeguard the unifying cultural memory of historical trauma itself is said to impose similar limits.[33]

From the 1970s until the early 2000s, for example, American television and print media universalized Indigenous historical suffering alongside Indigenous culture in the ubiquitous "Crying Indian" motif. The motif was first introduced into American consciousness in a 1971 "Keep America Beautiful" advertising campaign that was disseminated on television and in print media by the largest community activist non-profit organization in the country, composed largely of non-Indigenous people. Variations of the image and message appeared in public advertisements as late as 1998. In the most prominent image in the television commercial, a Native American man stood alone, beneath a pile of garbage that ruined the surrounding environment. As the camera focused on his tear, the commercial implored *all* Americans to "get involved now" to restore the pristine environment, to prevent waste, and to beautify outside spaces. Indigenous conceptions of environmental degradation are axiomatically associated with the massive contiguous loss of Indigenous lives following Euro-American colonization. Yet the Crying Indian motif supplanted the memory of those deaths with the suggestion that all Americans *share* Indigenous pain in the destruction of pristine environments. The universalization of historical Indigenous trauma accompanied the appropriation, dilution, and assimilation of Indigenous cultures of environmentalism, ecology, and spirituality in the same public media. Even the crying man's "Indianness" was complicated by the fact that Iron Eyes Cody, the figure in the film, was an Italian-American actor who had been falsely described as a descendent of Cherokee and Cree communities.[34]

The common association between cultural appropriation and universalized history has stimulated ongoing debates in the Indigenous world about the role of historical commemoration as a cultural ritual. The growing scholarly literature on "Plastic Shamanism" focuses on the transference of culture from surviving Indigenous populations to non-Native subjects, and its subsequent refraction back into those populations in attenuated forms. It has responded to statements such as those issued in the

1993 Declaration of War Against Exploiters of Lakota Spirituality, which asserted "a posture of zero-tolerance for any 'white man's shaman' who rises from within our own communities to 'authorize' the expropriation of our ceremonial ways by non-Indians; all such 'plastic medicine men' are enemies of the Lakota, Dakota and Nakota people." Since the 1990s, these and other statements have warned of the diminished meaning of Indigenous cultural and spiritual practices due to their popular appropriation outside Indian country.[35]

The Lakota statement should not be taken to represent the viewpoint of all Indigenous nations, nor even all Lakota. Even as culture is reoriented as a key measure of identity and belonging, including through the commemoration of traumatic historical memory, there is rarely one Indigenous viewpoint as to its exact association with external influences or the subsequent internal impact of its outward dissemination. Discussing the work of Eva Marie Garroutte and Circe Sturm, for example, Steve Russell notes how developing notions of Indigenous self-identification stimulate as many questions as they answer: "I see individuals defining Indian communities and Indian communities defining Indian individuals. I cannot comprehend the idea of an Indian being Indian as the only astronaut living on the moon. No community means no Indians. This gut-level answer . . . only leads to still more questions. In an esoteric sense, who gets to be the culture police? In an exoteric sense, who speaks for the community? 'Authenticity' remains problematic for tribes from within and from without." Russell explicitly notes how Indigenous cultural rituals cannot be divorced from their surrounding contexts, how they are likely to be disseminated to those contexts, and how they may then be refracted back to their own communities. In all these cases, Russell reminds us, it is erroneous to suggest that "authenticity" has come to enjoy one meaning and definition vis-à-vis the power of "culture" to bind Indigenous identity.[36] Still, the anxious response in the Lakota statements above do speak to broader tensions and debates among Indigenous people regarding the definition of "Indian" identity in an era of cultural appropriation, blood quantum, and DNA analysis.

These ongoing questions and debates over the nature of Indigenous cultural authenticity have not yet included much discussion of the outward dissemination and appropriation of traumatic historical memory as a discrete cultural form in and of itself. The literature has tended to focus on the ways that cultural and spiritual artefacts, rather than the history of suffering as a cultural form, have been appropriated by non-Indigenous sources.[37] A structural template for such a discussion can be found among a few of the recent critiques of the outward diffusion and requisition of Jewish spiritual edicts through the universalization of Holocaust memory. During the last decade, an increasingly heated debate in Jewish religious and intellectual circles has centered on the adoption of the *tikkun olam* edict to draw attention to and "heal" the suffering of non-Jewish victim groups, as well as to compare the Jewish experience during the Holocaust with historical examples from outside the Jewish world. The universalization of Jewish trauma and spirituality in these examples recalls a similar process in the trajectory of the Crying Indian motif in American public media. The Hebrew root תקן (t-k-n), according to most interpretations, appears in the Torah to define the repair or "straightening out" of objects. Rabbinical writings, to be sure, expand its meaning according to a full range of interpretations, referring to Jewish spiritual renewal, to fashioning superior objects from lesser forms, and even to societal amelioration. The phrase also appears somewhat ambiguously in Jewish liturgy in the *Aleinu* prayer. In that context, it likely refers to societal repair as a divinely led occurrence, rather than as that which humans can carry out under their own volition. But like many "traditional" terms that have migrated from Torah writings to rabbinical and liturgical texts, as Levi Cooper astutely notes, "we can expect that in different ages, under different circumstances, and in different contexts, *tikkun olam* will have different meanings." As liberal universalism has become increasingly common in public discourse, therefore, some Jewish leaders have marshaled the term to define their duty to perfect or repair the world beyond the communal needs of the Jewish community—just as some Indigenous figureheads have sometimes been accused (perhaps not always fairly) of positioning themselves to promote their spirituality to more universal public audiences. The edict has regularly been used to validate the entry of Jewish organizations into broader social justice movements, often through reference to the memory of the Holocaust. Recent work on the "assimilation" of *tikkun olam* in contemporary Jewish identity, including through approaches to Holocaust memory, has thus used the 2013 Pew Research Center Survey of US Jews to suggest that a focus on liturgy, ritual, and history has been superseded by a newer way of defining "liberal" Jewish identity: the promotion of ethical universalism in tandem with the deployment of Holocaust memory as a warning against all forms of injustice.[38]

Some culturally or religiously conservative Jewish commentators have issued a stinging response to such a "liberal" consensus. Jonathan Neumann, for example, has described his recent work on the appropriation of the *tikkun olam* edict under the following headline: "liberal Jews are destroying their own religion." The "sacred cow of Tikkun Olam," in Neumann's reading, has "isolated words in the Hebrew prayer 'Aleinu' as if all Jewish doctrine were designed to measure its worth before the moral perceptions of a 'universal audience.'" According to Neumann and several other commentators, cultural and religious edicts such as *tikkun olam* and Jewish rituals such as the Passover Seder are too often framed through the prism of contemporary "social justice" movements *outside* their community, rather than as religious works to be treated on their own terms. This commentary recalls earlier critiques of USHMM mission statements, which suggested their universalization of Exodus liturgy. Specifically inflected spiritual languages are said to be coarsened by their being filtered into secular homily, as is the memory of Jewish suffering during the Holocaust. Thus, the conjunction of *tikkun olam* with Holocaust terminology is defined as a facile example of post-war liberalism: first, Jews are required to secularize their religious edicts to situate themselves within a broader "progressive" social gospel; and second, the specificity of their historical suffering is minimized at just the point when other identity groups have begun to refer to their historical subjugation and its "intersectional" legacy in their lives.[39]

But however problematic the recent outward trajectory of the *tikkun olam* edict may have been, the criticisms above presuppose a historically authentic form of Jewish particularism that may not be entirely accurate—whether in relation to spiritual heritage or regarding the interaction between Jewish spirituality and the commemoration of historical trauma. Those who highlight excess universalism in the "liberal" Jewish appropriation of *tikkun olam* tend to claim its inspiration by nineteenth-century Jewish Enlightenment thought (the *Haskala*) as well as the classical Reform Judaism that soon germinated on both sides of the Atlantic. These influences are said to depart from and in turn threaten "traditional Judaism." But proclamations such as *tikkun olam*, which have been translated from scriptural to rabbinical texts, have always been codified and interpreted according to shifting societal contexts. The former interpretation, as Shaul Magid notes, employs an "essentialist definition" of "traditional Judaism" that "exhibits a significant lack of historical understanding of tradition as something that is continually made or re-made, rather than as a prepackaged gift bequeathed in turn to every generation." Contemporary proponents of "social-justice Judaism" such as Aryeh Cohen, Elliot Dorff, and Jill Jacobs use specific Jewish rituals to articulate what Magid, channeling the Jewish philosopher Emmanuel Levinas, describes as "a universalism that is performed through its particularism." Many critics of liberal Jewish universalism, then, employ ironically teleological interpretations of orthodoxy, traditionalism, and the ways that Reform, liberal, and Haskalah-influenced Jews have gone about defining ambiguous spiritual concepts.[40]

A similar interpretative tension can be detected in critiques of the link between Holocaust commemoration and the assimilation of Jewish spiritual culture in non-Jewish causes. Some proponents of the link may well have trivialized or diluted the specific horrors experienced by Jews during the Holocaust. But their opponents may also have overreached in their suggestion that pioneering Jewish legal theorists such as Raphael Lemkin avoided such a link entirely. We have already noted how Lemkin's engagement in comparative genocide analysis, including his reference to Indigenous history, was not dichotomous with his conception of the specific horror and magnitude of the Holocaust. But it is also germane to highlight the influence of *tikkun olam* on Lemkin's approach. Rather than suggesting that universalistic interpretations of Jewish spirituality were anathema to "pioneers" of genocide terminology such as Lemkin, more nuance is needed in tracing the moral philosophical and spiritual roots of comparative representations of genocide, including as they relate to public memorials and commemorative spaces.

Lemkin felt comfortable using Jewish spiritual heritage as a spur to compare the Holocaust with other cases of historical suffering and mass death, including in Indigenous North America. For example, he engaged with spiritual works that have governed rabbinical understandings of *tikkun olam*. In *Totally Unofficial Man*, Lemkin's unpublished autobiography, he incorporated the prophetic writings of Isaiah, which implored the Children of Israel to "Cease to do evil; learn to do well; relieve the oppressed; judge the fatherless; plead for the widow," both inside and outside their immediate religious sphere. Such a statement, according to Lemkin, "sounded to me so urgent, as if the oppressed stood now outside our door. The appeals for peace by converting swords into ploughshares seemed to recreate his presence." Universalism defined Lemkin's approach to comparative genocide in these examples not merely because group particularism was undervalued at the time. Specific spiritual edicts governed his approach, so that what "made his imagination cosmopolitan rather than merely tribal," as A. Dirk Moses points out, "was the Jewish tradition of *tikkun olam*: healing the world and caring for all the oppressed, irrespective of nationality." Lemkin was inspired to categorize and define the concept of genocide by events that preceded the Holocaust, as well as the Holocaust itself. And he channeled readings of ethical universalism that he could deduce from Jewish scripture, Rabbinical writings, and liturgy.[41]

Understandable opposition to the universalization of Holocaust terminology during the last few decades should not blind us to the manifestation of universalism in Jewish spiritual heritage, nor its contribution to foundational efforts in modern genocide studies that include Indigenous examples. Lemkin was influenced by Jewish spiritual precepts such as *tikkun olam* as he configured an approach that was itself affected by earlier assessments of Indigenous historical loss. While maintaining continued vigilance against facile universalism or egregious relativization, we do not need to jettison these aspects of Lemkin's legacy, including its potential contribution to an interpretative alliance between Holocaust Studies and Indigenous Studies. That alliance, we have begun to suggest, does not require either to relativize or minimize the specificity and scale of their respective subjects.[42]

These associations become even more germane considering a related phenomenon: the appropriation of cultural and spiritual ideas in regions where Indigenous nations and Jews once lived as the majority population but are now largely absent due to the legacy of historical displacement and mass death. A new body of work has begun to interrogate the ambiguous nature of ostensible philosemitism in Eastern European towns such as Krakow. There, as elsewhere, Jewish spiritual and cultural heritage is commemorated largely by non-Jews. The common "Lucky Jew" figurines sold in Polish towns and festivals, according to one assessment, can be compared to the problematic way "some view cigar store Indians in the

United States." These comparisons also recall the commodification of the Massasoit statue outside its region of provenance. The erection of the statue in Plymouth ignored the views of surviving Indigenous populations in the region. But copies of the statue also circulated in towns where far fewer Indigenous populations lived. Profits, marketing, and the pursuit of beneficial tax codes led to the proliferation of Massasoit statues alongside salt-and-pepper shakers and souvenirs that represented the Sachem as an interlocutor with the American people writ large. Cigar store Indians, salt and pepper shakers, and Lucky Jew figurines might suggest a positive climate in which Jews and Native Americans are venerated. But their proliferation also highlights the chasm between those who disseminate their cultural motifs and the permanently removed bodies of the people who created them in the first place. Cultural renewal in sites of loss may reduce the urge to commemorate mass death.[43]

North American Jews and Indigenous people both became more active in commemorating their histories of mass death during the second half of the twentieth century. Commentators in both communities fear the effects of continuous mourning. They also worry about the transformation of historical trauma into broader cultural motifs, which may refract back into their internal realms and dilute group consciousness. Rather than encouraging mournful fatalism, they claim, greater exposure to the extreme and specific nature of historical trauma will galvanize group identity and provide an impetus to rebuild culture and demography. But constant exposure to histories of trauma, other commentators warn, may encourage assimilation as a form of escapism.[44] Yet the reassertion—even the resurrection—of cultural and linguistic heritage can offer a more positive framework to resist assimilation, while offering more authentic ways to commemorate ancestral loss. Members of both communities retain archives of knowledge and culture that provide them with languages and concepts to grapple with—and represent—their traumatic histories while maintaining ongoing cultural cohesion.[45]

# PART THREE

# Europe

# CHAPTER FIVE

# "A permanent statement of our values."

# Indigenous Genocide, the Holocaust, and European Public Memory

In their attempt to distinguish the darkness of European history from the exceptional trajectories of the United States and Canada, North American civic institutions have often represented the Holocaust as an abstract and even de-Judaized icon while overlooking the confounding experiences of Indigenous people. This chapter explores a similar set of associations on the eastern side of the Atlantic, which have rarely been noted: European cultural institutions share structural tensions and lacunae with their North American counterparts in their approach to the public memory of the Holocaust and Indigenous genocide. Cultural media in Germany, France, and the UK have often represented Indigenous dispossession as an American rather than a European phenomenon or as a hazily defined occurrence without human causation. Others have simply ignored it altogether. Such representations make it easier for those sites and their civic supporters to marshal Holocaust memory as an aberrant counterpoint to the otherwise positive historical trajectory of European civilizational values—either in their national context or within supra-national frameworks that emphasize inclusivity and tolerance. The following sections thus consider differences as well similarities in the representation of the Holocaust and Indigenous genocide in Western European nations; how the contribution of those nations to European Union (EU) cultural institutions has impacted separate memory cultures in Eastern Europe; and how local cultural agents and curators have either supported or repudiated top–down approaches to the public representation of historical trauma in different parts of the continent.

## Germany: Ethnography and universalism

The curatorial culture of European museums has its origins in late-eighteenth-century royal collections that eventually became public displays, such as the Louvre in France, where artifacts from colonized or formerly colonized communities were said to be protected from vanishing. By extracting artifacts from their original context and defining their meaning from a European perspective, they reflected the assumptions of settler-colonists who privileged their needs over those of Indigenous people. Through the mid-nineteenth century, the German pioneers of ethnographic collecting reinforced these curatorial tendencies. Adolf Bastian, the first professor of ethnology in Germany, became the founding director of the Berlin Royal Museum of Ethnology (Königliches Museum für Völkerkunde), which opened its doors in 1886. Bastian stressed the importance of representing aesthetic and cultural systems that were not guaranteed to remain in their original context.[1]

From the late-nineteenth century, Bastian's developing ethnological approach coincided with and even influenced the German tendency to

**Figure 5.1** *The atrium of the Royal Museum of Ethnology in Berlin, Germany, 1887. © Getty Images.*

circulate abstract historical depictions of Indigenous people in writings, exhibitions, and popular re-enactments.[2] Germany, unlike many other European states, did not have much of a history of imperial expansion among indigenous people in the Americas. Why, then, would Germans have abstracted, universalized, and instrumentalized Indigenous histories of trauma to an even greater extent than other Europeans? We can begin to answer these questions by examining the preface to *Winnetou*, the first of a trilogy by the prolific German writer Karl May, which inspired an eponymous museum in Radebeul that stands today. The preface was published in 1892, and proclaimed: "Yes, the Indian is a sick, a dying man, and we now stand at his miserable bedside feeling sorry, with nothing left to do but to close his eyes. It is serious enough to witness the death of any human being—how much more serious, then, is it to see the destruction of an entire race! . . . The dying Indian could not be integrated into the white world, because of his unique character. Was that reason enough to kill him? Could he not have been saved? But what use are such questions in the face of certain death? . . . I can only lament, but change nothing; only grieve, but not bring a single dead back to life." Old Shatterhand, the book's protagonist, moved from Germany to become a blood brother with an Apache chief named Winnetou. Through that narrative, which May described as "a memorial to the red race," he defined what would become an increasingly common German nostalgia for pre-Industrial norms that were threatened by the global expansion of Anglo-American capitalism.[3] From the nineteenth century through the era of World War II, prominent German writers and philosophers displayed an interest in the history of Indigenous people in North America, often using vanishing motifs to describe the supposed rise and fall of their civilizations. By the early twentieth century, Indigenous culture was commonly valorized as a "noble" or "natural" alternative to nascent American capitalism and urbanism. German writers and commentators sometimes even broadened their own national identity to distinguish European civility from the aggressive capitalistic power of American settlers among the tragic "Red Man."[4]

By 1896, more than 400,000 copies of *Winnetou* had been published. They provided a template for later literary and ethnographic representations of Indigenous history that imagined a world where white Americans descended solely from Teutonic rather than Anglocentric stock. Their counterfactual narratives of irenic, civilized, and fraternal relations with Indigenous people rarely engaged Indigenous history and culture on its own terms. Instead, May and other later German writers distinguished German culture from the rapaciousness of Anglocentric power—including in its influence on American settler expansion during the nineteenth century. They sought to distinguish Germans from other European rivals, particularly the United Kingdom, rather than to examine the deeper character of Native American nations.[5]

Notwithstanding their tendency to distinguish Teutonic civilization from Anglocentric violence, German ethnographic ideas influenced the dissemination of similar traditions in the United States through pioneering anthropologists such as Franz Boas. On the one hand, Boas sought to distinguish himself from Eurocentric approaches by documenting Indigenous encounters with Europeans and by attempting to define those encounters from an Indigenous perspective. On the other hand, his fundraising and research activities purported to "salvage" Indigenous culture from vanishing and sometimes described the destruction of Indigenous populations in hazy and abstract ways. Through the first half of the twentieth century, indeed, North American "salvage anthropology" refracted its influence back to European museums and contributed to the "readymade Indian iconography" of their cultural displays.[6]

The rhetorical distinction between capitalistic American expansionism and European civility was of course belied by the actions of Germans and other Europeans in Africa, Asia, and elsewhere during the nineteenth and early twentieth centuries. The dissonance between cultural rhetoric and imperial reality can be detected in more recent attempts to distinguish Indigenous suffering as somehow external to the unfolding history of European civilization. Since the Holocaust, according to Jonathan Boyarin, "the German admiration and concern for the bitter fate of the 'Red Man'" has demonstrated an ambiguous "mise-en-abime of othering, brought forward into the present." The act of supplanting one historical "other" (Jews) by alluding to a different subjugated minority (Native Americans) has become "available, post-Holocaust, as a target of contemporary American sarcasm." Such acts may seem like mercenary attempts to reassert German moral capital by shifting focus to the actions of "American" populations on the western side of the Atlantic.[7] From the second half of the twentieth century until the present day, indeed, the distinction between German civility and Anglo-American violence has continued to be expressed through the writings of Karl May: to date, there are around one hundred million copies of his novels in print, translated into nearly forty languages. Ideas and motifs from the *Winnetou* trilogy have often been used to frame German museums, exhibitions, and popular hobbyist activities during the last several decades, most obviously in the Karl May Museum itself. The museum provides a case study in the way late-Romantic German accounts of Indigenous vanishing have interacted with the desire of contemporary Germans to position themselves at the vanguard of European multi-culturalism. In the Villa Bärenfett, which houses the Native American exhibit, a visitor pamphlet published in 2016 highlighted the "spirit of cross-cultural understanding, compassion, and tolerance" as a contrast to the negative experience of Native American populations at the hands of colonial and US settlers. Yet the exhibition chooses artifacts to represent the colonial world that Karl May sought to evoke, rather than reflecting Indigenous culture and history or Indigenous people today on their own terms.[8]

Similar problems can be detected at Berlin's Ethnologisches Museum, which is currently in the process of relocation to the Museumsinsel site to

Figure 5.2 *Karl May Museum, "Villa Shatterhand," in Radebeul bei Dresden, Germany, 1995. © Getty Images.*

become part of the Humboldt Forum. Prior to the first phase of its reopening in July 2021, much controversy focused on the Forum's plans to follow French and British institutions in housing sculptures that were looted from present-day Nigeria by British soldiers in 1897. Unlike museums in Paris and London, the Forum has recently stated its aim to return Benin Bronzes to Nigeria and to replace them with replicas or even empty space, following a 2022 exhibition. Interestingly, the museum has promised to exhibit the Bronzes before their return "to show Britain's 1897 violence and plunder in Benin." Its proposed display highlights British colonialism without attending to German atrocities in Southwest Africa a few years later, which some scholars have linked to later Nazi structures of power.[9] But whatever the exact motivations regarding the display and return of the Benin bronzes, similar public interventions about Indigenous materials from North America have been much rarer in Germany, despite their link to British and other European forms of dispossession. Some of the artifacts in the new Humboldt collection—including those drawn from Indigenous populations—can be traced to displays in the Prussian-Brandenburg Kingdom's 1794 Royal Cabinet and even earlier seventeenth-century *Kunstkammer* (Cabinets of Curiosity). But during early preparations for the move to the Humboldt site, in contrast to its discussions of the Benin Bronzes, museum representatives employed vanishing tropes in their claim to protect "non-occidental" objects that include Native American and First Nation artifacts as the last of their kind.[10]

By avoiding direct narrative representation of the violent imperial histories that dislocated Indigenous objects from their host populations, the proposed ethnographic displays at the Berlin Ethnologisches Museum overlook historical specificity and valorize the German context for the curation of objects. General descriptions of "white man" or "white settler" avoid accurate representations of perpetrator intent. Such passive descriptions accompany the tendency to define the impact of disease as a disembodied environmental phenomenon rather than as socially constructed. The pre-2017 exhibition on "Cultural Change: Horses, Traders, and Settlers" showed how the "sedentary village tribes died out almost completely as a result of imported diseases." The phrase "as a result of" led visitors to assume an unfortunate occurrence due to differing biological immunities about which colonial actors were unaware. Generalized adjectival descriptions remove national accountability from historical figures and siphon them off into a discrete past—distancing modern European states from the actions of their predecessors and the need for official apologies or reparations. Similar critiques can be applied to the recent displays at other museum sites in Germany, such as the permanent exhibit at MARKK in Hamburg—formerly the Museum of Ethnology (Völkerkunde)—*Indianer Nordamerikas: Eine Spurensuche* (Native Cultures of North America: Following the Trail).[11] Moreover, the failure to account for the specificity of the Indigenous experience of loss, the tendency to instrumentalize those losses in favor of contemporary German concerns, and the inability to represent the ongoing survival and development of Native societies can all be detected in other German public spaces, particularly where local organizations engage in "hobbyism" that reenacts purported "Indian" stories, battles, and rituals.[12] As Paul Williams has pointed out, memorial museums dedicated to "orchestrated violence" face the problem that the latter often "aims to destroy, and typically does so efficiently. The injured, dispossessed, and expelled are left object-poor." But where objects do remain in ethnographic collections, Eurocentric claims to protect them from vanishing offer a different set of problems.[13]

The universalization and abstraction of Indigenous population loss in German ethnographic displays has preceded and then accompanied structurally similar representations of the Holocaust. During the 1950s and 1960s, as ethnographic trends remained entrenched in the German museum landscape, public representations of the Holocaust were limited by the involvement of non-Jews who had been involved in the Nazi regime. Reflecting similar trends elsewhere in Europe, the tension between Jewish and German public memory was exacerbated by the ideological context of the early Cold War. Many European states used World War II sites and memorials to represent their national populations as victorious over, resistant to, or victims of Nazi fascism. Any reference to widespread collaboration with Nazi leaders against Jews risked reducing such narratives as well as the notion of moral superiority against Soviet communism or

Western capitalism, depending on the regional context for public memory work. As West Germany diverged from its East German neighbor, for example, civic leaders in both states sought to define their respective populations as passive victims of historical disorder rather than as bystanders or even perpetrators of genocide against Jews.[14]

Surviving Jews often responded to these repressive contexts by suppressing their traumatic experiences and memories to assimilate into broader European society. But in some cases, they objected to the invisibility of Jewish suffering at sites such as Auschwitz in Poland and Dachau in Germany. During the 1950s and 1960s they involved themselves in tense negotiations with curators and civic bodies at those sites to reduce their generalized representation of the Holocaust.[15] Through the 1970s their critiques became more vocal and provided an impetus for the *Historikerstreit* (historians' dispute) of the 1980s, which took place largely outside Jewish circles. West German intellectuals, academics, and politicians called for greater public representation of the Holocaust and for the German role in the destruction of European Jews to be more fully acknowledged in civic memory. These debates were accompanied by related scholarly disputes between functionalist understandings of the Holocaust, which suggested that the "Final Solution" was stimulated by broader events and concerns in the Nazi war effort, and intentionalist approaches that represented the elimination of Jews as a central ideological and strategic objective of Nazism. Intentionalist emphases contributed to what Germans have described as a process of *Vergangenheitsbewältigung* since the 1980s—the "struggle" to overcome and "work through" negative aspects of their past without treating those historical events in a facile way. But as Gavriel Rosenfeld reminds us, it:

> remains an ambiguous concept, for it uneasily embraces two diametrically opposed methods of coping with the past. On the one hand, *Vergangenheitsbewältigung* represents an effective means of countering the ineluctable tendency towards forgetting . . . At the same time, however, *Vergangenheitsbewältigung* implies a certain kind of forgetting. As Theodor Adorno argued in 1959, "coming to terms with the past does not imply a serious working through of the past . . ." Rather, it may suggest "wishing to turn the page and . . . wiping it from memory." This formulation "works through" the past only for a limited time, "at the end of which, it is "finished" and unable to affect the present as before.[16]

Through the 1980s, for example, Jürgen Habermas accused Germans such as Ernst Nolte of relativizing or minimizing the Holocaust to reassert German civic identity. Only true national accountability for Jewish suffering, according to Habermas, would continue "Germany's opening to the West." Yet Habermas's statements instrumentalized Holocaust memory by linking it to the acceptance of Germany back into Western civilization. The display of German contrition—rather than Jewish suffering itself—risked becoming the primary impetus for Holocaust memory work. German Jewish organizations made a similar point in their opposition to public plans for the construction of a National Memorial for the Victims of War and Terror in the Neue Wache ("New Guard") in Berlin, which were published in 1985. During the Weimar era, the site had been transformed from a royal guardhouse into a memorial for Germans who had fallen during World War I. In the German Democratic Republic, it had been used as a memorial for victims of World War II. But the plans for the new memorial used the site to define the universality of victimhood during World War II. Rather than representing the specificity and scale of Jewish loss, German chancellor Helmut Kohl's "historization agenda" seemed to depict the history of Nazism as a short aberration to display the moral virtue of West Germany's contemporary citizens by contrast.[17]

After the fall of the Berlin Wall in 1989, Germans led Europe in replacing Cold War liberalism with human rights discourse in their approach to public memory—a development that continued the trend to universalize the Jewish Holocaust experience. During the opening of the House of the Wannsee Conference Memorial and Educational Centre in 1992, for example, politicians and curators suggested the importance of Holocaust memorialization to the prevention of similar forms of racism and xenophobia against asylum seekers and a humane and "democratic" future. In 1993 the Neue Wache memorial finally opened in Berlin, dedicated to the "victims of war and tyranny"—an ambiguous generalization that failed to distinguish the Nazi role in causing the war from the defensive actions of allied forces, categorized fallen soldiers from all sides as universal victims, and overlooked the centrality of the Holocaust in Nazism.[18]

Similar approaches accompanied the flurry of memory work under the administration of German Chancellor Gerhard Schröder and Foreign Minister Joschka Fischer, which began in 1998. The 1999 German parliamentary resolution on the proposed construction of The Memorial to the Murdered Jews of Europe (Das Denkmal für die ermordeten Juden Europas) emphasized its contribution to the promotion of human rights and the prevention of persecution against *any* group who might suffer a similar fate: "With the memorial we intend to honor the murdered victims, keep alive the memory of these inconceivable events in German history, admonish future generations never again to violate human rights to defend the democratic constitutional state at all times, to secure equality before the law for all people and to resist all forms of dictatorship and regimes based on violence." These and similar statements allowed German leaders to define the events of World War II as a violation of universal human rights rather than as a specific tragedy for European Jews. As a signal of historical introspection, they demonstrated how far contemporary German values had come in their commitment to the protection of human rights through European integration. Among the memorial's planning committee, according to one member, there was even an initial suggestion to place "rupture in civilization" as one of the few quotations on the wall around the memorial.[19]

**Figure 5.3** *Prince Charles, Prince of Wales (L), Camilla, Duchess of Cornwall (second from R), German President Frank-Walter Steinmeier, and First Lady Elke Buedenbender visit the Neue Wache Memorial to Victims of War and Tyranny in Berlin, Germany, November 15, 2020. © Getty Images.*

The Memorial to the Murdered Jews of Europe and its subterranean Information Center eventually opened in Berlin on May 10, 2005, near the Brandenburg Gate and the Federal Parliament. Consisting of 2,711 gray concrete blocks (*Stelenfeld*) at different heights and angles over a large, maze-like 20,000m$^2$ site, the memorial was designed by the architect Peter Eisenman with collaborative input from the sculptor Richard Serra. The Information Center, which is situated underground at the southeastern side of the Memorial, incorporates an exhibition to facilitate greater awareness about the Holocaust in Europe and to highlight the broader meaning and context of the memorial and its German site. But the abstract concrete blocks dominate public consciousness of the memorial, avoiding specific representation of perpetrator intent or Jewish victimhood. Such generality, as Irit Dekel has noted, has often encouraged visiting students to link the site to universal anti-racism ideology.[20]

Similar universalistic frameworks were demonstrated in the public statements that accompanied the opening of the Jewish Museum in Berlin, which was designed by the star architect Daniel Libeskind. The first director of the museum, W. Michael Blumenthal, delivered a highly publicized speech on the opening of the permanent exhibition, *Two Millennia of German Jewish History*, on January 23, 1999, suggesting that Germans knew "little or nothing of Jews, apart from perhaps the Holocaust." By representing

**Figure 5.4** *A boy hops from one to another of the 2,711 stellae at the Memorial to the Murdered Jews of Europe, also called the Holocaust Memorial, on October 28, 2013, in Berlin, Germany. © Getty Images.*

Jews as "lively and creative citizens, who contributed a great deal to German life" before the Holocaust, Germans could "absorb this history, with all its glories and tragedies" to "learn how important it is to show tolerance to minorities—a relevant topic throughout the world today. They will also learn what price must be paid for intolerance, not only for the minorities and victims, but also for those who oppress and show intolerance." The museum, Blumenthal noted, "symbolizes a determination to confront the past and to gain a perspective on the societal problems of the present and the future" to create a "tolerant and peaceful society."[21] Scholars have used these and other similar examples to show how Germans have led Europeans through the early twenty-first century in defining the Holocaust as a "negative icon"—"de-Judaized" to become a "newly European 'cosmopolitan' memory [where] Holocaust future (and not the past) is now considered in absolutely universal terms: it can happen to anyone, at anytime, and everyone is responsible."[22]

The German examples above demonstrate meaningful similarities in the treatment of Indigenous and Jewish histories of trauma. Since the 1990s, Holocaust memory has often been instrumentalized to define the centrality of Germany in promoting the human rights discourse of EU integration. That process echoes the way Indigenous histories of death were used by Germans from the late-nineteenth century through the first half of the twentieth century. They were appropriated in literary and ethnographic motifs that defined the special attachment of Germans to civilized European ideals and distinguished those ideals from the rapaciousness of Anglo-Saxon interventions in North America. Having once used the memory of Indigenous dispossession to underscore their civility within Europe, many German public leaders now employ Holocaust memory to distinguish their espousal of universal rights within the context of European integration.

## France: Republican universalism and the abstraction of trauma

In France, the occlusion of the history of Indigenous population destruction can be compared and even connected to parallel developments in the representation of the Holocaust in public sites. Having influenced German ethnographic trends, the aesthetic approach of eighteenth- and nineteenth-century French museums can still be detected in contemporary French institutions. Since opening in 2006, for example, a Gallic understanding of universalism has underscored the refusal by Paris's Musée du quai Branly to represent the contextual specificity of its curated objects and its unwillingness to explain their possible connection to the history of French colonial dispossession in North America. In statements he delivered at the museum opening, President Jacques Chirac connected France's protection of universal values to the museum's promise to "preserve" cultural diversity. French national ideals, in Chirac's definition, were aligned with universalism rather than parochialism or subjectivity—including in the value they assigned to aestheticism as a comprehensive category to represent diverse cultures. Each indigenous object, according to Chirac, was understood by French curators as "a treasure that we must preserve" precisely because those curators cherished universal aesthetic standards. Chirac's classically French definition of diversity through universalism suggested that the museum offered "imagination, inspiration and dreaming against the temptation of disenchantment." Objects, like people, were equally protected by universal values. Through its display of non-French materials, therefore, Chirac proclaimed that the French institution provided "a vital lesson in humanity." Such operating assumptions conform to what Barbara Kirshenblatt-Gimblett has summarized as the "idea that those who produce culture do so by dint of their 'diversity', while those who come to own those cultural assets as world heritage do so by dint of their 'humanity." Though lauding its attention to universal and atemporal aesthetic values, the museum becomes *de facto* arbiter of those ideals and underlines France's distinct cultural development.[23]

More than a decade before President Chirac delivered his statement on the opening of the Musée du quai Branly, the French theorist Pierre Bourdieu examined the claim that proponents of aestheticism protected diverse cultural forms from disappearance. Such an approach, Bourdieu suggested in *The Rules of Art*, allowed institutions to remove objects from their original site without having to account for the colonial power structures that had often contributed to their dislocation. Bourdieu's insight is relevant to the curatorial approach adopted by the Musée du quai Branly and its exposition by President Chirac. By defining aestheticism as a timeless and borderless analytic mode, it becomes easier for the institution to overlook the historical provenance of the objects on display—including the potential French colonial contribution to their retrieval and the accompanying population losses of their origin communities. President Chirac's statements alluded to past injustices against "non-Western" people. But by claiming to "restore dignity" to diverse populations, the President and the museum curators underscored their special ability to protect universal ideals and avoided representing the French colonial contexts that contradicted them.[24]

The same Republic ideology that underlay President Chirac's statements at the Musée du quai Branly can be detected in representations of the Holocaust by French politicians and cultural leaders. As Henry Rousso's classic study of post-1945 French memory has shown, a "Vichy Syndrome" popularized the notion that all French citizens were victims of German fascism at the expense of their universally tolerant Republic values,

**Figure 5.5** *French President Jacques Chirac gives a speech, close to a reproduction of a Mexican Chupicuaro sculpture, as he inaugurates the Musée du quai Branly, which features the indigenous art and cultures of Africa, Asia, Oceania, and the Americas, Paris, France, 20 June, 2006. © Getty Images.*

overlooking the role of French collaborators in the liquidation of Jews. The Vichy administration was regularly described as an aberration in the French constitutional experience, wrought by external actors who bore sole responsibility for the destruction of Jews. In the two decades after the Holocaust, therefore, the universal Republican ideals of the French Revolution were reasserted in educational curricula and public memorials to repudiate the notion of French collaboration and to situate French resistance on a natural continuum with the spirit of 1789.[25]

Through the early 1990s, the universalism of French Revolutionary ideals remained central in the statements of French politicians as they responded to the proposed erection and subsequent foundation of the Monument de la rafle du Vél' d'Hiv' 16 et 17 Juillet 1942, commonly known as the Vél' d'Hiv' monument. The proposed memorial evoked the July 1942 "roundup" of more than 13,000 Jews by French police, who followed orders from German leaders in occupied Paris. They used a large velodrome (the Vélodrome d'hiver) to hold Jews before transferring them to a concentration camp at Drancy and then finally to Auschwitz. In 1993, the French President François Mitterrand explained his refusal to deliver a speech on the importance of the monument at its proposed site by referencing his commitment to the tradition of the French Republic since 1789. He depicted the Vichy regime as a historical aberration outside the republican constitution, which had been suspended from 1940–4, and suggested that the so-called "purges" of collaborators in 1944–5 had repaired and overcome that interruption. Mitterrand and his advisors thus objected to any memorial that represented the deportation of Jews as anything other than an externally induced anomaly from otherwise continuous French ideals.[26]

In 1995, a decade before he delivered his speech on the curation of indigenous objects at Musée du quai Branly, the newly appointed President Jacques Chirac spoke at the inauguration of the Vél' d'Hiv' monument. It had been designed by the Polish Holocaust survivor Walter Spitzer and erected on the side of the quai de Grenelle near the historical site of the velodrome. Only around $3m^2$ wide, the bronze sculpture is in a garden that is difficult to see at street level. The inscription on the monument, translated from French, reads as follows: "The French Republic in homage to victims of racist and antisemitic persecutions and of crimes against humanity committed under the authority of the so-called 'Government of the State of France.'" Though the inscription assigns a degree of specificity to the intent of the French state, it also lumps the experiences of Jews alongside broader crimes against humanity. To be sure, Chirac moved away from Mitterand's refusal to display introspection over the depth and scale of Vichy involvement in the deportation of Jews, acknowledging that the Republican parliament had itself voted for the dissolution of the constitution in July 1940. But rather than representing the specificity of Jewish trauma, Chirac spent more time stressing the monument's primary role in displaying the French commitment to the universal ideas of human rights that had been inspired by the spirit of 1789. Those ideals, according to Chirac, made it important to target other forms of "racism" in France and globally. As well as anticipating his discussions of the indigenous materials at the 2006 opening of the Musée du quai Branly, therefore, Chirac's speech at the Vél' d'Hiv' monument in 1995 can be compared with those of German ministers who described the foundation of the Berlin Holocaust Monument in 2000 as a restoration of the principles of universal human dignity and a sign of their protection in modern Germany.[27]

## Britain: The values of Holocaust memory and the occlusion of Empire

Though motivated by different historical legacies and ideological agendas, British public institutions have followed a structurally similar trajectory to their French counterparts in their representation of the Holocaust and Indigenous genocide. They have moved from relative silence about the destruction of European Jewry during the first few decades after World War II towards instrumentalizing Holocaust memory on behalf of contemporary civic concerns. As in France, that developing trajectory has not been accompanied by any parallel change in the treatment of Indigenous histories of trauma nor any acknowledgement of the British imperial role in Indigenous genocide.

Holocaust survivors such as Kitty Hart-Moxon have documented how unbearable it felt during the 1950s and 1960s when they were unable to find any British public audience or institution that was receptive to hearing about the specific horrors that she and millions of other Jews had so recently suffered. Her experiences mirrored the situation in North America during the same period, when the Holocaust had not even entered public discourse as an abstract icon.[28] That public silence was exacerbated by the perceived separation between British culture and the mainland European context for the liquidation of Jews, as well as the dominance of Bergen-Belsen rather than other death camps and concentration camps in British public representations of Nazi atrocities. In their role as liberators of Bergen-Belsen, British and Canadian armed forces tended to describe its victims in multinational terms rather than as disproportionately Jewish, owing to their lack of specific information about what they were witnessing rather than any concerted effort to obscure Jewish suffering. As the first broadcaster to enter Bergen-Belsen, Richard Dimbleby did reference "German and half a dozen other nationalities, thousands of them Jews" in his report, which the BBC initially refused to broadcast until he threatened to resign. "Here over an acre of ground," Dimbley continued, "lay dead and dying people. You could not see which was which . . . The living lay with their heads against the corpses and around them moved the awful, ghostly procession of emaciated, aimless people, with nothing to do and with no hope of life, unable to move out of your way, unable to look at the terrible sights around them . . . Babies had been born here, tiny wizened things that could not live . . . A mother, driven mad, screamed at a British sentry to give her milk for her child, and thrust the tiny mite into his arms, then ran off, crying terribly. He opened the bundle and found the baby had been dead for days. This day at Belsen was the most horrible of my life." As they circulated in British newspapers and broadcast media, these and other reports from media and soldiers were often framed without specific reference to Jews. By the 1950s, reflecting new Cold War concerns, they increasingly contributed to the representation of Belsen as an emblem of British liberation from totalitarianism.[29]

**Figure 5.6** *Dr. Fritz Klein (1888–1945), the Bergen-Belsen concentration camp "doctor," making a statement into a microphone set up by the BBC's Richard Dimbleby, in front of a mass grave of primarily Jewish victims, after the camp had been turned over to the Allied 21st Army Group, April 1945 (b&w photo). © Getty Images.*

In Britain during the 1970s, mirroring the situation in the United States more than in continental Europe, television media played a pivotal role in raising awareness of the Holocaust. British television documentaries such as *Kitty: Return to Auschwitz* (ITV 1979) complemented the US miniseries *Holocaust*, which aired in Britain a year earlier. The dominant public representation of Bergen-Belsen subsided in favor of the emblematic horror of industrialized murder at Auschwitz—at least offering the potential for the Jewish experience to be represented to a greater extent than before.[30] Yet it was only in 1995, thanks to the pioneering efforts of Steven Smith, James Smith, and their mother Marina Smith, that the Holocaust Centre was founded as Britain's "first dedicated Holocaust education and memorial institution."[31] During the same year, which marked the fiftieth anniversary of the liberation of Auschwitz, Holocaust commemoration crossed the threshold from educational settings to the broader non-Jewish public sphere. But British public officials increasingly framed Holocaust memory to correspond with other European approaches that emphasized tolerance and inclusivity for all marginalized or minority groups. The valorization of British values of tolerance alongside other modern Europeans culminated in the founding of the annual British Holocaust Memorial Day (HMD) in 2000, which influenced the approach of other nations in the enlarging European Union (EU).[32] Shortly after the unveiling of the HMD in early January 2000, Stephen Smith, the director of the Beth Shalom Holocaust Memorial Centre in Nottinghamshire, stated that "Britons still talk about the Holocaust in hushed tones . . . Sadly, it still remains a topic off-limits to those who mistakenly see it as a Jewish issue . . . This is no Jewish issue—it is everyone's." Smith and his family have done more than most to establish Holocaust memory in the United Kingdom, including by integrating Jewish archives of memory. His statements were well-meaning, drawing an important connection to modern human rights activism. But they risked reducing Holocaust memory to a generalized warning against intolerance rather than representing the Jewish context of the "Final Solution."[33]

In crossing the threshold from British school curricula to broader public settings such as the annual HMD, the instrumentalization of the Holocaust as a "usable past" to demonstrate the flourishing of "diversity" offered a model for supranational European cultural initiatives. Though the question of restitution and reparation for looted Jewish assets affected continental European nations to a far greater extent than Britain, the International Meeting on Nazi Gold took place in London in 1997. Britain's initiative at that meeting led to its invitation in 1998 to become a founder member of the International Task Force (ITF), a Swedish-inspired project to accomplish a European standard for Holocaust commemoration that had initially been sponsored by the Levande Historia (Living History) project.[34] It was a British delegate at the December 1998 Washington Conference on Holocaust-Era Assets who submitted the "Proposal for International Commemoration of the Holocaust" that stimulated much of the memory work at the 2000

Intergovernmental Conference on the Holocaust in Stockholm. Speaking to other European leaders in Stockholm, British Foreign Secretary Robin Cook linked the HMD to broader values shared outside Britain: "Our aim in the twenty-first century must be to work towards a tolerant and diverse society which is based upon the notions of universal dignity and equal rights and responsibilities for all citizens. The Holocaust Memorial Day is a symbol of this." Following Britain's lead, other European politicians extracted usable messages from Holocaust commemoration by outlining the nexus between tolerant European values and those that stemmed more specifically from local national identities. The resulting Stockholm Declaration, which became highly influential among European statesmen and officials, described the Holocaust as an affront to ideologies of tolerance that were central to European civilization. In reckoning with the memory of the "Final Solution," its membership sought to codify the universal tenets of human rights ideology to fight "genocide, ethnic cleansing, racism, antisemitism and xenophobia." The Declaration claimed that the "Holocaust (Shoah) fundamentally challenged the foundations of civilization. The unprecedented character of the Holocaust will always hold universal meaning."[35]

Universalistic trends in Holocaust representation continued during the ascent of Conservative governments under David Cameron from 2010. Prime Minister Cameron announced the founding of a new Holocaust Commission in September 2013 "to work harder than ever to preserve the memory of the Holocaust from generation to generation" and "to continue to learn and apply the lessons of the Holocaust to our society at home and abroad." Speaking on the twenty-fifth anniversary of Britain's Holocaust Educational Trust, Cameron suggested that the public memory of the Holocaust ought to stimulate the protection of vulnerable people throughout the world. The new commission would help British subjects to "remember the darkest hour of our human history, the Holocaust; a day when we decide to put away all and fight all forms of prejudice and hatred." The general reference to "all forms of prejudice" raised familiar fears among Jewish and allied groups that the Holocaust was represented as an abstract emblem of intolerance to mark contemporary pluralism rather than to allow a visceral understanding of the nature and scale of that which led 1.5 million Jewish children to be slaughtered alongside 4.5 million other Jews. Over the last decade, Labour as well as Conservative British politicians have regularly described the importance of Holocaust commemoration as an event that reminds citizens of the "dangers of intolerance" and "all forms of racism" rather than specifying the Jewish experience—despite repeated and often anguished protests from Jewish groups and institutions, some of whom have even defined such formulations as a new form of anti-Jewish prejudice.[36] In other forums, Prime Minister Cameron stressed his meetings with Jewish survivors, which made him "realize what a sacred task the Holocaust Commission has to carry out." But even these assertions can be distinguished from Jewish approaches to Holocaust memory in their allusion to the Holocaust as a sacred event.[37]

Cameron's statements were accompanied by a new tendency to marshal Holocaust memory to represent the exceptional British "values" that underlay the rescue and liberation of Jews from other European nations, either through the liberation of camps or the adoption of Jewish children. Such an emphasis had grown more apparent during the previous decade in the context of the Iraq and Afghanistan wars, British counter-terrorism offensives, and heated public statements about immigration.[38] The Terms of Reference of the Holocaust Commission, which were eventually published in 2018, highlighted the need for a "clear focus on the role that Britain played" in welcoming European Jews through the Kindertransport and through the settlement of older survivors, as well as the role of British soldiers in liberating Bergen-Belsen. It sought "deliverable recommendations" to "ensure the Holocaust and its lessons remain relevant for future generations." The use of Holocaust memory to underline "what it means to be British," according to Andy Pearce, came at a time when British leaders demonstrated a "deep craving" to define their nation's exceptional and deep-rooted "post-Imperial" moral authority in a post-Brexit context. Thus a "striking and prominent new Memorial" was proposed in London as focal point for national commemoration of the Holocaust" and "as a permanent affirmation of the values of British society." In a Press Release delivered a year after the Commission delivered its recommendations, Prime Minister Cameron described the proposed Memorial's place "beside Parliament . . . as a permanent statement of our values as a nation."[39]

The instrumentalization of Holocaust memory to support contemporary British values is also worthy of critique because it privileges historical cases of rescue and liberation without accounting for the ambiguity of British civic and political engagement with European Jewry. In a 2014 letter to the Holocaust Commission, several British scholars suggested that it was "not at all clear that programmes such as the Kindertransport were representative of British reactions to the Holocaust, especially at the level of government policy. If the Holocaust Commission is to be a success then it must make an effort to review and represent the full range of British experiences and responses, including those we would perhaps prefer not to remember, and not just those we can remember positively."[40]

The desire to secure the exceptional values of Britishness through Holocaust memory can also be connected to ongoing tensions and controversies over Britain's historical role as an imperial nation—including among Indigenous people in North America. British Imperial violence joined the Holocaust in its absence from the British imagination during the 1950s and 1960s, even while the British public suddenly became more aware of global efforts to de-colonize states from British rule. But unlike the subsequent trajectory of Holocaust memory, histories of Indigenous genocide under British imperial jurisdiction have rarely even been adopted as abstract icons. The recent flurry of activity and discussion about statues in British cities and universities, which has been inspired in part by the efforts of the BLM movement, has most often related to British engagement with the slave trade or colonization in Africa and India rather than Indigenous people in North America. Following recent revelations about the death of Indigenous children in Canadian Residential Schools, activists in cities such as Winnipeg have gone as far as removing statues of Queen Victoria. During Australia's ongoing "History Wars," there is at least a discussion about integrating atrocities against Aboriginal people into the mainstream public narrative of Australian history and memory. But in mainland Britain, similar efforts have not yet begun to consider Britain's role in North American genocides—whether in popular forums or in cultural institutions and museums. The failure to represent British imperial atrocities, according to Michelle Gordon, can even be linked to a contiguous lack of understanding regarding the chaotic forms of murder and dispossession that many Jews faced during the Holocaust. By focusing solely on "industrialized" forms of Nazi murder rather than the bloody violence of local perpetrators, it becomes easier to overlook organizationally similar atrocities under British colonial rule and to ignore the need for their public representation in museums and cultural institutions.[41]

The comparative trajectories of the Holocaust exhibition at the Imperial War Museum (IWM) in London, which opened in 2000, and the separate "Crimes against Humanity" section that was launched in 2002 before eventually being discontinued, illustrate the tendency to instrumentalize Holocaust memory while overlooking the specific British role in Indigenous genocide altogether. The many positive aspects of IWM displays will be examined in the following chapter. But at this point, it is worth examining universalistic motifs at the institution during the early twenty-first century. According to Suzanne Bardgett, a project director at the IWM, curators had originally envisioned a single exhibition about "Man's Inhumanity to Man" but eventually decided to divide it "into two" so that the upper floor exhibition would consider the role of "genocide as a general theme." Yet by defining the Holocaust with a greater degree of specificity than other global genocides, albeit with significant lacunae, the museum avoided the thorny issue of accountability for the actions of the "first British Empire" in North America and later iterations of British violence in Australasia, the Indian subcontinent, and Kenya. During these stages of the IWM's development, the Holocaust provided archetypical motifs that found their way into the exhibition on global genocides. Generalized depictions of humanitarian catastrophes distracted from specific accounts of perpetrator intent and did not require a more comprehensive index of genocides, particularly those that occurred before the 1990s. *Any* case study could be used to illustrate the universal danger of inhumanity, rather than attending to similarities and differences among myriad examples—including those associated with British imperial interventions among Indigenous people from New England to the Great Lakes and beyond.[42]

## Indigenous history, the Holocaust, and the material of European integration

During the last three decades, supra-national institutions such as the EU parliament, the Council of Europe, the Organization for Security and Cooperation in Europe (OSCE), and the Office for Democratic Institutions and Human Rights (ODIHR) have often represented the Holocaust as an aberrant counterpoint to otherwise contiguous European values of pacifism and tolerance. Yet as those cultural institutions have sought to influence EU enlargement, they have unintentionally exacerbated the pre-existing tendency to obscure the Jewish dimension of the Holocaust in Eastern Europe, the Balkans, and the Baltic. The role of Holocaust commemoration in EU enlargement is particularly worrisome for Eastern Europeans who perceive its connection to restitution and reparation for the confiscation of Jewish land and property in Budapest, Bucharest, Odessa, Riga, Vilnius, Split, and many other cities and towns.[43] Unsurprisingly, therefore, cultural sites with national and EU funding have defined the identity of non-Jewish Latvians, Estonians, Lithuanians, Ukrainians, Croatians, and Hungarians according to their own victimhood under Nazis, de-specifying the experiences of Jews and occluding the collusion of their own national communities in deportation and murder. Even The House of European History, a public institution sponsored by the EU that opened in Brussels, Belgium, in May 2017, defines Nazism and Communism as "two European totalitarianisms" in its central exhibition, reducing the specificity and scale of Jewish suffering during the Holocaust.[44]

Given the scarcity of ethnographic displays of Indigenous material in Eastern European states, it is more difficult to connect their obfuscation of Holocaust memory to the erroneous representation of North American genocide. But there are other ways that the Eastern European context for Holocaust memory can speak to Indigenous concerns, and vice versa. For example, consider how the fear of reparations has contributed to counter-memorial efforts by non-Jewish Eastern Europeans. That phenomenon is germane to ongoing North American debates on compensation for Indigenous dispossession. The present (inchoate) discussion of European retribution for the Atlantic trade in enslaved Africans is instructive. Europeans were once content to memorialize slavery and black dispossession as an "American" problem that culminated in the US Civil War and the subsequent era of Jim Crow. Reparations to the African-American descendants of enslaved people from US federal, state, and private institutions did not affect European cultural identity, nor European finances. But since activists, legal experts, and scholars have begun to emphasize the European role in the consolidation of racial slavery in the Americas, contiguous debates about reparations in North America have been met with a rather more muted European reception. By defining Indigenous population loss as a nineteenth-century American

**Figure 5.7** *Soviet-built memorial to Holocaust victims adjacent to the IX fort (out of thirteen), where thousands of Jewish people were executed, Kaunas, Lithuania. January, 2017. © Alamy Images.*

phenomenon, or simply by overlooking European colonization altogether, European public bodies have so far avoided a similar reckoning with the question of reparations for Indigenous loss, whether symbolic or financial. Examining the tension between European Holocaust memory and the call for reparations offers a useful template for Indigenous people as they approach the question of restitution from European as well as North American institutions.[45]

Another comparative context is also worth interrogating further: the relatively recent formulation of inter-state standards on the display of Indigenous artifacts in North America, which has not yet been matched by any supra-national European standard. Through the 1970s and 1980s Indigenous artists, activists, and commentators critiqued the Euro-American curatorial claim to revive Indigenous culture through the neutral protection of artifacts. Such an approach, they noted, ignores the deadly colonial interventions that led those artifacts to become disconnected from their originating communities. By the 1990s, these critiques influenced public bodies in North America as they began to effect important legislative changes regarding the display of Indigenous materials. In Canada, the legally sanctioned repatriation of Indigenous objects was described as a necessary response to the legacy of violence and dispossession that accompanied their removal under the 1876 Indian Act. In the United States, growing public awareness of the continuity between European imperial dispossession and American settler expansion provided an important impetus for the 1990 *Native American Graves Protection and Repatriation Act* (NAGPRA). The Act began with the question of Indigenous human remains and broadened its scope to encompass the inventorying and repatriation of other Native American cultural artifacts in US federally funded institutions.[46]

But although acts such as NAGPRA tacitly recognize the European colonial roots of Indigenous dispossession, they do not apply any jurisdictional force to the curation of Indigenous objects in European nations themselves. Consider, then, the ongoing controversy over the display of human scalps at the Karl May Museum in Radebeul, close to Dresden. In 2014 Cecil Pavlat, member of the Sault St. Marie Tribe of Chippewa Indians, spearheaded a call for repatriation of the remains. Supported by the global organization Survival International, several members of the Oneida Nation soon visited the museum to negotiate their potential return. Though museum curators strongly reiterated their ownership of the original remains under German law, they eventually agreed to replace the scalps with replicas while the original scalps remained on site. But even the display of replicas reinforced European stereotypes about Indigenous culture and exaggerated the centrality of scalping rituals in historical communities. The refusal to repatriate the items also demonstrated the institution's failure to work according to the spirit of NAGPRA.[47]

The Eurocentric categorization of objects in British, French, and German museums has often overlooked Indigenous cultural traditions that imbue them with a spiritual life-force, as more than merely inert artifacts. As intermediaries between human spirits and the rest of creation, they are thought to serve as "witnesses" to historical events in contemporary Indigenous memory work. Their removal, therefore, constitutes an affront to the way that living "beings" are defined in many Indigenous communities, situating their role in repatriation controversies on a continuum with those that have related to human remains such as scalps.[48] Many artifacts, moreover, are often associated with Indigenous burial rituals, linking them to the display of human remains in other ways. Devon Mihesuah, Cressida Forde, Jane Hubert, Paul Turnbull, Robert E. Bieder, Suzanne J. Crawford, and many others have thus connected the treatment of human remains to the necessary reorientation of curatorial techniques with respect to non-human—but nonetheless sacred—objects. Though there are no Indigenous scalps on display in other European museums, therefore, the issue of repatriation has become more prominent in tense interchanges between Indigenous people and institutional leaders in Britain, France, and Germany.[49]

Consider also the British controversy over the display of a Ghost Dance Shirt, which occurred during the early 1990s at Glasgow's Kelvingrove Museum. The shirt was thought to have been obtained by a US solder from the body of a deceased Native American at the Wounded Knee Massacre, which took place on December 29, 1890,. The item was later stored by

Lakota representatives before then being given to George Crager, who incorporated it in Buffalo Bill's Wild West Show. Along with several other artifacts, the shirts were sold to Kelvingrove in 1892. In campaigning for the shirt's repatriation, The Wounded Knee Survivors' Association highlighted its retrieval from a fallen man and its subsequent treatment as a "curiosity" at the museum. Lakota representatives underscored their conception that all objects and elements retained a life force and that fallen community members were traditionally buried in their own garments. The shirt, they argued, was to be treated in the same way as human remains. Yet, two years after NAGPRA was passed in the United States, the director of the museum in Glasgow rejected the call for repatriation and suggested that the shirt was not unique, despite no Lakota arguments having rested on the relative uniqueness of objects. In a slight contradiction, the director also reminded petitioners that the shirt in question was the only one held in any British institution and that it was "the duty of the museum to the modern Lakota to tell the story of the Massacre, and that this story would reflect the Lakota point of view." With such a statement, the director reflected Eurocentric assumptions about the protection of Indigenous artifacts by neutral institutional bodies.[50]

These examples can be compared with ongoing European controversies over the representation of the material culture of the Holocaust. Indigenous literatures on the spiritual dimension of non-human objects can inform more recent and inchoate discussions of Holocaust artifacts as somehow "sacred" in their connection to traumatic memories. They are also relevant to discussions about the treatment of spiritual objects such as Torah scrolls, which are often buried in ceremonial ways that reflect the handling of deceased human bodies.[51] Insights from Mihesuah and other Indigenous scholars complement the pioneering work of European scholars such as Zuzanna Dziuban and Caroline Sturdy Colls and have even influenced their assessments of the link between Jewish spirituality, forensic archaeology, and Holocaust memory. Those insights are also worth considering in relation to work by Chloe Paver on the curation of objects such as the shoes or spectacles removed from Jews at death camps as well as materials that were looted from ghettos or removed from inmates at camps, such as scrolls, *teffilin*, prayer shawls, mezuzahs, menorahs, and *havdalah* spice holders. The representation of Holocaust artifacts as somehow "sacred" risks incorporating Christological understandings of suffering to reorient memory work away from Jewish spiritual practices. But the approaches above re-engage Jewish materials in more complex ways that are less distinct from Jewish traditions, complementing separate Indigenous templates.[52]

Finally, the colonial and imperial contexts for the removal and display of Indigenous objects can speak to the link between material culture and Holocaust memory in even broader ways. Indigenous materials often entered Euro-American ethnographic collections due to the contiguous dispossession or death of the people who owned them. Scholars in settler-colonial studies have highlighted the deadly connection between the objectification of

Indigenous bodies and the frenzied search for material wealth in North America, and its analogue in the subsequent display of Indigenous materials in European museums. These discussions are germane to ongoing tensions regarding the display of objects from Nazi death camps and their possible connection to the extractive economies that developed around sites of Jewish murder in Eastern Europe during and immediately after the Holocaust. In a 2009 interview, Marek Kucia noted that "even in the 1980s, on the terrain of the former [Auschwitz] camp, so-called *kanadziarze* were active, who, in search of gold, were digging over the grounds around the crematoria and around the places where the ashes of victims were thrown in." As they discussed the recent theft of the sign above the Auschwitz entrance, Kucia reminded the interviewer of those occurrences to highlight the objectification of murdered Jews and the economic opportunity it offered to other groups. The *Kanada* term appears in concentration camp stones by Tadeusz Borowski. It is thought to have been used by forced workers to describe the context in which baggage was removed from new transports to camps such as Auschwitz II-Birkenau. The luggage and personal articles made its way into Nazi hands as well as a network of expanding markets throughout the surrounding Polish community. In the decades after World War II, the term also became connected to the public memory of Euro-American settlers who went in search of gold in Northern Canada and Alaska after local Indigenous populations lost their land. In Poland, according to Kucia, the *kanadziarze* were "searchers of treasures, who looked for valuables sold later on the market." Hazy memories of the North American gold rush influenced those who described the excavation of gold from dead Jewish bodies, which were redefined as territories to mine resources. The interviewer thus wondered whether the market for gold extracted from the teeth of murdered Jewish corpses inspired the subsequent theft of the "museum's showpiece"—another material object from the Holocaust that could be circulated for potential profit.[53]

Influenced by the writings of Zygmunt Bauman on the dehumanization of Jews in Nazi ideology, Dean Neu and Richard Therrien have discussed the tendency for Indigenous nations in Canada to be described as "weeds" to be extracted from an "ideal garden."[54] Referring to Auschwitz's "Kanada," Jan Tomasz Gross and Irena Grudzinska Gross have also used Bauman's framework to suggest that "the Shoah was a result of a 'gardener's' vision of society, a vision in which some people are considered weeds and efforts to eliminate them rational, purposeful. The persistent, decades-long digging, raking, sifting through the camp areas can be seen as constituting such 'gardening' activities. These activities—digging out human bodies, ashes, and bones in search of valuables—are performed outside of any moral context. These places are not considered burial grounds but fields open to gleaners." Such horrifying allusions remind us how the curation of material objects can be placed on a continuum with the display of human remains. They also remind us how in Europe as well as in North America, representations of trauma have so often overlooked horrifying specificities in favor of alternative public agendas.[55]

Such discussions provide a fitting way to end this chapter, which has examined structural similarities between the way Europeans have universalized the Holocaust and the ways they have occluded Indigenous genocide. Universalistic depictions of the Holocaust as an anomalous benchmark are likely to overlook the massive European contribution to the destruction of indigenous people in the Americas, including the massive losses incurred under Spanish, French, Dutch, and British settlement among Indigenous people in North America. Imperial histories of genocide and dispossession preceded and even contributed to the foundation of the various states that now make up the European Union. Yet during the last few decades, supra-national civic bodies have often joined national institutions in defining the Holocaust as an aberration in continental European history and an anathema to the deep-rooted civilizational tenets of its constituent states. Identifying the continuity of violent dispossession in European imperial history unsettles the ideological vision expressed in national and EU memory work—even in more nuanced examples such as the recent contributions of the EU Agency for Fundamental Rights. That unsettling potential helps to explain why multi-lateral European institutions have so often joined national European bodies in ignoring Indigenous genocide altogether. Far from threatening Jewish Holocaust memory with relativism, such a comparative insight clarifies how European civilizational narratives have allowed it to be instrumentalized as an abstract benchmark rather than as a specifically Jewish trauma.

# CHAPTER SIX

# "The void has made itself apparent as such." Placing Group Memory in Public History

This final chapter recognizes and compares recent positive developments in the integration of Indigenous and Jewish archives of memory in European public institutions. It shows how they can inform the memory work of museums and public officials on both sides of the Atlantic. North American cultural sites have often been influenced by Eurocentric curatorial methods and assumptions in their representation of the Holocaust and Indigenous genocide. But they can also integrate better practices from several recent European cultural initiatives, which have countered the notion that group memories of trauma lack the neutral stance of historical methodology. Some of those initiatives have even been influenced by Indigenous critiques from the western side of the Atlantic. Many emphasize the importance of ongoing historical education and avoid the allure of shorthand icons that replace specific historical knowledge with abstract motifs. Comparing them allows us to gauge how far—and why—other public sites on both sides of the Atlantic have favored universal, abstract, or instrumentalized representations of Indigenous genocide and the Holocaust.

## The dialectical turn in European Holocaust memory

There are several positive trends in the representation of the Holocaust in national and supra-national European contexts. Consider, for example, the

European Union Agency for Fundamental Rights project, *Discover the Past for the Future: A Study on the Role of Historical Sites and Museums In Holocaust Education and Human Rights Education in the EU*. Jolanta Ambrosewicz-Jacobs, who contributed to the study, has called for educational curricula and museologists to work with public leaders in states such as Poland to integrate EU standards on Holocaust memory without jettisoning discussions of perpetrator intent or specific Jewish experiences.[1] Consider also the lengthy 2020 Swedish Government Official Report, *Holocaust Remembrance and Representation: Documentation from a Research Conference, Sweden, 2020*. The conference and resulting document incorporated insights from Henry Greenspan on victim-centered approaches ("On Listening to Holocaust Survivors: Beyond Testimony"). The report acknowledges that "conversation" about the occlusion of Jewish memory may be a necessary component of exhibitions and museums, whether in Sweden or elsewhere, including the failure to account for "Outsider, Bystander, [and] Insider" intent against Jews. In contemporary memory work, the document notes, "Holocaust memorialization" is too often "politicized and distorted by states, and this is a potential problem for all Holocaust museums."[2] Both initiatives highlight the need for cultural sites to educate citizens about the common shortcomings in public memory. They signal the importance of remembrance as active, ongoing, and didactic, rather than passive, fleeting, and subject-centered.

Considering these curatorial recommendations, we can return to our discussion of subjectivity and abstraction at sites such as The Memorial to the Murdered Jews of Europe and the Berlin Jewish Museum to view them in a new more positive light. According to Sybille Quack, the "openness" at The Memorial "bears the risk of being perceived merely as an attractive perhaps even adventurous space in the city center," hence forfeiting what Marion Klein describes as its proposed "function as a cultural representation of the Holocaust." In this sense, "the Holocaust Memorial, or rather its being used in this way, represents the forgetting of the Holocaust in today's society."[3] Yet, counterintuitively, the representation of "forgetting" at the site can be viewed as a useful educational tool. The concrete stelae, as Brigitte Sion notes, "expresses the ephemeral and fragile nature of memory as it is experienced in the presence."[4] They allow visitors to come to terms with the subjective nature of their encounter with these and other singular memorials, raising awareness of the need for ongoing education about the Holocaust rather than relying on shorthand symbols or icons.

Precisely by stimulating a subjective response, then, the stelae highlight the requirement for more concrete historical education, which can be accessed at the subterranean Information Center at the same site. The Center offers detailed historical narratives and access to primary source documents. An exhibition focuses on other European Jewish communities, less familiar to the German public, showing the intersection between national and imperial frameworks of power in their destruction. The Room of Families

**Figure 6.1** *Visitors at the entrance to the underground Information Centre at the Memorial to The Murdered Jews of Europe, Berlin, Germany, 2005. © Alamy Images.*

shows different social, national, and religious Jewish contexts through the fates of fifteen families. The dialectical relationship between abstraction in the stelae and specificity in the subterranean Information Center is further reinforced by interactive portals that challenge visitors to supplement their knowledge of the Holocaust with ongoing research and education long after they depart the site. Located in the exit foyer, another portal allows visitors to find other exhibitions at perpetrator sites in Germany and throughout Europe, as well as digitally. It provides access to Yad Vashem databases and its "Pages of Testimony" and the ability to print out any information, stimulating ongoing knowledge development. In signaling remembrance as active and ongoing, the center aligns its agenda more closely with Jewish group memory, countering the abstract public message of the stelae.[5]

Daniel Libeskind's controversial design for the Jewish Museum in Berlin, which opened for initial viewing in 1999, can be viewed in a similarly dialectical way. Libeskind's use of empty spaces at the heart of the museum—a deliberate refusal to curate with objects—allows visitors to acknowledge common limitations in the refraction of the Holocaust through public memory. Those limitations, which are rarely acknowledged at other sites, are represented by what Libeskind describes as the "impenetrability . . . around which the exhibitions are organized." In another description of his design, Libeskind delineates an "emblem wherein the invisible, the void, has made itself apparent as such." Representing the "void," according to Libeskind, "refers to that which can never be exhibited in this museum, no matter how many objects are brought to it and stories told in it." In another part of the museum, a "Memory Void" (Leerstelle des Gedenkens), is filled with hundreds of iron faces with open mouths and empty eye sockets, over which visitors walk. Rather than representing total absence, this section of the museum uses abstract forms to signal the depersonalization and de-specification of victims that is so common in public memory—educating visitors about problems in museology and prompting them to seek supplementary forms of historical education. By representing the tension between historical trauma and contemporary memorialization, the museum repudiates the common impetus for institutions to "come to terms" with the Holocaust merely to underline the moral introspection of their contemporary context. The gaps and crevices preclude comforting contemporary messages and require further work to understand the histories that led to such irrevocable losses.[6]

These insights are helpful to understand positive developments at other prestigious European sites, such as the Imperial War Museum (IWM) in London. As an institution that receives public funding from British government grants-in-aid and a large proportion of its visitors from state-funded schools, it is unsurprising that the IWM has sometimes incorporated universalistic or instrumentalized approaches in its representation of the Holocaust from the mid-1990s through the 2000s. Several displays, for example, defined the actions of Nazis and their allies as monstrous archetypes of universal evil.[7] During its early years, the Holocaust exhibit also included motifs that distinguished the British values and heroism that contributed to the defeat of the Nazis. By the second decade of the twentieth century, as Tom Lawson has noted, the "museum visitor's literal journey in the exhibition" moved "from the darkness of Auschwitz to the light of British victory and the ephemera of war in the main atrium." But these tendencies have never been dominant at the IWM. Rigorous and detailed memory work has accompanied powerful video and oral testimony from survivors as well as sections that align more closely with the specific experiences of Jews. Those sections reflect the approach of Jewish organizations at the local level of archiving, memory, and memorialization, particularly their focus on the need for ongoing education following site visits. Thus, the IWM has been able to offset universalistic approaches with more detailed exhibitions that exert a similar role to the Information Center at the Berlin Memorial.[8]

These positive trends are set to continue in the new IWM Holocaust Exhibition, which opened in October 2021. It has refocused its displays to prompt visitors towards ongoing educational research rather than to evoke an immediate understanding of abstract values and norms. It has prioritized the education of students and partnerships with teachers in its display of primary sources and detailed historical narratives, rather than contextualizing the Holocaust as a part of contemporary civic memory. New exhibits in the Second World War and the Holocaust galleries are set to immerse visitors in individual victim narratives and to focus on the various layers of perpetrator intent that led to the destruction of Jews.[9] By promoting in-depth engagement

**Figure 6.2** *Interior architecture of the Memory Void room at the Jewish Museum in Kreuzberg, Berlin, Germany, 2001. © Getty Images.*

with historical sources rather than relying on shorthand representations, those sections of the museum are set to continue its transformation into a far more comfortable space for European and British Holocaust survivors and their families. As in the Berlin examples, abstract approaches at the IWM are counterbalanced by those that align the exhibition more closely with the focus on historical specificity and ongoing education that is more commonly associated with Jewish group memory of the Holocaust.[10]

Other British institutions have also begun to alter their approach to encourage long-term educational engagement with Holocaust history rather than exhibiting shorthand memorial techniques. In 2005, for example, the Holocaust Educational Trust's (HET) Lessons from Auschwitz Project (LFA) initiated a one-day visit to Auschwitz for students that followed visits to UK museums and regular classroom work. The project received more funding and expanded in scope until 2008.[11] The nature of the association between museums and schools will always be influenced by political administrations and broader public discourse. But more independent initiatives such as the UCL Centre for Holocaust Education are now well placed to counter universalistic tendencies in civic culture. Though jointly funded by the government and the Pears Foundation, the Center was founded in 2008 to provide research output and pedagogical frameworks that are aligned more closely with Jewish archives of memory than public agendas. It reflects what Andy Pearce describes as the principle of "research-informed practice" in Holocaust education, mirroring the work of museums such as the IWM in its aim to motivate ongoing engagement during and after school careers. In a 2009 report, the Center warned that most teachers held what Pearce describes as "inclusive understandings of victimhood at the same time as pursuing abstract, civic-centered, 'lessons'-laden, teaching aims." But the publication of the report itself also showed the potential for new qualitative controls that are now backed by British government-funded institutions.[12]

The promotion of educational research through public memory work has also influenced the design of the controversial new Holocaust Memorial in London, which was initially proposed under the administration of Prime Minister David Cameron and which now faces ongoing public scrutiny in its final stages of planning and acceptance. Having assuaged anxieties that it will compete with output at the IWM, the design for the Memorial now includes an Information Center that is similar to that which can be found at the Berlin Memorial. Though suggesting the use of Holocaust memory to define a "British narrative" and to "oppose prejudice and hatred," a December 2018 updated mission statement by The War Memorial commission also promised to use the Information Center to address "the complexities of Britain's ambiguous responses to the Holocaust, avoiding simplistic judgements and encouraging visitors to critically reflect on whether more could have been done, both by policymakers and by society as a whole." As in Berlin, therefore, different parts of the proposed site incorporate universalism and specificity, acknowledging and even mitigating the former though nuanced educational strategies. It remains to be seen how far this design is finally implemented.[13]

Greater alignment between Jewish memory and public memory can even be detected in the subsequent trajectory of the Paris Vél' d'Hiv' monument. We have noted the universalistic political statements that accompanied the founding of the monument in 1995. But as a result, the site became a place for French Jews to challenge public memory of the Holocaust during subsequent years—whether in speeches adjacent to the sculpture or in public media that interrogated its contested meaning. Precisely *because* the memorial had been defined as a site for political discourse, French Jews found a space to challenge political assumptions about Holocaust memory that public officials displayed in its vicinity. They redefined commemoration as an evolutionary process; an ongoing give-and-take between group memory and public memory rather than a medium to arouse an immediate and singular response. The Paris sculpture thus joins the Berlin Memorial, the Berlin Jewish Museum, and the proposed British Holocaust Memorial, as well as other sites such as the Topography of Terror, the Neue Wache, the Memorial of German Resistance, and the House of the Wannsee Conference,

**Figure 6.3** *A picture taken on July 18, 2010, shows the monument commemorating the victims of racist and anti-Semitic persecutions in Paris, during a ceremony marking the anniversary of infamous Vél' d'Hiv' round-up of 13,000 French Jews. On July 16 and 17, 1942, some 13,000 Jews, mostly of non-French origin, were detained and taken to the Vélodrome d'Hiver cycling stadium near the Eiffel Tower, where they spent a week in appalling conditions, before being deported to Nazi concentration camps. © Getty Images.*

by encouraging *memory work* through questions, critiques, and ongoing approaches to education.[14]

## Indigenous counter-memory and the reconfiguration of European ethnography

By raising awareness of the subjectivity of public memory and aligning their offerings more closely with Jewish archives of knowledge, the European examples above can be compared with recent (and less recent) Indigenous responses to North American memory work. Since the early twentieth century, we have noted, Indigenous commemorative activities have often reoriented problematic public representations towards alternative sites. The former have often become teachable spaces to highlight the problem of public memory and inspire alternative approaches. Recall, for example, the critical literature on the Massasoit statue in the decades following the Plymouth Rock tercentenary. The Plymouth "counter-memorial" by local Indigenous activists and the United American Indians of New England was stimulated by the attempt to have the statue represent the inclusivity of early Euro-American settlers who negotiated with the Massasoit. It confirmed Gerald Vizenor's definition of survivance by using erroneous representations of Indigenous history to stimulate and signpost more comprehensive memory work by surviving communities. The commemoration of loss thus avoided signaling the notion of a vanished people. But rather than returning to discussions of Indigenous counter-memory in North American sites, it is worth considering the recent influence of Indigenous communities on curators and public historians at European ethnographic collections.[15]

Let us revisit, for example, the controversy over the display of a Ghost Dance Shirt at Glasgow's Kelvingrove Museum. During the early 1990s the North American NAGPRA model failed to move the museum leaders, who rejected requests by Indigenous activists for the shirt's repatriation. But the story did not end with their rejection and their attendant claim to protect the shirt from inevitable loss. Lakota people continued to exert pressure on the institution by highlighting the role of the shirts and other similar items in their mourning rituals, including in ceremonies that recalled their removal during Euro-American wars and colonization. According to a statement from Wounded Knee Survivors' Association representative Marcella LeBeau, who was of Sioux descent:

> The Lakota people have lived under oppression, broken Treaties when the Lakota people were ruthlessly massacred at Wounded Knee—250 Lakota people died and something else happened—the sacred hoop was broken—the spirit was broken. It is up to us to solve our destiny—it is our choice—the choice of my son Richard and myself, on behalf of the

> Lakota Nation . . . The Sacred Ghost Dance Shirt of Wanagni Wacipi Agee Wakan was taken off a dead body at Wounded Knee and the body was buried naked in a mass grave. No culture in the world would do this as it simply is not the proper thing to do. Native Americans have the greatest respect for their dead. Today on the reservation, we, as veterans of World War II, Vietnam, and the Korean conflict pay our respect and tribute to each cemetery on the Reservation on Memorial Day, yearly. Memorial feeds and Give Aways are common to honor their dead. It follows the natural law of society that a Ghost Dance Shirt taken off the body of a massacred Lakota should be returned to the Lakota.

By connecting objects to historical dispossession *as well as* subsequent cultural renewal, the Lakota statement redefined the museum's collection as a contested site. Its artifacts were central to Lakota commemorative efforts, including in the way those efforts contributed to cultural survival. By linking the objects to ongoing rituals of commemoration among surviving community members, the statement undermined the museum director's claim to protect the items from vanishing or obscurity.[16]

Trauma, according to the statement, was exacerbated by the inability of surviving community members to commemorate historical suffering using Indigenous methods. By removing objects from surviving host communities, the statement suggested, the cultural education of younger generations would be stymied:

> The younger generation are identifying their Bands, taking their place in history and picking their roads . . . We want our youth to know firsthand their own history, to bring meaning to their lives, build self-esteem, honor and respect into their lives, which is our culture, to eliminate the devastation of alcoholism, suicide and other negative influences . . . Longstanding grief and sadness prevails with the descendants and it would help in some small measure to bring closure and healing to a sad and horrible event in the history of the Lakota Nation.

As more-than-inert objects, the shirts were doubly important because their possession signified the ongoing survival of spiritually infused entities and the human communities that hosted them. Though used to commemorate the traumatic loss of historical subjects, their continued employment displayed the demographic and cultural survival of their host populations. As the medium of commemoration expressed a message about survivance, the Lakota statement thus underscored the role of its people as caretakers of the shirt alongside non-Indigenous institutions: "The Cheyenne River and Pine Ridge Wounded Knee Survivors' Association have an agreement with the Heritage Cultural Centre in Pierre, South Dakota, to hold the Sacred Ghost Dance Shirt until such time as the Pine Ridge and Cheyenne River Sioux Tribe have a suitable museum for the Ghost Dance Shirt." So long as the shirt remained close to them, they did not require any other external entity to protect it from oblivion.[17]

These statements and continued activism from Lakota communities eventually led the Kelvingrove Museum to accept the call for repatriation and reverse its earlier rejection. In an unwritten agreement with the director and the Glasgow City Council, Lakota representatives promised an ongoing conversation and relationship with the museum and provided it with a replica of the Ghost Dance shirt. The original shirt was moved to the South Dakota State Historical Society Museum in Pierre, South Dakota, where it could be preserved in appropriate ways, but also accessed by the Lakota people in less formal ways. It was also agreed that the shirt might be loaned temporarily to the Glasgow museum in the future.[18]

The importance of Indigenous community involvement in redefining European approaches to material culture has also been demonstrated at the Berlin Ethnologisches Museum. Countering universalistic and Eurocentric tendencies at the museum, a 1997 Native North American exhibit initiated

**Figure 6.4** *Richard LeBeau from South Dakota looks at a Ghost Dance Shirt that had been held in the Kelvingrove Art Gallery in Glasgow since 1882, November 1998. Glasgow City Council decided to return the shirt, which was worn at the Battle of Wounded Knee, to the Lakota Sioux. © Alamy Images.*

an important and ongoing collaborative exercise with Yup'ik elders from present-day Alaska. The elders educated museum curators about the role of objects in the commemoration of historical trauma under European colonization as well in the demonstration of subsequent cultural survival. They defined the importance of the museum holdings for the ongoing education of *their* community members, allowing them to align their group memory more closely with the projection of public memory at the institution. As Yu'pik representative Andy Paukan summarized, "I'm thinking that coming to Germany to examine these objects will make it easier for us to explain our culture to our young people and to our children. We will be able to tell them things with no reservations. Our work will make it easier to prepare teaching material about our culture for our younger generations, our children, our grandchildren, to our peers and even our own parents and grandparents. With this work, our roots and culture will come closer to us." These activities were facilitated by the provision of working space to examine the objects, including by touching them in ways that had hitherto been forbidden in museum settings.[19]

By freeing themselves from European ethnographic restrictions, Yup'ik people used the Berlin museum objects to stimulate their ongoing discussion of Indigenous sovereignty and decolonization in Alaska. While listening to discussions about the artifacts in the museum, Ann Fienup Riordan noted their connection to the autonomy of Yup'ik people outside Europe: "I was listening to a political statement about what it meant to be Yup'ik in the modern world which would certainly be re-stated in public hearings back in Alaska." According to Yup'ik elder Paul John, "When we were looking at the objects that were once used by our ancestors, I began to realize . . . Gosh, our ancestors took charge of their lives, truly living in their traditional culture. . . . Since we have no understanding, we've abandoned our cultural ways. But those of us that came here have been granted more understanding regarding our people. We have a better understanding that we should retain our cultural ways until the end of the world. . . . I hope the objects would be exhibited in the villages or at a museum in Bethel. . . . If our people begin to see them and begin to understand the culture of our ancestors, they might begin to believe and gain pride in their own identity. I envision our people gaining more faith in their own identity by seeing the objects or seeing their pictures or reading about them in books. My hope is that our work will bring our people closer to their own culture."[20]

Expanding the collaborative model offered by the Berlin Yup'ik exhibition, the Blackfoot Shirts Project in Oxford, England, offers an even more recent redefinition of Indigenous community involvement in European museum work. Initiated in 2010, the project allowed collaboration between the Pitt Rivers Museum in Oxford, the University of Oxford, and Blackfoot communities from present-day Canada and the United States, including the Siksika, Piikani, and Kainai in Alberta and the Blackfeet Tribe in northern Montana. The project was initially spearheaded by Blackfoot "ceremonial leader" Rufus Good Striker, from the Kainai Nation, and Louis Soop, who taught at Red Crow Community College on the Kainai reserve. During a visit to the Pitt Rivers Museum in 2000, Good Striker openly prayed for ancestral communities who wore one of the shirts on display at the institution, having also gained permission to "smudge" it by burning sweetgrass and sage in its vicinity. Taking place over a single hour in the museum, these activities, according to Laura Peers, "changed the meanings of the shirts, completely ignoring their designation as ethnological specimens and inserting them into a living cultural tradition."[21]

The shirts found their way into European hands during an 1841 trip to Blackfoot territory in Alberta and Montana by Sir George Simpson, the governor of the Hudson's Bay Company. Though Simpson purchased the shirts at a time of ostensible peace, the spontaneous activities of the Blackfoot visitors in 2000 remind us of the broader context in which Simpson's intervention had taken place: ongoing disruption and dispossession with roots in colonial British policy and a subsequent era of Anglo-American settlement in the region. In his first encounter with the shirts, Good Striker noted the war honors that were painted on one of them. He taught museum representatives about similar shirts that were worn in conflicts between Indigenous communities within the disruptive context of Anglo-American settlement in 1832. Though Blackfoot commemoration ceremonies regularly recall inter-Indigenous warfare, those conflicts were often rooted in the unruly context of prior European interference.[22]

In the decades after its founding in 1884, the Pitt Rivers Museum had obscured such traditions in its Eurocentric approach to ethnography, which used objects from Indigenous cultures to define the notion of "end on evolution." Ethnographic displays charted the development of societies in relation to civilized ideals that the museum defined from a European (often British) perspective. Acting as a curator for the Americas Collections at the Pitt Rivers Museum as well as Professor of Museum Anthropology at the University of Oxford, Peers was quickly educated in the definition of objects as more-than-inert beings and their important role in commemorating population loss. Material objects, the Blackfoot delegations explained, were treated as witnesses to events—whether historical acts of dispossession and murder or happier occurrences that preceded those acts. Like all objects, the shirts were integral to Indigenous memory work as an ongoing process. Peers and her colleagues were thus persuaded to loan the shirts to the Glenbow and Galt museums in Alberta, where Blackfoot elders and Blackfoot students could "visit" them without their being held behind barriers or glass casing.[23]

In 2010, during the first visits with the shirts, Blackfoot members immediately demonstrated their dual role as bridges to ancestral traditions and a means to overcome the subsequent disruption of those traditions by colonization. Ramona Big Head asked rhetorically:

> How long have they been gone from Blackfoot territory and now they are back and they are hearing the language . . . And I'm not talking about the shirts themselves, but I'm talking about the people that made the shirts. That's what I mean by the spirits behind the shirt. How long had it been since someone had admired their work? Can you imagine what that must have felt like?

As more-than-inert entities, the shirts were said to channel the spirit and voices of ancestors. The ability to "hear" those voices through the shirts allowed them to function as intermediaries between the past and present and expressed the survival of the population who could use them in such ways.[24]

The Blackfoot Shirts Project provided a model for similar collaborative networks between the Pitt Rivers Museum, the British Museum, and Haida people from present-day Canada. The Pitt Rivers Museum had previously displayed Haida materials as neutral entities that had no connection to European colonial dispossession and no role in the subsequent memory and commemoration of that trauma.[25] Yet colonial processes that led to hairlock shirts and other sacred items leaving Blackfoot communities made those populations less cohesive by preventing the subsequent ceremonial use of the items. Contiguously, the communities became likelier to suffer the synergistic effects of disease and societal fragmentation, leading them to give up further remaining artifacts in periods of ostensible peace. The legacy of colonial disruption in apparently irenic periods led items to be sold to feed and clothe

**Figure 6.5** *Interior gallery, Pitt Rivers Museum, Oxford. © Getty Images.*

community members. According to Lea Whitford (Blackfeet), "I talked with my friend about why they would give such a sacred item up, for some people it was a matter of survival. Being able to have a meal. And when your children are not eating, you're going to do whatever it takes to feed them." Though the loss of the items may have prevented poverty among individuals and families, it also removed a key medium for demographic cohesion among those surviving populations and thus conforms to recent definitions of cultural genocide.[26]

The decolonizing role of the Blackfoot Shirts Project becomes even more acute if we recall the ban on the use of ceremonial shirts by white colonial agents in the Confederation of Canada in the decades after the 1867 British North America Act. Through the early decades of the twentieth century, ceremonial clothing required the consent of British-Canadian officials who oversaw assimilationist policies. The prevention of such ceremonial work during the era of the Canadian Confederation represented a clear colonial imposition. By re-engaging and "re-remembering" with the shirts, Blackfoot people underscored the importance of the ceremonial transfer of shirts within and between generations.[27]

During the post-colonial era, therefore, institutions such as the Pitt Rivers Museum risked preventing the commemoration of historical trauma from facilitating cultural renewal—a connection that lies at the heart of survivance. Consider the words of Herman Yellow Old Woman, an elected and ceremonial leader from the Siksika Nation who was interviewed in 2010 by Alison Brown and Laura Peers after the Blackfoot shirts arrived in Canada: "This is part of that connection, that missing link that our people don't understand. Our people, things from the past, way back, these shirts come from way back . . . There was a connection to where my people are today. They came back together . . . when I see them, I can picture in my mind who was where, who was under those shirts at one time. . . ." As Herman Yellow Old Woman (Siksika) noted elsewhere: "We still speak the language. We still call on our ancestors, where these shirts come from. We might have suffered some loss, but it's coming back strong." Touching the shirts, according to Ramona Big Head, "became a kind of opening up of all these questions. The answers were already there and already within us. We just hadn't asked those questions yet. We hadn't had the voice to really articulate what we needed to know . . . The way I see it, the knowledge was always there. But no one really opened that box, because we hadn't had the opportunity to think about it. And bringing the shirts here, all of a sudden these questions started coming up and we were being led to people who knew what they were talking about . . . And it's like we opened up a box of knowledge that we didn't realize we had." Another Blackfoot member, Shirlee Crowshoe, suggested that cultural ideas were "stored in someone's memory" and that access to sensory objects such as the shirts "triggers something where they go back and they remember. Not right away. It takes time for them to reflect, and time for that to come back." These responses support the recent scholarly turn to consider the role of sensory stimulation in exciting collective memory among surviving communities.[28]

As in the Lakota statement that was delivered to Glasgow's Kelvingrove Museum, many Blackfoot community members described the ceremonial renewal of memory as crucial to prevent social problems such as depression and hopelessness among younger generations. Such "social loss," according to older community members, reflected the legacy of earlier periods of cultural restriction, even cultural genocide. Their conclusions corroborate the use of museum objects as a form of "Reminiscence therapy" among communities with ancestral histories of trauma and dislocation. They redefine objects from ethnographic artifacts to more-than-inert beings—an expression of survivance through Indigenous memory work. They join other collaborative efforts between Indigenous nations and non-Indigenous institutions on both sides of the Atlantic. They are influenced by Indigenous and allied critiques of North American ethnographic museums as "contact zones." James Clifford, for example, has described the role of Tlingit elders in redefining historic artifacts in the Portland Museum of Art, and their emphasis that the institution "act on behalf of Tlingit communities, not simply to represent the history of tribal objects."[29] The efforts in Europe are also influenced by the interventions and critiques of Indigenous curators on the western side of the Atlantic, such as those who contributed to the launch of the Oneida Nation Museum (ONM) in Wisconsin in 1979, the eventual opening of the Forest County Potawatomi Museum in Wisconsin in 2002, and the unveiling of the Ziibiwing Center of Anishinabe Culture and Lifeways in Michigan in 2004.[30]

**Figure 6.6** *The Ziibiwing Center of Anishinabe Culture & Lifeways, Mt. Pleasant, Michigan, 2019. The museum is operated by the Saginaw Chippewa Indian Tribe of Michigan. © Alamy Images.*

## An Indigenous-Jewish template for public memory work

Museum practitioners, public historians, and civic leaders in the examples above have been careful to avoid defining "collaboration" from Eurocentric or Euro-American perspectives. Ostensibly progressive memory work can easily veer towards underlining the special inclusivity of the non-Indigenous contexts that "allow" collaboration with Indigenous cultural techniques.[31] Critiques usually leveled at Canadian and American institutions are thus relevant to recent developments in European museums. Deriving from Native American and First Nations scholarship, they offer pertinent insights for Holocaust Studies.[32] Cultural institutions, after all, often focus on the progressive context for their introspection rather than representing the specificity, scale, and legacy of the Holocaust from a Jewish perspective.[33] By avoiding such pitfalls, positive developments in the representation of Indigenous history and culture can speak to better practices at sites of Holocaust memory, and vice versa. But before we consider such a comparative template, it is important to note two key differences in Indigenous and Jewish approaches to the public representation of their historical trauma in the case studies explored in this chapter.

First, Indigenous people have tended to refute curatorial representations that emphasize an irrevocable void as the legacy of historical genocide. Such an emphasis in some European sites of Holocaust memory does not easily transfer to Indigenous representations of trauma, given its potential to reinforce the notion of "vanishing" and to obscure the agency of surviving nations. Second, Jewish critiques of public memory have rarely denied the right of European states to incorporate them under their constitutional jurisdiction. French Jews, for example, criticized the instrumentalization of Holocaust memory at the Paris Vél' d'Hiv' monument without questioning the overall authority of the French state to carry out memory work on their behalf. By acknowledging the important role of the Vichy regime in the Holocaust, Jewish petitioners suggested, public authorities would make French Jews feel more comfortably integrated by the modern French state.[34] Though they have sometimes objected to the instrumentalization of Holocaust memory in public institutions since the late 1990s, most British Jews have been more than happy to support their incorporation by the British state. A similar response can be detected among Jews in Germany, most of whom descend from later migrations to the country since the 1990s. Indigenous people in the United States and Canada have often shown greater nuance—even ambivalence—in their critiques of public memory practices. Most have avoided the notion that improved public history will guarantee their greater allegiance to the United States or Canada. Though some Indigenous people are happy to define themselves as citizens of those states, framing their critique in such a way would risk undermining notions of tribal sovereignty and Indigenous autonomy.

Several public historians have suggested that museums on both sides of the Atlantic should commemorate the illegitimate liquidation of Indigenous land sovereignty while charting the survival of national identity in a "diasporic" form, akin to the way Jewish identity has manifested through much of global history.[35] But the diasporic metaphor risks overlooking differences between Jewish and Indigenous conceptions of nationhood in the present day. Many Jews accept or even cherish their incorporation in North American and European states while also envisioning their attachment to broader notions of Jewish nationhood. Indigenous people, conversely, are more likely to use the diasporic metaphor to define a more specific constitutional goal: strengthening the notion of tribal sovereignty *alongside* the multicultural American and Canadian states.[36]

Without overlooking these important caveats and distinctions, positive developments at European sites of Holocaust memory can speak to those in Indigenous memory work, and vice versa. By aligning European ethnographic collections more closely with Indigenous group memory, for example, the Blackfoot Shirts Project and the Haida collaboration provide a model that is germane to the treatment of Holocaust artifacts and former Jewish property across Europe. Zuzanna Dziuban has recently described the unsettling role of "Jewish ghosts" in the "Post-Holocaust Imaginaire" of nations such as Poland. Surviving Jews haunt European communities by reminding them of the Jewish provenance of objects and spaces that had hitherto been obscured by their occupiers. Marianne Hirsch and Leo Spitzer have described the effect of Jewish visitors in Polish towns who appear "like ghostly revenants or haunting reminders of a forgotten world . . . unsettle[ing] the present by refusing to allow the past to disappear into oblivion."[37] Tomasz Majewski has thus called for the "relocalization of memory" in sites such as the former Lodz ghetto in Poland, to prevent objects being removed from their community context under the guise of institutional protection. Having initially been ignored by non-Jewish civic leaders, for example, objects from a hospital building in the ghetto were transferred to the United States Holocaust Memorial Museum (USHMM) where they were "transformed into an element of universal memory of the Holocaust" as a "condition for preserving memory." Yet local Jewish survivor groups and European Jewish agencies might have preserved the objects on site, aligning their archives of memory with the specific context in which those memories were rooted. But instead, under the auspices of preservation from decay, the gate and other objects were excised from their local framework and used to memorialize abstract motifs on the other side of the Atlantic.[38]

There are other ways that Indigenous collaboration with European cultural institutions can speak to recent developments at sites of Holocaust memory. We have noted how the educational and archival sections at institutions such as the Imperial War Museum in London have inadvertently become places of memorialization for Holocaust survivors, their descendants, and other Jews. At the museum and at other sites such as the Berlin War

Memorial Information Center, commemoration has been redefined as an ongoing educational process rooted in direct engagement with archives, source collections, and manuscripts. These developments align the institutions more closely with Jewish group memory, which has always distinguished itself from the shorthand motifs and icons of non-Jewish public memorials.[39] Yet as the Blackfoot and Haida collaborations show, such processes need not be inadvertent, but rather by design. What Cara Krmpotich and Laura Peers describe as a "significant shift in museum attitudes" led Haida delegations to stipulate that collaboration between British museums and their community include younger and older "learners" rather than only experts and knowledgeable elders. The synthesis between expert study and "green" learning emphasized the educational role of commemoration in transferring culture across generations.[40] The Haida and Blackfoot projects also show how artifacts from happier cultural contexts can contribute to the commemoration of traumatic histories, adding a sensory aspect to visitor engagement with manuscripts and archives. Combined with their emphasis on educational development, they offer a template for Jewish communities to express their own commemorative agendas in new and unexpected ways, including by using curated objects and materials that are not directly associated with the Holocaust.[41]

As the literature on the counter-memorialization of the Massasoit statue shows, it has been more common for Indigenous than Jewish communities to use egregious public memorials to direct visitors to more comprehensive sites that align more closely with their archives of memory. But of course, the Massasoit statue was not initially designed with such a dialectical process in mind. Indigenous communities, therefore, might find a useful template in The Memorial to the Murdered Jews of Europe and the Jewish Museum in Berlin, which are intentionally designed to allow visitors to understand the subjectivity of public history and the need for ongoing education *on-site*. Indigenous people might also find an adaptable model in the Stolpersteine project, which is designed to raise awareness about the tension between public representations of the Holocaust and Jewish group memory. Since 1996, more than 5,000 stones have been laid in Berlin and other German cities, forcing walkers to "stumble" or watch their footing in particular areas with historical resonance.[42] Public memory tends to smooth over past traumas to suggest they have been overcome by contemporary inclusivity. As counter-memorials, stumbling blocks are designed to interrupt such convenient narratives, literally tripping up visitors or unsuspecting bystanders and forcing them to acknowledge the discomfort that public memory has so often sought to erase.[43] They contribute further to what James Young has defined as the "memory-work" that is necessary to counter the common claim that public sites have "resolved" the remembrance of trauma.[44] Similar approaches, which are designed to display the problems of commemoration, would complement existing counter-memorials in the Indigenous world. The National Museum of the American Indian, indeed,

**Figure 6.7** *Stolpersteine (stumbling blocks) erected in memory of the Jewish Marcuse family in Gipsstrasse, Mitte, Berlin. © Getty Images.*

may have been ahead of its time in some of its early exhibitions, such as those curated by Jolene Rickard (Tuscarora). The "'uninterpreted" display of objects in Rickard's exhibition refused to conform to Euro-American categories of order. Instead, their lack of context provided what Ruth Phillips has described as the "evidence" of the disruption of Indigenous culture by colonial interventions.[45]

These comparative insights provide a template for European public sites as well as North American institutions whose representations are rooted in Eurocentric assumptions and practices. All must avoid the pitfalls of *Vergangenheitsbewältigung*—a "working through" of the past to display the moral worth of contemporary culture. In Eastern Europe, Holocaust memory has often been relativized or deliberately superseded. In the multilateral institutions of the European Union and in nations such as Germany, France, and Britain, displays of introspection and soul-searching risk becoming the primary impetus for Holocaust memory work. In Germany, the history of Indigenous population loss has often been appropriated to define contemporary civic agendas or to distinguish German moral valor from the historical behavior of other Europeans. But European ethnographic institutions have begun to counter the representation of Indigenous culture as lost or vanishing. German, French, and British museums have increasingly claimed to produce a more honest account of the meaning and context of their curated materials. They have begun to grapple with their contribution to the occlusion or abstraction of Indigenous history and culture, trying to break the legacy of earlier colonial dispossession and instances of cultural genocide. Their debates over the representation of Indigenous history and the importance of group memory are well worth considering alongside similar discussions about the representation of the Holocaust. Through their comparison, they demonstrate what Peter Carrier has described as the broader role of "monuments as vehicles of historical ambivalence." So long as separate spaces exist to acknowledge and then counter the shortcomings in existing public sites, it is precisely their subjectivities and lacunae that transform them into ironic "spurs to participate in history through its formal mediation." An important part of that mediation relates to the respect and intellectual weight that is accorded to group memories of trauma in those separate spaces.[46]

# Conclusion

This book has compared and connected the way North American and European cultural institutions have represented the Holocaust and North American genocide using metaphors, motifs, and icons that de-specify and replace the events of which they are supposed to be the reminder. It has traced the movement of memory from local contexts around perpetrator sites to other public forums on both sides of the Atlantic. It has examined the contiguous move from group archives of memory to national and supranational frameworks that have often appropriated traumatic histories to define contemporary ideological agendas. The occlusion of the nature and scale of Euro-American perpetrator intent in Indigenous population loss has often preceded and then coincided with structurally similar depictions of the Holocaust. Indigenous commentators are primed to repudiate the abstraction of historical suffering on behalf of unrelated agendas—including those cases that have de-specified Holocaust memory while overlooking Indigenous histories of trauma altogether.

Along with the forced movement and deaths of millions of enslaved Africans during the Middle Passage, the historical destruction of Jewish and Indigenous communities confounds the progressive and humanistic stories that European-descended people often connect to the cultural trajectory of the nations in which they live. By de-specifying both histories, political and cultural institutions can more easily avoid such an unsettling phenomenon. Public representations of Indigenous genocide and the Holocaust are thus connected rather than merely comparable. They converge in structurally similar ways to support common narratives of Euro-American civilization. Examining that convergence—rather than assessing each case separately—provides a powerful critique to stimulate more accurate and detailed representations among public historians, cultural agents, political bodies, and educators.

From the eighteenth century, non-Indigenous writers represented Native American population loss as an abstract environmental occurrence as they sought to provide a contrast with the arrival of European civilization. English and other European settlers, they suggested, asserted their control over nature rather than allowing degeneration by environmental phenomena within its bounds. Through the nineteenth century, European ethnographic displays were influenced by those descriptive trends as they represented Indigenous population loss as an abstract occurrence without perpetrator intent. On the eastern side of the Atlantic during the early twentieth century, especially in Germany, public media began to relate the demographic decline of Indigenous nations to specifically Anglo-American rather than continental European interventions. Those representations continued during the early Cold War era and were accompanied by organizationally similar trends in the representation of the Holocaust: In France, West Germany, and Britain, direct reference to the perpetrator intent of European populations in the attempted elimination of Jews risked unsettling their perceived moral distinction from Soviet communism. More recently, the near erasure of Indigenous histories of genocide and the de-specification of Holocaust memory has allowed European public institutions to represent the "Final Solution" as an abstract counterpoint to the otherwise contiguous humanitarian roots of European civilization.

From the nineteenth century through the first half of the twentieth century, ethnographic trends influenced the tendency for North American cultural institutions to overlook the role of their European forebears in the destruction of Indigenous communities. At best, they purported to salvage Indigenous culture from vanishing and commonly represented the obliteration of Indigenous populations in hazy and abstract ways. During the early Cold War, they often distinguished the trajectories of American and Canadian liberty from the threat of Communism in Europe. While mostly overlooking the history of Indigenous population loss, some represented it as an aberrant contrast to the flourishing of American civil rights through the mid-twentieth century or the special Canadian attachment to pluralism and tolerance during the same period. Since the 1970s, those ongoing tendencies in the representation of North American genocide have been accompanied by the comparable inclination to instrumentalize Holocaust memory to show the exceptional protection offered by the Canadian and American states against "man's inhumanity to man." To draw such a distinction, the Holocaust has often been represented as an abstract icon of Old World horror rather accounting for the specificity and scale of the Jewish experience on its own terms. Moreover, by overlooking the connection between the imperial European dispossession of Indigenous people and subsequent eras of North American state-building, it becomes easier for American and Canadian public bodies to distinguish the special course of rights-based pluralism on the western side of the Atlantic from its inevitable repudiation in the Holocaust. Through the present day, such public memory work contradicts Indigenous conceptions of tribal autonomy by emphasizing the protection of Native Americans or First Nations people by state jurisdiction rather than their legal independence *alongside* states such as the US and Canada. It has also tended to require the de-specification of historical Jewish trauma to distinguish the universal protection offered by contemporary North American pluralism.

Like Indigenous people in colonial North America and in the nineteenth-century American West, Jews in Nazi-occupied Europe were conceived as transnational forces that threatened alternative imperial structures of authority. Both lived within the various constituent states of imperially structured unions, without being considered as full citizens or subjects in either regional or supra-regional contexts. When Nazis deployed the terminology of an anti-colonization movement to oppose the existence of Jews in each of the European states they occupied, they ironically reinforced their imperial authority over non-Jewish people in those same places. Jews were said to threaten Germans as well as the non-Jewish populations whom Germans occupied, stimulating widespread collaboration between centralized Nazi directives and improvised local anti-Semitic violence. In previous centuries, imperial European powers asserted metropolitan control over outlying white settler populations in North America while also offering those populations a degree of leeway to dispossess and massacre Indigenous people. In both cases an imperial perspective clarifies the structural frameworks that allowed ordinary people and grassroots organizations rather than merely a few leaders to become perpetrators. It also helps to explain why it has been so common for Indigenous and Jewish histories of trauma to be described in abstract ways or overlooked altogether. Convenient civilizational narratives risk being unsettled by the ubiquity of imperial frameworks of power—whether in the connection between European colonizers and the later trajectory of US and Canadian expansion or in the way that Nazis allied with occupied non-Germans to consolidate the destruction of Jews.

Future studies ought to consider whether structural similarities in the representation of Jewish and Indigenous histories of trauma since the nineteenth century are rooted in early modern narratives of destruction and othering, which accompanied the imperial expansion of Europeans. Some scholars have begun to suggest a conceptual bridge between late-medieval Iberian notions of "purity of blood" (*limpieza de sangre*) and the definitive categories that were used to describe Ashkenazi Jews in other parts of Europe from the early modern era. Even more controversially, a few have drawn tentative links with the later deployment of anti-Semitism against Jews during the nineteenth and twentieth centuries and during the Holocaust.[1] More work is needed to assess the impact of such associations on the classifications and historical narratives that Europeans used to justify the subjugation of indigenous people in the Americas, including in continental North America, as well as the destruction of Jewish populations in pogroms. The occlusion of Jewish and Indigenous death in early modern European memory work may well have contributed to the descriptive categories that led later generations of Europeans and Euro-Americans to misrepresent or overlook the perpetrator intent of their ancestors—whether in accounts of Inquisitions and massacres of Jews in Europe, in narratives of Indigenous death, or in representations of the Holocaust.[2]

Deeper historical comparisons might also stimulate a joint discussion among Indigenous people and Jews about residual animosity in post-genocidal frontier communities. Writing about ongoing tensions in American reservation border towns during the post-colonial era, Winona LaDuke and Jennifer Nez Denetdale have connected the sudden eruption of violence against Indigenous people to the common desire to suppress visceral feelings of guilt. Ongoing frontier fears highlight the legacy of earlier imperial frameworks, in which the loyalty of settlers to colonial authority was often contingent on their ability to dispossess local Indigenous populations.[3] These discussions might speak to troubling insights from the recent historiography of post-1945 European frontier-towns in Ukraine, Romania, Lithuania, and even Poland. In nations such as the Netherlands, whose Jewish populations were removed to death camps, later generations have experienced the Holocaust as a distant memory, both spatially and temporally. But in the aftermath of World War II in towns such Kielce in Poland, non-Jewish inhabitants experienced unsettling feelings of guilt due to their perceived local collaboration with Nazi authorities. The return of surviving Jews to Kielce made those feelings more visceral, contributing to a brutal pogrom by some of the town's inhabitants.[4] A "new form of Jew-hatred," according to Lars Rensmann, "originates in the political and psychological desire to split off, repress, and downplay the memory of the Holocaust because such memory, with which Jews are often identified, evokes unwelcome guilty feelings. As Holocaust memory undermines the uncritical identification with a collective, family, or nation tainted by anti-Jewish mass atrocities, the repression of national guilt may unconsciously motivate the reproduction of resentments that helped cause the Shoah"—even in the twenty-first century.[5]

These insights should stimulate other related comparative discussions. Future work in memory studies, for example, might examine the tension between centralized cultural initiatives and the identity of local populations in supra-regional entities such as the European Union (EU) or the United States. EU institutions have often instrumentalized the Holocaust as a negative memory to facilitate European integration under the banner of anti-racism, multi-culturalism, and inclusivity. In response, public leaders in Eastern European and Balkan nations have sometimes emphasized alternative narratives of victimhood that supersede or even deny the role of Holocaust memory in their local context. They have also often demonstrated disdain for the perceived imposition of historical guilt by the centralizing authority of EU cultural institutions. Similarly, non-Indigenous North Americans often fear and resent any reminder of their role in the historical dispossession of Indigenous people. In counter-response, some have defined themselves as victims of overreach by federal and state cultural agencies—including through educational curricula—rather than grappling with the potential role of their ancestors in dispossessing Indigenous people.[6]

This book can also speak to several contemporary concerns and their possible future trajectories. During its last decade of research and writing, the longstanding tendency to de-specify Holocaust memory in civic and cultural representations has accompanied increasing alarm from Jewish and allied commentators about a seemingly related phenomenon. They have suggested that the specific and horrific experiences of Jews and the Nazi obsession to erase all forms of Jewishness from the world has deliberately rather than merely inadvertently been obscured. Historians and social scientists such as Deborah Lipstadt have begun to describe such a tendency as a form of "Softcore Denial" leading to the "de-Judaization of the Holocaust"—"a form of historiographic pornography" in which politicians, cultural leaders, and activists from myriad ideological backgrounds purposely relativize the Holocaust or define it according to broad and general categories that eschew Jewish specificity.[7] Lipstadt responded to the Trump administration's 2017 statement on Holocaust Memorial Day, which jettisoned an earlier statement mentioning Jews in order to commemorate the "victims, survivors, heroes of the Holocaust." Neo-Nazi websites lauded the statement in online media. Yet according to Lipstadt and others, it is erroneous to assume that the minimization or relativization of the Holocaust as a Jewish experience has been restricted to mischievous elements of the Far Right. The dilution, universalization, or replacement of Jewish Holocaust memory, they suggest, has provided language and terminology for the parallel phenomenon of a "New Antisemitism" among a broad ideological spectrum of people—a worrying trend among those who consciously displace the representation of Jewish suffering to prevent a purported Jewish purchase on power.[8]

Given the large and growing literature on the New Anti-Semitism, this book has been less concerned with two of its main facets: the unsettling ways that Holocaust motifs may have been used in tropes, memes, and sometimes openly hostile statements against Jews (often online); and the overt exclusion of Jews in ostensibly more progressive statements that nonetheless provide evidence of Softcore Denial.[9] To be sure, the tendencies towards occlusion and abstraction identified in this book may have provided language and terminology for more deliberate or nefarious attempts to obscure the specificity of Jewish suffering as an overtly anti-Semitic act. Moreover, the obfuscation of Holocaust memory in civic and cultural sites has also sometimes been rooted in the longstanding anti-Semitic inclination to overlook Jewish suffering in many societal contexts. Nonetheless, this book has focused on less overt misuse of Holocaust memory through metaphorical or abstract icons that dilute Jewish content even while claiming to represent it.

During the research and writing of this book, clear instances of racism and chauvinism have also appeared in the misrepresentation or deliberate obfuscation of Indigenous genocide in the United States and Canada. Former US President Donald J. Trump has regularly referred to Senator Elizabeth Warren of Massachusetts as "Pocahontas"—a catch-all, Euro-American stereotype of an Indigenous woman, perhaps the only historical name familiar to many non-Indigenous people, most likely due to its cartoonish association with the eponymous Disney character. Coupled with President Trump's avowed admiration for President Andrew Jackson, and his jokey allusions to Indigenous history (including, potentially, the Trails of Tears) in relation to Senator Warren, his words have caused understandable consternation and pain in many Indigenous circles.[10] Mirroring the scholarly discussion of the New Anti-Semitism, Indigenous and allied commentators have used the Trump–Warren dispute to show how the misrepresentation of Indigenous archives of memory has often transcended party lines or distinctions between liberals and conservatives. Senator Warren, they note, has employed problematic lines of reasoning in her past claims to Indigenous heritage and in her more recent attempts to defend those ambiguous assertions from President's Trump's attacks. In a poorly advised statement, Senator Warren published the results of a DNA test to prove that, as an exceedingly small percentage of her overall DNA, she has some "Native American ancestry." But in her use of such a test to discount the jibes of a Republican president, Senator Warren reflected white rather than Indigenous understandings of citizenship, demonstrating a degree of entitlement that some Indigenous commentators defined to be as insidious—even threatening—as President Trump's tweets.[11] Rebecca Nagle has issued a stark summary of the repudiation of Native American history, memory, and ethno-cultural identity in the Trump–Warren discourse: "[a]s contemporary Native Americans, we live in the space between Donald Trump and Elizabeth Warren, between the stereotypes that were created to excuse the wholesale slaughter of our people and the stereotypes that were created to excuse the wholesale appropriation of our identity and cultures. . . ." At a time when the identity of marginalized groups is valorized, at least on the surface, Senator Warren expanded the definition of Native American nationhood to unsettle its coherent meaning altogether, as defined by Indigenous frameworks.[12]

As in the case of anti-Semitic discourse, these and many other similar instances of chauvinism have drawn language and terminology from ostensibly more measured cultural and civic representations of Indigenous history. They are rooted in longstanding anti-Indigenous trends that contributed to the more formal civic and cultural representations examined in this book. The ongoing Indigenous response to such representations provides a useful critical framework and set of terms to describe the Trump–Warren disputation—just as Lipstadt's discussion of Softcore Denial has drawn on earlier scholarly critiques of the dilution of Jewish memory in ostensibly progressive cultural sites. The "presumption of the *absence* of Indigenous archives" of memory noted by Alyssa Mt. Pleasant in Senator Warren's reasoning has appeared for more than a century in museums, civic bodies, and cultural sites.[13]

During the final stages of this book, more people have become aware of the occlusion of imperial histories of trauma in public memory thanks to the ongoing global response to the Black Lives Matter movement. North American and British activists have campaigned for the removal of statues and memorials to historical figures who are connected to the transatlantic enslavement and deaths of Africans. These new movements might encourage cultural institutions to avoid instrumentalizing Holocaust memory on behalf of European, Euro-American, or Western values. Whether or not that is the case, recent events have certainly made it more difficult for British or other European institutions to define racism and slavery as an "American" issue that is disconnected from their own historical trajectory. It has also made North Americans less likely to overlook the colonial European origins of slavery and racism and their contribution to ongoing structural imbalances in their societies. The global effect of the BLM movement has shown that memory cannot easily be bound to one region or state, just as past injustices often traduced boundaries across the Atlantic world.[14]

In Europe—and particularly Britain—a similar reckoning with histories of Indigenous dispossession and genocide has not yet influenced popular discourse or more formal public sites, memorials, and educational curricula. Distinct from the sea-change in the public memory of transatlantic slavery and colonial European atrocities in Africa, Indigenous death is still often connected to American rather than Euro-American contexts. As this book goes to press, hundreds (perhaps even more than 1,000) unmarked graves are in the process of being uncovered at former Residential Schools for Indigenous children in Canada. In June 2021 in Winnipeg, statues of Queen Victoria were removed during events that coincided with these discoveries.[15] But so far British public media and civic institutions have been silent about the connection between these events and the imperial interventions that often set in motion such deadly practices. This book has tried to show how identifying structural similarities in the occlusion of the histories of the Holocaust and Indigenous genocide might prevent such lacunae. We have seen, for example, how the Indigenous-supported Truth and Reconciliation Commission responded to the memory of cultural genocide in Canadian Residential Schools to underline how for "members of the Jewish community, their experience of the Holocaust is a source of empathy in approaching the topic . . ." The trajectory of Holocaust memory has allowed the experience of cultural genocide at Residential Schools to be examined and acknowledged without encouraging competitive tensions between Jews and Indigenous people.[16]

During the last year the multidirectional nature of memory has become even more apparent at the site where I began to think about this book project, when I considered my personal relationship to Holocaust history while also learning about the representation of Indigenous histories of trauma. Near the Colorado Capitol Building, where I often sat eating my lunch, a large statue erected in the first decade of the twentieth century honored the Colorado soldiers who fought and sometimes died for the Union in the US Civil War, in part to prevent the expansion of slavery in the United States. The statue framed the War as a sacrifice on behalf of American liberty to remove the aberration of racial slavery. Yet on June 25, 2020, it was toppled by protestors. Demonstrating the ambiguity and contingency of memory, some Coloradans accused white supremacists and sympathizers with the Confederacy of toppling the statue, given its representation of Union soldiers. But some of the names on the monument, such as Colonel Chivington, also recalled those who had massacred Indigenous people in Sand Creek. Harvey Pratt, a Sand Creek descendant, has been commissioned to create a replacement for the 1907 US Civil War monument in Denver. The idea for the replacement statue—a grieving Native American mother—came to him in a dream: "It's really about the women. The women carry the men in the tribes on their backs. [After the dream] I wanted to depict a woman . . . She's in mourning and she's kneeling, just sitting down. She's lost her baby and maybe her grandparents. She's got cuts on her legs and she's cut her finger off . . . She's not asking to be spared . . . She's saying 'Remember us. don't forget us. I've lost my whole family.'" Initial assumptions about the removal of the statue reflected an ongoing trend in the public memory of the Civil War in states such as Colorado. They suggested the purification of the United States from racial slavery while overlooking the dispossession of Indigenous people that occurred during the same period and ignoring the memories that remain for people like Harvey Pratt.[17]

This book has questioned the common notion that group memories such as those of Harvey Pratt depart from the attention to specificity and causation of neutral archival research. It has identified how similarities in the public treatment of Indigenous genocide and the Holocaust can provide a powerful baseline for public historians and cultural agents to adapt alternative knowledge and insights from group memories of trauma. It has compared recent positive developments in the incorporation of Indigenous and Jewish archives of memory in public institutions and sites where they were once evaded. Some of those initiatives have demonstrated what Indigenous scholars such as Gerald Vizenor describe as "survivance"—the ability to remember and represent historical suffering while avoiding the assumption that communities are prone to vanish or endure the irrevocable loss of cultural vitality. They emphasize the capacity for survival without overlooking the external role of perpetrator intent in fomenting historical trauma. When used in counter-memorials, they often direct people to alternative and more accurate sites. Some initiatives even stimulate visitors to acknowledge the subjective nature of public memory and the need for ongoing education rather than shorthand symbols and icons.

As well as reminding us of the work of Gerald Vizenor, these insights bring us back to the words of Halina Birenbaum, who still lives despite having once been trapped in Majdanek. She has written works such as *Dopóki Ich wspominamy Oni żyją, jestem ich nagrobkiem, turystka grobów, szukam życia u umarłych, nie daję umrzeć (They live as long as they are remembered, I am their tomb, tourist of the graves, I am looking for life in the dead, I do not let them die)*. Her words speak to the way the memory of murdered Ashkenazi Jews is kept alive by surviving communities in the synagogue in St. Thomas, US Virgin Islands. By the late-seventeenth century, behind large bushes of tropical pink flowers, Sephardic Jews covered the floors of their synagogue on the island with white beach sand to muffle their prayers, fearing deadly Iberian pogroms. The synagogue is now the oldest in continual use under an American flag, situated on an island where the lives of indigenous people from Taino and Island-Carib communities were once severely and often lethally disrupted by the arrival of Europeans. Hidden behind pink bougainvillea, the St. Thomas synagogue uses Torah scrolls that were rescued from the small town of Budyně nad Ohří in the Czech Republic, where Jews lived from the thirteenth century until their extermination by bullets and gas and typhus and starvation, by strict and structural genocidal intent and by all the banal and horrific intentions in between.[18]

# NOTES

## Preface

1. See David Svaldi, *Sand Creek and the Rhetoric of Extermination: A Case Study in Indian-White Relations* (Lanham, MD: University Press of America, 1989), 149–50; Laurelyn Whitt and Alan W. Clarke, *North American Genocides: Indigenous Nations, Settler Colonialism, and International Law* (Cambridge: Cambridge University Press, 2019), 10–11.
2. Tiffany Midge, "After Viewing the Holocaust Museum's Room of Shoes and a Gallery of Plains' Indian Moccasins, Washington D.C.," *Cold Mountain Review* 34, no. 1 (2005): 18–19.
3. Kazimierz Sakowicz, *Ponary Diary, 1941–1943: A Bystander's Account of Mass Murder* (New Haven, CT: Yale University Press, 2005), 13, 16, 19, 40. See the account of this entry in Jan Tomasz Gross and Irena Grudzinska Gross, *Golden Harvest: Events at the Periphery of the Holocaust* (Oxford: Oxford University Press, 2012), 37, 38.
4. See the account from Jerzy Królikowski cited in Jan Tomasz Gross and Irena Grudzinska Gross, *Golden Harvest: Events at the Periphery of the Holocaust* (Oxford: Oxford University Press, 2012), 30.
5. Sławomir Buryła, *Tematy (Nie)opisane, (Un)described Subjects* (Kraków: Universitas, 2013), cited in Zuzanna Dziuban, "The Politics of Human Remains at the Peripheries of the Holocaust," Dapim: *Studies on the Holocaust*, vol. 29 (2015): 7.

## Introduction

1. According to Rabbi Feshbach of the Saint Thomas synagogue: "When we have a bar mitzvah here—and it's a strange phrase, but we have 'destination bar mitzvahs'—the sand on the floor connects us to the worst moment of Sephardic history, when they were kicked out of Spain . . . The Hebrew Congregation's Torah scrolls come from synagogues destroyed during the Holocaust, a connection to the worst moment in the history of the Ashkenazi Jews of central and Eastern Europe." See https://www.washingtonpost.com/local/from-a-chevy-chase-md-synagogue-to-one-in-the-path-of-hurricane-irma/2017/09/18/171b18f2-9c65-11e7-8ea1-ed975285475e_story.html; https://synagogue.vi/our-historic-synagogue/.

2 On these migrations see, for example, the essays in Paolo Bernardini and Norman Fiering (eds), *The Jews and the Expansion of Europe to the West, 1450 to 1800* (New York: Berghahn Books, 2001).

3 On "Vast Early America" see Karin Wulf, "Vast Early America: Thee Simple Words for a Complex Reality," *Humanities*, vol. 40, no. 1 (Winter 2019). On the continuation of candle lighting rituals and converso identity in these regions more generally, see Barbara Kessel, *Suddenly Jewish: Jews Raised as Gentiles Discover Their Jewish Roots* (Lebanon, New Hampsire: University Press of New England, 2012), 17–39.

4 On the tricky representation of these coinciding phenomena, see Alejandro Caeque, "On Modernity, Colonialism, and the Spanish Inquisition: Reflections on the Spanish Empire in the New World," *January 2011 Conference: 125th Annual Meeting American Historical Association*; George Mariscal, "The Role of Spain in Contemporary Race Theory," *Arizona Journal of Hispanic Cultural Studies,* vol. 2 (1998): 7–22; Francois Soyer, *Antisemitic Conspiracy Theories in the Early Modern Iberian World Narratives of Fear and Hatred* (Leiden: Brill, 2019).

5 José de Acosta responded to the popularity of the Jewish–Indian link among Spanish imperial thinkers and sought to discount it. See José de Acosta, *Natural & Moral History of the Indies, Reprinted from the English Translated Edition of Edward Grimston, 1604*, Vol. 1: *The Natural History* (New York: Burt Franklin, 1880), chap. 23. See also Elizabeth Fenton, *Old Canaan in a New World: Native Americans and the Lost Tribes of Israel* (New York: NYU Press, 2020), esp. Introduction; Matthew W. Dougherty, *Lost Tribes Found: Israelite Indians and Religious Nationalism in Early America* (Norman, OK: University of Oklahoma Press, 2021).

6 This book uses the word "Indigenous" as a general term to describe the first peoples of North America, some of whose descendants find the border between Montana and Alberta, or Alaska and British Columbia, or Manitoba and Minnesota, to be somewhat arbitrary from their perspective. It uses a capital "I" to distinguish from the more general category to define the first people of the Americas and the Caribbean more generally. On the ambiguous North American borders from an Indigenous perspective, see Elspeth Martini, "Borderlands, Indigenous Homelands and North American Settler Colonialism," *Reviews in American History,* vol. 45 (2017): 416–22; Adam Jones, "The Great Lakes Genocides: Hidden Histories, Hidden Precedents," in Alexander Laban Hinton, Thomas La Pointe, and Douglas Irvin-Erickson (eds), *Hidden Genocides: Power, Knowledge, Memory* (New Brunswick, NJ: Rutgers University Press, 2014), 129–48.

7 See for example Laurelyn Whitt and Alan W. Clarke, *North American Genocides: Indigenous Nations, Settler Colonialism, and International Law* (Cambridge: Cambridge University Press, 2019); Alexander Laban Hinton, Andrew Woolford, and Jeff Benvenuto (eds), *Colonial Genocide in Indigenous North America* (Durham, NC: Duke University Press, 2014); Benjamin Madley, "Reexamining the American Genocide Debate: Meaning, Historiography, and New Methods," *The American Historical Review,* vol. 120, no. 1 (February 2015): 108. On the Canadian settler colonial context for the genocide of Indigenous people, see for example Matthew Wildcat,

"Fearing Social and Cultural Death: Genocide and Elimination in Settler Colonial Canada—an Indigenous Perspective," *Journal of Genocide Research,* vol. 17, no. 4 (2015): 391–409; Andrew Woolford and Jeff Benvenuto (eds), *Canada and Colonial Genocide* (Milton, UK: Routledge, 2017).

**8** On the Indigenous demographic "nadir" at the end of the nineteenth century, see J. David Hacker and Michael R. Haines, "American Indian Mortality in the Late Nineteenth Century: The Impact of Federal Assimilation Policies on a Vulnerable Population," *Annales de démographie historique,* vol. 2, no. 110 (2005): 17; Suzanne A. Alchon, *A Pest in the Land: New World Epidemics in a Global Perspective* (Albuquerque: University of New Mexico Press, 2003), 147–72; Douglas H. Ubelaker, "Population Size, Contact to Nadir," in Douglas H. Ubelaker and William C. Sturtevant (eds), *Handbook of North American Indians, vol. 3, Environment, Origins and Population* (Washington, D.C.: Smithsonian Institution, 2007), 694–701.

**9** "Jewish Massacre Denounced," *The New York Times,* April 28, 1903, 6. See also Steven J. Zipperstein, *Pogrom: Kishinev and the Tilt of History* (New York and London: Liveright Publishing Co., 2018).

**10** David Brody, "American Jewry, the Refugees and Immigration Restriction, (1932–1942)," *Publications of the American Jewish Historical Society,* vol. 45, no. 4 (1956): 219.

**11** On the Guernsey context, see Frederick E. Cohen, *The Jews in the Channel Islands During the German Occupation, 1940–1945* (London, 1998), 46; "Guernsey's Holocaust role 'should be marked'," BBC News, January 15, 2015, https://www.bbc.co.uk/news/world-europe-guernsey-30811115.

**12** On the Nazi obsession with eradicating "Jewishness" from the world, even after Jewish bodies were destroyed, see the recent discussions in Dan Michman, "What is the Core of the Shoah—the 'Final Solution of the Jewish Question' or 'Total Removal of the Jews' and of Judaism?" in Emanuel Etkes, David Asaf and Yosef Kaplan (eds), *Milestones: Essays and Studies in Jewish History in Honor of Zvi (Kuti) Yekutiel* (Jerusalem: Shazar Center, 2015), 397–409.

**13** Alain Finkielkraut, *The Future of a Negation: Reflections on the Question of Genocide* (Lincoln, NE: University of Nebraska Press, 1998), 59.

**14** On the notion of "man's inhumanity to man" as a problematic phenomenon, as well as contiguous trajectory and universalization of Anne Frank imagery, see Yehuda Bauer, "Against Mystification: The Holocaust as a Historical Phenomenon" (1978), in Michael R. Marrus (ed.), *The Nazi Holocaust: Perspectives on the Holocaust* (Berlin: De Gruyter, 1989), 106; Francine Prose, *Anne Frank: The Book, the Life, the Afterlife* (New York: HarperCollins, 2009), 85; Jeffrey Shandler, "From Diary to Book: Text, Object, Structure," in Barbara Kirshenblatt-Gimblett and Jeffrey Shandler (eds), *Anne Frank Unbound: Media, Imagination, Memory* (Bloomington: Indiana University Press, 2012), 53. On the "Crying Indian" motif in broader context, see David Rich Lewis, "American Indian Environmental Relations," in A *Companion to American Environmental History*, ed. Douglas C. Sackman (Chichester, West Sussex: Wiley-Blackwell, 2010), 191–92; Maureen Konkle, *Writing Indian Nations: Native Intellectuals and the Politics of Historiography, 1827–1863*

(Chapel Hill: University of North Carolina Press, 2004), 295. On the often overlooked Canadian context, see Tricia Logan, "National Memory and Museums: Remembering Settler Colonial Genocide of Indigenous Peoples in Canada," in Nigel Eltringham and Pam Maclean (eds), *Remembering Genocide* (London: Routledge, 2014), 112–30.

**15** See A. Dirk Moses, "Genocide and the Terror of History," *Parallax*, vol. 17, no. 4, (2012): 90; Marvin Hurvich, "The Place of Annihilation Anxieties in Psychoanalytic Theory," *Journal of the American Psychoanalytic Association*, vol. 51, no. 2 (2003): 581.

**16** Steven T. Katz has suggested the "merciless, exceptionless, biocentric intentionality of Hitler's 'war against the Jews'" as that which distinguishes the Holocaust in comparative exercises. See Steven T. Katz, *The Holocaust in Historical Context: Volume I: The Holocaust and Mass Death before the Modern Age* (New York: Oxford University Press, 1994), 59. On the debate over concentrated periods of loss versus longer scales, see Benjamin Madley, "Reexamining the American Genocide Debate: Meaning, Historiography, and New Methods," *The American Historical Review,* vol. 120, no. 1 (February 2015): 108. On these vexed definitional debates since the 1990s, including in response to Katz's interventions, see David B. MacDonald, *Identity Politics in the Age of Genocide: The Holocaust and Historical Representation* (London and New York: Routledge, 2008); A. Dirk Moses, "The Holocaust and Genocide," in Dan Stone (ed.), *The Historiography of the Holocaust* (Basingstoke, UK: Palgrave Macmillan, 2004), 546; Gavriel D. Rosenfeld, "The Politics of Uniqueness: Reflections on the Recent Polemical Turn in Holocaust and Genocide Scholarship," *Holocaust and Genocide Studies*, vol. 13, no. 1 (Spring 1999): 28–61. On the ambiguous trajectory of the Holocaust as normative category, see Daniel Blatman, "The Holocaust as Genocide: Milestones in the Historiographical Discourse," in *The Wiley Companion to the Holocaust,* 95–114; A. Dirk Moses, "The Holocaust and Genocide," in Dan Stone (ed.), *The Historiography of the Holocaust* (Basingstoke, UK: Palgrave Macmillan, 2004), 546; Rebecca Jinks, *Representing Genocide: The Holocaust as Paradigm?* (London and New York: Bloomsbury, 2016).

**17** Such tensions thus occlude the "multidirectional" and "transcultural" ways their separate memories have subsequently been appropriated by cultural and civic bodies. See Michael Rothberg, *Multidirectional Memory: Remembering the Holocaust in the Age of Decolonization* (Stanford, CA: Stanford University Press, 2009), 3; Richard Crownshaw, *The Afterlife of Holocaust Memory in Contemporary Literature and Culture* (Basingstoke, UK: Palgrave Macmillan, 2010); Richard Crownshaw (ed.), *Transcultural Memory* (London and New York: Routledge, 2014); Stef Craps, *Postcolonial Witness: Trauma Out of Bounds* (Basingstoke, UK: Palgrave Macmillan, 2013); Stef Craps, "Holocaust Literature: Comparative Perspectives," in Jenni Adams (ed.), *The Bloomsbury Companion to Holocaust Literature* (London: Bloomsbury Academic, 2014), 199–218.

**18** See Peter Carrier, "Holocaust Memoriography and the Impact of Memory on the Historiography of the Holocaust," in Bill Niven and Stefan Berger (eds), *Writing the History of Memory*, (London: Bloomsbury, 2014), 199.

**19** This book can be placed alongside Susan Neiman's recent attempt to show how Germans and Americans might gain new insights about their national identities by comparing their approaches to Holocaust memory and the memory of the enslavement of Africans. Neiman seeks to avoid relativizing or directly comparing the Holocaust and the Middle Passage by examining similarities in their subsequent public representation. See Susan Neiman, *Learning from the Germans: Race and the Memory of Evil* (New York: Farrar, Straus and Giroux, 2019). See also the important work comparing memory cultures as they relate to the enslavement of Africans in the Atlantic world, in Ana Lucia Araujo, *Slavery in the Age of Memory: Engaging the Past* (London: Bloomsbury, 2020).

20 Sara de Leeuw, Margo Greenwood and Nicole Lindsay, "Troubling Good Intentions," *Settler Colonial Studies*, vol. 3, nos. 3–4 (2013): 381–94; Bonita Lawrence, "Rewriting Histories of the Land: Colonization and Indigenous Resistance in Eastern Canada," in Sherene H. Razack (ed.), *Race, Space, and the Law: Unmapping a White Settler Society* (Toronto: Between the Lines, 2002), 24; Andrew Woolford & Jeff Benvenuto, "Canada and Colonial Genocide," *Journal of Genocide Research*, vol. 17, no. 4 (2015): 384. See also Alyssa Mt. Pleasant, Caroline Wigginton, and Kelly Wisecup, "Materials and Methods in Native American and Indigenous Studies: Completing the Turn," *The William and Mary Quarterly*, vol. 75, no. 2 (2018): 207–36; Christine M. DeLucia, "Continuing the Intervention: Past, Present, and Future Pathways for Native Studies and Early American History," *The American Historical Review*, vol. 125, no. 2 (April 2020): 528–32; Jean M. O'Brien, "What Does Native American and Indigenous Studies (NAIS) Do?" *The American Historical Review*, vol. 125, no. 2 (April 2020): 542–5. For the stakes in museum studies more specifically, see Lisa Michelle King, *Legible Sovereignties: Rhetoric, Representations, and Native American Museums* (Corvallis: Oregon State University Press, 2017); Natchee Blu Barnd, *Native Space Geographic Strategies to Unsettle Settler Colonialism* (Corvallis: Oregon State University Press, 2017).

21 Scott Richard Lyons, "Rhetorical Sovereignty: What Do American Indians Want from Writing?," *College Composition and Communication*, vol. 51, no. 3 (February 2000): 447–68.

22 Gerald Vizenor, *Fugitive Poses: Native American Indian Scenes of Absence and Presence* (Lincoln: University of Nebraska Press, 1998), 27. As David J. Silverman notes in a recent discussion of the Thanksgiving saga in history and myth, "Wampanoags today commonly tell of their parents objecting to the performance of Thanksgiving pageants and associated history lessons that the New England Indians were all gone . . ." See David J. Silverman, *This Land Is Their Land: The Wampanoag Indians, Plymouth Colony, and the Troubled History of Thanksgiving* (London and New York: Bloomsbury, 2019), 10.

23 James E. Young, *The Texture of Memory: Holocaust Memorials and Meaning* (New Haven, CT: Yale University Press, 1993).

24 Those representations include the "Arbeit macht frei" slogan and gateway, the persona of Anne Frank, and the number "six million." See Oren Baruch Stier, *Holocaust Icons: Symbolizing the Shoah in History and Memory* (New Brunswick, NJ: Rutgers University Press, 2015), 2–3. See also Marianne Hirsch, *The Generation of Postmemory: Writing and Visual Culture After the Holocaust* (New York: Columbia University Press, 2012), 5, 113–16; Dominik

Bartmanski and Jeffrey C. Alexander, "Introduction: Materiality and Meaning in Social Life: Toward an Iconic Turn in Cultural Sociology," in Jeffrey C. Alexander, Dominik Bartmanski, and Bernhard Giesen (eds), *Iconic Power: Materiality and Meaning in Social Life* (New York: Palgrave Macmillan, 2012), 1–2; Peter Carrier, *Holocaust Monuments and National Memory Cultures in France and Germany since 1989: The Origins and Political Function of the Vél d'Hiv' in Paris and the Holocaust Monument in Berlin* (New York: Bergahn Books, 2005), 41; Alejandro Baer, *Holocausto: Recuerdo y Representación* (Madrid: Losada, 2006); Alejandro Baer and Nathan Sznaider, *Memory and Forgetting in the Post-Holocaust Era: The Ethics of Never Again* (Milton, UK: Routledge, 2017); Dominick LaCapra, *Representing the Holocaust: History, Theory, Trauma* (Ithaca, NY: Cornell University Press, 1996); Berel Lang, *Holocaust Representation: Art Within the Limits of History and Ethics* (Baltimore, MD: Johns Hopkins University Press, 1996); Carolyn J. Dean, "History and Holocaust Representation," *History and Theory*, vol. 41, no. 2, (2002): 239–49.

25 A. Dirk Moses, "Anxieties in Holocaust and Genocide Studies," in Claudio Fogu, Wulf Kansteiner, and Todd Presner (eds), *Probing the Ethics of. Holocaust Culture* (Cambridge, MA: Harvard University Press, 2016), 336; Levy and Sznaider, "Memory Unbound: The Holocaust and the Formation of Cosmopolitan"; Daniel Levy and Natan Sznaider, "Memories of Europe: Cosmopolitanism and Its Others", in Chris Rumford (ed.), *Cosmopolitanism and Europe* (Liverpool: Liverpool University Press, 2007), 167; Daniel Levy and Natan Sznaider, *The Holocaust and Memory in the Global Age* (Philadelphia: Temple University Press, 2006), 8; Jeffrey C. Alexander, "On the Social Construction of Moral Universalist: the "Holocaust" from Mass Murder to Trauma Drama," *European Journal of Social Theory*, vol. 5, no. 1 (2002): 5–86; Ross Poole, "Misremembering the Holocaust: Universal Symbol, Nationalist Icon or Moral Kitsch?," in Yifat Gutman, Adam Brown and Amy Sodaro (eds), *Memory and the Future: Transnational Politics, Ethics and Society* (Basingstoke, UK: Palgrave MacMillan, 2010), 31–49; Aleida Assmann, "The Holocaust—A Global Memory? Extensions and Limits of a New Memory Community," in Aleida Assmann and Sebastian Conrad (eds), *Memory in a Global Age: Discourses Practices and Trajectories* (London: Palgrave, 2010), 109, 113; Alon Confino, *Foundational Pasts: The Holocaust as Historical Understanding* (Cambridge: Cambridge University Press, 2012), 1.

26 Harold Marcuse, "Holocaust Memorials: The Emergence of a Genre," *The American Historical Review*, vol. 115, no. 1 (February 2010): 55. See also work such as Michael Meng, *Shattered Spaces: Encountering Jewish Ruins in Postwar Germany and Poland* (Cambridge, MA: Harvard University Press, 2011). On Holocaust universalization, see for example, Levy and Sznaider, *The Holocaust and Memory in the Global* Age; Jeffrey C. Alexander, "On the Social Construction of Moral Universalist: the "Holocaust" from Mass Murder to Trauma Drama," *European Journal of Social Theory*, vol. 5, no. 1, (2002): 5–86; Ross Poole, "Misremembering the Holocaust: Universal Symbol, Nationalist Icon or Moral Kitsch?," in Yifat Gutman, Adam Brown and Amy Sodaro (eds), *Memory and the Future: Transnational Politics, Ethics and Society* (Basingstoke, UK: Palgrave MacMillan, 2010), 31–49; Aleida

Assmann, "The Holocaust—A Global Memory? Extensions and Limits of a New Memory Community," in Aleida Assmann and Sebastian Conrad (eds), *Memory in a Global Age: Discourses Practices and Trajectories* (London: Palgrave, 2010), 109, 113; Alon Confino, *Foundational Pasts: The Holocaust as Historical Understanding* (Cambridge: Cambridge University Press, 2012), 1; Alvin H. Rosenfeld, *The End of the Holocaust* (Bloomington: Indiana University Press, 2013); Gavriel D. Rosenfeld, *Hi Hitler! How the Nazi Past is Being Normalized in Contemporary Culture* (Cambridge: Cambridge University Press, 2015); A. Huyssen, "Monument and Memory in a Postmodern Age," in J. E. Young (ed.), *The Art of Memory: Holocaust Memorials in History* (New York: Prestel–Verlag/The Jewish Museum New York, 1994), 13; J. E. Young, *At Memory's Edge: After-Images of the Holocaust in Contemporary Art and Architecture* (New Haven, CT: Yale University Press, 2000), 198. On the Americanization and Canadianization of Holocaust memory, see Peter Novick, *The Holocaust and Collective Memory* (London: Bloomsbury, 1999), 10–13, 20; Hilene Flanzbaum (ed.), *The Americanization of the Holocaust* (Baltimore: Johns Hopkins University Press, 1999); Jason Chalmers, "Canadianising the Holocaust: Debating Canada's National Holocaust Monument," *Canadian Jewish Studies* 24 (2016), 149–65; Dorota Glowacka, ""Never Forget": Intersecting Memories of the Holocaust and the Settler Colonial Genocide in Canada," 388.

27 As David Stirrup notes, echoing insights from Vizenor, "the Native American in Europe is too often a specter, a ghostly image of a past actualized by the always already anomalous appearance of the Indian." See David Stirrup, "Introduction," in James Mackay and David Stirrup (eds), *Tribal Fantasies: Native Americans in the European Imaginary, 1900–2010* (New York: Palgrave, 2010), 9.

28 In Europe, according to Deborah Madsen, the "category of "Native" is effectively "melted" into another category of cultural experience (with the attendant loss of Indigenous identities, historical experiences, and claims to justice) . . ." See Deborah Madsen, "Out of the Melting Pot, into the Nationalist Fires: Native American Literary Studies in Europe," *American Indian Quarterly*, vol. 35, no. 3 (Summer 2011): 353. On genocide and memory more generally, see Simone Gigliotti, *The Memorialization of Genocide* (London and New York: Routledge, 2016); Alex Hinton and Devon Hinton (eds), *External Genocide and Mass Violence: Memory, Symptom, Recovery* (Cambridge: Cambridge University Press, 2015); Jutta Lindert and Armen T. Marsoobian (eds), *Multidisciplinary Perspectives on Genocide and Memory* (Basingstoke, UK: Palgrave Macmillan, 2018).

29 Omer Bartov, "The Holocaust as Genocide: Experiential Uniqueness and Integrated History," in *Probing the Ethics of Holocaust Culture*; Omer Bartov, "Genocide and the Holocaust: Arguments over History and Politics," in *Lessons and Legacies*, vol. XI, ed. Karl Schleunes and Hilary Earl (Evanston, IL: Northwestern University Press, 2014), 15. On the potential links between the occlusion of the memory of British imperial atrocities and the universalization of Holocaust memory, see several of the recent essays in Tom Lawson and Andy Pearce (eds), *The Palgrave Handbook of Britain and the Holocaust* (Basingstoke, UK: Palgrave, 2021).

30 Christine M. DeLucia, *Memory Lands: King Philip's War and the Place of Violence in the Northeast* (New Haven, CT: Yale University Press, 2018), 2–3. For attention to oral record as well a place and locality in Holocaust Studies, see Shoshana Felman, "The Return of the Voice: Claude Lanzmann's Shoah," in Shoshana Felman and Dori Laub, *Testimony: Crises of Witnessing in Literature, Psychoanalysis, and History* (New York: Routledge, 1992), 205; Saul Friedländer, *Memory, History, and the Extermination of the Jews of Europe* (Bloomington and Indianapolis: Indiana University Press, 1993), viii; Hannah Pollin-Galay, *Ecologies of Witnessing: Language, Place, and Holocaust Testimony* (New Haven, CT: Yale University Press, 2018).

31 On the coining of the term "genocide" in 1944 by Raphael Lemkin, see Raphael Lemkin, *Axis Rule in Occupied Europe: Laws of Occupation, Analysis of Government, Proposals for Redress* (Washington, D.C.: Carnegie Endowment for International Peace, Division of International Law, 1944), xi–xii, chap. 9. On the origins of the Genocide Convention, including Lemkin's manifold involvement, see Hirad Abtahi and Philippa Webb, *The Genocide Convention: The Travaux Préparatoires* (2 vols) (Leiden: Brill, 2008). See also: Convention on the Prevention and Punishment of the Crime of Genocide, Adopted by the General Assembly of the United Nations on 9 December 1948, United Nations—Treaty Series, vol. 78, no. 1021: 280; Anna-Vera Sullam Calimani, "A Name for Extermination," *The Modern Language Review*, vol. 94, no. 4 (October 1999): 983. On broader "settler-colonial" dynamics for genocide and population destruction in Indigenous communities, which move beyond strict notions of genocidal intent as often defined by the UN definition of genocide, see for example Patrick Wolfe, "Settler Colonialism and the Elimination of the Native," *Journal of Genocide Research,* vol. 8 (Dec. 2006): 387–409; Lorenzo Veracini, "Introducing Settler Colonial Studies," *Settler Colonial Studies,* vol. 1, no. 1 (2011): 1–12; Jeffrey Ostler, "'To Extirpate the Indians': An Indigenous Consciousness of Genocide in the Ohio Valley and Lower Great Lakes, 1750s–1810,' *The William and Mary Quarterly,* vol. 72, no. 4 (October 2015): 587; Frederick E. Hoxie, "Retrieving the Red Continent: Settler Colonialism and the History of American Indians in the US," *Ethnic and Racial Studies*, vol. 31, no. 6 (2008): 1153–67, Walter L. Hixson, *American Settler Colonialism: A History* (New York: Palgrave Macmillan, 2013); Bethel Saler, *The Settlers' Empire: Colonialism and State Formation in America's Old Northwest* (Philadelphia: University of Pennsylvania Press, 2014). On the genocide term from a moral and philosophical perspective, see Berel Lang, *Genocide: The Act as Idea* (Philadelphia: University of Pennsylvania Press, 2016). On the problem of using UN-definitions that sidestep Indigenous ways of understanding cultural destruction, see Andrew Woolford, "Ontological Destruction: Genocide and Canadian Aboriginal Peoples," *Genocide Studies & Prevention,* vol. 4 (2009): 81, 89, 90

32 TRC Canada, *Truth and Reconciliation Commission of Canada Final Report: Reconciliation,* vol. 6 (Montreal: McGill-Queens University Press, 2015), 212. See the discussion in David B. MacDonald, "Indigenous Genocide and Perceptions of the Holocaust in Canada," in S. Gigliotti and H. Earl (eds), *The Wiley Companion to the Holocaust* (London: Wiley-Blackwell, 2020), 588.

33 On cultural genocide and the Canadian context, see for example David B. MacDonald, "Indigenous Genocide and Perceptions of the Holocaust in Canada," 577–97; David B. MacDonald, *The Sleeping Giant Awakens: Genocide, Indian Residential Schools, and the Challenge of Conciliation* (Toronto: University of Toronto Press, 2019); David B. MacDonald, "Canada's History War: Indigenous Genocide and Public Memory in the United States, Australia, and Canada," *Journal of Genocide Research*, vol. 17, no. 4 (2015): 411–31; Dean Neu and Richard Therrien, *Accounting for Genocide: Canada's Bureaucratic Assault on Aboriginal People* (Blackpoint, Nova Scotia: Fernwood Publishing, 2003); Lindsey Kingston, "The Destruction of Identity: Cultural Genocide and Indigenous Peoples," *Journal of Human Rights*, vol. 14, no. 1 (2015): 63–83. In Holocaust Studies, see Bianca Gaudenzi and Astrid Swenson, "Looted Art and Restitution in the Twentieth Century—Towards a Global Perspective," *Journal of Contemporary History*, vol. 52, no. 3 (2017): 491–518; Leora Bilsky and Rachel Klagsbrun, "The Return of Cultural Genocide?" *European Journal of International Law*, vol. 29, no. 2 (May 2018): 373–96; Benedicte Savoy, "Plunder, Restitution, Emotion and the Weight of Archives: A Historical Approach," in Ines Rotermund-Reynard (ed.), *Echoes of Exile: Moscow Archives and the Arts in Paris 1933–1945* (Berlin and Boston: De Gruyter, 2015), 27–44; Martin Dean, Constantin Goschler, and Philipp Ther (eds), *Robbery and Restitution: The Conflict over Jewish Property in Europe* (New York and Oxford: Berghahn Books, 2007).

34 Marianne Hirsch has compared "familial and 'affiliative' postmemory" to distinguish between "the process of identification, imagination, and projection of those who grew up in survivor families, and of those less proximate members of their generation or relational network who share a legacy of trauma and thus the curiosity, the urgency, the frustrated need to know about a traumatic past." See Marianne Hirsch, *The Generation of Postmemory*, 35–6.

35 See, for example, the discussions in Kathleen Brown-Rice, "Examining the Theory of Historical Trauma Among Native Americans," *The Professional Counselor*, vol. 3, no. 3 (2013): 117–30; M. Brave Heart, J. Chase, J. Elkins, and D. B. Altschul, "Historical Trauma among Indigenous Peoples of the Americas: Concepts, Research, and Clinical Considerations," *Journal of Psychoactive Drugs*, vol. 43, no. 4 (2012): 282–90; J. Jacobs, "The Cross-Generational Transmission of Trauma: Ritual and Emotion among Survivors of the Holocaust," *Journal of Contemporary Ethnography*, vol. 40, no. 3 (2011): 342–61; Jenny Edkins, "Remembering Relationality: Trauma Time and Politics," in Duncan Bell (ed.), *Memory, Trauma, and World Politics: Reflections on the Relationship between Past and Present* (New York: Palgrave Macmillan, 2006), 99–115.

36 On the question of agency relative to perpetrator intent in Native American studies, see Alyssa Mt. Pleasant, Caroline Wigginton, and Kelly Wisecup, "Materials and Methods in Native American and Indigenous Studies," 207–36. For the tricky representation of agency in Holocaust Studies, see Dan Stone, "Beyond the 'Auschwitz Syndrome': Holocaust Historiography after the Cold War," *Journal Patterns of Prejudice*, vol. 44, no. 5 (2010): 454–68.

37 Elizabeth Fine, "The Absent Memory: The Act of Writing In Post-Holocaust French Literature," in Berel Lang (ed.), *Writing and the Holocaust* (New York: Holmes and Meier, 1998), 41–57.

38 See Dagmar Wernitznig, *Europe's Indians, Indians in Europe: European Perceptions and Appropriations of Native American Cultures from Pocahontas to the Present* (Lanham, MD: University Press of America, 2007), 132; Lisa Aldred, "Plastic Shamans and Astroturf Sun Dances: New Age Commercialism of Native American Spirituality," *American Indian Quarterly,* vol. 24, no. 3. (2000): 342. On the Jewish context for similar debates about outward dissemination of cultural ideas at a time when historical suffering has itself been appropriated, see for example, Levi Cooper, "The Assimilation of Tikkun Olam," *Jewish Political Studies Review,* vol. 25, no. 3–4 (Fall 2013): 10-42

39 Kitty Millet, *The Victims of Slavery, Colonization, and the Holocaust: A Comparative History of Persecution* (New York and London: Bloomsbury, 2017), 2.

## Chapter One "Humanitarian feelings . . . crystallized in formulae of international law."

1 See, for example, Ward Churchill, *A Little Matter of Genocide: Holocaust and Denial in the Americus, 1492 to the Present* (San Francisco: City Lights, 1997); David E. Stannard, *American Holocaust: The Conquest of the New World* (New York: Oxford University Press, 1992); Russell Thornton, *American Indian Holocaust and Survival: A Population History since 1492* (Norman, OK: University of Oklahoma Press, 1987).

2 Australian literatures on Indigenous genocide have often engaged Holocaust studies in productive ways. Those examples have often been marshaled in discussions of Indigenous loss in North America as well as in discussions of the European imperial framework for the Nazi persecution of Jews during the Holocaust. See for example James Belich, "Riders of the Whirlwind: Tribal Peoples and European Settlement Booms, 1790s–1900s," in *Raupatu: The Confiscation of Maori Land* (Wellington: Victoria University Press, 2009); A. Dirk Moses, "Genocide and Settler Society in Australian History," in A. Dirk Moses (ed.), *Genocide and Settler Society: Frontier Violence and Stolen Indigenous Children in Australian History* (New York: Berghahn, 2004), 3–48; Patrick Wolfe, "Settler Colonialism and the Elimination of the Native," *Journal of Genocide Research*, vol. 8 (December 2006): 387–409; Margaret Jacobs, *White Mother to a Dark Race: Settler Colonialism, Maternalism, and the Removal of Indigenous Children in the American West and Australia, 1880–1940* (Lincoln, NE: University of Nebraska Press, 2009); Paul Bartropp, "The Holocaust, the Aborigines and the bureaucracy of destruction: An Australian dimension of genocide," *Journal of Genocide Research*, vol. 3, no. 1 (2001): 77; Tony Barta, "After the Holocaust: Consciousness of Genocide in Australia," *Australian Journal of Politics and History,* vol. 31, no. 1 (1985): 154–61; Rowan Savage, "The Political Uses of Death-as- Finality in Genocide Denial: The Stolen Generations and the Holocaust," *Borderlands,* vol. 12, no. 1 (2013): 1–22.

3 Michael Rothberg, *Multidirectional Memory: Remembering the Holocaust in the Age of Decolonization* (Palo Alto, CA: Stanford University Press, 2009), 17–19.

4 Bruce G. Trigger and William R. Swagerty, "Entertaining Strangers: North America in the Sixteenth Century," in Bruce G. Trigger and Wilcomb E. Washburn, eds. *The Cambridge History of the Native Peoples of The Americas: Volume I: North America: Part I* (Cambridge, UK: Cambridge University Press, 1996), 363.

5 See Russell Thornton, "Health, Disease, and Demography," in Philip J. Deloria and Neal Salisbury (eds), *A Companion to American Indian History* (Malden, MA: Wiley Blackwell 2002), 72–3; Gideon Mailer and Nicola Hale, *Decolonizing the Diet: Nutrition, Immunity, and the Warning from Early America* (New York and London: Anthem Press, 2018), 1–30.

6 Mailer and Hale, *Decolonizing the Diet*, 1–30.

7 Mailer and Hale, *Decolonizing the Diet,* chap. 3.

8 Christian Gerlach, "Extremely Violent Societies: An Alternative to the Concept of Genocide," *Journal of Genocide Research,* vol. 8, no. 4 (2006): 464.

9 Steven Katz, "The Uniqueness of the Holocaust: The Historical Dimension," in *Is the Holocaust Unique?: Perspectives on Comparative Genocide*, ed. Alan Rosenbaum (Boulder, CO: Westview Press, 1996), 21, 26, 30–4; S. Katz, "The Depopulation of the New World in the Sixteenth Century" in *The Holocaust in Historical Context: Volume I: The Holocaust and Mass Death before the Modern Age* (New York: Oxford University Press, 1994), 87–9.

10 Churchill, *A Little Matter of Genocide,* 30–1, 36, 50, 63–80, esp. 64; Stannard, *American Holocaust*, 167; David Stannard, "Uniqueness as Denial: The Politics of Genocide Scholarship," in *Is The Holocaust Unique?*, 89, 258–60. On the tensions in partial response to Katz, see Friedberg, "Dare to Compare: Americanizing the Holocaust," 360; Gavriel D. Rosenfeld, "The Politics of Uniqueness: Reflections on the Recent Polemical Turn in Holocaust and Genocide Scholarship ," *Holocaust and Genocide Studies*, vol. 13, no. 1 (Spring 1999): 28–61; MacDonald, *Identity Politics in the Age of Genocide*, 82–5. These controversies were revived in a March 2020 public exchange: See Steven T. Katz, "Comparing Causes of Death in the Holocaust with the Tragedy of the Indigenous Peoples of Spanish America: The View of David E. Stannard"; David E. Stannard, "True Believer: The Uniqueness of Steven T. Katz"; Jan Burzlaff, "The Holocaust and Slavery? Working Towards A Comparative History of Genocide and Mass Violence". On the "migration" of the "Stannard-Churchill style of argumentation" to Canada, see David B. MacDonald, "Indigenous Genocide and Perceptions of the Holocaust in Canada," in S. Gigliotti and H. Earl (eds), *The Wiley Companion to the Holocaust* (London: Wiley-Blackwell, 2020), 578.

11 Brenden Rensink, "Genocide of Native Americans: Historical Facts and Historiographic Debates," in Samuel Totten and Robert Hitchcock (eds), *Genocide of Indigenous Peoples, Vol. 8 in Genocide: A Critical Bibliographic Series* (New Brunswick, NJ: Transaction Publishers, 2011), 17; Madley, "Reexamining the American Genocide Debate," 108.

12 Steven T. Katz, "The "Unique" Intentionality of the Holocaust," *Modern Judaism—A Journal of Jewish Ideas and Experience*, vol. 1, no. 2 (September 1981): 161–83; J. Roth and E. Maxwell (eds), *Remembering for the Future: 3 Volume Set: The Holocaust in an Age of Genocide* (Basingstoke, UK: Palgrave

Macmillan, 2001), 19–153; Thomas W. Simon, "The Holocaust's Moral 'Uniqueness', *in Contemporary Portrayals of Auschwitz*, eds. Alan Rosenberg et al. (Amherst: Humanity Press, 2000); Lewi Stone, "Quantifying the Holocaust: Hyperintense Kill Rates During the Nazi Genocide," *Science Advances*, January 2, 2019, eaau7292. The common notion that "[p]hysical genocide seems more characteristic of years and decades than of centuries" would apply to the overall Jewish experience in mainland Europe during the Holocaust, given the scale of loss within a short period of time. See Russell Thornton, "Native American Demographic and Tribal Survival into the Twenty-First Century," *American Studies,* vol. 46, no. 4 (Fall/Winter 2005): 32. See also David MacDonald, "First Nations, Residential Schools, and the Americanization of the Holocaust: Rewriting Indigenous History in the United States and Canada," *Canadian Journal of Political Science/Revue canadienne de science politique*, vol. 40, no. 4 (December 2007): 1000.

**13** Madley, "Reexamining the American Genocide Debate," 108.

**14** Stannard, *American Holocaust*, 118, 151, 180–1; Friedberg, "Dare to Compare," 397.

**15** David Bernstein, "The Holocaust as 'White On White Crime' and Other Signs of Intellectual Decay," *The Washington Post,* February 5, 2016, https://www.washingtonpost.com/news/volokh-conspiracy/wp/2016/02/05/the-holocaust-as-white-on-white-crime-and-other-signs-of-intellectual-decay/

**16** Most publicly, Timothy Snyder has attempted to draw attention to those Jewish communities who were murdered in "Bloodlands" of Eastern Europe, and who have not always received the same attention as those who perished in death camps. See Timothy Snyder, *Bloodlands: Europe Between Hitler and Stalin* (New York: Basic Books, 2010). Others have focused on the differing experiences and outcomes among North African, Greek, and Balkan Jews, as well as differences between Western European Jewish communities. See for example, Henry Abramson, "A Double Occlusion: Sephardim and the Holocaust," in Zion Zohar (ed.), *Sephardic and Mizrahi Jewry: From the Golden Age of Spain to Modern Times* (New York: New York University Press, 2005), 285–99.

**17** Primo Levi, *If This Is a Man* (1947) (New York: Orion Press, 1959), 59; Paris Papamichos Chronakis, "'We Lived as Greeks and We Died as Greeks': Thessalonican Jews in Auschwitz and the Meanings of Nationhood," in Giorgos Antoniou and A. Dirk Moses (eds), *The Holocaust in Greece* (Cambridge, UK: Cambridge University Press, 2018), 157–80. See also Cecil Roth, "The Last Days of Jewish Salonica: What Happened to a 450-Year-Old Civilization," *Commentary,* vol. 10 (July 1950): 49–55; Steven B. Bowman, *The Agony of Greek Jews, 1940–1945* (Palo Alto, CA: Stanford University Press, 2009), 132.

**18** For an introduction to these ongoing conflicts over memory in Salonika, see Giorgos Antoniou and A. Dirk Moses, "Introduction: The Holocaust in Greece," in *The Holocaust in Greece*, 8. On contingent economic and business interests and their lethality for Jews in Salonika, see Leon Saltiel, "A City against Its Citizens? Thessaloniki and the Jews," in ibid, 113–34; Maria Kavala, "The Scale of Jewish Property Theft in Nazi-occupied Thessaloniki," in ibid., 183–207; Stratos N. Dordanas, "The Jewish Community of Thessaloniki and the Christian Collaborators: 'Those that are Leaving and What They are Leaving Behind,'" in ibid, 208–27; Kostis Kornetis, "Expropriating the Space of the Other: Property Spoliations of Thessalonican Jews in the 1940s," in ibid, 228–52.

**19** Devin E. Naar, "'You are Your Brother's Keeper': Rebuilding the Jewish Community of Salonica from Afar," in ibid, 273–303.

**20** Tzvetan Todorov, *The Fragility of Goodness: Why Bulgaria's Jews Survived the Holocaust: a Collection of Texts* (Princeton, NJ: Princeton University Press, 2001); Norman H. Gershman, *Besa: Muslims Who Saved Jews in World War II* (Syracuse, NY: Syracuse University Press, 2008).

**21** Mark Levene, "The Bulgarians Were the Worst!" Reconsidering the Holocaust in Salonika within a Regional History of Mass Violence," in *The Holocaust in Greece*, 36–57.

**22** Andrew Apostolou, "Greek Collaboration in the Holocaust and the Course of the War," in ibid, 89–112.

**23** Pekka Hämäläinen, "The Politics of Grass: European Expansion, Ecological Change, and Indigenous Power in the Southwest Borderlands," *William and Mary Quarterly*, vol. 67, no. 2 (2010): 173–208; Jones, *Rationalizing Epidemics*, 173–4; Joshua L. Reid, "Indigenous Power in The Comanche Empire," *History and Theory*, vol. 52, no. 1 (February 2013): 54–9; Patricia K. Galloway, *Choctaw Genesis: 1500–1700* (Lincoln, NE: University of Nebraska Press, 1995), 183–99; Jeff Benvenuto, "Revisiting Choctaw Ethnocide and Ethnogenesis: The Creative Destruction of Colonial Genocide," in Andrew Woolford, Jeff Benvenuto, and Alexander Laban Hinton (eds), *Colonial Genocide in Indigenous North America* (Durham, NC: Duke University Press, 2014), 208–25; David J. Silverman, *Thundersticks: Firearms and the Violent Transformation of Native America* (Cambridge, MA: Belknap Press of Harvard University Press, 2016).

**24** The pluralistic and complex nature of Indigenous life following the arrival of Europeans, and the role of contingency in their response, is also shown in work such as Michael Witgen, *An Infinity of Nations: How the Native New World Shaped Early North America* (Philadelphia: University of Pennsylvania Press, 2012).

**25** See Shoshana Felman, "The Return of the Voice: Claude Lanzmann's Shoah," in Shoshana Felman and Dori Laub (eds), *Testimony: Crises of Witnessing in Literature, Psychoanalysis, and History* (New York: Routledge, 1992), 205; Julia Epstein and Lori Lefkovitz (eds), *Shaping Losses: Cultural Memory and the Holocaust* (Urbana and Chicago: University of Illinois Press, 2001). Thanks to the work of Lanzmann, according to Andrzej Żbikowski, a "Rubicon had been crossed" that allowed the question of local bystander intent to become publicly discussed in nations such as Poland. See Andrzej Żbikowski, "The Dispute over the Status of a Witness to the Holocaust: Some Observations on How Research into the Destruction of the Polish Jews and into Polish–Jewish Relations during the Years of Nazi Occupation Has Changed since 1989," in *New Directions in the History of the Jews in the Polish Lands*, 404. See also Erin McGlothlin, Brad Prager, and Markus

Zisselsberger (eds), *The Construction of Testimony: Claude Lanzmann's Shoah and Its Outtakes* (Detroit: Wayne State University Press, 2020).

26 Hannah Pollin-Galay, *Ecologies of Witnessing: Language, Place, and Holocaust Testimony* (New Haven, CT: Yale University Press, 2018); Amit Pinchvevski, "The Audiovisual Unconscious: Media and Trauma in the Video Archive for Holocaust Testimonies," *Critical Inquiry,* vol. 39, no.1 (Autumn 2012): 142–66; Julia Epstein and Lori Lefkovitz, *Shaping Losses: Cultural Memory and the Holocaust*; Caroline Wake, "Regarding the Recording: The Viewer of Video Testimony, the Complexity of Copresence and the Possibility of Tertiary Witnessing," *History and Memory,* vol 25, no. 1 (Spring–Summer 2013): 111–44; Omer Bartov, "The Voice of your Brother's Blood: Reconstructing Genocide on the Local Level," in Norman J. W. Goda (ed.), *Jewish Histories of the Holocaust New Transnational Approaches* (New York and Oxford: Berghahn, 2014), 105–35; Claire Zalc and Tal Bruttmann (eds), *Toward a Microhistory of the Holocaust* (New York and Oxford: Berghahn Books, 2016), 2; Natalia Aleksiun, "On Humanizing Victims and Perpetrators of the Holocaust in Eastern Europe," *Journal of Genocide Research*, vol. 20, no. 4 (2018): 645; Żbikowski, "The Dispute over the Status of a Witness to the Holocaust,", 404.

27 Pim Griffioen and Ron Zeller, *Jodenvervolging in Nederland, Frankrijk en België 1940–1945* (Amsterdam: Boom, 2011); Jan Grabowski, "The Role of 'Bystanders' in the Implementation of the 'Final Solution' in Occupied Poland," *Yad Vashem Studies,* vol. 43, no. 1 (2015): 113–32; Victoria J. Barnett, "The Changing View of the "Bystander," *Utah Law Review*, vol. 2017, no. 4: Article 1; Jared Orsi, "Construction and Contestation: Toward a Unifying Methodology For Borderlands History," *History Compass*, vol. 12 (2014): 433–43; Christina Morina and Krijn Thijs (eds), *Probing the Limits of Categorization: The Bystander in Holocaust History* (New York: Berghahn Books, 2018); Frank Bajohr and Andrea Löw (eds), *The Holocaust and European Societies: Social Processes and Social Dynamics* (Cambridge, UK: Cambridge University Press, 2016); Laura Jokusch, *Collect and Record: Jewish Holocaust Documentation in Early Postwar Europe* (Oxford, UK: Oxford University Press, 2012). Victoria Khiterer (ed.), *The Holocaust: Memories and History* (Newcastle, UK: Cambridge Scholars Publishing, 2014). In the above, see especially Jacqueline Cherepinsky, "Babi Yar: The Absence of the Babi Yar Massacre from Popular Memory," and Eric D. Miller, "The Double–Edged Sword of Remembering the Holocaust: The Case of Jewish Self–Identity." On the Eastern context, see Yitzhak Arad, *The Comprehensive History of the Holocaust: The Soviet Union and the Occupied Territories* (Lincoln, NE: University of Nebraska Press; Jerusalem: Yad Vashem, 2010); Patrick Desbois, *The Holocaust by Bullets: A Priest's Journey to Uncover the Truth Behind the Murder of 1.5 Million Jews* (New York: Palgrave Macmillan, 2008); Yad Vashem, *The Untold Stories: The Murder Sites of the Jews in the Occupied Territories of the Former USSR*; http://www.yadvashem.org/untoldstories/homepage.html; Timothy Snyder, *Bloodlands: Europe between Hitler and Stalin* (New York: Basic Books, 2010). For a critique of these trends, see Thomas Kühne, "Great Men and Large Numbers. Undertheorizing a History of Mass Killing," *Contemporary European History,* vol. 21, no. 2 (2012): 133–43. Michman, "Historiography on the Holocaust in Poland," 390.

**28** David W. Grua, *Surviving Wounded Knee: The Lakotas and the Politics of Memory* (New York: Oxford University Press, 2016); Lisa Blee, "Struggles Over Memory: Indigenous People and Commemorative Culture," *Reviews in American History*, vol. 46, no. 4 (December 2018): 597–604; Lisa Blee, *Framing Chief Leschi: Narratives and the Politics of Historical Justice* (Chapel Hill: University of North Carolina Press, 2014),, 21; Ari Kelman, *A Misplaced Massacre: Struggling over the Memory of Sand Creek* (Cambridge, MA: Harvard University Press, 2013), 136–44. Though as Blee also notes, oral archives may have become influenced by colonial frameworks and assumptions.

**29** See Christine M. DeLucia, *Memory Lands: King Philip's War and the Place of Violence in the Northeast* (New Haven, CT: Yale University Press, 2018), 2–3. See also "Fugitive Collections in New England Indian Country: Indigenous Material Culture and Early American History Making at Ezra Stiles's Yale Museum," *The William and Mary Quarterly*, 3rd ser., vol. 75, no. 1 (January 2018): 109–50; "An 'Indian Fishing Weir' at Musketaquid: Marking Northeastern Indigenous Homelands and Colonial Memoryscapes," *Environmental History*, vol. 23, no. 1 (January 2018): 184–98; "Antiquarian Collecting and the Transits of Indigenous Material Culture: Rethinking 'Indian Relics' and Tribal Histories," *Common-place: The Journal of Early American Life*, vol. 17, no. 2 (Spring 2017); "Locating Kickemuit: Springs, Stone Memorials, and Contested Placemaking in the Northeastern Borderlands," *Early American Studies: An Interdisciplinary Journal, special issue on early American environments*, vol. 13, no. 2 (Spring 2015): 467–502; Lisa Brooks, *The Common Pot: The Recovery of Native Space in the Northeast* (Minneapolis: University of Minnesota Press, 2008); Lisa Brooks, *Our Beloved Kin: A New History of King Philip's War* (New Haven, CT: Yale University Press, 2019). See also the digital companion to Brooks' book at https://ourbelovedkin.com/awikhigan/about?path=index.

**30** On Indigenous regionalism in survivor oral testimony, see also Brian Calliou, "Methodology for Recording Oral Histories in the Aboriginal Community," *Native Studies Review,* vol. 15, no. 1 (2004): 73–105; Angela Cavender Wilson, "Grandmother to Granddaughter: Generations of Oral History in a Dakota Family," *American Indian Quarterly,* vol. 20, no. 1 (Winter 1996): 7–13. Recent Indigenous discussions of local space and memory might speak to developing insights on Holocaust memory and spatial categories of analysis, particularly through new techniques in digital humanities. See for example the contributions of Waitman Wade Beorn and others at the Holocaust Geographies Collaborative, at https://holocaustgeographies.org/

**31** On definitions of intent in these strict ways, see for example A. Dirk Moses, "The Holocaust and Genocide," 546.

**32** Lilian Friedberg, "Dare to Compare: Americanizing the Holocaust," *The American Indian Quarterly,* vol. 24, no. 3 (Summer 2000): 359; Jeffrey Ostler, "Genocide and American Indian History," *Oxford Research Encyclopedia of American History*, 2015, http://oxfordre.com/americanhistory/view/10.1093/acrefore/9780199329175.001.0001/acrefore-9780199329175-e-3; Churchill, *A Little Matter of Genocide,* 154–56; Barbara Mann, *The Tainted Gift: The Disease Method of Frontier Expansion* (Santa Barbara, CA: ABC CLIO,

2009), 1–18, 43–81. See also Philip Ranlet, "The British, the Indians, and Smallpox: What Actually Happened at Fort Pitt in 1763?," *Pennsylvania History: A Journal of Mid-Atlantic Studies,* vol. 67, no. 3, (Summer 2000): 427–41.

33 See Ostler, "Genocide and American Indian History,"; Guenter Lewy, "Were American Indians the Victims of Genocide?," *Commentary* (September 2004), 55–63.

34 Ostler, "Genocide and American Indian History,"; "Report of Brigadier General Scott, June 28, 1791," *American State Papers: Indian Affairs,* 1: 129–32; Michael Mann, *The Dark Side of Democracy: Explaining Ethnic Cleansing* (Cambridge, UK: Cambridge University Press, 2005); A. Dirk Moses, "An Antipodean Genocide? The Origins of the Genocidal Moment in the Colonization of Australia," *Journal of Genocide Research,* vol. 2 (2000): 89–106; Rensink, "Genocide of Native Americans," 20–1; Paul Andrew Hutton, *Phil Sheridan and His Army* (Lincoln: University of Nebraska Press, 1985), 180; Grua, *Surviving Wounded Knee*, 49; Blee, "Struggles Over Memory," 597–604.

35 Benjamin Madley, "California's Yuki Indians: Defining Genocide in Native American History," *Western Historical Quarterly,* vol. 39 (Autumn 2008): 309; Albert L. Hurtado, *Indian Survival on the California Frontier* (New Haven, CT: Yale University Press, 1988), 1, 136, 144, 194, 212. In California, according to Ostler, "[d]irect killing was a significant factor and may have explained the majority of deaths for some nations, such as the Yukis and Yanas" even while others died from the effects of societal disruption and disease (mortality outcomes that were still related to settler interventions). See Ostler, "Genocide and American Indian History,"; Frank H. Baumgardner, *Killing for Land in Early California: Indian Blood at Round Valley, 1856–1863* (New York: Algora Publishing, 2005), 34; Lynwood Carranco and Estle Beard, *Genocide and Vendetta: The Round Valley Wars of Northern California* (Norman: University of Oklahoma Press, 1981); Jack Norton, *When Our Worlds Cried: Genocide in Northwestern California* (San Francisco: Indian Historian Press, 1979), x, 107.

36 See Ostler, "Genocide and American Indian History,"; Gary Clayton Anderson, *The Conquest of Texas: Ethnic Cleansing in the Promises Land, 1820–1875* (Norman: University of Oklahoma Press, 2005); Brenden Rensink, "The Sand Creek Phenomenon: The Complexity and Difficulty of Undertaking a Comparative Study of Genocide vis-à-vis the North American West," *Genocide Studies and Prevention: An International Journal,* vol. 4, no. 1 (Spring 2009): 9–27.

37 At the USHMM, for example, Geoffrey Megargee and Martin Dean have suggested the need to reassess the role of bloody chaos in Eastern frontiers, which was primed by Nazi propaganda, but also reflected murderous chauvinism closer to home. See Eric Lichtblau, "The Holocaust Just Got More Shocking," *New York Times*, March 1, 2013, https://www.nytimes.com/2013/03/03/sunday-review/the-holocaust-just-got-more-shocking.html.

38 Cited in Dee Brown, *Bury My Heart at Wounded Knee* (New York: Pan Macmillan, 1970), 86–7. See the discussion of these statements in Rensink,

"Genocide of Native Americans: Historical Facts and Historiographic Debates," 19.

39 See Giorgio Agamben, *Homo Sacer: Sovereign Power and Bare Life*, trans. Daniel Heller-Roazen (Palo Alto, CA: Stanford University Press, 1998), 114.

40 See Friedberg, "Dare to Compare," 363. See also Stannard, *American Holocaust,* x.

41 Carroll P. Kakel, III, *The American West and the Nazi East: A Comparative and Interpretive Perspective* (New York: Palgrave Macmillan, 2011), 22, 34, 44, 59–60, 128 Thomas Kühne, "Colonialism and the Holocaust: Continuities, Causations, and Complexities," *Journal of Genocide Research*, vol. 15, no. 3 (2013): 347. See also Robert F. Berkhofer, Jr., *The White Man's Indian: Images of The American Indian from Columbus to the Present* (New York: Vintage Books, 1978).

42 Ostler, "Genocide and American Indian History"; Thomas Kühne, "Colonialism and the Holocaust," 343; Adam Jones, *Genocide: A Comprehensive Introduction* (New York: Routledge, 2006), 38, 125–6; Alex Alvarez, *Governments, Citizens, and Genocide: A Comparative and Interdisciplinary Approach* (Bloomington: Indiana University Press, 2001), 52; A. Dirk Moses, "Genocide and Settler Society in Australian History," in A. Dirk Moses, ed., *Genocide and Settler Society: Frontier Violence and Stolen Indigenous Children in Australian History* (New York: Berghahn, 2004), 3–48; Tony Barta, "Relations of Genocide: Land and Lives in the Colonization of Australia," in Isidor Wallimann and Michael N. Dobkowski (eds), *Genocide and the Modern Age: Etiology and Case Studies of Mass Death* (New York: Greenwood Press, 1987), 237–51; Patrick Wolfe, "Settler Colonialism and the Elimination of the Native," 387–409.

43 On "Structural Intent" as societally induced frameworks that pre-figure genocide, see Thomas Simon, *The Laws of Genocide: Prescriptions for a Just World* (Westport, CT: Praeger Security International, 2007), 73; A. Dirk Moses, "The Holocaust and Genocide," 546; "Introduction," in *Genocide and the Modern Age Etiology and Case Studies of Mass Death*, xvi.

44 Walter Laqueur, "In the Ghettos: Starvation and Disease," in Walter Laqueur (ed.), *The Holocaust Encyclopedia* (New Haven, CT: Yale University Press, 2001), 269–71; S. G. Massry and M. Smogorzewski, "The Hunger Disease of the Warsaw Ghetto," *American Journal of Nephrology,* vol. 22 (2002): 197–201.

45 See Michael Shermer and Alex Grobman, *Denying History: Who Says the Holocaust Never Happened and Why Do They Say It?* (rev. ed., Berkeley, CA: University of California Press, 2009), 100; Ted Gottfried, *Deniers of the Holocaust: Who They Are, What They Do, Why They Do It* (Brookfield, CT: Twenty-First Century Books, 2001), 39–41; Friedberg, "Dare to Compare," 359; Lord Jeffrey Amherst, cited in Churchill, *Matter of Genocide*, 154; Stannard, *American Holocaust,* xii.

46 On the contingency of disease mortality, and attempts to respond to constraints imposed by Nazis, see the essays in Michael A. Grodin (ed.), *Jewish Medical Resistance in the Holocaust* (New York and Oxford: Berghahn Books, 2014). On Nazi "annihilation through work," see Donald Bloxham, "Jewish Slave Labour and its Relationship to the 'Final Solution,'" in John K. Roth and

Elisabeth Maxwell (eds), *Remembering for the Future: The Holocaust in an Age of Genocide* (New York: Palgrave Macmillan, 2001), 163–86; Wolf Gruner, *Jewish Forced Labor Under the Nazis: Economic Needs and Racial Aims, 1938–1944* (New York: Cambridge University Press, 2006); Shmuel Krakowski, "Forced Labor," in *The Holocaust Encyclopedia*, 210–13; Michael Thad Allen, *The Business of Genocide: The SS, Slave Labor, and the Concentration Camps* (Chapel Hill: University of North Carolina Press, 2002).

47 See Michael Shermer and Alex Grobman, *Denying History: Who Says the Holocaust Never Happened and Why Do They Say It?* (rev. ed., Berkeley: University of California Press, 2009), 100; Ted Gottfried, *Deniers of the Holocaust*, 39–41; Robbie Ethridge and Sherie M. Shuck-Hall (eds), *Mapping the Mississippian Shatter Zone: The Colonial Indian Slave Trade and Regional Instability in the American South* (Lincoln: University of Nebraska Press, 2009), 1–62. For a recent discussion of the question and representation of Indigenous agency in the "colonial" North American world, see Joshua Reid, "AHR Forum Introduction: Indigenous Agency and Colonial Law," *American Historical Review*, vol. 124, no. 1 (February 2019): 20–7. Reid has shown how in the Pacific Northwest, Indigenous groups were able to adapt technological and commercial cultures to withstand the interventions of external Euro-American settler colonialism. See Joshua L. Reid, *The Sea Is My Country: The Maritime World of the Makahs* (New Haven, CT: Yale University Press, 2015).

48 Ostler, "Genocide and American Indian History"; Alfred A. Cave, *The Pequot War* (Amherst: University of Massachusetts Press, 1996), 1–7; John S. Marr and John T. Cathey, "New Hypothesis for Cause of Epidemic among Native Americans, New England, 1616–1619," *Emerging Infectious Diseases*, vol. 16 (February 2012): 281–6; Jones, *Rationalizing Epidemics*, 29–31; Russell Thornton, *American Indian Holocaust and Survival*, 71.

49 Ostler, "Genocide and American Indian History."

50 Ostler, "Genocide and American Indian History"; Paul Kelton, *Epidemics and Enslavement: Biological Catastrophe in the Native Southeast, 1492–1715* (Lincoln, NE: University of Nebraska Press, 2007).; Stannard, *American Holocaust*, xii.

51 As Whitt and Clark argue, the "genocidal tendencies" in settler-colonialism "may manifest themselves at a particular historical moment, then lapse into abeyance," before taking on new forms as settler colonial frameworks structurally limit population vitality in the medium to long term. See Whitt and Clarke, *North American Genocides*, 54.

52 Laurelyn Whitt and Alan W. Clarke, *North American Genocides: Indigenous Nations, Settler Colonialism, and International Law* (Cambridge: Cambridge University Press, 2019), 4; Jeffrey Ostler, "Locating Settler Colonialism in Early American History," *The William and Mary Quarterly*, vol. 76, no. 3 (July 2019): 443–50; Patrick Wolfe, "Structure and Event," in A Dirk Moses (ed.), *Empire, Colony, Genocide*, 387–8; Lorenzo Veracini, *Settler Colonialism: A Theoretical Overview* (New York: Palgrave Macmillan, 2010), vii; Circa Sturm, "Reflections on the Anthropology of Sovereignty and Settler Colonialism," 340–2, cited in Whitt and Clark, *North American Genocide*, 47.

53 Alfred A. Cave, *Lethal Encounters: Englishmen and Indians in Colonial Virginia* (Santa Barbara, CA : Praeger, 2011), xiii, xiiii, 170; Whitt and Clarke, *North American Genocides*, 55; A. D. Moses, "Conceptual Blockages and Definitional Dilemmas In the "'Racial Century'": Genocides of Indigenous Peoples and the Holocaust," *Patterns of Prejudice*, vol. 36, no. 4 (2002): 7, 27.

54 Whitt and Clarke, *North American Genocides*, 62. See especially Laurelyn Whitt, *Science, Colonialism and Indigenous Peoples: The Cultural Politics of Law and Knowledge* (Cambridge, UK: Cambridge University Press, 2009), chapter 1 and chapter 2.

55 Leanna Betasamosake Simpson, "As We Have Always Done: Indigenous Freedom Through Radical Resistance," (2017), cited in Whitt and Clarke, *North American Genocides*, 62. "Within such knowledge systems," according to Whitt and Clarke, "knowledge is always knowledge of relations; it is the relations that hold between entities and processes that are basic, not the entities and processes themselves." See also Christopher Powell and Julia Peristerakis, "Genocide in Canada: A Relational View," in *Colonial Genocide in Indigenous North America*, 71

56 Glen Coulthard, *Red Skin, White Masks: Rejecting the Colonial Politics of Recognition* (Minneapolis: University of Minnesota Press, 2014), 61, 13.

57 Great Britain, *Report from the Select Committee on Aborigines (British Settlements) with Minutes of Evidence, Appendix and Index 5* (1837) at 5 and 9, https://catalog.hathitrust.org/Record/008589606 https://catalog.hathitrust.org/Record/008589606. See also Whitt and Clarke, *North American Genocides*, 45.

58 On differences see, for example, Andrew Woolford and Jeff Benvenuto, "Canada and Colonial Genocide," *Journal of Genocide Research*, vol. 17, no. 4 (2015): 379–80.

59 Robert A. Williams, *Linking Arms Together: American Indian Treaty Visions of Law & Peace*, 1600–1800 (New York and Oxford: Oxford University Press, 1997); Matthew Wildcat, "Fearing Social and Cultural Death: Genocide and Elimination in Settler Colonial Canada—An Indigenous Perspective," *Journal of Genocide Research*, vol. 17, no. 4 (2015): 391–3; Whitt and Clarke, *North American Genocides*, 42–3, 53–4; Whitt and Clarke, *North American Genocides*, 42–3; Dorota Glowacka, "'Never Forget,'" 409.

60 On the paradigmatic importance of the Armenian genocide for Lemkin, see V. N. Dadrian, "The Historical and Legal Interconnections between the Armenian Genocide and the Jewish Holocaust," *Yale Joumal or International Law*, vol. 23, no. 2 (1998): 504; A. Dirk Moses, "The Holocaust and Genocide," in Dan Stone (ed.), *The Historiography of the Holocaust* (Basingstoke, UK: Palgrave MacMillan, 2004), 543.

61 Anna-Vera Sullam Calimani, "A Name for Extermination," *The Modern Language Review*, vol. 94, no. 4 (October 1999): 983

62 On the coining of the term "genocide" in 1944 by Raphael Lemkin, see Raphael Lemkin, *Axis Rule in Occupied Europe: Laws of Occupation, Analysis of Government, Proposals for Redress* (Washington, D.C.: Carnegie Endowment for International Peace, Division of International Law, 1944), xi–xii, chap. 9. For the convention itself, see Convention on the Prevention

and Punishment of the Crime of Genocide, Adopted by the General Assembly of the United Nations on 9 December 1948, United Nations—Treaty Series, vol. 78, no. 1021: 280.

63 A. Dirk Moses, "Lemkin, Culture, and the Concept of Genocide," in *The Oxford Handbook of Genocide Studies*, 19; Raphael Lemkin, *Axis Rule in Occupied Europe* (Washington, DC: Carnegie Council, 1944), 80 n.3, cited in A. Dirk Moses, "The Holocaust and World History: Raphael Lemkin and Comparative Methodology," in Dan Stone, ed., *The Holocaust and Historical Methodology* (New York and Oxford: Berghahn Books, 2012), 278; John Cooper, *Raphael Lemkin and the Struggle for the Genocide Convention* (Basingstoke, UK: Palgrave Macmillan, 2008), 54. Citations from Lemkin in A. Dirk Moses, "Genocide," *Australian Humanities Review*, vol. 55 (November 2013): 33. See also Yehuda Bauer, "The Place of the Holocaust in History," *Holocaust and Genocide Studies,* vol. 2 (1987): 211–15.

64 According to Moses, for "some Holocaust specialists, his definition of genocide is too broad, illegitimately associating the Holocaust with other crimes by trivializing the former and miscategorizing the latter." See Moses, "Lemkin, Culture, and the Concept of Genocide," 21. See also Yehuda Bauer, "The Place of the Holocaust in History," 211–15. According to Moses, "The implicit charge that he neglected the metahistorical significance of the Holocaust is also based on the proposition that he did not fully understand the ambition of the Nazi genocide of Jews when he coined the term genocide." See A. Dirk Moses, "Genocide," *Australian Humanities Review*, vol. 55 (November 2013): 32. On this charge, see also John Cooper, *Raphael Lemkin and the Struggle for the Genocide Convention*, 10, 23, 58–9.

65 Donna-Lee Frieze has begun important work on Lemkin's correspondence in the Papers at New York Public Library. See also Donna Lee Frieze (ed.), *Totally Unofficial: The Autobiography of Raphael Lemkin* (New Haven: Yale University Press, 2013), xxvi–vii.

66 Lemkin, "Spain Colonial Genocide," Folder 12, cited in Mcdonnell and Moses, "Raphael Lemkin as Historian of Genocide in the Americas," *Journal of Genocide,* vol. 7, no. 4 (December 2005): 501; Lemkin, "Proposal," Cited in A. Dirk Moses, "Genocide," *Australian Humanities Review*, vol. 55 (November 2013): 37.

67 Mcdonnell and Moses, "Raphael Lemkin as Historian of Genocide in the Americas," 516–18; David E. Stannard, "Disease and Infertility: A New Look at the Demographic Collapse of Native Populations in the Wake of Western Contact," *Journal of American Studies*, vol. 24, no. 3 (1990): 325–50. Las Casas's neglect of disease has also been noted in David Noble Cook and W. George Lovell (eds), *"Secret Judgments of God": Old World Disease in Colonial Spanish America* (Norman: University of Oklahoma Press, 1991), 241. Lemkin, according to Jürgen Zimmerer, was "the progenitor of the school of structural genocide." See Jürgen Zimmerer, "Foreword," *International Journal of Human Rights,* vol. 18 (2004): 263–4.

68 Thomas M. Butcher, "A 'Synchronized Attack': On Raphael Lemkin's Holistic Conception of Genocide," *Journal of Genocide Research*, vol 15, no. 3 (2013): 253.

69 This is connected to "Physical Genocide, by which is meant killing members of the targeted group(s)" and "Biological Genocide, by which is meant the prevention of births within the target group(s) . . . ". See Churchill, *A Little Matter of Genocide*, 432–4. See also David Moshman, "Conceptual constraints on thinking about genocide," *Journal of Genocide Research*, vol. 3, no. 3 (2001): 438–9.

70 Donald W. Beachler, *The Genocide Debate: Politicians, Academics, and Victims* (New York: Palgrave Macmillan, 2011), 84; A. Dirk Moses, "Lemkin, Culture, and the Concept of Genocide," in Donald Bloxham and A. Dirk Moses (eds), *The Oxford Handbook of Genocide Studies* (Oxford, UK: Oxford University Press, 2010), 21; A. Dirk Moses, "The Holocaust and Genocide," in Dan Stone (ed.), *The Historiography of the Holocaust* (Basingstoke, UK: Palgrave Macmillan, 2004), 541.

71 A. Dirk Moses, "Lemkin, Culture, and the Concept of Genocide," 21; A. Dirk Moses, "The Holocaust and Genocide," 541; Raphael Lemkin, *Axis Rule in Occupied Europe*, 79; Michael A. McDonnell and A. Dirk Moses, "Raphael Lemkin as historian of genocide in the Americas," *Journal of Genocide*, vol. 7, no. 4 (December 2005): 514. See also Raphael Lemkin, "Genocide as a Crime under International Law", *American Journal of International Law* 41:1 (1947), 147; Caroline Fournet, *The Crime of Destruction and the Law of Genocide: Their Impact on Collective Memory* (Aldershot: Ashgate, 2007); Churchill, *A Little Matter of Genocide*, 432.

72 John Docker, "Raphael Lemkin's History of Genocide and Colonialism," Paper delivered to U.S. Holocaust Memorial Museum, February 26, 2004), https://www.ushmm.org/m/pdfs/20040316-docker-lemkin.pdf; Lemkin, "Genocide: A Modern Crime," 39–43, cited in Moses, "The Holocaust and Genocide," 539; Raphael Lemkin, "Totally Unofficial Man," in Samuel Totten and Steven Leonard Jacobs (eds), *Pioneers of Genocide Studies* (New York: Routledge, 2002), 393. See also Leora Bilsky and Rachel Klagsbrun, "The Return of Cultural Genocide?," *European Journal of International Law*, vol. 29, no. 2 (May 2018): 373–96.

73 See also Jürgen Zimmerer and Dominik J. Schaller (eds), *The Origins of Genocide: Raphael Lemkin as a Historian of Mass Violence* (Milton, UK: Routledge, 2009).

74 Lindsey Kingston, "The Destruction of Identity: Cultural Genocide and Indigenous Peoples," *Journal of Human Rights*, vol. 14, no. (2015): 63–83; David B. MacDonald, "Indigenous Genocide and Perceptions of the Holocaust in Canada," in S. Gigliotti and H. Earl (eds), *The Wiley Companion to the Holocaust* (London: Wiley-Blackwell, 2020): 577–97; Moses, "The Holocaust and Genocide," 535. On Lemkin and the connections between biological loss and cultural loss, see A. Dirk Moses, "Lemkin, Culture, and the Concept of Genocide," in Donald Bloxham and A. Dirk Moses (eds), *The Oxford Handbook of Genocide Studies* (Oxford, UK: Oxford University Press, 2010), 21. On the same connection from the perspective of Indigenous Studies, see Kingston, "The Destruction of Identity: Cultural Genocide and Indigenous Peoples." On cultural genocide and biological genocide from a demographic perspective, see Leora Bilsky and Rachel Klagsbrun, "The Return of Cultural

Genocide?," 373–96; Damien Short, "Cultural Genocide and Indigenous Peoples: A sociological Approach," *The International Journal of Human Rights*, vol. 14, no. 6 (2010): 833–48; Jeff Benvenuto, "What Does Genocide Produce? The Semantic Field of Genocide, Cultural Genocide, and Ethnocide in Indigenous Rights Discourse," *Genocide Studies and Prevention: An International Journal*, vol. 9, no. 2: (2015): 26–40; Douglas Irvin-Erickson, "Genocide, the 'Family of Mind' and the Romantic Signature of Raphael Lemkin," *Journal of Genocide Research,* no. 15 (2013): 273, 278. On the UN definition in David MacDonald, "First Nations, Residential Schools, and the Americanization of the Holocaust: Rewriting Indigenous History in the United States and Canada," *Canadian Journal of Political Science/Revue canadienne de science politique*, vol. 40, no. 4 (December 2007): 1003.

75 For Emerson's statement on Language as Fossil Poetry, and the association with the evolution of national identity, see Tony Crowley, *Language in History: Theories and Texts* (London and New York: Routledge, 1996), 154.

76 Renée Levine Melammed, *An Ode to Salonika The Ladino Verses of Bouena Sarfatty* (Bloomington, Indiana University Press, 2013).

77 William A. Geiger, "From the Logic of Elimination to the Logic of the Gift: Towards a Decolonial Theory of Tlingit Language Revitalization," *Open Linguistics*, vol. 3, no. 1 (2017): 219–35; Lance Twitchell, *Haa Wsineix̲ Haa Yoo X̲'atángi, Our Language Saved Us: A Guidebook for Learning the Tlingit Language* (Juneau, AK: Goldbelt Heritage Foundation and Alaska Native Language Center, 2016), http://tlingitlanguage.com/wp-content/uploads/2015/09/haa-wsineixh-1.pdf (11.5.2016).

78 On Yiddish linguistic destruction, and potential renewal, see Jan Schwarz, *Survivors and Exiles: Yiddish Culture after the Holocaust* (Detroit, MI: Wayne State University Press, 2015). See also the important work carried out by Suzan Shown Harjo on the preservation of Indigenous languages: "Native Languages Archives Repository Project: Reference Guide: American Indian Higher Education Consortium, April 13, 2015, http://www.aihec.org/our-stories/docs/NativeLanguagePreservationReferenceGuide.pdf.

79 Dirk Moses, "Coming to Terms with Genocidal Pasts in a Comparative Perspective," *Aboriginal History* 25, no. 1 (2001): 106; Robert Manne, "In Denial: The Stolen Generations and the Right," *Australian Quarterly* Essay 1 (2001): 27; Paul Bartropp, "The Holocaust, the Aborigines and the bureaucracy of destruction: An Australian dimension of genocide," *Journal of Genocide Research*, vol. 3, no. 1 (2001): 77; Colin Tatz, "Confronting Australian Genocide," *Aboriginal History* 25, no. 1 (2001): 18–19; Dirk Moses, "Coming to Terms with Genocidal Pasts in a Comparative Perspective," 95–8; MacDonald, "First Nations, Residential Schools, and the Americanization of the Holocaust," 1003; Isabel C. Barrows (ed.), *Proceedings of the National Conference of Charities and Correction at the Nineteenth Annual Session Held in Denver, Col., June 23–29, 1892* (Boston: George H. Ellis, 1892), 4; Ward Churchill, *Kill the Indian, Save the Man: The Genocidal Impact of American Indian Residential Schools* (San Francisco: City Lights, 2004); David Wallace Adams, *Education for Extinction: American Indians and the Boarding School Experience, 1875–1928* (Lawrence: University of Kansas Press, 1995).

80 Andrew Woolford, "Nodal Repair and Networks of Destruction: Residential Schools, Colonial Genocide, and Redress in Canada," *Settler Colonial Studies*, vol. 3, no. 1 (2013): 72–3; MacDonald, "Indigenous Genocide and Perceptions of the Holocaust in Canada," 579; David B. MacDonald, "Genocide in the Indian Residential Schools: Canadian History Through the Lens of the UN Genocide Convention," in Andrew Woolford, Jeff Benvenuto, and Alexander Laban Linton (eds), *Colonial Genocide in Indigenous North America* (Durham: Duke University Press, 2014), 465–6; David B. MacDonald and Graham Hudson, "Contextualizing Aboriginal Residential Schools in Canada: How International and Domestic Law Can Help Us Interpret Genocide Claims," *Canadian Journal of Political Science*, no. 45 (2012): 427–49; TRC Canada, Honouring the Truth, Reconciling the Future: Summary of the Final Report of the Truth and Reconciliation Commission of Canada (Winnipeg: Truth and Reconciliation Commission of Canada (2015); Jim Miller, *Lethal Legacy: Current Native Controversies in Canada* (Toronto: McClelland & Stewart, 2004), 35; Christopher Powell and Julia Peristerakis, "Genocide in Canada: A Relational View," in *Colonial Genocide in Indigenous North America*, 71; Andrew Woolford, "Ontological Destruction: Genocide and Canadian Aboriginal Peoples," *Genocide Studies & Prevention*, vol. 4 (2009): 81–97.

81 MacDonald, "Genocide in the Indian Residential Schools: Canadian History Through the Lens of the UN Genocide Convention," 465–6; David B. MacDonald and Graham Hudson, "Contextualizing Aboriginal Residential Schools in Canada,"427–49; TRC Canada, *Honouring the Truth, Reconciling the Future: Summary of the Final Report of the Truth and Reconciliation Commission of Canada* (Winnipeg: Truth and Reconciliation Commission of Canada, 2015), 1, 264. See the discussion of the "convoluted" statement in MacDonald, "Indigenous Genocide and Perceptions of the Holocaust in Canada," 587. On the Australian work that has influenced North American discussions, see Ann Curthoys and John Docker, "Introduction: Genocide: Definitions, questions, settler-colonies," *Aboriginal History*, vol. 25 (2001): 1. These broader definitions contributed to the Australian Human Rights Commission's 1997 report "Bringing Them Home" in its use of the term genocide to describe the effects on the stolen generation.

82 Whitt and Clarke, *North American Genocides*, 63; Andrea Smith, *Conquest: Sexual Violence and American Indian Genocide* (Brooklyn, NY: South End Press, 2005), 122.

83 Dean Neu and Richard Therrien, *Accounting for Genocide: Canada's Bureaucratic Assault on Aboriginal People* (Blackpoint, Nova Scotia: Fernwood Publishing, 2003), 5, 13, 15, 100. See the discussion of these statements in Whitt and Clarke, *North American Genocides*, 48. See also David B. MacDonald, ""Canada's History War: Indigenous Genocide and Public Memory in the United States, Australia, and Canada," *Journal of Genocide Research*, vol. 17, no. 4 (2015): 411–31.

84 MacDonald, "First Nations, Residential Schools, and the Americanization of the Holocaust," 1004; David B. MacDonald, *The Sleeping Giant Awakens: Genocide, Indian Residential Schools, and the Challenge of Conciliation* (Toronto: University of Toronto Press, 2019); Kevin Annett, "Program of the

Truth Commission into Genocide in Canada Approved and Ratified May 8, 2002," http:00canadiangenocide.nativeweb.org0program.html; *~TCGC, 2001: 32~TCGC, 2001: 37–8;* Neu and Therrien, *Accounting for Genocide*, 14–15, 22; Phil Fontaine and Bernie Faber, "What Canada Committed against First Nations Was Genocide. The UN Should Recognize It," *Globe and Mail* (Toronto), October 14, 2013, cited in Dorota Glowacka, ""Never Forget": Intersecting Memories of the Holocaust and the Settler Colonial Genocide in Canada," 398.

85 Dorota Glowacka, "Sexual Violence against Men and Boys during the Holocaust: A Genealogy of (Not-So-Silent) Silence," *German History*, vol. 38, no. 4 (December 2020): 8–9; Nate Leipciger, *The Weight of Freedom* (Toronto: The Azrieli Foundation, 2015), 260.

86 MacDonald, "Indigenous Genocide and Perceptions of the Holocaust in Canada," 585.

## Chapter Two "Metaphysical Jew Hatred" and the "Metaphysics of Indian-hating."

1 Much conceptual slippage, according to A. Dirk Moses, offers a "source of postwar morality . . . both unique and universal" to frame "Western" humanitarianism in public approaches to Holocaust memory in Europe and North America. Such a rhetorical formulation underlies a degree of triumphalism that belies the universalistic language it promotes: the "West is culturally superior because memory of the Holocaust in the West led to the criminalization of genocide in International law and to the field of genocide studies itself." By publicly confronting a horrific event that took place in Europe—the continent where Western civilization is said to have emerged—Europeans and Euro-Americans display their special cultural capacity to comprehend universal human concerns and to apply them to the experiences of people outside their cultural realm. See A. Dirk Moses, "Anxieties in Holocaust and Genocide Studies," in Claudio Fogu, Wulf Kansteiner, and Todd Presner (eds), *Probing the Ethics of. Holocaust Culture* (Cambridge, MA: Harvard University Press, 2016), 336. See also Stef Craps, "Holocaust Literature: Comparative Perspectives," in Jenni Adams (ed.), *The Bloomsbury Companion to Holocaust Literature* (London: Bloomsbury Academic, 2014), 203–04.

2 For an introduction to some of these trends, see A. Dirk Moses, "Conceptual Blockages and Definitional Dilemmas in the 'Racial Century': Genocides of Indigenous Peoples and the Holocaust", *Patterns of Prejudice*, vol. 36, no. 2 (2007): 7–36.

3 See, for example, Andrew Woolford, Jeff Benvenuto, and Alexander Laban Hinton (eds), *Colonial Genocide in Indigenous North America* (Chapel Hill, NC: Duke University Press, 2014); Laurelyn Whitt and Alan W. Clarke, *North American Genocides: Indigenous Nations, Settler Colonialism, and International Law* (Cambridge, UK: Cambridge University Press, 2019); Matthew Wildcat, "Fearing Social and Cultural Death: Genocide and

Elimination in Settler Colonial Canada—An Indigenous Perspective," *Journal of Genocide Research,* vol. 17, no. 4 (2015): 391–409. Frederick E. Hoxie, "Retrieving the Red Continent: Settler Colonialism and the History of American Indians in the US," *Ethnic and Racial Studies,* vol. 31 (2008): 1153–67; Patrick Wolfe, "Corpus Nullius: The Exception of Indians and Other Aliens in US Constitutional Discourse," *Postcolonial Studies*, vol. 10 (2007): 127–51; Patrick Wolfe, "After the Frontier: Separation and Absorption in US Indian Policy," *Settler Colonial Studies,* vol. 1 (2011): 13–51.

4 See Carrol P. Kakel, III, *The American West and the Nazi East: A Comparative and Interpretive Perspective* (Basingstoke, UK: Palgrave Macmillan, 2011). See also Edward B. Westermann, *Hitler's Ostkrieg and the Indian Wars: Comparing Genocide and Conquest* (Norman: University of Oklahoma Press, 2016); James Q. Whitman, *Hitler's American Model: The United States and the Making of Nazi Race Law* (Princeton, NJ: Princeton University Press, 2018). For a broader overview of this trend, see Thomas Kühne, "Colonialism and the Holocaust: Continuities, Causations, and Complexities," *Journal of Genocide Research*, vol. 15, no. 3 (2013): 347–52; Jens-Uwe Guettel, "The US Frontier as Rationale For the Nazi East? Settler Colonialism and Genocide in Nazi-occupied Eastern Europe and the American West," *Journal of Genocide Research*, vol. 15, no. 4 (2013): 415.

5 On the potential link between German imperialism and the Holocaust, see Christopher R. Browning, "Contextualizing the Holocaust: Modernization, Modernity, Colonialism, and Genocide," in Michael Meng and Adar R. Seipp (eds), *Modern Germany in Transatlantic Perspective* (New York, Berghahn Books, 2017), 73–95; Richard J. Evans, *The Third Reich in History and Memory* (New York: Oxford University Press, 2015), 355–400; Mark Mazower, *Hitler's Empire: Nazi Rule in Occupied Europe* (London: Allen Lane, 2008), 581–8; Dirk Moses, "Empire, Colony, Genocide: Keywords and the Philosophy of History," in A. D. Moses (ed.), *Empire, Colony, Genocide: Conquest, Occupation, and Subaltern Resistance in World History* (New York: Berghahn Books, 2008), 3–54; Aimé Césaire, *Discourse on Colonialism* (New York: Monthly Review Press, 2000); Hannah Arendt, *The Origins of Totalitarianism* (New York: Harcourt Brace, 1951); Stef Craps et al., "Decolonizing Trauma Studies Round-Table Discussion," *Humanities,* vol. 4 (2015), 909–10. On the critique of the colonial turn in Holocaust history, see A. Dirk Moses has summarized the anxious response of Holocaust scholars to the colonial turn in A. Dirk Moses, "Anxieties in Holocaust and Genocide Studies," in Claudio Fogu, Wulf Kansteiner, and Todd Presner (eds), *Probing the Ethics of Holocaust Culture* (Cambridge, MA: Harvard University Press, 2016), 340–5; Tom Lawson, "Coming to Terms with the Past: Reading and Writing Colonial Genocide in the Shadow of the Holocaust," *Holocaust Studies: A Journal of Culture and History,* vol. 20, 1–2 (2014): 129–56; David Furber and Wendy Lower, "Colonialism and Genocide in Nazi-occupied Poland and Ukraine," in *Empire, Colony, Genocide*, 376–7; Kühne, "Colonialism and the Holocaust," 354; Roberta Pergher et al., "The Holocaust: A Colonial Genocide? A Scholars' Forum," *Dapim: Studies on the Holocaust,* vol. 27, no. 1 (2013), 42–9; Raphael Ahren, "Academics Go to War over the Study of Mass Killings," *The Times of Israel*, June 26, 2016, https://

www.timesofisrael.com/academics-go-to-war-over-the-study-of-mass-killings/; Omer Bartov, "The Holocaust as Genocide: Experiential Uniqueness and Integrated History," in *Probing the Ethics of Holocaust Culture;* Omer Bartov, "Genocide and the Holocaust: Arguments over History and Politics," in *Lessons and Legacies*, vol. XI, eds. Karl Schleunes and Hilary Earl (Evanston: Northwestern University Press, 2014), 15; Thomas Kühne, "Colonialism and the Holocaust. Continuities, Causations, and Complexities," *Journal of Genocide Research*, vol. 15, no. 3 (2013): 354; Christian S. Davis, *Colonialism, Antisemitism, and Germans of Jewish Descent in Imperial Germany* (Ann Arbor: University of Michigan Press, 2012), 250–1. According to Davis, "colonialism complemented the antisemitic movement at the same time that it partly undermined it."

6 See A. D. Moses, "Conceptual Blockages and Definitional Dilemmas in the "Racial Century": Genocides of Indigenous Peoples and the Holocaust," *Patterns of Prejudice*, vol. 36, no. 4 (2002): 7–36; Jens-Uwe Guettel, "Review of Kakel, The American West and the Nazi East," *Journal of Genocide Research*, vol. 14, nos. 3/4 (2012): 514–19. Guettel, *German Expansionism, Imperial Liberalism, and the United States, 1776–1945* (Cambridge, UK: Cambridge University Press, 2013), 16, 19.

7 See Guettel, "The US Frontier as Rationale for the Nazi East?," 415; Adolf Hitler, *Hitler's Table Talk, 1941–1944* (New York: Enigma Books, 2008), 55, 469 (October 17, 1941, and August 8, 1942); Jens-Uwe Guettel, "Review of Kakel," 514–19; Guettel, *German Expansionism,* 19, 16. See also Klaus P. Fischer, *Hitler and America* (Philadelphia: University of Pennsylvania Press, 2011); Matthew P. Fitzpatrick, *Liberal Imperialism in Germany: Expansionism and Nationalism, 1848–1884* (New York: Berghahn Books, 2008).

8 See Mark Roseman, "National Socialism and the End of Modernity," *The American Historical Review*, vol. 116, no. 3 (June 2011): 688–701; Helmut Walser Smith, "When the Sonderweg Debate Left Us," *German Studies Review,* vol. 31, no. 2 (2008): 225–40; Jürgen Kocka, "Asymmetrical Historical Comparison: The Case of the German Sonderweg," *History and Theory,* vol. 38, no. 1 (1999): 40–51; Matthew P. Fitzpatrick, "The Pre-History of the Holocaust? The Sonderweg and Historikerstreit Debates and the Abject Colonial Past," *Central European History,* vol. 41, no. 3 (September 2008): 477–503; Volker Berghahn, "German Colonialism and Imperialism from Bismarck to Hitler," *German Studies Review,* vol. 40, no. 1 (2017): 147–62. See also Kühne, "Colonialism and the Holocaust," 350; Guettel, *German Expansionism, Imperial Liberalism, and the United States*; Guettel, "The US Frontier as Rationale for the Nazi East?" 404, 415; Guettel, *German Expansionism*, 93–111, 164–71, 201–02. On US Free Soil liberalism in colonial expansion into the US frontier, see Eric Foner, *Free Soil, Free Labor, Free Men: The Ideology of the Republican Party before the Civil War* (Oxford, UK: Oxford University Press, 1970).

9 Nineteenth-century Western expansion, after all, was often deadly for Native Americans—"genocidal," even, in the case of California Indigenous communities who suffered mass killing and land dispossession by individual settlers and state representatives. See Albert L. Hurtado, *Indian Survival on the*

*California Frontier* (New Haven, CT: Yale University Press, 1988), 136; Benjamin Madley, "California's Yuki Indians: Defining Genocide in Native American History," *Western Historical Quarterly,* vol. 39 (Autumn 2008), 303–32.

**10** Omer Bartov, "The Holocaust as Genocide: Experiential Uniqueness and Integrated History," in *Probing the Ethics of Holocaust Culture;* Omer Bartov, "Genocide and the Holocaust: Arguments over History and Politics," in *Lessons and Legacies*, 15. Michman and Bartov, according to Moses, "are anxious about 'false or facile parallels,' and they ultimately end up arguing against any colonial connections . . . After all, France and Britain had longer-lasting and larger empires but did not unleash a Holocaust, avers Bartov." See A. Dirk Moses, "Anxieties in Holocaust and Genocide Studies," 342. On broader connections, see Roberta Pergher and Mark Roseman, "The Holocaust: An Imperial Genocide?," *Dapim—Studies on the Holocaust* 27, no. 1 (2013): 42–9.

**11** See Robert Eaglestone, *The Holocaust and the Postmodern* (New York and Oxford: Oxford University Press, 2004), esp. 166–72; Richard Evans, *In Defence of History* (London: Granta, 1997), 125–8.

**12** Marshall McLuhan, *Understanding Media* (London: Routledge, 1964), 9; Marshall McLuhan, "McLuhan: Now the Medium Is the Message," *New York Times*, March 3, 1967.

**13** A. Dirk Moses, "The Holocaust and Colonialism," in Peter Hayes and John Roth (eds), *The Oxford Handbook of Holocaust Studies* (Oxford, UK: Oxford University Press, 2010), 68–80; A. Dirk Moses, "Empire, Colony, Genocide: Keywords and the Philosophy of History," 3–54; Moses, "Redemptive Anti-Semitism and the Imperialist Imaginary"; Moses, "Anxieties in Holocaust and Genocide Studies," 342.

**14** On linguistic determinism, from a Kantian perspective, see George Bealer, "The A Priori," in John Greco and Ernest Sosa (eds), *The Blackwell Guide to Epistemology* (Oxford, UK: Blackwell, 1999), 243–70. W. Stegmuller, *Collected Papers on Epistemology, Philosophy of Science and History of Philosophy,* vol. 1 (Boston: De Reidel, 1977), 104–14. On these discursive influences in the Holocaust, see Moses, "Anxieties in Holocaust and Genocide Studies," 342; A. D. Moses, "Conceptual Blockages and Definitional Dilemmas in the 'Racial Century': Genocides of Indigenous Peoples and the Holocaust," *Patterns of Prejudice*, vol. 36, no. 4 (2002): 7–36.

**15** Donald Bloxham and A. Dirk Moses, "Introduction: Changing Themes in the Study of Genocide," *The Oxford Handbook of Genocide Studies* (Oxford, UK: Oxford University Press, 2010), 8; Mark Roseman, "Beyond Conviction? Perpetrators, Ideas and Action in the Holocaust In Historiographical Perspective," in Frank Biess, Mark Roseman, and Hanna Schissler (eds), *Conflict, Catastrophe and Continuity: Essays on Modern German History* (Oxford and New York: Berghahn Press, 2007), 81–103; Mark Roseman, "Racial Discourse, Nazi Violence, and the Limits of the 'Racial State' Model," in Devin Pendas, Mark Roseman, and Richard Wetzel (eds), *Beyond the Racial State* (Cambridge, UK: Cambridge University Press, 2017), 31–57; Mark Roseman, "The Holocaust in European History," in Nicholas Doumanis (ed.),

*Oxford Handbook of Modern Europe 1914–1945* (Oxford, UK: Oxford University Press, 2016), 518–36; Christian Gerlach, *Extremely Violent Societies: Mass Violence in the Twentieth Century* (Cambridge, UK: Cambridge University Press, 2010), 237; Dan Diner, "The Irreconcilability of an Event: Integrating the Holocaust into the Narrative of the Century," in Dan Michman (ed.), *Remembering the Holocaust in Germany, 1945–2000* (New York and Oxford: Berghahn Books, 2002).

**16** Moses, *Empire, Colony, Genocide*, 31–2; Nicholas A. Robins and Adam Jones (eds), *Genocides by the Oppressed: Subaltern Genocide in Theory and Practice* (Bloomington: Indiana University Press, 2009); Moses (ed.), *Empire, Colony, Genocide*, Section III; Martin Shaw, "Britain and Genocide: Historical and Contemporary Parameters of National Responsibility," *Review of International Studies*, vol. 37, no. 5 (2011): 2417–38; Dan Stone, "Genocide and Memory," in Donald Bloxham and A. Dirk Moses (eds), *The Oxford Handbook of Genocide Studies* (Oxford University Press, 2010), accessed online at http://www.oxfordhandbooks.com/view/10.1093/oxfordhb/9780199232116.001.0001/oxfordhb-9780199232116-e-6.

**17** See Steven T. Katz, "The Pequot War Reconsidered," *New England Quarterly*, vol. 64, no. 2 (1991): 206–24; Michael Freeman, "Puritans and Pequots: The Question of Genocide," *New England Quarterly*, vol. 68, no. 2 (1995): 278–93; Steven T. Katz, "Pequots and the Question of Genocide: A Reply to Michael Freeman," *New England Quarterly*, vol. 68, no. 4 (1995): 641–9.

**18** Laurence M. Hauptman and James D. Wherry (eds), *The Pequots in Southern New England: The Fall and Rise of an American Indian Nation* (Norman: University of Oklahoma Press, 1990).

**19** See the various cutting-edge essays in Nicole Eustace and Fredrika J. Teute (eds), *Warring for America: Cultural Contests in the Era of 1812* (Chapel Hill, NC: Omohundro Institute of Early American History and Culture and the University of North Carolina Press, 2017).

**20** Albert L. Hurtado, *Indian Survival on the California Frontier*, 136; Benjamin Madley, "California's Yuki Indians: Defining Genocide in Native American History," 303–32; Richard Drinnon, *Facing West: The Metaphysics of Indian-Hating and Empire Building* (Minneapolis: University of Minnesota Press, 1980), 463; Aziz Rana, *The Two Faces of American Freedom*; Bulmer-Thomas, *Empire in Retreat*, chap. 1; Mark Rifkin, *Manifesting America: The Imperial Construction of U.S. National Space* (Oxford, UK: Oxford University Press, 2009), 3–36; Richard Slotkin, *Regeneration Through Violence: The Mythology of the American Frontier, 1600-1860* (Norman, OK: University of Oklahoma Press, 2000).

**21** See Moses, "Paranoia and Partisanship: Genocide Studies, Holocaust Historiography, and the 'Apocalyptic Conjuncture,'" *The Historical Journal*, vol. 54, no. 2 (2011): 580. On the fear of white colonial American settlers that metropolitan British power would reduce their control of non-white subjects, including enslaved people, see Robert G. Parkinson, *The Common Cause: Creating Race and Nation in the American Revolution* (Chapel Hill, NC: Omohundro Institute of Early American History and Culture and the University of North Carolina Press, 2016).

22 Hannah Arendt, *The Origins of Totalitarianism,* ix; Lilian Friedberg, "Dare to Compare: Americanizing the Holocaust," *The American Indian Quarterly,* vol. 24, no. 3 (Summer 2000): 361.

23 Alon Confino, "Fantasies about the Jews: Cultural Reflections on the Holocaust', *History and Memory*, vol. 17 (2005): 296–322; Alon Confino, *A World without Jews: The Nazi Imagination from Persecution to Genocide* (New Haven, CT: Yale University Press, 2015); Brendan Simms, *Hitler: Only the World Was Enough* (London and New York, Penguin, 2019); Moses, "Empire, Colony, Genocide," 39.

24 See Segal Raz, "Beyond Holocaust Studies: Rethinking the Holocaust in Hungary, *Journal of Genocide Research*, 16:1, (2014): 1–23; Ivo Goldstein and Slavko Goldstein, *The Holocaust in Croatia* (Pittsburgh, PA: University of Pittsburgh Press in association with the United States Holocaust Memorial Museum, 2016).

25 Moses, "Empire, Colony, Genocide", 36–7; Kühne, "Colonialism and the Holocaust. Continuities, Causations, and Complexities," 355.

26 See Timothy Snyder, *Bloodlands: Europe Between Hitler and Stalin* (New York: Basic Books, 2010); Timothy Snyder, *Black Earth: The Holocaust as History and Warning* (New York: Penguin, 2015); Jan Burzlaff, "Confronting the Communal Grave: A Reassessment of Social Relations During the Holocaust in Eastern Europe," *The Historical Journal*, vol. 63, no. 4 (2019): 1054–77; Waitman Wade Beorn, "All the Other Neighbors: Communal Genocide in Eastern Europe," in Hilary Earl and Simone Gigliotti (eds), *The Wiley Blackwell Companion to the Holocaust* (Hoboken, NJ: Wiley and Sons, 2020), 153–72; Waitman Wade Beorn, *The Holocaust in Eastern Europe At the Epicenter of the Final Solution* (London and New York: Bloomsbury, 2018).

27 Dan Stone, "The Holocaust and 'the Human'" in Richard H. King and Dan Stone (eds), *Hannah Arendt and the Uses of History: Imperialism, Nation, Race, and Genocide* (New York: Berghahn Books, 2007), 236–9; Stephen J. Whitfield, "Hannah Arendt and the Banality of Evil," *The History Teacher,* vol. 14, no. 4 (August 1981): 469–77; A. Dirk Moses, "Genocide and Modernity," 162–4; A. Rabinbach, "Why Were the Jews Sacrificed? The Place of Anti-Semitism in Dialectic of Enlightenment," *New German Critique*, vol. 81 (2000): 55.

28 Dan Michman, "Historiography on the Holocaust in Poland: An Outsider's View of its Place within Recent General Developments in Holocaust Historiography," in Antony Polonsky, Hanna Węgrzynek and Andrzej Żbikowski (eds), *New Directions in the History of the Jews in the Polish Lands* (Academic Studies Press, 2017), 394–5.

29 The "cultural history" of imperial "images and processes is important," according to Moses, "and new research into them is underway." See A. Dirk Moses, "Paranoia and Partisanship: Genocide Studies, Holocaust Historiography, and the 'Apocalyptic Conjuncture,'" 575

30 McDonnell and Moses, "Raphael Lemkin as Historian of Genocide in the Americas," 503, 513. For the most recent evaluation of Amherst and the smallpox debate, see Elizabeth A. Fenn, "Biological Warfare in Eighteenth-

Century North America: Beyond Jeffrey Amherst," *Journal of American History*, vol. 86, no. 4 (2000): 1552–80.

31 Kühne, "Colonialism and the Holocaust. Continuities, Causations, and Complexities," 344; Moses, "Empire, Colony, Genocide", 9, 37; John Docker, "Are Settler-colonies Inherently Genocidal? Rereading Lemkin", in *Empire, Colony, Genocide,* 86–8; Lemkin, *Axis Rule*, 81 ,cited in A. Dirk Moses, "Genocide," *Australian Humanities Review*, vol. 55 (November 2013): 37; McDonnell and Moses, "Raphael Lemkin as Historian of Genocide in the Americas," 501; Lemkin, *Axis Rule,* 79. See also A. Dirk Moses, "Raphael Lemkin, Culture, and the Concept of Genocide," 19–41; Jürgen Zimmerer and Dominik Schaller (eds), *The Origins of Genocide: Raphael Lemkin as a Historian of Mass Violence* (London: Routledge, 2007).

32 See Kühne, "Colonialism and the Holocaust. Continuities, Causations, and Complexities," 344.

33 Michael A. McDonnell and A. Dirk Moses, "Raphael Lemkin as Historian of Genocide in the Americas," *Journal of Genocide,* vol. 7, no. 4 (December 2005): 501; Robert S. Frey (ed.), *The Genocidal Temptation* (Dallas: University Press of America, 2004), 69; A. Dirk Moses, "The Holocaust and Genocide," 533–55; A. Dirk Moses, "Genocide," *Australian Humanities Review*, vol. 55 (November 2013): 37; A. D. Moses, "Empire, Colony, Genocide: Keywords and the Philosophy of History"; Geoff Eley, "Empire, Ideology, and the East: Nazism's Spatial Imagery," in Claus-Christian W. Szejnman and Maiken Umbach (eds), *Heimat, Region, and Empire: Spatial Identities under National Socialism* (Houndmills, UK: Palgrave Macmillan, 2012), 252–75.

34 Mark Roseman "Beyond Conviction? Perpetrators, Ideas and Action in the Holocaust in Historiographical Perspective"; Mark Roseman, "Racial Discourse, Nazi Violence, and the Limits of the 'Racial State' Model," 31–57; Mark Roseman, "The Holocaust in European History."

## Chapter Three "We are waiting for the construction of our museum."

1 Brett Williams, "A River Runs Through Us," *American Anthropologist*, vol. 103, no. 2 (June 2001): 346–57.

2 Sherman Alexie, "Inside Dachau," *The Beloit Poetry Journal,* vol. 46, no. 4 (Summer 1996), https://warwick.ac.uk/fac/cross_fac/ehrc/events/sherman_alexie_-_inside_dachau.pdf. On Alexie's work in this regard, see Nancy J. Peterson, "'If I Were Jewish, How Would I Mourn the Dead?': Holocaust and Genocide in the Work of Sherman Alexie," *MELUS,* vol. 35, no. 3, *Crime, Punishment, and Redemption* (FALL 2010), 63–84; Rachel Rubinstein, *Members of the Tribe: Native America in the Jewish Imagination* (Detroit, MI: Wayne State University Press, 2010), 162–3. See also the recent discussion in Stef Craps, "Holocaust Literature: Comparative Perspectives," in Jenni Adams (ed.), *The Bloomsbury Companion to Holocaust Literature* (London and New

York: Bloomsbury, 2015), 205–12. On Jewish–Indigenous encounters since the nineteenth century, see the following important recent work: David S. Koffman, *The Jews' Indian: Colonialism, Pluralism, and Belonging in America* (New Brunswick, NJ: Rutgers University Press, 2019), chap. 5.

3 According to Rubinstein, "In the contemporary moment, Alexie's poems suggest, it has become possible for the Native poet to become "American" by simultaneously invoking and distancing himself from the Jews and their Holocaust." See Rubinstein, *Members of the Tribe,* 162–3.

4 On initial Indigenous tensions regarding the USHMM, see Edward Tabor Linenthal, *Preserving Memory: The Struggle to Create America's Holocaust Museum* (New York: Columbia University Press, 2001), 63–4; Jonathan Boyarin, Greg Sarris and Menahem Prywes, "Europe's Indian, America's Jew: Modiano and Vizenor," *Boundary* 2, Special Issue: 1492–1992: American Indian Persistence and Resurgence, vol. 19, no. 3 (Autumn 1992): 207. For a summary of the perceived link to Indigenous history, see David B. MacDonald, *Identity Politics in the Age of Genocide: The Holocaust and Historical Representation* (New York: Routledge, 2008), 91; Peter Novik, *The Holocaust in American Life* (New York: Houghton Mifflin, 1999), 10–13. See also Lilian Friedberg, "Dare to Compare: Americanizing the Holocaust," *The American Indian Quarterly,* vol. 24, no. 3 (Summer 2000): 354.

5 Carol A. Horton, *Race and the Making of American Liberalism* (New York: Oxford University Press, 2005); Boyarin, Sarris, and Prywes, "Europe's Indian, America's Jew: Modiano and Vizenor," *Boundary* 2, vol. 19, no. 3: 1492–1992: *American Indian Persistence and Resurgence* (Autumn, 1992): 198, 203.

6 Rubinstein, *Members of the Tribe*, 165; Linenthal, *Preserving Memory*, 63–4; Lilian Friedberg, "Dare to Compare: Americanizing the Holocaust," 354–9; Peter Novick, *The Holocaust and Collective Memory* (London: Bloomsbury, 1999), 20; Hilene Flanzbaum (ed.), *The Americanization of the Holocaust* (Baltimore: Johns Hopkins University Press, 1999); Greig Crysler and Abidin Kusno, "Angels in the Temple: The Aesthetic Construction of Citizenship at the United States Holocaust Memorial Museum," *Art Journal,* vol. 56, no. 1 (Spring 1997): 52–64; Tim Cole, "The United States Holocaust Memorial Museum, Washington, D.C.," in *Selling the Holocaust: From Auschwitz to Schindler: How History Is Bought, Packaged, and Sold* (New York: Routledge, 1999), 146–71. For separate literatures on the origins and foundation of these two museums in Washington, D.C., see Linenthal, *Preserving Memory;* Amy Lonetree, *Decolonizing Museums: Representing Native America in National and Tribal Museums* (Chapel Hill: University of North Carolina Press, 2012).

7 See the discussions in Lonetree, *Decolonizing Museums*, 108–10; MacDonald, *Identity Politics in the Age of Genocide*, 90–2.

8 Jason Chalmers, "Canadianising the Holocaust: Debating Canada's National Holocaust Monument," *Canadian Jewish Studies,* vol. 24 (2016): 149–65; Tricia Logan, "Memory, Erasure, and National Myth," in Andrew Woolford, Jeff Benvenuto, and Alexander Laban Hinton (eds), *Colonial Genocide in Indigenous North America* (Durham, NC: Duke University Press, 2014), 149–65; Tricia Logan, "National Memory and Museums: Remembering Settler Colonial Genocide of Indigenous Peoples in Canada," in Nigel Eltringham and

Pam Maclean (eds), *Remembering Genocide* (London: Routledge, 2014), 112–30; A. Dirk Moses, "Does the Holocaust Reveal or Conceal Other Genocides? The Canadian Museum for Human Rights and Grievable Suffering," in Alexander Laban Hinton, Thomas La Pointe, and Douglas Irvin-Erickson (eds), *Hidden Genocides: Power, Knowledge, Memory* (New Brunswick, NJ: Rutgers University Press, 2014), 21–51; David B. MacDonald, "Indigenous Genocide and Perceptions of the Holocaust in Canada," in S. Gigliotti and H. Earl (eds), *The Wiley Companion to the Holocaust* (London: Wiley-Blackwell, 2020), 578 David B. MacDonald, "Canada's History War: Indigenous Genocide and Public Memory in the United States, Australia, and Canada," *Journal of Genocide Research*, vol. 17, no. 4 (2015): 411–31.

9 On "de-judaization," see Deborah E. Lipstadt, *Antisemitism: Here and Now* (New York: Schocken Books, 2019), 156.

10 Michael Rothberg, *Multidirectional Memory: Remembering the Holocaust in the Age of Decolonization* (Palo Alto, CA: Stanford University Press, 2009), 3. On the tricky balance between survival and loss in Holocaust commemoration, which must show that "although Jews were not simply passive victims, as an older stereotype had it, nevertheless their fate was ultimately out of their hands," see Dan Stone, "Holocaust Historiography and Cultural History," in Dan Stone (ed.), *The Holocaust and Historical Methodology* (New York: Berghahn Books, 2012), 47. In addition to the seminal critiques of the NMAI by Lonetree and others engaged below, as well as conceptually similar critiques of the treatment of Holocaust memory in North America, see also the essays in Susan Sleeper-Smith, *Contesting Knowledge: Museums and Indigenous Perspectives* (Lincoln: University of Nebraska Press, 2009); Kristine Ronan, "Native Empowerment, the New Museology, and the National Museum of the American Indian," *Museum and Society,* vol. 12, no. 2 (2014): 132–47; Catherine D. Chatterley, "Canada's Struggle with Holocaust Memorialization: The War Museum Controversy, Ethnic Identity Politics, and the Canadian Museum for Human Rights," *Holocaust and Genocide Studies*, vol. 29, no. 2) (2015), 189–211.

11 Linenthal, *Preserving Memory*, 12; Jon Catlin, "How Jewish was the Holocaust?" *Makom* (2013), 2; Novick, The *Holocaust in American Life*, 133–4.

12 Cited in Deborah E. Lipstadt, *Holocaust: An American Understanding* (New Brunswick, NJ: Rutgers University Press, 2016), 112.

13 Yehuda Bauer, "Whose Holocaust?," *Midstream,* vol. 26, no. 9 (November 1980): 35, 38; A. Dirk Moses, "The Holocaust and Genocide," in *The Historiography of the Holocaust*, 533.

14 Ron Kampeas, "'Remember the 11 Million'? Why an Inflated Victims Tally Irks Holocaust Historians," *Times of Israel,* February 1, 2017, http://www.timesofisrael.com/remember-the-11-million-why-an-inflated-victims-tally-irks-holocaust-historians/.

15 Linenthal, *Preserving Memory,* 44–5; Avril Alba, *The Holocaust Memorial Museum: Sacred Secular Space* (Basingstoke, UK: Palgrave Macmillan, 2015). See also the discussions in the works by Novick referenced above.

**16** Yehuda Bauer, "Against Mystification: The Holocaust as a Historical Phenomenon" (1978), in Michael R. Marrus (ed.), *The Nazi Holocaust: Perspectives on the Holocaust* (Berlin: De Gruyter, 1989), 106.

**17** Saul Friedländer, *Reflections of Nazism: An Essay on Kitsch and Death* (Bloomington and Indianapolis: Indiana University Press, 1984).

**18** William Styron, *Sophie's Choice* (New York: Random House, 1979), 237; Jon Catlin, "How Jewish Was the Holocaust?," 28–9; Franciszek Piper, "Estimating the Number of Deportees to and Victims of the Auschwitz-Birkenau Camp," *Yad Vashem Studies,* vol. 21 (1991): 49–103; Martin Gilbert, *Atlas of the Holocaust* (Oxford, UK: Pergamon, 1988), 242–4; D. G. Myers, "Jews Without Memory: 'Sophie's Choice' and the Ideology of Liberal Anti-Judaism," *American Literary History*, vol. 13, no. 3 (Autumn 2001): 500; Alan L. Berger, *Crisis and Covenant: The Holocaust in American Jewish Fiction* (Albany: State University of New York Press, 1985), 33; "Stealing the Holocaust," in Alexander Edward, *The Holocaust and the War of Ideas* (New Brunswick, NJ: Transaction, 1994), 195.

**19** See Franjo Tudjam, *Wastelands of Historical Truth*, cited in Robert S. Wistrich, *Holocaust Denial: The Politics of Perfidy* (Berlin: De Gruyter, 2012), 54.

**20** See the seminal discussion of these critiques in Jan T. Gross, *Neighbors: The Destruction of the Jewish Community in Jedwabne, Poland* (Princeton, NJ, and Oxford, UK: Princeton University Press, 2001).

**21** See Clemens Heni, "The Prague Declaration, Holocaust Obfuscation, and Anti-Semitism," 8, http://www.clemensheni.net/the-prague-declaration-holocaust-obfuscation-and-antisemitism/.

**22** Zofia Woycicka, *Przerwana Zaloba: Spory wokol pamigci i upamiqtnienia nazis-towskich obozdw koncentracyjnych i zaglady w Polsce 1944–1950 [Ruptured Mourning: Polish Debates about Memory and Commemoration of Nazi Concentration and Annihilation Camps in Poland 1944–1950]* (Warsaw: Trio, 2009). See also the discussion of Woycicka's work in comparison to Huener in Karen Auerbach, "Review Essay: Holocaust Memory in Polish Scholarship," *AJS Review* , vol. 35, no. 1 (April 2011): 147.

**23** See W. T. Bartoszewski, *The Convent at Auschwitz* (New York: George Braziller, 1991); E. Klein, *The Battle for Auschwitz: Catholic–Jewish Relations under Strain* (London: Vallentine Mitchell, 2001).

**24** Molly Crabapple has recently noted such a phenomenon in popular discourse, at least among some Polish-American communities. See Josh Marshall, "Anti-Semitic Rally in New York City," April 2, 2019, https://talkingpointsmemo.com/edblog/anti-semitic-rally-in-new-york-city?fbclid=IwAR1CTn5tRs0PPHGtI-wGUgVs169f3GldAIu7-bKaOLELXyBsKt8_5s70Gcc. See also James Kirchick, *The End of Europe: Dictators, Demagogues, and the Coming Dark Age* (New Haven, CT: Yale University Press, 2017), 43; James Kirchick, "The Holocaust Without Jews," *Tablet Magazine*, May 3, 2016, http://www.tabletmag.com/jewish-news-and-politics/201420/the-holocaust-without-jews.

**25** Judith Goldstein, "Anne Frank: the Redemptive Myth," *Partisan Review,* vol. 70, no. 1. (Winter 2013) 16–17; Oren Baruch Stier, *Holocaust Icons:*

*Symbolizing the Shoah in History and Memory* (New Brunswick, NJ: Rutgers University Press, 2015), 148.

26 Andreas Huyssen, *Twilight Memories: Marking Time in a Culture of Amnesia* (London: Routledge, 1995), 255; Rosenfeld, *The End of the Holocaust*; MacDonald, *Identity Politics in the Age of Genocide*, 24–6; Alvin H. Rosenfeld, "The Americanization of the Holocaust," in Deborah Dash Moore (ed.), *American Jewish Identity Politics* (Ann Arbor: University of Michigan Press, 2008), 55; Tim Cole, *Images of the Holocaust: The Myth of the "Shoah Business"* (London: Duckworth, 1999), 156. See also Dan Stone, "Memory, Memorials and Museums," in Dan Stone (ed.), *The Historiography of the Holocaust* (Basingstoke, UK: Palgrave Macmillan, 2004), 519.

27 See Rubinstein, *Members of the Tribe*, 165; Linenthal, *Preserving Memory*, 63–4.

28 See the discussion in Lonetree, *Decolonizing Museums*, 105–10.

29 Jean M. O'Brien, *Firsting and Lasting: Writing Indians Out of Existence in New England* (Minneapolis: University of Minnesota Press, 2010); Michel-Rolph Trouillot, *Silencing the Past: Power and the Production of History* (Boston: Beacon Press, 1995).

30 Philip J. Deloria, *Playing Indian* (New Haven, CT: Yale University Press, 1998), 25–8; Alexander Saxton, *The Rise and Fall of the White Republic: Class Politics and Mass Culture* (London: Verso, 2003), 153; Richard Drinnon, *Facing West: The Metaphysics of Indian-Hating and Empire Building* (Norman: University of Oklahoma Press, 1997), 463; Lilian Friedberg, "Dare to Compare: Americanizing the Holocaust," 361.

31 See Claudio Saunt, *Unworthy Republic: The Dispossession of Native Americans and the Road to Indian Territory* (New York: W. W. Norton, 2020).

32 Margaret D. Jacobs, "Seeing Like a Settler Colonial State," *Modern American History*, vol. 1, no. 2 (July 2018): 270; Jodi A. Byrd, "Introduction" to "Forum: Indigeneity's Difference: Methodology and the Structures of Sovereignty," *J19: The Journal of Nineteenth-Century Americanists*, vol. 2, no. 1 (Spring 2014): 131–61; Frederick E. Hoxie, "Sovereignty's Challenge to Native American (and United States) History," *J19: The Journal of Nineteenth-Century Americanists*, vol 2, no. 1 (Spring 2014): 137–42; Taiawagi Helton and Lindsay G. Robertson, "The Foundations of Federal Indian Law and Its Application in the Twentieth Century," in Daniel M. Cobb and Loretta Fowler (eds), *Beyond Red Power: American Indian Politics and Activism Since 1900* (Santa Fe, NM: School for Advanced Research Press 2007), 33–55.

33 Jerome A. Greene, *American Carnage: Wounded Knee, 1890* (Norman: University of Oklahoma Press, 2014), 236; Michael A. Elliott, "Not Over: The Nineteenth Century Indian Wars," *Reviews in American History*, vol. 44 (2016), 279; David W. Grua. *Surviving Wounded Knee: The Lakotas and the Politics of Memory* (New York: Oxford University Press, 2016), 40–61, 52.

34 The spelling of the name *8sâmeeqan* here is as presented by the Wôpanâak Language Reclamation Project, and as cited in Christine M. DeLucia, "Memory on the Move: Confronting Indigenous and Settler Colonial Commemorations in Stone and Bronze," *Reviews in American History*, vol.

48, no. 1 (March 2020): 82; Lisa Blee and Jean M. O'Brien, *Monumental Mobility: The Memory Work of Massasoit* (Chapel Hill: The University of North Carolina Press, 2019). On the trajectory of the Thanksgiving motif in history and memory, see also David J. Silverman, *This Land Is Their Land: The Wampanoag Indians, Plymouth Colony, and the Troubled History of Thanksgiving* (London and New York: Bloomsbury, 2019).

**35** Blee and Jean M. O'Brien, *Monumental Mobility*, 44–5; DeLucia, "Memory on the Move," 86.

**36** Ibid., 47, 88, 62–3, 91–3, 112–13; DeLucia, "Memory on the Move," 86. During the early decades of the twentieth century Indigenous archives of memory were also ignored in other regions, including the Midwest. See Doug Kiel, "Competing Visions of Empowerment: Oneida Progressive-Era Politics and Writing Tribal Histories," *Ethnohistory*, vol. 61, no. 3 (2014): 419–44.

**37** Andrew Denson, "Native Americans in Cold War Public Diplomacy: Indian Politics, American History, and the US Information Agency," *American Indian Culture and Research Journal,* vol. 36 (Fall 2012): 3–22; Daniel M. Cobb, *Native Activism* in *Cold War America: The Struggle for Sovereignty* (Lawrence: University Press of Kansas, 2008).

**38** Andrew Denson, *Monuments to Absence: Cherokee Removal and the Contest Over Southern Memory* (Chapel Hill: University of North Carolina Press, 2017), 27, 9, 112–13. As Christina Snyder has noted, "whites framed removal as the tragic end of Native history in the South. Monuments to absent peoples were politically cheap, allowing southern elites to claim moral authority in crafting a narrative of progress." Christina Snyder, "Review of Monuments to Absence: Cherokee Removal and the Contest over Southern Memory by Andrew Denson," *Journal of the Civil War Era*, vol. 8, no. 1 (March 2018): 167–9. On the complex interaction between anti-black racism and the occlusion of Indigenous archives of memory, see also Malinda Maynor Lowery, "Racial Science and Federal Recognition: Lumbee Indians in the Jim Crow South," in Jean M. O'Brien and Amy Den Ouden (eds), *Recognition, Sovereignty Struggles, and Indigenous Rights in the United States: A Sourcebook* (Chapel Hill: University of North Carolina Press, 2013), 65–94; Malinda Maynor Lowery, *Lumbee Indians in the Jim Crow South: Race, Identity, and the Making of a Nation* (Chapel Hill: University of North Carolina Press, 2010).

**39** Denson, *Monuments to Absence*, 91, 11, 219; Boyd Cothran, *Remembering the Modoc War: Redemptive Violence and the Making of American Innocence* (Chapel Hill: University of North Carolina Press, 2014), 15.

**40** Kevin M. Bruyneel, *The Third Space of Sovereignty: The Postcolonial Politics of U.S.–Indigenous Relations* (Minneapolis: University of Minnesota Press, Indigenous Americas Series, 2007); Jacobs, "Seeing Like a Settler Colonial State," 262.

**41** Margaret D. Jacobs, "Seeing Like a Settler Colonial State," 270; Jodi A. Byrd, "Introduction" to "Forum: Indigeneity's Difference: Methodology and the Structures of Sovereignty," *J19: The Journal of Nineteenth-Century Americanists,* vol. 2, no. 1 (Spring 2014): 131–61; Frederick E. Hoxie,

"Sovereignty's Challenge to Native American (and United States) History," *J19: The Journal of Nineteenth-Century Americanists,* vol 2, no. 1 (Spring 2014): 137–42; Taiawagi Helton and Lindsay G. Robertson, "The Foundations of Federal Indian Law and Its Application in the Twentieth Century," 33–55. As Sarah B. Shear has argued in her study of US textbooks, the confinement of Indigenous history to the pre-twentieth century context "silences the connection between that past and the everyday struggle for sovereignty in the twenty-first century." See Sarah B. Shear, "Cultural Genocide Masked as Education: U.S. History Textbooks' Coverage of Indigenous Education Policies," in Prentice T. Chandler (ed.), *Doing Race in Social Studies: Critical Perspectives* (Charlotte, NC: Information Age Publishing, 2015), 13–40.

42 Ari Kelman, *A Misplaced Massacre: Struggling Over the Memory of Sand Creek* (Cambridge, MA: Harvard University Press, 2015), 1, 13–14, 34–5, 66–8.

43 See Andrew Denson, "Memories of Western Violence, Lost and Found," *Reviews in American History,* vol. 42, no. 2 (2014): 277. See also Michael A. Elliot, *Custerology: The Enduring Legacy of the Indian Wars and George Armstrong Custer* (Chicago: University of Chicago Press, 2007); Karl Jacoby, *Shadows at Dawn: An Apache Massacre and the Violence of History* (New York: Penguin, 2008); Waziyatawin Angela Wilson, *In the Footsteps of Our Ancestors: The Dakota Commemorative Marches of the 21st Century* (St. Paul, MI: Living Justice Press, 2006).

44 These depictions culminated in a memorial stone placed in 1964 near the site of Leschi's hanging. See Lisa Blee, *Framing Chief Leschi: Narratives and the Politics of Historical Justice* (Chapel Hill: University of North Carolina Press, 2014), 123–8. On Moses, see ibid., 9, 72, 194.

45 See Lisa Blee, *Framing Chief Leschi*, 78, 147–54.

46 Ibid., 9–10, 152–8, 182. See also David Chang, *The Color of the Land: Race, Nation, and the Politics of Land Ownership in Oklahoma, 1832–1929* (Chapel Hill: University of North Carolina Press, 2010).

47 Paulette Regan, *Unsettling the Settler Within: Indian Residential Schools, Truth Telling, and Reconciliation in Canada* (Vancouver: UBC Press, 2010), 83–4.

48 See Ruth B. Phillips, "Can National Museums Be Postcolonial?: The Canadian Museum for Human Rights and the Obligation of Redress to First Nations," in Annie. E. Coombes and Ruth B. Phillips (eds), *The International Handbook of Museum Studies: Museum Transformations* (Hoboken, NJ: Wiley-Blackwell, 2020), 549; Ruth B. Phillips and Sherry Brydon, "'Arrow of Truth: The Indians of Canada Pavilion at Expo 67," in Ruth B. Phillips (ed.), *Museum Pieces: Toward the Indigenization of Canadian Museums* (Montreal: McGill-Queens University Press, 2011), 27–47.

49 Phillips (ed.), *Museum Pieces*, 61.

50 Phillips, "Can National Museums Be Postcolonial?," 545–6.

51 According to Phillips, this represents a "multi-cultural" approach to citizenship that follows "British imperial, Anglo-Canadian, [and] bicultural . . . collective

constructs of national identity" that are "inherently antithetical to Aboriginal affirmations of sovereignty." See ibid.

52 Jonathan Dewar, "'Where are the Children?' And 'We were so far away . . . ': Exhibiting the Legacies of Residential Schools, Healing, and Reconciliation," in *The International Handbook of Museum Studies,* 85–111.

53 Phillips, "Can National Museums Be Postcolonial?," 561.

54 D. Blue Spruce (ed.), *Spirit of a Native Place: Building the National Museum of the American Indian* (Washington, D.C.: National Museum of the American Indian, 2004), 45; D. Blue Spruce and T. Thrasher (eds), *The Land Has Memory: Indigenous Knowledge, Native Landscapes, and the National Museum of the American Indian* (Washington, D.C.: National Museum of the American Indian, 2008), 1–2, 14; Amanda Cobb, "The National Museum of the American Indian as Cultural Sovereignty," *American Quarterly,* vol. 57, no. 2 (2005): 502; Ira Jacknis, "A New Thing? The NMAI in Historical and Institutional Perspective," *American Indian Quarterly*, vol. 30, nos. 3/4 (2006): 511–42; Whitney Kerr, "Giving up the 'I': How the National Museum of the American Indian Appropriated Tribal Voices,' *American Indian Law Review*, vol. 29, (2004): 421–42.

55 For a recent summary of the vanishing trope, see Gordon M. Sayre, *The Indian Chief as Tragic Hero: Native Resistance and the Literatures of America, From Moctezuma to Tecumseh* (Chapel Hill: University of North Carolina Press, 2005), 4–5. According to Lonetree, the museum "problematically us[es] an event caused by nature as a metaphor for what happened to Indigenous people at the hands of the U.S. government and its citizens." See Lonetree, *Decolonizing Museums*, 108–10. A critical literature on the early curatorial offerings of the NMAI has suggested that the institution allowed visitors to conceive Indigenous notions of sovereignty and autonomy as protected by the US State rather than as necessarily distinct and parallel. See Kerr, "Giving Up the 'I',"422–3; Amy Lonetree, "Continuing Dialogues: Evolving Views of the National Museum of the American Indian," *The Public Historian*, vol. 28, no. 2 (2006): 57–61; Sonya Atalay, "No Sense of the Struggle: Creating a Context for Survivance at the NMAI," *American Indian Quarterly*, vol. 30, no. 3/4 (2006), 597–618, Myla Vicenti Carpio, "(Un)disturbing Exhibitions: Indigenous Historical Memory at the NMAI," *American Indian Quarterly*, vol. 30, no. 3/4 (2006): 619–31; Amy Lonetree, "Missed Opportunities: Reflections on the NMAI," *American Indian Quarterly*, vol. 30, no. 3/4 (2006): 632–63; Steven Conn, "Heritage vs. History at the National Museum of the American Indian," *The Public Historian*, vol. 28, no. 2 (2006): 69–73; Elizabeth Archuleta, "Gym Shoes, Maps, and Passports, Oh My!: Creating Community or Creating Chaos at the National Museum of the American Indian?" in Amy Lonetree and Amanda Cobb (eds), *The National Museum of the American Indian: Critical Conversations* (Lincoln: University of Nebraska Press, 2008); Pauline Wakeham, "Performing Reconciliation at the National Museum of the American Indian: Postcolonial Rapprochement and the Politics of Historical Closure," in ibid., 354; Lonetree, "Acknowledging the Truth of History": Missed Opportunities at the National Museum of the American Indian," in *The National Museum of the American Indian: Critical Conversations*, 312; Carpio, "(Un)disturbing Exhibitions," 296; D. Fixico,

"Change Over Time: The National Museum of the American Indian," *The Public Historian*, 28 (2) (2006): 81–4. See also Steven Conn, *Do Museums Still Need Objects?* (Philadelphia: University of Pennsylvania Press, 2010), 45, 48; "At the Intersection of Apology and Sovereignty: The Arctic Exile Monument Project." *Cultural Critique*, vol. 87, no. 1.

56 Monika Siebert, *Indians Playing Indian: Multiculturalism and Contemporary Indigenous Art in North America* (Tuscaloosa: University of Alabama Press, 2015), 22, 26–7; Lonetree, *Decolonizing Museums*, 105–10. See also Jacki Thompson Rand, "Why I Can't Visit the National Museum of the American Indian," *Common-place.org*, vol. 7, no. 4 (July 2007).

57 Lonetree, *Decolonizing Museums*, 110; Lonetree and Cobb, *The National Museum of the American Indian*, 311.

58 Lonetree, *Decolonizing Museums*, 110–12.

59 Tricia Logan, "National Memory and Museums," 112–30. On the tendency for Canadian public officials to extract universal moral ideals from historical aberrations in the European realm, and to distill those ideals in their conception of the positive historical evolution of Canadian civic identity, see also A. Dirk Moses, "Does the Holocaust Reveal or Conceal Other Genocides? The Canadian Museum for Human Rights and Grievable Suffering," in Alexander Laban Hinton, Thomas La Pointe, and Douglas Irvin-Erickson (eds), *Hidden Genocides: Power, Knowledge, Memory*, 21–51; Jason Chalmers, "Settled Memories on Stolen Land: Settler Mythology at Canada's National Holocaust Monument," *American Indian Quarterly*, vol. 43, no. 4 (Fall 2019), 379–407; Sunera Thobani, *Exalted Subjects: Studies in the Making of Race and Nation in Canada* (Toronto: University of Toronto Press, 2007), 247–9. Very recently, at the time of writing this book, the CMHR has expanded its definition of genocide to include Indigenous experiences.

60 Standing Senate Committee on Social Affairs, Evidence of Proceedings, 21; Canada, House of Commons Debates, 8 December 2009 (Tim Uppal, Con.), 7814; Canada, House of Commons Debates, 8 December 2010 (Dennis Bevington, NDP), 6984, all cited in Chalmers, "Settled Memories on Stolen Land," 385, 388. See also A. Dirk Moses, "Does the Holocaust Reveal or Conceal Other Genocides?," 21–51.

61 Gail Lord, Daniel Libeskind, Edward Burtynsky, Claude Cormier, and Doris Berger (Team Lord), "National Holocaust Monument: Landscapes of Loss, Memory and Survival," *designboom*, March 4, 2014, 2; Nadine Blumer, "Memorials Are Built of Public Discussion as Much as Stone," *Ottawa Citizen*, May 8, 2015, cited in Chalmers, "Settled Memories on Stolen Land," 388–90. See the discussion in Chalmers, "Settled Memories on Stolen Land," 388.

62 Volpe, as Chalmers notes, "framed the Canadian government as the rightful owner of land and all legal residents of the country as 'legitimate' residents." See Canada, Parliament, House of Commons, Standing Committee on Transport, Infrastructure and Communities, Evidence of Proceedings (3rd sess., 40th Parliament, Meeting No. 21, 2010), 9, cited in Chalmers, "Settled Memories on Stolen Land," 391.

63 Erica Lehrer, "Thinking through the Canadian Museum for Human Rights," *American Quarterly,* vol. 67, no. 4 (2015): 1195–1216; Karen Busby, Adam Muller, and Andrew Woolford (eds), *The Idea of a Human Rights Museum* (Winnipeg: University of Manitoba Press, 2015), 3–6; Dorota Glowacka, '"Never Forget': Intersecting Memories of the Holocaust and the Settler Colonial Genocide in Canada," in Shirli Gilbert and Avril Alba (eds), *Holocaust Memory and Racism in the Postwar World* (Detroit, MI: Wayne State University Press, 2019), 400–02.

64 Pauline Wakeham, "Performing Reconciliation at the National Museum of the American Indian: Postcolonial Rapprochement and the Politics of Historical Closure," 354. See also Pauline Wakeham, "At the Intersection of Apology and Sovereignty: The Arctic Exile Monument Project," *Cultural Critique,* vol. 87, number 1 (Spring 2014): 84–143; Pauline Wakeham, "Reconciling 'Terror': Managing Indigenous Resistance in the Age of Apology," *American Indian Quarterly,* vol. 36, no. 1 (Winter 2012): 1–33; Jennifer Henderson and Pauline Wakeham, "Colonial Reckoning, National Reconciliation?: First Peoples and the Culture of Redress in Canada," *ESC: English Studies in Canada*, vol. 35, no. 1 (March 2009): 1–26; Jennifer Henderson and Pauline Wakeham (eds), *Reconciling Canada: Critical Perspectives on the Culture of Redress* (Toronto: University of Toronto Press, 2013).; Glen Coulthard, *Red Skin, White Masks: Rejecting the Colonial Politics of Recognition* (Minneapolis: University of Minnesota Press, 2014), 107–12.

65 Canadian Tribute to Human Rights, "Statement of the Algonquin Anishnabe People" (2008), cited in Chalmers, "Settled Memories on Stolen Land," 391.

66 See Catherine D. Chatterley, "Canada's Struggle with Holocaust Memorialization," 189–211; Karyn Ball and Per Anders Rudling, "The Underbelly of Canadian Multiculturalism: Holocaust Obfuscation and Envy in the Debate about the Canadian Museum for Human Rights," *Holocaust Studies: A Journal of Culture and History,* vol. 20, no. 3 (2014): 33–80.

67 It has done so through its affiliated research agenda, its press releases, its online presence, and its influential set of recommended readings. For an example of Berenbaum's nuanced approach, see Michael Berenbaum and Abraham J. Peck, *The Holocaust and History: The Known, the Unknown, the Disputed, and the Reexamined* (Bloomington and Indianapolis: Indiana University Press, 2nd ed., 2002).

68 See Omer Bartov et al., "An Open Letter to the Director of the US Holocaust Memorial Museum," *New York Review of Books*, July 1, 2019, https://www.nybooks.com/daily/2019/07/01/an-open-letter-to-the-director-of-the-holocaust-memorial-museum/.

69 See Edward Rothstein, "The Problem with Jewish Museums," *Mosaic Magazine*, February 2016, https://mosaicmagazine.com/essay/2016/02/the-problem-with-jewish-museums/.

70 Dan Stone, "Memory, Memorials and Museums," 521; S. Milton, Jr., *Fitting Memory: The Art and politics of Holocaust Memorials* (Detroit, MI: Wayne State University press, 1991), 16, cited in Linenthal, *Preserving Memory*, 199.

71 Canada, Debates of the Senate, March 22, 2011 (Hon. Joan Fraser), 2081, cited in Chalmers, "Settled Memories on Stolen Land," 385.

72 For these citations, see Edward Rothstein, "The Problem with Jewish Museums."

73 Walter Reich, "Holocaust Museums and the Itch to Universalize," *Mosaic Magazine*, February 15, 2016, https://mosaicmagazine.com/response/2016/02/holocaust-museums-and-the-itch-to-universalize/.

74 James Kirchick, "The Bad-Faith Analogy Between Syrian Refugees and Jews Fleeing Nazi Germany," *Tablet Magazine*, December 4, 2015, http://www.tabletmag.com/jewish-news-and-politics/195469/syrian-refugees-analogy. ; Edward Rothstein, "The Problem with Jewish Museums."

75 The NMAI, to be sure, has also evolved in its curatorial strategy since Lonetree's 2012 assessment. Some very recent commentaries have even called for the museum and other allied institutions to highlight Indigenous survival and vitality to a greater extent. They worry that their emphases have veered towards somber accounts at the expense of other aspects of Native American history and culture. See for example the account in Ernest Stromberg, "Intergenerational Cultural Trauma and the National Museum of the American Indian," in Roger C. Aden (ed.), *US Public Memory, Rhetoric, and the National Mall*, (New York: Lexington Books, 2018), 135–55.

76 Philip J. Deloria, *Indians in Unexpected Places* (Lawrence: University Press of Kansas, 200), 9–11. See also Siebert, *Indians Playing Indian*, 22–7; Circe Sturm, "Reflections on the Anthropology of Sovereignty and Settler Colonialism: Lessons from Native North America," *Cultural Anthropology*, vol. 32, no. 3 (2017): 340–8. Nick Estes has begun to show how the ongoing occlusion of Indigenous archives of memory necessarily repudiates Indigenous activism and assertions of sovereignty, including in the present conflict over the Dakota Access Pipeline. See Nick Estes, *Our History Is the Future: Standing Rock Versus the Dakota Access Pipeline, and the Long Tradition of Indigenous Resistance* (New York: Verso, 2019).

77 Erika Doss, *Memorial Mania: Public Feeling in America* (Chicago: University of Chicago Press, 2010), 26–37.

## Chapter Four "The shrines of the soul of a nation."

1 Lewis Mumford, "The Culture of Cities" (1938), in Donald L. Miller (ed.), *The Lewis Mumford Reader* (New York: Pantheon Books, 1986), 104.

2 Dan Stone, "Introduction: The Holocaust and Historical Methodology," in Dan Stone (ed.), *The Holocaust and Historical Methodology* (New York: Berghahn Books, 2012), 9; Alain Finkielkraut, *The Future of a Negation: Reflections on the Question of Genocide* (Lincoln, NE: University of Nebraska Press, 1998), 59; James E. Young, *The Texture of Memory: Holocaust Memorials and Meaning* (New Haven, CT: Yale University Press, 1993), 6–7. "None of the existing concepts of Holocaust trauma," according to Kansteiner,

"is well suited to explain the effects of Holocaust representations on individuals or collectives who encounter the Final Solution only as a media event for educational or entertainment purposes.'" See Wulf Kansteiner, "Testing the Limits of Trauma: The Long-Term Psychological Effects of the Holocaust on Individuals and Collectives," *History of the Human Sciences,* vol. 17, no. 2–3 (2004): 97; Wulf Kansteiner, "Genealogy of a Category Mistake: A Critical Intellectual History of the Cultural Trauma Metaphor," *Rethinking History,* vol. 8, no. 2 (2004): 193–221; Dan Stone, "Genocide and Memory," in *The Oxford Handbook of Genocide Studies*, 102–19. See also Saul Friedländer, *Reflections of Nazism: An Essay on Kitsch and Death* (Bloomington and Indianapolis: Indiana University Press, 1984); Gavriel D. Rosenfeld, "The Normalization of Memory: Saul Friedländer's Reflections of Nazism Twenty Years Later," in Dagmar Herzog (ed.), *Lessons and Legacies, Vol. VII: The Holocaust in International Perspective* (Evanston, IL: Northwestern University Press 2006), 400–10. We can apply a similar observation in discussing Indigenous histories of suffering in in public media. See for example, Robert F. Berkhofer Jr., *The White Man's Indian: Images of the American Indian from Columbus to the Present* (New York: Knopf, 1978), 6–8; Paul Chaat Smith, *Everything You Know About Indians in Wrong* (Minneapolis: University of Minnesota Press, 2009); Kiara Vigil, *Indigenous Intellectuals: Sovereignty, Citizenship, and the American Imagination, 1880–1930* (Cambridge and New York: Cambridge University Press, 2015).

3 J. E. Young, *At Memory's Edge: After-Images of the Holocaust in Contemporary Art and Architecture* (New Haven, CT: Yale University Press, 2000), 198.

4 Rachel Rubinstein, *Members of the Tribe: Native America in the Jewish Imagination* (Detroit, MI: Wayne State University Press, 2010), 7. See also Brian W. Dippie, *The Vanishing American: White Attitudes and U.S. Indian Policy* (Lawrence: University Press of Kansas, 1991); Jean M. O'Brien, *Firsting and Lasting: Writing Indians Out of Existence in New England* (Lincoln: University of Nebraska Press, 2010), 145–201.

5 Rubinstein, *Members of the Tribe*, 157. On Cooper and the Vanishing Indian trope, see George D. Pappas, *The Literary and Legal Genealogy of Native American Dispossession: The Marshall Trilogy Cases* (New York: Routledge, 2017), 95–124.

6 On the American context for this phenomenon see Peter Novik, *The Holocaust in American Life* (New York: Houghton Mifflin, 1999), 35, 37, 65, 100, 306. For the potential role of trauma studies in understanding the phenomenon more globally, see for example Larissa Allwork, "Interrogating Europe's Voids of Memory: Trauma Theory and Holocaust Remembrance Between the National and the Transnational," *Quest: Issues in Contemporary Jewish History,* vol. 10 (2016): 1–22.

7 Ange-Marie Hancock, *Intersectionality: An Intellectual History* (New York: Oxford University Press, 2016); Novick, *The Holocaust in American Life*, 35–40, 65–8, 100–02, 306.

8 Eric J. Sundquist, *Strangers in the Land: Blacks, Jews, Post-Holocaust America* (Cambridge, MA: Harvard University Press, 2005), 193. See also Novik, *The*

*Holocaust in American Life,* 83–98, 9–16. On the rise of American consciousness of the Holocaust, see also Stephen J. Whitfield, "The Holocaust and the American Jewish Intellectual," *Judaism* 28 (Fall 1979), 391–401; Jeffrey Shandler, *While America Watches: Televising the Holocaust* (New York: Oxford University Press, 1999), 127–32. For a comparative look at Anglo-American responses to the Holocaust, see Tony Kushner, *The Holocaust and the Liberal Imagination* (Cambridge, MA: Blackwell, 1994), 205–69.

9 See Sundquist, *Strangers in the Land*, 209; Melvin Jules Bukiet, "In the Beginning Was Auschwitz," *Chronicle of Higher Education,* vol. 48, March 8, 2002.

10 Benjamin Nathans and Gabriella Safran (eds), *Culture Front: Representing Jews in Eastern Europe* (Philadelphia: University of Pennsylvania Press, 2007), 2; Salo W. Baron, "Newer Emphases in Jewish History," *Jewish Social Studies,* vol. 25, no. 4 (1963): 245–58; Adam Teller, "Revisiting Baron's "Lachrymose Conception": The Meanings of Violence in Jewish History," vol. 38, no. 2 (November 2014): 431–9; David Engel, "Crisis and Lachrymosity: On Salo Baron, Neobaronianism, and the Study of Modern European Jewish History," *Jewish History,* vol. 20 (2006): 243–264; Zachary Braiterman, "(Anti-Lachrymose Jewish History) A Lachrymose, Theological, Reactionary Object (Salo Baron)," Dec 26, 2018, https://jewishphilosophyplace.com/2018/12/26/anti-lachrymose-jewish-history-a-lachrymose-theological-reactionary-object-salo-baron/. Engel argues that historians of Jewish history have negated the negative experience of the Holocaust in recent years, in favor of a more positive historical vision, which is not entirely appropriate. See David Engel, *Historians of the Jews and the Holocaust* (Palo Alto, CA: Stanford University Press, 2010).

11 These excerpts from Dayksel are cited from Rubinstein, *Members of the Tribe*, 149, 154.

12 Rubinstein, *Members of the Tribe,* 157.

13 Ibid., 155–6. See also the depiction of Native Americans in Yiddish graphic novels. See Laurence Roth, "Contemporary American Jewish Comic Books: Abject Pasts, Heroic Futures," in Samantha Baskind and Ranen Omer-Sherman (eds), *The Jewish Graphic Novel: Critical Approaches* (Newark, NJ: Rutgers University Press, 2008), 13–14.

14 Jews "born after the catastrophe" on both sides of the Atlantic, in Finkielkraut's assessment, have turned over "their" history to such "symbols." See Finkielkraut, *Future of a Negation*, 59. See also Yitzchak Schwartz, "An Anti-Anti-Lachrymose Approach to Jewish History?" *Journal of the History of Ideas Blog*, Feb 22, 2017, https://jhiblog.org/2017/02/22/an-anti-anti-lachrymose-approach-to-jewish-history/ (Schwartz is not concerned with the effects on assimilation).

15 Alan M. Dershowitz, *The Vanishing American Jew: In Search of Jewish Identity for the Next Century* (New York, Little Brown and Company, 1996), 1.

16 Jacob Neusner, *Stranger at Home: "The Holocaust," Zionism and American Judaism* (Chicago: University of Chicago, 1981), 89; Robert Alter, "Deformation of the Holocaust," *Commentary,* vol. 71, no. 2 (1981): 53.

17 Nathans and Safran (eds), *Culture Front: Representing Jews in Eastern Europe*, 2.

18 Emil L. Fackenheim, *God's Presence in History: Jewish Affirmations and Philosophical Reflections* (First Jason Aronson Edition. Northvale, N.J: Jason Aronson Inc., 1997), 84. See also the comparison between Fackenheim and Neusner in Michael Oppenheim, "Between Halle and Jerusalem," in Sharon Portnoff, James A. Diamond, and Martin D. Yaffe (eds), *Emil L. Fackenheim: Philosopher, Theologian, Jew* (Leiden and Boston: Brill: 2008), 32–3.

19 Edna Friedberg, "Does the Holocaust Play an Outsized Role in Contemporary Jewish Identity?," 2019, http://www.jtsa.edu/stuff/contentmgr/files/1/271f91ea975bce4d8eed02ac2444f4fb/pdf/yomhashoah5779.pdf.

20 Ibid. Neusner, according to Friedberg, "argued that an emotional connection to the Holocaust and the State of Israel had come to supplant a more substantive and positive sense of Jewishness based on faith and learning."

21 See Maria Yellow Horse Brave Heart, *Historical Trauma and Unresolved Grief: Implications for Clinical Research and Practice with Indigenous Peoples of the Americas,* Smith College School for Social Work, 2015, https://www.ihs.gov/telebehavioral/includes/themes/newihstheme/display_objects/documents/slides/education/historicaltrauma_100412.pdf; Kathleen Brown-Rice, "Examining the Theory of Historical Trauma Among Native Americans," *The Professional Counselor* vol. 3, no. 3 (2013): 117–30; M. Brave Heart, J. Chase, J. Elkins, and D. B. Altschul, "Historical Trauma Among Indigenous Peoples of the Americas: Concepts, Research, and Clinical Considerations," *Journal of Psychoactive Drugs,* vol. 43, no. 4 (2012): 282–90. See also, more generally, Jenny Edkins, "Remembering Relationality: Trauma Time and Politics," in Duncan Bell (ed.), *Memory, Trauma, and World Politics: Reflections on the Relationship between Past and Present* (New York: Palgrave Macmillan, 2006), 99–115.

22 Lisa Blee and Jean M. O'Brien, *Monumental Mobility: The Memory Work of Massasoit* (Chapel Hill: The University of North Carolina Press, 2019), 113, 140; Christine M. DeLucia, "Memory on the Move: Confronting Indigenous and Settler Colonial Commemorations in Stone and Bronze," *Reviews in American History,* vol. 48, no. 1 (March 2020): 92.

23 Frederick E. Hoxie, *A Final Promise: The Campaign to Assimilate the Indians, 1880–1920* (Lincoln: University of Nebraska Press, 2001), chap. 8; Daniel M. Cobb, *Native Activism in Cold War America: The Struggle for Sovereignty* (Lawrence: University Press of Kansas, 2008); Bradley G. Shreve, *Red Power Rising: The National Indian Youth Council and the Origins of Native Activism* (Norman: University of Oklahoma Press, 2011); Kent Blansett, *A Journey to Freedom: Richard Oakes, Alcatraz, and the Red Power Movement* (New Haven: Yale University Press, 2018); Ellen S. Fine, "The Absent Memory: The Act of Writing in Post-Holocaust French Literature," in Berel Lang (ed.), *Writing and the Holocaust* (New York: Holmes and Meier, 1988), 41–57; Jennifer Lemberg, "Transmitted Trauma and 'Absent Memory' in James Welch's The Death of Jim Loney," Studies in American Indian Literatures, vol. 18, no. 3 (2006): 67; P. Lerner and M. Micale, "Trauma, Psychiatry, and History: A Conceptual and Historiographical Introduction," in P. Lerner and M. Micale (eds), *Traumatic Pasts: History, Psychiatry, and*

*Trauma in the Modern Age, 1870–1930* (Cambridge, UK: Cambridge University Press, 2001), 4; Vamik Volkan, *Bloodlines: From Ethnic Pride to Ethnic Terrorism* (London: Farrar, Strauss and Giroux, 1997), 43.

24 Traditional Hunkpapa Lakota Elders Council (Blackcloud, 1990), cited in Maria Yellow Horse Brave Heart, *Historical Trauma and Unresolved Grief: Implications for Clinical Research and Practice with Indigenous Peoples of the Americas*; Brave Heart and DeBruyn, "The American Indian Holocaust: Healing Historical Unresolved Grief," 60; Brave Heart et al., "Historical Trauma Among Indigenous Peoples of the Americas."

25 Maria Yellow Horse Brave Heart, *Historical Trauma and Unresolved Grief.*

26 On the problem of the Holocaust's "negative" identity formation in Jewish circles, see Shaul Magid, "The American Jewish Holocaust 'Myth' and 'Negative Judaism': Jacob Neusner's Contribution to American Judaism," in A. Avery Peck, B. Chilton, W. S. Green and G. G. Porton (eds), *A Legacy of Learning: Essays in Honor of Jacob Neusner* (Leiden, Brill, 2014), 321–40.

27 See Cindy L. Ehlers, Ian R. Gizer, David A. Gilder, Jarrod M. Ellingson, and Rachel Yehuda, "Measuring Historical Trauma in an American Indian Community Sample: Contributions of Substance Dependence, Affective Disorder, Conduct Disorder and PTSD," *Drug and Alcohol Dependence,* vol. 133, no. 1 (2013): 180; Amy Bombay, Kim Matheson, and Hymie Anisman, "Intergenerational Trauma: Convergence of Multiple Processes among First Nations People in Canada," *Journal de la santé autochtone* (November 2009), 15. There is not yet a consensus on the validity of generational trauma theory due to the ambiguity of some of its organizing concepts and the need for further study. For the discussion, see for example T. Evans-Campbell, "Historical Trauma In American Indian/Native Alaska Communities: A Multilevel Framework for Exploring Impacts on Individuals, Families, and Communities," *Journal of Interpersonal Violence*, vol. 23, no. 3, (2008): 316–38; J. P. Gone, "A Community-Based Treatment for Native American historical trauma: Prospects for Evidence-Based Practice," *Journal of Counseling and Clinical Psychology*, vol. 77, no. 4, (2009): 751–62; J. P. Gone and C. Alcántara, "Identifying Effective Mental Health Interventions for American Indians and Alaska Natives: A Review of the Literature," *Cultural Diversity & Ethnic Minority Psychology*, vol. 13, no. 4, (2007): 356–63.

28 Lisa Blee, "Struggles Over Memory: Indigenous People and Commemorative Culture," *Reviews in American History*, vol. 46, no. 4, (December 2018): 603; Blee and O'Brien, *Monumental Mobility*, 63–5, 76.

29 DeLucia, "Memory on the Move," 9, 87, 90; Waziyatawin Angela Wilson (ed.), *In the Footsteps of Our Ancestors: The Dakota Commemorative Marches of the 21st Century* (St. Paul, MN: Living Justice Press, 2006); Coll Thrush, *Indigenous London: Native Travelers at the Heart of Empire* (New Haven, CT: Yale University Press, 2016); Christine M. DeLucia, *Memory Lands: King Philip's War and the Place of Violence in the Northeast* (New Haven, CT: Yale University Press, 2018), 22–9; Kent Blansett, "How Alcatraz became a powerful monument for Indigenous peoples," Washington Post (Nov. 20, 2019), www.washingtonpost.com/outlook/2019/11/20/how-alcatraz-became-powerful-monument-indigenous-peoples/; Blansett, *A Journey to Freedom*;

Gerald Vizenor, *Manifest Manners: Narratives on Postindian Survivance* (Lincoln: University of Nebraska Press, 1999), vii; Lisa Blee, "Struggles Over Memory," 603. Sonya Atalay makes similar arguments about public archaeology and Indigenous approaches. See Sonya Atalay, *Community-Based Archaeology: Research with, by and for Indigenous and Local Communities* (Berkeley: University of California Press, 2012). N. Bruce Duthu has suggested the importance of reconfiguring Indigenous memory to show its ongoing legacy in contemporary tribal sovereignty. See N. Bruce Duthu, "Commentary: Reconciling Our Memories in Order to Re-envision Our Future," in Catherine Bell and David Kahane eds., *Intercultural Dispute Resolution in Aboriginal Contexts* (Vancouver: University of British Columbia Press, 2004), 232–7; N. Bruce Duthu, *Shadow Nations: Tribal Sovereignty and the Limits of Legal Pluralism* (New York and Oxford, UK: Oxford University Press, 2013). For the Canadian context for counter-assimilationist strategies in Indigenous worlds, see Victoria Jane Freeman, "'Toronto Has No History!' Indigineity, Settler Colonialism and Historical Memory in Canada's Largest City," PhD diss., University of Toronto, 2010, chap. 8.

30 Katherine Ellinghaus, *Blood Will Tell: Native Americans and Assimilation Policy* (Lincoln: University of Nebraska Press, 2017); Norbert S. Hill, Jr. and Kathleen Ratteree (eds), *The Great Vanishing Act: Blood Quantum and the Future of Native Nations* (Golden, CO: Fulcrum Publishing, 2017); Elspeth Martini, "Borderlands, Indigenous Homelands and North American Settler Colonialism," *Reviews in American History,* vol. 45 (2017): 416, 422; Whitt and Clarke, *North American Genocides*, 60; Sarah E. Hammill, "McIvor v. Canada and the 2010 Amendments to the Indian Act: A Half-Hearted Remedy to Historical Injustice," *Const. F,* vol. 19 (2011): 75–80; John Borrows, *Freedom and Indigenous Constitutionalism* (Toronto: University of Toronto Press, 2016).

31 Henrietta Mann, "Foreword," in Kathleen Ratteree and Norbert S. Hill Jr. (eds), *The Great Vanishing Act: Blood Quantum and the Future of Native Nations* (Golden, CO: Fulcrum Publishing, 2017), xv. For another important voice on the role of blood quantum in unsettling Indigenous approaches to cultural sovereignty, see the work of Jill Doerfler, such as "'Making ourselves whole with words': A Short History of White Earth Anishinaabeg Tribal Citizenship Criteria," in Ratteree and Hill Jr., *The Great Vanishing Act: Blood Quantum and the Future of Native Nations,* 189–209. See also Jill Doerfler, *Those Who Belong: Identity, Family, Blood, and Citizenship Among the White Earth Anishinaabeg* (East Lansing: Michigan State University Press, 2015); Beth Piatote, *Domestic Subjects: Gender, Citizenship, and Law in Native American Literature* (New Haven, CT: Yale University Press, 2013).

32 Dershowitz, *The Vanishing American Jew*, 2; Ratteree and Hill Jr., *The Great Vanishing Act*, xvii; Kim TallBear, *Native American DNA: Tribal Belonging and the False Promise of Genetic Science* (Minneapolis: University of Minnesota Press, 2013); Krystal Tsosie, "Elizabeth Warren's DNA Is Not Her Identity," *The Atlantic*, October 17, 2018, https://www.theatlantic.com/ideas/archive/2018/10/what-make-elizabeth-warrens-dna-test/573205/; Krystal Tsosie and Matthew Anderson. "Two Native Americans Geneticists Interpret Elizabeth Warren's DNA test." *The Conversation.* October 22, 2018, https://

theconversation.com/two-native-american-geneticists-interpret-elizabeth-warrens-dna-test-105274. See also the excellent bibliography on this phenomenon, complied by Adrienne Keene, Rebecca Nagle, and Joseph M. Pierce, at http://www.criticalethnicstudiesjournal.org/blog/2018/12/19/syllabus-elizabeth-warren-cherokee-citizenship-and-dna-testing.

33 On the intergenerational and ongoing transmission of Holocaust trauma from a literary perspective, see Victoria Aarons and Alan L. Berger, *Third-Generation Holocaust Representation Trauma, History, and Memory* (Evanston, IL: Northwestern University Press, 2017).

34 Keep America Beautiful, Inc. 2006; Ad Council 2009; Finis Dunaway, *Seeing Green: The Use and Abuse of American Environmental Images* (Chicago: University of Chicago Press, 2015), 79–96; David Rich Lewis, "American Indian Environmental Relations," in Douglas C. Sackman (ed.), A *Companion to American Environmental History* (Chichester, UK: Wiley-Blackwell, 2010), 191–32; Maureen Konkle, *Writing Indian Nations: Native Intellectuals and the Politics of Historiography, 1827–1863* (Chapel Hill: University of North Carolina Press, 2004), 295; Paul Nadasky, "Transcending the Debate over the Ecologically Noble Indian: Indigenous Peoples and Environmentalism," *Ethnohistory,* vol. 52, no. 2 (2005): 291–331; Shepard Krech III, *The Ecological Indian: Myth and History* (New York: W.W. Norton, 1999), 23–7.

35 Dagmar Wernitznig, *Europe's Indians, Indians in Europe: European Perceptions and Appropriations of Native American Cultures from Pocahontas to the Present* (Lanham, MD: University Press of America, 2007), 132; Wilmer Mesteth et al., "Declaration of War Against Exploiters of Lakota Spirituality," June, 10, 1993; Maureen Trudelle Schwarz, *Fighting Colonialism with Hegemonic Culture: Native American Appropriation of Indian Stereotypes* (Albany, NY: SUNY Press, 2013); Suzanne Owen, *The Appropriation of Native American Spirituality* (London: Bloomsbury, 2011); Lisa Aldred, "Plastic Shamans and Astroturf Sun Dances: New Age Commercialism of Native American Spirituality," *American Indian Quarterly*, vol. 24, no. 3. (2000): 342.

36 Eva Marie Garroutte, *Real Indians: Identity and the Survival of Native America* (Berkeley: University of California Press, 2003); Circe Sturm, *Blood Politics: Race, Culture, and Identity in the Cherokee Nation of Oklahoma* (Berkeley: University of California Press, 2002); Steve Russell, "Review of Real Indians: Identity and the Survival of Native America by Eva Marie Garroutte," *Political and Legal Anthropology Review*, vol. 27, no. 1 (May 2004): 147–53. In addition to the work of Jill Doerfler discussed above, see also Wallace Coffey and Rebecca Tsosie, "Rethinking the Tribal Sovereignty Doctrine: Cultural Sovereignty and the Collective Future of Indian Nations," *Stanford Law and Policy Review,* vol. 12, no. 1, (2001): 191–210.

37 See, for example, the various essays in Carter Jones Meyer and Diana Royer (eds), *Selling the Indian: Commercializing & Appropriating American Indian Cultures* (Tucson: University of Arizona Press, 2001); Owen, *The Appropriation of Native American Spirituality.*

38 On the use of *Tikkun Olam* in these ways, see Levi Cooper, "The Assimilation of Tikkun Olam," *Jewish Political Studies Review,* vol. 25, no. 3–4 (Fall 2013):

11-12; Gilbert S. Rosenthal, "Tikkun ha-Olam: The Metamorphosis of a Concept," *Journal of Religion,* vol. 85, no. 2 (2005): 214–40; http://www.pewforum.org/files/2013/10/jewish-american-survey-full-report.pdf.

**39** Liberal Jews Are Destroying Their Own Religion," *New York Post*, June 23, 2018, https://nypost.com/2018/06/23/liberal-jews-are-destroying-their-own-religion/; Jonathan Neumann, *To Heal the World?: How the Jewish Left Corrupts Judaism and Endangers Israel* (New York: All Point Books and St. Martin's Press, 2018), xvii, 207–10; Avril Alba, *The Holocaust Memorial Museum: Sacred Secular Space* (Basingstoke, UK: Palgrave Macmillan, 2015); Cathy Young, "What They Talk About When They Talk About Intersectionality," *Tablet Magazine*, January 30, 2019.

**40** Shaul Magid, "Social Justice and the Future of Judaism," *Tablet Magazine*, June 13, 2018, https://www.tabletmag.com/jewish-arts-and-culture/264145/social-justice-and-the-future-of-judaism.

**41** On the association between Holocaust memory, Lemkin's genealogy of influence, and Tikkun Olam, including as argued by Moses and Jacobs, see Douglas Irvin-Erickson, *Raphael Lemkin and the Concept of Genocide* (Philadelphia: University of Pennsylvania Press, 2017), 18; Lemkin, *Totally Unofficial Man,* cited in A. Dirk Moses, "Genocide," *Australian Humanities Review*, 55 (November 2013), 28; A. Dirk Moses, "Genocide," *Australian Humanities Review*, 55 (November 2013), 28. See also the discussion n Gilbert S. Rosenthal, "'Tikkun ha-Olam: The Metamorphosis of a Concept," *Journal of Religion,* vol. 85, no. 2 (2005): 214–40.

**42** Neumann, *To Heal the World?;* Magid, "Social Justice and the Future of Judaism."

**43** Cnaan Liphshiz, "Why 'Lucky Jew' Imagery Is So Popular in Poland," *The Times of Israel*, August 18, 2018, https://www.timesofisrael.com/why-lucky-jew-imagery-is-so-popular-in-poland/; Blee and O'Brien, *Monumental Mobility*, 58–9; Ruth Ellen Gruber, *Virtually Jewish: Reinventing Jewish Culture in Europe* (Berkeley and Los Angeles: University of California Press, 2002); Geneviève Zubrzycki, "Nationalism, "Philosemitism," and Symbolic Boundary-Making in Contemporary Poland," *Comparative Studies in Society and History*, vol. 58, no. 1 (2016): 66–98; Doug Saunders, "A Jewish Revival In Poland Without Any Jews," *The Globe and Mail*, January 26, 2005, updated April 21, 2018, https://www.theglobeandmail.com/news/world/a-jewish-revival-in-poland-without-any-Jews/article18213965; Sander Gilman and Karen Remmler (eds., *Reemerging Jewish Culture in Germany: Life and Literature since 1989* (New York: New York University Press, 1994): 15–45; Wendy Rose, "The Great Pretenders: Further Reflections on Whiteshamanism," in M. Annette Jaimes, *The State of Native North America* (Boston: South End Press, 1992), 403–21. On earlier approaches to the "simultaneous repression and evocation of Jewish difference" in Viennese cultural allusions to Jews and Judaism, see Lisa Silverman, "Absent Jews and Invisible Antisemitism in Postwar Vienna: *Der Prozeß* (1948) and *The Third Man* (1949)," *Journal of Contemporary History,* vol. 52, no. 2 (2017): 211–28. For an attempt to document the "vanishing" of Jewish cultural artifacts in Eastern Europe and the failure to commemorate its loss, see also the important photographic work and writings of Christian Herrmann, which notes the increasing blurring of "traces" of old Jewish life in Europe. See Christian Herrmann, *In schwindendem Licht. Jüdische Spuren im Osten Europas* (Lukas Verlag, 2018); Christian Herrmann, "I Have Nothing to Say, Just to Show: Traces of a Genocide," https://www.bh.org.il/blog-items/nothing-say-just-show-traces-genocide. (2018) See also the website for Herrmann's work at https://vanishedworld.blog/.

44 On the problem of the Holocaust's "negative" identity formation in Jewish circles, see Shaul Magid, "The American Jewish Holocaust 'Myth' and 'Negative Judaism': Jacob Neusner's Contribution to American Judaism," in A. Avery Peck, B. Chilton, W. S. Green, and G. G. Porton (eds), *A Legacy of Learning: Essays in Honor of Jacob Neusner* (Leiden: Brill, 2014), 321–40.

45 We should not overlook the resurgence of interest among younger Jews of their cultural and linguistic heritage, including the Yiddish language, and their comfort with a more open form of Jewish identity. See Sally Kalson, "Yiddish Language and Culture Enjoying a Worldwide Resurgence," *Pittsburgh Post-Gazette*, April 21, 2013, https://www.post-gazette.com/life/lifestyle/2013/04/21/Yiddish-language-and-culture-enjoying-a-worldwide-resurgence/stories/201304210199.

## Chapter Five "A permanent statement of our values."

1 Carol Duncan and Alan Wallach, "The Universal Survey Museum," in Bettina Messias (ed.), *Museum Studies* Malden, MA: Blackwell, 2004), 55.; Miriam Jordan and Julian Halaydn, "Formations of 'Indian' Fantasies: European Museums and the Decontextualization of Native American Art and Artifacts," in Karsten Fitz (ed.), *Visual Representations of Native Americans: Transnational Contexts and Perspectives* (Heidelberg: Universitätsverlag Winter [American Studies Monograph Series], 2012), 179–93; Ruth B. Philips, "A Proper Place for Art or the Proper Arts of Place? Native North American Objects and the Hierarchies of Art, Craft, and Souvenir," in Lynda Jessup (ed.), *On Aboriginal Representation in the Gallery* (Hull, Quebec: Canadian Museum of Civilization, 2002), 45. See also the discussion of Phillips' assessments in Miriam Jordan and Julian Halaydn, "Formations of 'Indian' Fantasies," 180–2. These ideas, according to Rainer Hatoum, "paired with the widely shared assumption of the rapid disappearance of Indigenous peoples in the face of civilization, led to the establishment of the Berlin Museum." See Rainer Hatoum, "'The First Real Indians That I Have Seen': Franz Boas and the Disentanglement of the Entangled," *ab-Original: Journal of Indigenous Studies and First Nations and First Peoples' Culture*, vol. 2, no. 2 (2018): 18.

2 Jens-Uwe Guettel, *German Expansionism, Imperial Liberalism and the United States, 1776–1945* (Cambridge, UK: Cambridge University Press, 2012), 83; Christian Feest, "Germany's Indians in a European Perspective," in Colin G. Calloway, Gerd Gemuenden, and Susanne Zantop (eds), *Germans and Indians: Fantasies, Encounters, Projections* (Lincoln, NE: University of Nebraska Pres,

2002), 29–31; Kate Flint, *The Transatlantic Indian, 1776–1930* (Princeton, NJ: Princeton University Press, 2009). Nonetheless, the situation is more marked in Germany. See Hartmut Lutz, *Approaches: Essays in Native North American Studies and Literatures* (Augsburg: Wissner Verlag, 2002), 168–9. Nicole Perry has recently described a particularly acute "German framework from which to analyze the German preoccupation with North American Indigeneity." See Nicole Perry, "Verwoben in 'Indianthusiasm': A Uniquely German Entanglement," *ab-Original*, vol. 2, no. 2 (2018): 210.

3 Karl May, preface to Winnetou (1892). See the discussion of this preface in Lisa Michelle King, "Revisiting Winnetou: The Karl May Museum, Cultural Appropriation, and Indigenous Self-Representation," *Studies in American Indian Literatures*, vol. 28, no. 2, (Summer 2016): 25–55. See also Nicole Perry, "Verwoben in 'Indianthusiasm': A Uniquely German Entanglement," *ab-Original*, vol. 2, no. 2 (2018): 233–6.

4 See Frank Usbeck, *Fellow Tribesmen: The Image of Native Americans, National Identity, and Nazi Ideology in Germany* (New York: Berghahn Books, 2015), esp. chaps. 1 and 2; H. Glenn Penny, *Kindred by Choice: Germans and American Indians since 1800* (Chapel Hill, NC: University of North Carolina Press, 2013), chaps. 1–6; Alfred Vagts, "The Germans and the Red Man," *American–German Review*, vol. 24 (1957): 17.; Jace Weaver, *The Red Atlantic: American Indigenes and the Making of the Modern World 1000–1927* (Chapel Hill: University of North Carolina Press, 2014), 254–7.

5 Perry, "Verwoben in "Indianthusiasm," 232–3; Karl May, *Winnetou: Erster Band. Historisch-Kritische Ausgabe.* ed. J. Biermann and U. Scheinhammer-Schmid (Radebeul: Karl May Verlag, 2003); Lutz, *Approaches: Essays in Native North American Studies and Literatures*, 168–9; Hartmut Lutz, "German Indianthusiam: A Socially Constructed German National(ist) Myth," in *Germans and Indians: Fantasies, Encounters*, 167–84; Susanne Zantop, "Close Encounters: Deutsche and Indianer," in *Germans and Indians*, 3–14; Susanne Zantop, *Colonial Fantasies: Conquest, Family, and Nation in Precolonial Germany, 1770–1870* (Durham, NC: Duke University Press, 1997), 193; King, "Revisiting Winnetou," 29–30; Perry, "Verwoben in "Indianthusiasm", 232–3.

6 Hatoum, ""The First Real Indians That I Have Seen," 18, 51; Gerald McMaster, Julia Lum, and Kaitlin McCormick, "The Entangled Gaze: Indigenous and European Views of Each Other," *ab-Original: Journal of Indigenous Studies and First Nations and First Peoples' Culture,* Vol. 2, no. 2 (2018): 18; Laura Mulvey, "Changing Objects, Preserving Time," in Laura Mulvey (ed.), *Jimmie Durham* (London: Phaidon, 1995), 64–5; Miriam Jordan and Julian Halaydn, "Formations of 'Indian' Fantasies," 180–2. Amanda Cobb highlights the tendency for European ethnographic displays to follow non-Indigenous institutions in the United States by emphasizing "Native Americans as peoples of a distant past; this is particularly true of dioramas, which 'freeze' Native people in a particular moment in time . . . [and which] tend to establish Native American peoples as 'other' and frequently, whether intentionally or not, as exotic and inferior." See Amanda Cobb, "The National Museum of the American Indian as Cultural Sovereignty," in Amy Lonetree and Amanda J. Cobb (eds), *The National Museum of the American Indian: Critical*

*Conversations* (Lincoln, NE: University of Nebraska Press. 2008), 342. In new work on American "salvage tourism," Katrina Phillips has shown how European ethnography has often influenced museums and public sites on the western side of the Atlantic as they have supplanted Indigenous concerns with multi-cultural approaches to public memory. See Katrina Phillips, *Staging Indigeneity: Salvage Tourism and the Performance of Native American History* (Chapel Hill: University of North Carolina Press, forthcoming).

7 Jonathan Boyarin, "Europe's Indian, America's Jew: Modiano and Vizenor," *Boundary*, vol. 19, no. 3 (Autumn 1992): 207.

8 Zantop, "Close Encounters: Deutsche and Indianer," 4, Klaus Walther, *Karl May* (Munich: Deutscher Taschenbuch Verlag, 2002), 10–11; King, "Revisiting Winnetou," 29, 34, 37; Evan Maurer, "Presenting the American Indian: From Europe to America," in W. Richard West Jr. (ed.), *The Changing Presentation of the American Indian* (Seattle: University of Washington Press, 2000), 24; King, "Revisiting Winnetou," 31.

9 Catherine Hickley, "Humboldt Forum to show Britain's 1897 violence and plunder in Benin exhibition next year," *The Art Newspaper*, March 31, 2021, https://www.theartnewspaper.com/interview/humboldt-forum-to-show-britain-s-1897-violence-and-plunder-in-benin-exhibition.

10 Chip Colwell, *Plundered Skulls and Stolen Spirits: Inside the Fight to Reclaim Native America's Culture* (Chicago: University of Chicago Press, 2017); Courtney Cottrell, "Competing Discourses, Developing Partnerships: Navigating Differences Between Ethnographic Museums and Tribal Museums," PhD diss., University of Michigan, (2017), 16–17.

11 See Cottrell, "Competing Discourses, Developing Partnerships," ix, 9, 15, 42-3, 115, 125 132; "Cultural Change: Horses, Traders, and Settlers" exhibit at the Berlin Ethnologisches Museum, cited in Cottrell, "Competing Discourses, Developing Partnerships," 128–30. See also Barbara Kirshenblatt-Gimblett, *Destination Culture: Tourism, Museums, and Heritage* (Berkeley and Los Angeles: University of California Press, 1998).

12 H. Glenn Penny, "Elusive Authenticity: The Quest for the Authentic Indian in German Public Culture," *Comparative Studies in Society and History*, vol. 48, no. 4, (October 2006), 798–818; Petra Kalshoven, *Crafting "the Indian": Knowledge, Desire & Play in Indianist Reenactment* (New York: Berghahn Books, 2012); Glenn Penny, *Objects of Culture: Ethnology and Ethnographic Museums in Imperial Germany* (Chapel Hill and London: University of North Carolina Press, 2002); Glenn Penny, *Kindred by Choice: Germans and American Indians since 1800* (Chapel Hill: University of North Carolina Press, 2013); Martin Hermansky, "War Bonnets and Calumets in the Heart of Europe: Native American Exhibition in Rosenheim, Germany," *Lidé města / Urban People,* vol. 13 (2011): 281–2, 288, 293. Some more balanced and accurate exhibitions at the Rosenheim site likely resulted from the involvement of Christian Feest, one of the exhibition curators, who has published volumes of nuanced scholarship on European perceptions of Indigenous people.

13 Paul Williams, *Memorial Museums: The Global Rush to Commemorate Atrocities* (Oxford, UK: Berg Publishers, 2007), 25.

**14** On non-Jewish memorialization see Dan Michman, "Historiography on the Holocaust in Poland: An Outsider's View of its Place within Recent General Developments in Holocaust Historiography," *New Directions in the History of the Jews in the Polish Lands*, 396; Nicolas Berg, *The Holocaust and the West German Historians: Historical Interpretation and Autobiographical Memory* (Madison: University of Wisconsin Press, 2015); Chris Lorenz, "Border-crossings: Some Reflections on the Role of German Historians in Recent Public Debates on Nazi History," in Dan Michman (ed.), *Remembering the Holocaust in Germany, 1945–2000: German Strategies and Jewish Responses* (New York: Peter Lang Inc., 2002), 59–94. On Cold War contexts see Mercer, "The Memory of Europe's Age of Catastrophe 1914–2014," 621. In France, "the nation as victim and martyr took on new importance as a theme of commemoration" after 1945. See Sarah Farmer, *Martyred Village: Commemorating the 1944 Massacre at Oradour-sur-Glane* (Berkeley and Los Angeles: University of California Press, 1999), 10. See also A. A. Assmann, "Europe's divided memory," in U. Blacker, A. Ėtkind, and J. Fedor (eds), *Memory and Theory in Eastern Europe* (New York: Palgrave, 2013), 25–41; A. Assmann, "Transnational Memories," *European review*, vol. 22 (2014): 546–56; C. Kinnvall, I. Manners, and J. Mitzen, "Introduction to 2018 Special Issue of European Security: "Ontological (In)Security in the European Union," *European Security*, vol. 27, no. 3 (2018): 249–65; Gößwald, "Politics and Memory," 448, 450; Mercer, "The Memory of Europe's Age of Catastrophe 1914–2014," 621.

**15** On the early genealogy for conflicts over the occlusion of Jewish suffering at such public sites, see Jonathan Huener, *Auschwitz, Poland, and the Politics of Commemoration, 1945–1979* (Athens: Ohio University Press, 2003); Harold Marcuse, *Legacies of Dachau: The Uses and Abuses of a Concentration Camp, 1933–2001* (Cambridge, UK: Cambridge University Press, 2001).

**16** Richard Bessel, "Functionalists vs. Intentionalists: The Debate Twenty Years on or Whatever Happened to Functionalism and Intentionalism?" *German Studies Review*, vol. 26, no. 1 (2003): 16; Gavriel D. Rosenfeld, *Munich and Memory Architecture, Monuments, and the Legacy of the Third Reich* (Berkeley: Univerity of California Press, 2000), 2.

**17** Jürgen Habermas, "A Kind of Settlement of Damages: On Apologetic Tendencies in German History Writing," in Ernst Piper (ed.), *Forever in the Shadow of Hitler?* (Atlantic Highlands, N.J: Humanities Press, 1993), 43; Siobhan Kattago, *Ambiguous Memory: The Nazi Past and German National Identity* (Westport, CT: Praeger Press, 2001), 56–62; Małgorzata Pakier and Bo Stråth, A *European Memory?: Contested Histories and Politics of Remembrance* (New York, Berghahn Books, 2010), 264; Gößwald, "Politics and Memory," 451; Wulf Kansteiner, "Losing the War, Winning the Memory Battle," in Claudio Fogu, Wulf Kansteiner, and Richard Lebow (eds), *The Politics of Memory in Postwar Europe* (Durham, NC: Duke University Press, 2006), 125.

**18** Michelle Magin, "Toward a Globalised Memory of the Holocaust: An Exploration of the Exhibition Spaces and Educational Programmes at Four Sites of Remembrance in Post-Unification Berlin," PhD diss., University of Manchester, 2015, 61; Peter Carrier, *Holocaust Monuments and National*

*Memory Cultures in France and Germany since 1989: The Origins and Political Function of the Vél' d'Hiv' in Paris and the Holocaust Monument in Berlin* (New York: Bergahn Books, 2005), 24. See also Derek Dalton, *Encountering Nazi Tourism Sites* (New York: Routledge, 2020); Daniel P. Reynolds, *Postcards from Auschwitz: Holocaust Tourism and the Meaning of Remembrance* (New York: NYU Press, 2018); Michael Meng, *Shattered Spaces: Encountering Jewish Ruins in Postwar Germany and Poland* (Cambridge, MA: Harvard University Press, 2011).

19 Sibylle Quack, "The Holocaust Memorial in Berlin and Its Information Center: Concepts, Controversies, Reactions," in Annie E. Coombes and Ruth B. Phillips (eds), *Museum Transformations: Decolonization and Democratization* (Hoboken, NJ: Wiley Blackwell, 2020), 15.

20 "German Bundestag Resolution," cited in Sibylle Quack, "The Holocaust Memorial in Berlin and Its Information Center," 7, 8, 14; Kansteiner, "Losing the War, Winning the Memory Battle," 129–30, 138; Sibylle Quack, "The Holocaust Memorial in Berlin and Its Information Center," 15; Irit Dekel, "Jews and Other Others at the Holocaust Memorial in Berlin," *Anthropological Journal of European Cultures*, vol. 23, no. 2 (2014): 77; Irit Dekel, *Mediation at the Holocaust Memorial in Berlin* (New York: Palgrave, 2013).

21 W. Michael Blumenthal, "Inauguration speech," cited Jennifer Hansen-Glucklich, *Holocaust Memory Reframed: Museums and the Challenges of Representation* (New Brunswick, NJ: Rutgers University Press, 2014), 38; Hansen-Glucklich, *Holocaust Memory Reframed,* 38.

22 Daniel Levy and Natan Sznaider, *The Holocaust and Memory in the Global Age* (Philadelphia: Temple University Press, 2006), 195; D. Levy and N. Sznaider, "Memory Unbound: The Holocaust and the Formation of Cosmopolitan," *European Journal of Social Theory*, vol. 5, no. (2002), IOCf. 8. On the idea of a negative icon, see Dan Diner, *Gegenläufige Gedächtnisse. Über Geltung und Wirkung des Holocaust* (Göttingen: Vandenhoeck & Ruprecht., 2007), 7. See also Tom Lawson, "The Myth of the European Civil War," in Richard Littlejohns and Sara Soncini (eds), *Myths of Europe* (Amsterdam: Editions Rodopi BV, 2007), 287.

23 Nelia Dias, "Double Erasures: Rewriting the Past at the Musée du quai Branly." *Social Anthropology,* vol. 16 (2008): 302, 304–05; Barbara Kirshenblatt-Gimblett, "World Heritage and Cultural Economics," in I. Karp, Corinne A. Kratz, Lynn Szwaja, and Tomas Ybarra-Frausto (eds), *Museum Frictions: Public Cultures/Global Transformations* (Durham: Duke University Press, 2006), 183. Octave Debary and Melanie Roustana, "A Journey to the Musée du Quai Branly: The Anthropology of a Visit," *Museum Anthropology*, vol. 40, no. 1 (2017): 5.

24 Pierre Bourdieu, *The Rules of Art: Genesis and Structure of the Literary Field*, cited in Jordan and Halaydn, "Formations of 'Indian' Fantasies," 180; Dias, "Double Erasures," 304–05, 307, 309. See also Anthony Alan Shelton, "The Public Sphere as Wilderness: Le Musée du quai Branly," *Museum Anthropology* vol. 32, no. 1 (2009): 1–16; Natasha Ruiz-Gomez, "The (Jean) Nouvel Other: Primitivism and the Musée du quai Branly," *Modern and*

*Contemporary France,* vol. 14, no. 4 (2006): 17–32; Sally Price, *Paris Primitive: Jacques Chirac's Museum on the Quai Branly* (Chicago: Chicago University Press, 2007), 169; James Clifford, "Quai Branly in Process," *October Magazine,* vol. 120 (Spring 2007), 18.

25 Mercer, "The Memory of Europe's Age of Catastrophe 1914–2014," 621. See also Farmer, *Martyred Village,* 10.

26 François Mitterrand's annual presidential declaration on July 14, this time in 1992, "'De mauvaises moeurs se sont répandues partout, y compris dans la justice,'" *Le Monde*, July 16, 1992, 6–7; Peter Carrier, *Holocaust Monuments and National Memory: France and Germany since 1989*, 162.

27 Carrier, *Holocaust Monuments and National Memory: France and Germany since 1989*, 24–5, 41, 160–2. See also Eric Langenbacher and Friederike Eigler, "Introduction: Memory Boom or Memory Fatigue in Twenty-first Century Germany?," *German Politics and Society,* vol. 23, no. 3 (2005): 1–15.

28 Tom Lawson and Andy Pearce, "Britain and the Holocaust: An Introduction," in *The Palgrave Handbook of Britain and the Holocaust*, 3.

29 "Richard Dimbleby Describes Belsen", BBC News, April 15, 1945, https://www.bbc.co.uk/archive/richard-dimbleby-describes-belsen/zvw7cqt; Caroline Sharples, "'Where, Exactly, Is Auschwitz?' British Confrontation with the Holocaust Through the Medium of the 1945 'Belsen' Trial," in *The Palgrave Handbook of Britain and the Holocaust,* 182–3; Dan Stone, "Belsen and the British," in ibid, 160. On the parallel tendency in American public discourse during the late 1940s and 1950s, in which scenes at death camps were described in multinational terms given the confusion of the soldiers that liberated them, and the few number of surviving Jews, see Peter Novick, *The Holocaust in American Life* (New York: Houghton Mifflin, 1999), 63–4.

30 Andy Pearce, *Holocaust Consciousness in Contemporary Britain* (London: Routledge, 2014), 165–85; Barry Langford, "British Cinema and the Holocaust," in *The Palgrave Handbook of Britain and the Holocaust,* 270–1; Isabel Wollaston, "'I Belong Here. I Know I Ought Never to Have Come Back, Because It Has Proved I've Never Been Away': Kitty Hart-Moxon's Documentaries of Return," in ibid, 347–66.

31 See Stephen Smith, *Making Memory: Creating Britain's First Holocaust Centre* (Newark, NJ: 2002); https://www.holocaust.org.uk/our-history; "The brothers behind the UK's only Holocaust museum," BBC News Website, Jan 27, 2020, https://www.bbc.com/news/uk-england-nottinghamshire-51239945.

32 Kara Critchell, "From Celebrating Diversity to British Values: The Changing Face of Holocaust Memorial Day in Britain," in *The Palgrave Handbook of Britain and the Holocaust*, 429–48; Stone, "From Stockholm to Stockton," 212; Andy Pearce, "An Emerging "Holocaust Memorial Problem?: The Condition of Holocaust Culture in Britain," *The Journal of Holocaust Research,* vol. 33, no. 2 (2019), accessed on page 12 of preprint; Mark Donnelly, "'We Should Do Something for the Fiftieth': Remembering Auschwitz, Belsen and the Holocaust in Britain in 1995," in *Britain and the Holocaust,* 171–89; Steven Cooke, "Negotiating Memory and Identity: the Hyde Park Holocaust Memorial, London," *Journal of Historical Geography* vol. 26, no. 3 (July 2000): 449–65; Andy Pearce, "Britain and the Formation

of Contemporary Holocaust Consciousness: A Product of Europeanization, or Exercise in Triangulation?," in Lucy Bond and Jessica Rapson (eds), *The Transcultural Turn: Interrogating Memory Between and Beyond Borders* (Berlin: De Gruyter, 2014), 119–39. See also Adam Sutcliffe, "The Politics of Holocaust Memory," in Anna Maerker, Simon Sleight, and Adam Sutcliffe (eds), *History, Memory and Public Life: The Past in the Present* (London; New York: Routledge, 2018), chapter 12.

33 "Blair unveils Holocaust memorial plan," Jan 26, 2000, http://news.bbc.co.uk/2/hi/uk_news/politics/619244.stm. According to Pearce, at the beginning of the twenty-first century, Britain's Holocaust culture was "conflicting and conflictual." See Andy Pearce, *Holocaust Consciousness in Contemporary Britain*, 209.

34 John P. Fox, *Teaching the Holocaust: A Report of a Survey in the United Kingdom* (Leicester: National Yad Vashem Charitable Trust and The Centre for Holocaust Studies, 1989), 12–13; Pearce, "An Emerging "Holocaust Memorial Problem?:" (accessed on pp. 12 and 15 of preprint); Stone, "From Stockholm to Stockton," 219, 221; Pearce, "The Development of Holocaust Consciousness in Contemporary Britain, 1979–2001", 71–94; Stephen Smith, "Proposal for International Commemoration of the Holocaust", in J. D. Bindenagel (ed.), *Proceedings of the Washington Conference on Holocaust-Era Assets* (Washington, 1999), 998; Klas-Göran Karlsson, "Public Uses of History in Contemporary Europe," in Harriet Jones, Kjell Östberg and Nico Randeraad (eds), *Contemporary History on Trial: Europe since 1989 and the Role of the Expert Historian* (Manchester: Manchester University Press, 2007), 27–45.

35 Larissa Allwork, *Holocaust Remembrance between the National and the Transnational: The Stockholm International Forum and the First Decade of the International Task Force* (London: Bloomsbury, 2015), 111–31; Stone, "From Stockholm to Stockton," 217; Pearce, "Britain and the Formation of Contemporary Holocaust Consciousness," 119–39. Some have connected these British commemorative activities to the context of the Iraq war and the desire to change the narrative of British bellicosity. See Mark Levene, "Britain's Holocaust Memorial Day: A Case of Post-Cold War Wish-Fulfillment, or Brazen Hypocrisy?," *Human Rights Review*, vol. 7, no. 3 (2006): 53. See the declaration at https://www.holocaustremembrance.com/stockholm-declaration.

36 For one interpretation of this phenomenon among Labour party members and progressive activists see Alan Johnson, *Institutionally Antisemitic: Contemporary Left Antisemitism and the Crisis in the British Labour Party* (2019), http://fathomjournal.org/wp-content/uploads/2019/03/Institutionally-Antisemitic-Report-for-event.pdf. To be sure, scholars and commentators have not yet achieved a settled consensus on the nature and degree of the link between Holocaust obfuscation and anti-Jewish prejudice in progressive or activist circles, or the validity of concepts such as "The New Antisemitism" among "the Left."

37 David Cameron, "25th anniversary of the Holocaust Educational Trust: Prime Minister's Speech," September 16, 2013; David Cameron, "David Cameron's Holocaust Speech," January 27, 2014, https://www.gov.uk/government/speeches/david-camerons-holocaust-commission-speech. The use of Holocaust

memory to prevent misdeeds by the Syrian and Iranian governments, according to Pearce, "infused Cameron's announcement with an unwelcome and unshakeable scent of instrumentalization." See Pearce, "An Emerging "Holocaust Memorial Problem?" (accessed on p. 29 of preprint). https://www.gov.uk/government/speeches/25th-anniversary-of-the-holocaust-educational-trust-prime-ministers-speech. See the discussion of the Holocaust Commission's proposed Holocaust memorial in London, in David Tollerton, "'A New Sacred Space in the Centre of London': The Victoria Tower Gardens Holocaust Memorial and the Religious-Secular Landscape of Contemporary Britain," *Journal of Religion and Society*, vol. 19, no. 4 (2017): 1–22. These trends, which synthesize secular languages of human rights with Christological understandings of universal suffering, can be detected elsewhere in European memory work—ranging from Polish discussions of Auschwitz to the redefinition of Anne Frank in public media. See Stier, *Holocaust Icons*, 148.

**38** Critchell, "From Celebrating Diversity to British Values," 440–7.

**39** The Prime Minister's Holocaust Commission, "Terms of Reference," accessed May 12, 2018, https://assets.publishing.service.gov.uk/government/uploads/system/uploads/attachment_data/file/275198/Terms-of-Reference-PM-Holocaust-Commission.pdf. Cited in Pearce, "An Emerging "Holocaust Memorial Problem?" (accessed on p. 29 of preprint). David Cameron, quoted in "Press release: PM: Holocaust Memorial Will Stand Beside Parliament As Permanent Statement of Our British Values,"; Cabinet Office, *Britain's Promise to Remember*, 21–3, 41. On the use of Belsen as a part of British identity, see also Levene, "Britain's Holocaust Memorial Day," 26–59; Tony Kushner, "Belsen for Beginners: The Holocaust in British Heritage," in Monica Riera and Gavin Schaffer (eds), *The Lasting War: Society and Identity in Britain, France and Germany after 1945* (Basingstoke, UK: Palgrave; 2008), 226–47. See also Kara Critchell, "Remembering and Forgetting: The Holocaust in 21st Century Britain," *Quest. Issues in Contemporary Jewish History. Journal of Fondazione CDEC*, no 10 (December 2016), 23–59; David Tollerton, "Visions of Permanence, Realities of Instability: The Prime Minister's Holocaust Commission and the United Kingdom Holocaust Memorial Foundation," in *The Palgrave Handbook of Britain and the Holocaust,* 449–68; Andy Pearce, "Britishness, Brexit, and the Holocaust," in ibid, 469–506.

**40** Extract from a letter sent to the Prime Minister's Holocaust Commission, May 12, 2014, cited in Andy Pearce and Tom Lawson, "Britain and the Holocaust: An Introduction," in *The Palgrave Handbook of Britain and the Holocaust,* 3; Louise London, "The Agenda of British Refugee Policy, 1933–48," in ibid, 57–74; Anthony Grenville, "The Immigration and Reception of Jewish Refugees from the Third Reich," in ibid, 75–92; Andrea Hammel, "'I Remember Their Labels Round Their Necks' Britain and the Kindertransport," in ibid, 93–112.

**41** Michelle Gordon, "Selective Histories: Britain, the Empire and the Holocaust," in *The Palgrave Handbook of Britain and the Holocaust,* 219–42. See the recent commentaries of Niigaanwewidam James Sinclair on the British imperial involvement in atrocities in present-day Canada, including the toppling of the Queen Victoria statue in summer 2021, in Rachel Bergen, "Mother figure or colonial oppressor? Examining Queen Victoria's legacy after Winnipeg statue toppled," *CBC News*, July 7, 2021, https://www.cbc.ca/news/canada/manitoba/queen-victoria-winnipeg-statues-residential-schools-colonialism-british-empire-1.6090322. On the gap in British museums, see for example Elizabeth Edwards and Matt Mead, "Absent Histories and Absent Images: Photographs, Museums and the Colonial Past," *Museum & Society*, vol. 11, no. 1 (2013): 31–4; Afua Hirsch, "Britain's Colonial Crimes Deserve a Lasting Memorial: Here's Why", *The Guardian*, November 22, 2017. On Australian genocide and the (often overlooked) British connection, see Tom Lawson, *The Last Man: A British Genocide in Tasmania* (London: I.B. Tauris, 2014). See also A. Dirk Moses, 'Empire, Colony, Genocide: Keywords and the Philosophy of History', in Moses (ed.), *Empire, Colony, Genocide: Conquest, Occupation, and Subaltern Resistancein World History* (New York: Berghahn, 2010 [2008]), 26; Dan Stone, *Histories of the Holocaust* (Oxford, UK: Oxford University Press, 2010), 153; Dan Stone, "Britannia Waives the Rules: British Imperialism and Holocaust Memory," in *History, Memory and Mass Atrocity: Essays on the Holocaust and Genocide* (London: Valentine Mitchell, 2006); Michelle Gordon, *Extreme Violence and the 'British Way': Colonial Warfare in Perak, Sierra Leone and Sudan* (London: Bloomsbury, 2020), chap. 1.

42 Lawson, *The Holocaust and Colonial Genocide at the Imperial War Museum*, 160–68; Rebecca Jinks, "Holocaust Memory and Contemporary Atrocities: The Imperial War Museum's Holocaust Exhibition and Crimes Against Humanity Exhibition," in *Britain and the Holocaust*, 143–5, 153; Tony Kushner, *The Holocaust and the Museum World*, 21–4; Tony Kushner, "From 'This Belsen Business' to 'Shoah Business': History, Memory and Heritage, 1945–2005," 189–216; Tony Kushner, "Oral History at the Extremes of Human Experience: Holocaust Testimony in a Museum Setting," *Oral History*, vol. 29, no. 2 (2001): 83–94; Suzanne Bardgett, "Witness Statements: Testimonies at the Holocaust Exhibition," *Museum Practice*, vol. 1, no. 1 (2004): 54–6; Suzanne Bardgett and Annie Dodds, "Exploring the Common Threads of Genocide: The Crimes Against Humanity Exhibition at the Imperial War Museum," in Toby Haggith and Joanna Newman (eds), *Holocaust and the Moving Image: Representations in Film and Television since 1933* (London and New York: Wallflower, 2005), 281; Tom Lawson, "Memorializing colonial genocide in Britain: the case of Tasmania," *Journal of Genocide Research*, vol, 16, no. 4 (2014): 441–61; Tom Lawson, "Coming to Terms with the Past: Reading and Writing Colonial Genocide as a Holocaust Historian," *Holocaust Studies: a Journal of Culture and History*, vol. 20 (2014): 129–56; Donald Bloxham, "Exhibiting Racism: Cultural Imperialism and Representation," *Rethinking History*, vol. 2, no. 3 (1998), 349–58.

43 Kucia, "The Europeanization of Holocaust memory and Eastern Europe," 30, 97–119, 103; Subotic, "Political Memory, Ontological Security, and Holocaust Remembrance in Post-Communist Europe," 300; J. P. Himka, "Obstacles to the Integration of the Holocaust Into Post-Communist East European Historical Narratives," *Canadian Slavonic Papers*, vol. 50, (2008): 359–72; Littoz-Monnet, "The EU Politics of Remembrance: Can Europeans Remember Together?," *West European Politics,* vol. 35, no. 5 (2012): 1183; Oliver Plessow, "The Interplay of the European Commission, Researcher and Educator Networks and Transnational Agencies in the Promotion of a

Pan-European Holocaust Memory," *Journal of Contemporary European Studies,* vol. 23, no. 3 (2015): 388.

44 Kucia, "The Europeanization of Holocaust Memory and Eastern Europe," 97, 103–04; Ljiljana Radonić, "From 'Double Genocide' to 'the New Jews': Holocaust, Genocide and Mass Violence in Post-Communist Memorial Museums," *Journal of Genocide Research*," vol. 20, no. 4, (2018): 515 103–04; Subotic, "Political Memory, Ontological Security, and Holocaust Remembrance in Post-communist Europe," 303; A. Littoz-Monnet, "The EU Politics of Remembrance: Can Europeans Remember Together?" *West European Politics*, vol. 35 (2012): 1182–1202; A. Littoz-Monnet, "Explaining Policy Conflict Across Institutional Venues: European Union-Level Struggles Over the Memory of the Holocaust," *JCMS: Journal of Common Market Studies* (2013), 51, 489–504; L. Neumayer, "Integrating the Central European Past Into a Common Narrative: The Mobilizations Around the 'Crimes of Communism' in the European Parliament," *Journal of Contemporary European Studies*, vol. 23 (2015): 344–63; Éva Kovács, "Limits of Universalization: The European Memory Sites of Genocide," *Journal of Genocide Research*, vol. 20, no. 4, (2018): 490–509. These EU measures exacerbated pre-existing representations that minimized Jewish suffering under national regimes. See Dovid Katz, "On Three Definitions: Genocide; Holocaust Denial: Holocaust Obfuscation," in Leonidas Donskis (ed.), *A Litmus Test Case of Modernity: Examining Modern Sensibilities and the Public Domain in the Baltic States at the Turn of the Century* (New York: Peter Lang, 2009), 365; Dovid Katz, "Is Eastern European 'Double Genocide' Revisionism Reaching Museums?" in *Dapim: Studies on the Holocaust*, vol. 30, no. 3 (November 2016): 18; Natalia Aleksiun, "On Humanizing Victims and Perpetrators of the Holocaust in Eastern Europe," *Journal of Genocide Research*, vol. 20, no. 4 (2018): 645, 648; Mercer, "The Memory of Europe's Age of Catastrophe 1914–2014," 622. Katz has also noted more positive recent developments. See Dovid Katz, "The Extraordinary Recent History of Holocaust Studies in Lithuania," *Dapim: Studies on the Holocaust,* vol. 31, no. 3 (December 2017): 285–95.

45 Hilary Beckles, *Britain's Black Debt: Reparations for Caribbean Slavery and Native Genocide* (Barbados: University of West Indies Press, 2013); William A. Darity, A. Kirsten Mullen, *From Here to Equality: Reparations for Black Americans in the Twenty-First Century* (Chapel Hill: University of North Carolina Press, 2020); Ana Lucia Araujo, *Reparations for Slavery and the Slave Trade: A Transnational and Comparative History* (London: Bloomsbury Publishing, 2017).

46 Jordan and Halaydn, "Formations of 'Indian' Fantasies," 182, 188–9; Gerald McMaster, Julia Lum, and Kaitlin McCormick, "The Entangled Gaze: Indigenous and European Views of Each Other," 8. Congress described NAGPRA as a means to "strike a balance between the interest in scientific examination of skeletal remains and the recognition that Native Americans, like people from every culture around the world, have a religious and spiritual reverence for the remains of their ancestors." See R. Kosslak, "The Native American Graves Protection and Repatriation Act: The Death Knell for Scientific Study?," *American Indian Law Review*, vol. 151 (2000): 130. On

NAGPRA, see for example, Chip Colwell, *Plundered Skulls and Stolen Spirits: Inside the Fight to Reclaim Native America's Culture* (Chicago: University of Chicago Press, 2017); Kathleen Fine-Dare, *Grave Injustice: The American Indian Repatriation Movement and NAGPRA* (Lincoln, NE and London: University of Nebraska Press, 2002). Canadian policy work such as *Turning the Page, A Task Force on Repatriation*, has sought to effect similar recommendations in Canadian museums.

47 See Lisa Michelle King, "Revisiting Winnetou," 26.

48 Gerald Conaty and Clifford Crane Bear, "History, Connections, and Cultural Renewal," in S. Boehm (ed.), *Powerful Images: Portrayals of Native America* (Seattle: University of Washington Press, 1998), 73.

49 Devon Mihesuah (ed.), *Repatriation Reader: Who Owns American Indian Remains?* (Lincoln, NE: University of Nebraska Press, 2000); Cressida Forde, Jane Hubert, and Paul Turnbull (eds), *The Dead and Their Possessions: Repatriation in Principle, Policy in Practice* (New York and London: Routledge, 2004); Robert E. Bieder, "Representations of Indian Bodies in Nineteenth-Century American Anthropology," in *Repatriation Reader*, 19–36; Suzanne J. Crawford, "(Re)constructing Bodies: Semiotic Sovereignty and the Debate over Kennewick Man," in *Repatriation Reader*, 211–36.

50 See the discussion in Neillian MacLachlan, "Sacred and Secular: An Analysis of the Repatriation of Native American Sacred Items from European Museums," MA diss., University of Aberdeen, 2012, 11; UK Parliament. (2000) Memorandum Glasgow City Council, 2.2), available at http://www.publications.parliament.uk/pa/cm199900/cmselect/cmcumeds/371/0051808.htm.

51 As the New York Times noted in 1952, "A collection of damaged sacred objects, looted from Jewish temples in World War II by the Nazis, was buried today in Beth-El Cemetery in ceremonies that go back to Biblical times," "Burying Jewish Religious Objects in Jersey," *The New York Times*, January 14, 1952.

52 Caroline Sturdy Colls, "Holocaust Victims, Jewish Law and the Ethics of Archaeological Investigations," *Accessing Campscapes: Inclusive Strategies for Using European Conflicted Heritage E-Bulletin*, vol. 3 (Autumn 2018); Caroline Sturdy Colls and M. Branthwaite, "This is Proof"? Forensic Evidence and Ambiguous Material Culture at Treblinka Extermination Camp," *International Journal of Historical Archaeology*, vol. 22 (2018): 430–53; Caroline Sturdy Colls, "Holocaust Archaeology: Archaeological Approaches to Landscapes of Nazi Genocide and Persecution," *Journal of Conflict Archaeology*, vol. 7, no. 2 (2012): 71–105; Caroline Sturdy Colls, *Holocaust Archaeologies: Approaches and Future Directions* (London: Springer, 2015); Zuzanna Dziuban (ed.), *Mapping the "Forensic Turn": Engagements with Materialities of Mass Death in Holocaust Studies and Beyond* (Vienna: New Academic Press 2017); Zuzanna Dziuban, "Between Subjectification and Objectification: Theorizing Ashes," in *Mapping the "Forensic Turn,"* 261–88; Zuzanna Dziuban, "(Re)politicising the Dead in Post-Holocaust Poland: The Afterlives of the Human Remains at the Belzec Extermination Camp," in E. Anstett and J-M. Dreyfus (eds), *Human Remains in Society: Curation and*

*Exhibition in the Aftermath of Genocide and Mass-Violence* (Manchester: Manchester University Press, 2016), 38–65; Zuzanna Dziuban, "The Politics of Human Remains at the Peripheries of the Holocaust," *Dapim—Studies on the Holocaust,* vol. 29 (2015): 3; Chloe Paver, *Exhibiting the Nazi Past: Museum Objects Between the Material and the Immaterial* (New York: Palgrave Macmillan, 2018); Ewa Domanska, "The Environmental History of Mass Graves," *Journal of Genocide Research*, vol. 22, no. 2 (2020): 241–55. See also Ivar Schute, "Collecting Artifacts on Holocaust Sites: A Critical Review of Archaeological Research in Ybenheer, Westerbork, and Sobibor," *International Journal of Historical Archaeology,* vol. 22 (2018): 593–613; Bozena Shallcross, *The Holocaust Object in Polish and Polish-Jewish Culture* (Bloomington: Indiana University Press, 2011); Oren Baruch Stier, "Torah and Taboo: Containing Jewish Relics and Jewish Identity at the United States Holocaust Memorial Museum," *Numen,* vol. 57 (2010): 505–36.

53 Marek Kucia, interview in Tygodnik Powszechny (December 28, 2009) in Jan Tomasz Gross and Irena Grudzinska Gross, *Golden Harvest: Events at the Periphery of the Holocaust* (Oxford, UK: Oxford University Press, 2012), 30. See also Andrzej Strzelecki, "The Plunder of Victims and Their Corpses," in Michael Berenbaum and Yisrael Gutman (eds), *Anatomy of the Auschwitz Death Camp* (Bloomington: Indiana University Press, 1998), 246–66, esp. 250–1; Rudolf Vrba, "Claude Lanzmann Shoah Collection, Interview with Rudolf Vrba, November 1978," New York: Steven Spielberg Film and Video Archive, United States Holocaust Memorial Museum, 03:23:30; Rudolf Vrba, *I Escaped from Auschwitz* (Fort Lee, NJ: Barricade Books., 2002), 90–1, 160–6.

54 Dean Neu and Richard Therrien, *Accounting for Genocide: Canada's Bureaucratic Assault on Aboriginal People* (Blackpoint, Nova Scotia: Fernwood Publishing, 2003), 13.

55 Gross and Grudzinska Gross, *Golden Harvest: Events at the Periphery of the Holocaust*, 38–40.

## Chapter Six "The void has made itself apparent as such."

1 *Discover the Past for the Future: A Study on the Role of Historical Sites and Museums in Holocaust Education and Human Rights Education in the EU* (Vienna: European Union Agency for Fundamental Rights, 2010); Jolanta Ambrosewicz-Jacobs, "The Challenges of New Work in History and Education about the Holocaust in Poland," in Antony Polonsky, Hanna Węgrzynek and Andrzej Żbikowski (eds), *New Directions in the History of the Jews in the Polish Lands* (Boston: Academic Studies Press, 2017), 170–82.

2 *Holocaust Remembrance and Representation: Documentation from a Research Conference, Sweden, 2020* (Swedish Government Official Reports SOU 2020: 21, Elanders Sverige AB: Stockholm, 2020).

3 Sibylle Quack, "The Holocaust Memorial in Berlin and Its Information Center: Concepts, Controversies, Reactions," in Annie E. Coombes and Ruth

B. Phillips, *Museum Transformations: Decolonization and Democratization* (Hoboken, NJ: Wiley, 2020), 23; Marion Klein, *Schülerinnen und Schüler am Denkmal für die ermordeten Juden Europas* (Berlin: VS Verlag für Sozialwissenschaften, 2012), 138, 141.

4 Brigitte Sion, "Absent Bodies, Uncertain Memorials: Performing Memory in Berlin and Buenos Aires," PhD diss., New York University, 2008, 171.

5 Quack, "The Holocaust Memorial in Berlin and Its Information Center," 22. On the ambiguous link between abstract memorials and detailed archival centers on the same sites, see also Irit Dekel, "Subjects of Memory? On Performing Holocaust Memory in Two German Historical Museums," *Dapim: Studies on the Holocaust*, vol. 30, no. 3 (2016): 296–314; Gad Yair, "Neutrality, Objectivity, and Dissociation: Cultural Trauma and Educational Messages in German Holocaust Memorial Sites and Documentation Centers," *Holocaust and Genocide Studies,* vol. 26, no. 3 (2014): 487; Irit Dekel, "Jews and Other Others at the Holocaust Memorial in Berlin," *Anthropological Journal of European Cultures*, vol. 23, no. 2 (2014): 71–84; Heidemarie Uhl, "Going Underground; Der ort der Information' des Berliner Holocaust-Denkmals" [The Information Center Of the Berlin Holocaust Memorial], *Zeithistorische Forschuwn/Studies in Contemporary History*, 2 available at http://www.zeithistorische-forschungen.de/16126041-Uhl-3-2008; Irit Dekel, *Mediation at the Holocaust Memorial Berlin* (Basingstoke, UK: Palgrave Macmillan, 2013); Peter Carrier, *Holocaust Monuments and National Memory Cultures in France and Germany since 1989: The Origins and Political Function of the Vél' d'Hiv' in Paris and the Holocaust Monument in Berlin* (New York: Berghahn Books, 2005).

6 Daniel Libeskind, *Space of Encounter* (New York: Universe, 2000), 28; Jennifer Hansen-Glucklich, *Holocaust Memory Reframed: Museums and the Challenges of Representation* (New Brunswick, NJ: Rutgers University Press, 2014), 47; Daniel Libeskind, "Between the Lines: Extension to the Berlin Museum, with the Jewish Museum," *Assemblage*, vol. 12 (1990): 48; Hansen-Glucklich, *Holocaust Memory Reframed*, 54; James E. Young, *At Memory's Edge: After-images of the Holocaust in Contemporary Art and Architecture* (New Haven: Yale University Press, 2000), 37–8, 165.

7 The new redesign may alter these dynamics, including by using narrative techniques that emphasize personalized storytelling. It will be interesting to examine whether those changes reinforce or change existing methods at the exhibit, whether for good or for bad.

8 Tom Lawson, "Ideology in a Museum of Memory: A Review of the Holocaust Exhibition at the Imperial War Museum," *Totalitarian Movements and Political Religions*, vol. 4, no. 2 (2003): 173–83; Hannah Holtschneider, "Holocaust Representation in the Imperial War Museum, 2000–2020," in *The Palgrave Handbook of Britain and the Holocaust*, 390; Tom Lawson, "The Holocaust and Colonial Genocide at the Imperial War Museum," in Caroline Sharples and Olaf Jensen (eds), *Britain and the Holocaust: Remembering and Representing War and Genocide* (Basingstoke, UK: Palgrave Macmillan, 2013), 161; Tom Lawson, "Ideology in a Museum of Memory: A Review of the Holocaust Exhibition at the Imperial War Museum," *Totalitarian Movements and Political Religions,* vol. 4, no. 2 (2003): 182; Tim Cole,

"Nativization and Nationalization: A Comparative Landscape Study of Holocaust Museums in Israel, the US and the UK," *Journal of Israeli History*, vol. 23, no. 1 (2004): 136. The IWN Holocaust exhibition underwent even further redesign, before opening finally on October 20, 2021. See https://www.iwm.org.uk/history/new-gallery-concepts-for-iwms-future-revealed.

**9** Suzanne Bardgett, "The Genesis and Development of the Imperial War Museum's Holocaust Exhibition Project," *Journal of Holocaust Education*, vol. 7, no. 3 (1998): 36; K. Hannah Holtschneider, *The Holocaust and Representations of Jews: History and Identity in the Museum* (London and New York: Routledge, 2011), 21; Andy Pearce, "An Emerging "Holocaust Memorial Problem?: The Condition of Holocaust Culture in Britain," *The Journal of Holocaust Research*, vol. 33, no. 2 (2019): 117–37 (accessed on p. 17 of preprint); Andy Pearce, "Introduction: Education, Remembrance, and the Holocaust: Towards Pedagogic Memory-Work," in Andy Pearce (ed.), *Remembering the Holocaust in Educational Settings* (London and New York: Routledge, 2018), 8–11. As K. Hannah Holtschneider noted as early as 2011, the Imperial War Museum has begun to provide a "a strong narrative that guides the visitor through a very complex and historiographically challenging terrain . . . [to make sure they are] helpfully initiated into the history of the Holocaust." See Holtschneider, *The Holocaust and Representations of Jews*, 41. On the new 2021/2022 galleries at the IWM, see Caroline Davies, "Imperial War Museums gallery to question way Holocaust understood," *The Guardian*, Jan 27, 2021, https://www.theguardian.com/world/2021/jan/27/imperial-war-museums-gallery-to-question-way-holocaust-understood; Hannah Holtschneider, "Holocaust Representation in the Imperial War Museum, 2000–2020," in *The Palgrave Handbook of Britain and the Holocaust*, 390–2.

**10** As Rachel Donnelly notes, "While IWM did not set out to create a memorial space, for many survivors and their families the exhibition became precisely that: a place of memory." See Rachel Donnelly, "Imperial War Museums: Reflecting and shaping Holocaust memory," in *Remembering the Holocaust in Educational Settings*, 110. For a related discussion about group and communal memory at regional Holocaust museums in Australia, see Avril Alba, Steven Cooke, and Donna-Lee Frieze, "'Community Museums and the Creation of a 'Sense of Place': Holocaust Museums in Australia," *Recollections: A Journal of Museums and Collections*, vol. 9, no. 1 (2014).

**11** Kara Critchell, "Remembering and Forgetting: The Holocaust in 21st Century Britain," *Quest: Issues in Contemporary Jewish History*, vol. 10 (2016), http://www.quest-cdecjournal.it/focus.php?issue=10&id=383; Pearce, "An Emerging "Holocaust Memorial Problem?" (accessed on p. 23 of preprint).

**12** Stuart Foster, Alice Pettigrew, Andy Pearce, Rebecca Hale, Adrian Burgess, Paul Salmons, and Ruth-Anne Lenga, *What Do Students Know and Understand about the Holocaust? Evidence from English Secondary Schools* (London: UCL IOE, 2016), 7–9; Andy Pearce, "An Emerging "Holocaust Memorial Problem? (accessed on p. 23 of preprint).

**13** Ministry of Housing, "Press release: UK Holocaust Memorial to reaffirm," https://www.gov.uk/government/news/uk-holocaust-memorial-to-reaffirm-britains-commitment-to-stand-up-against-antisemitism-prejudice-and-hatred.

Of course, some such as Gad Yair warn against the other extreme: excess information leading to a malaise among visitors. See Gad Yair, "Neutrality, Objectivity, and Dissociation: Cultural Trauma and Educational Messages in German Holocaust Memorial Sites and Documentation Centers," *Holocaust and Genocide Studies,* vol. 26, no. 3 (2014): 487.

**14** Peter Carrier, *Holocaust Monuments and National Memory: France and Germany since 1989*, 9, 29. The more recent post-2007 exhibition House of the Wannsee Conference Memorial and Educational Site in Germany has attempted to assess "the alternatives for action presented to the bystanders and the fight for survival of the victims," reinforcing the notion that alternative views and actions were possible and could have prevented the escalation of violence and persecution. See Michael Haupt, Wolf Kaiser, Gaby Müller-Oelrichs, Caroline Pearce (eds), *The Wannsee Conference and the Genocide of the European Jews: Catalogue of the Permanent Exhibition* (Berlin: House of the Wannsee Conference Memorial and Educational Site, 2009), 7.

**15** Lisa Blee and Jean M. O'Brien, *Monumental Mobility: The Memory Work of Massasoit* (Chapel Hill: The University of North Carolina Press, 2019), 113, 140; Christine M. DeLucia, "Memory on the Move: Confronting Indigenous and Settler Colonial Commemorations in Stone and Bronze," *Reviews in American* History vol. 48, no. 1 (March 2020): 92; Gerald Vizenor, *Manifest Manners: Narratives on Postindian Survivance* (Lincoln, NE: University of Nebraska Press, 1999), vii.

**16** "Speech by Marcella LeBeau," UK Parliament. (2000) Memorandum Glasgow City Council, available at http://www.publications.parliament.uk/pa/cm199900/cmselect/cmcumeds/371/0051808.htm. See also the discussion in Neillian MacLachlan, "Sacred and Secular: An Analysis of the Repatriation of Native American Sacred Items from European Museums," MA diss., University of Aberdeen, 201, 12.

**17** Ibid.

**18** See Neil G. W. Curtis, "Repatriation from Scottish Museums: Learning from NAGPRA," *Museum Anthropology*, vol. 33, no. 2 (2010): 237; Memorandum submitted by Glasgow City Council to the House of Commons Culture, Media and Sport Committee. Electronic document, 2000, http://www.publications.parliament.uk/pa/cm199900/cmselect/cmcumeds/371/0051808.htm.

**19** "Innumerable stories, dances and songs were reawakened while the old people passed Jacobsen's Yup'ik objects from hand to hand." See the discussion in Courtney Cottrell, *Competing Discourses, Developing Partnerships: Navigating Differences Between Ethnographic Museums and Tribal Museums.* PhD diss., The University of Michigan, 2017, 106; Ann Fienup-Riordan, "Yup'ik Elders in Museums: Fieldwork Turned on Its Head," in Alison K. Brown and Laura Peers (eds), *Museums and Source Communities: A Routledge Reader* (London and New York: Routledge: 2003), 28–9.

**20** Riordan, "Yup'ik Elders," 33, 38.

**21** Alison K. Brown and Laura Peers, "The Blackfoot Shirts Project: 'Our Ancestors Have Come to Visit'," in Sharon Macdonald and Helen Leahy (eds), *The International Handbooks of Museum Studies* (Hoboken, NJ: John Wiley & Sons, 2014), 4.

22 Brown and Peers, "The Blackfoot Shirts Project," 5.

23 Brown and Peers, "The Blackfoot Shirts Project," 6. See also Walter McClintock, *The Old North Trail: Life, Legends and Religion of the Blackfeet Indians* [1910] (Lincoln, NE: University of Nebraska Press, 1999), 491–505.

24 Ramona Big Head, interview with Alison Brown and Laura Peers, August 18, 2010, in Brown and Peers, "The Blackfoot Shirts Project," 7.

25 These activities demonstrated what Peers describes as the role of "decolonization as permanent process." See Laura Peers, "Decolonization as a Permanent Process: PRM Relations with the Haida Nation, 1998–2018," in Laura Peers, *Decolonizing the Museum in Practice: Papers from Annual Conference of the Museum Ethnographers Group Held at the Pitt Rivers Museum 12–13 April 2018* (Museum Ethnographers Group, 2019); Laura Peers, "Museums and Source Communities: Reflections and implications," in W. Modest, N. Thomas, and C. Augustat (eds), *Matters of Belonging: Ethnographic Museums in a Changing Europe* (Leiden: Sidestone Press, 2019); Cara Krmpotich and Laura Peers, *This Is Our Life: Haida Material Heritage and Changing Museum Practice* (Vancouver: University of British Columbia Press, 2013), 9, 320; Douglas Cole, *Captured Heritage: The Scramble for Northwest Coast Artifacts* (Vancouver: University of British Columbia Press, 1995); J. C. H. King, *First Peoples, First Contacts: Native Peoples of North America* (London: British Museum Press, 1999).

26 Lea Whitford, Blackfeet, in Laura Peers, "'Ceremonies of Renewal': Visits, Relationships, and Healing in the Museum Space," *Museum Worlds: Advances in Research,* vol. 1 (2013): 140. See the discussions of cultural genocide in Chapter 4 of this book.

27 See Brown and Peers, "The Blackfoot Shirts Project," 5. ; Laura Peers, "'Ceremonies of Renewal," 145. See also Katherine Pettipas, *Severing the Ties that Bind: Government Repression of Indigenous Religious Ceremonies on the Prairies* (Winnipeg: University of Manitoba Press, 1994).

28 Herman Yellow Old Woman, interview with Alison Brown and Laura Peers, in "The Blackfoot Shirts Project," 9; Robert Archibald, "A Place to Remember: Using History to Build Community" (Walnut Creek, CA: AltaMira, 1999) 133; Peers, "'Ceremonies of Renewal," 141, 147-9; S. Crowshoe, interview with Alison Brown, August 11, 2010, in Brown and Peers, "The Blackfoot Shirts Project," 10; Maria Zedeno, "Bundled Worlds: The Roles and Interactions of Complex Objects from the North American Plains," *Journal of Archaeological Method and Theory,* vol. 15 (2008), 362–78; Kenneth H. Lokensgard, *Blackfoot Religion and the Consequences of Cultural Commoditization* (Burlington, VT: Ashgate, 2010); Elizabeth Edwards, Chris Gosden, and Ruth B. Phillips (eds), *Sensible Objects: Colonialism, Museums and Material Culture* (Oxford and New York: Berg Publishers, 2006).

29 Laura Peers, "'Ceremonies of Renewal," 138, 141; Alison K. Brown, "Material Histories: Scots and Aboriginal Peoples in the Canadian Fur Trade," Department of Anthropology, University of Aberdeen, 2008, http://www.abdn.ac.uk/materialhistories/proceedings.php; James Clifford, "Museums as Contact Zones," in James Clifford, *Routes: Travel and Translation in the Late Twentieth Century* (Cambridge, MA: Harvard University Press, 1997), 190–3.

See also James Waldram (ed.), *Aboriginal Healing in Canada: Studies in Therapeutic Meaning and Practice* (Ottawa: Aboriginal Healing Foundation, 2014); Michael Chandler and Christopher Lalonde, "Cultural Continuity as a Moderator of Suicide Risk Among Canada's First Nations," in Laurence J. Kirmayer and Gail G. Valaskaskis (eds), *Healing Traditions: The Mental Health of Aboriginal Peoples in Canada* (Vancouver: University of British Columbia Press, 2008), 221–48; Bernie Arigho, "Getting a Handle on the Past: The Use of Objects in Reminiscence Work," in Helen Chatterjee (ed.), *Touch in Museums: Policy and Practice in Object Handling* (Oxford, UK: Berg, 2008), 205–12; Helen Chatterjee, Sonjel Vreeland, and Guy Noble, "Museopathy: Exploring the Healing Potential of Handling Museum Objects," *Museum and Society,* vol. 7 (2009): 164–77; Elizabeth Hallam and Jenny Hockey, *Death, Memory and Material Culture* (Oxford, UK: Berg: 2001), 7; David Parkin, "Mementoes as Transitional Objects in Human Displacement," *Journal of Material Culture,* vol. 4 (1999): 303–20; Daniel Miller and Fiona Parrott, "Loss and Material Culture in South London," *Journal of the Royal Anthropological Institute,* vol. 15 (2009): 502; Claire Lyons, "Objects and Identities: Claiming and Reclaiming the Past," in Elazar Barkan and Ronald Bus (eds), *Claiming the Stones/Naming the Bones: Cultural Property and the Negotiation of National and Ethnic Identity* (Los Angeles: Getty Research Institute, 2002), 116; Alison K. Brown, "Material Histories: Scots and Aboriginal Peoples in the Canadian Fur Trade," Department of Anthropology, University of Aberdeen, 2008, http://www.abdn.ac.uk/materialhistories/proceedings.php; James Clifford, "Looking Several Ways: Anthropology and Native Heritage in Alaska," *Current Anthropology,* vol. 45, no. 1 (2004): 5–30; Ann Fienup-Riordan, "Yup'ik Elders in Museums: Fieldwork Turned on Its Head," in Laura Peers and Alison K. Brown (eds), *Museums and Source Communities: A Routledge Reader* (London: Routledge, 2003), 28–41; Ann Fienup-Riordan, *Ciuliamta akluit/Things of Our Ancestors: Yup'ik Elders Explore the Jacobsen Collection at the Ethnologisches Museum Berlin.* Trans. Marie Meade (Seattle: University of Washington Press, 2005); Judy Thompson and Ingrid Kritsch, *Long Ago Sewing We Will Remember: The Story of the Gwich'in Traditional Caribou Skin Clothing Project* (Hull, Quebec: Canadian Museum of Civilization, 2005); Chantal Knowles, "Object Journeys: Outreach Work Between National Museums Scotland and the Tlicho," in A. Brown (ed.), *Material Histories: Proceedings of a Workshop Held at Marischal Museum, University of Aberdeen, 26–27 April 2007* (Aberdeen, Scotland: Marischal Museum, University of Aberdeen, 2008), 37–56; Mary Louise Pratt, *Imperial Eyes: Travel Writing and Transculturation*, 2nd ed. (London: Routledge, 1992), 8; Gerald McMaster, Julia Lum, and Kaitlin McCormick, "The Entangled Gaze: Indigenous and European Views of Each Other," *ab–Original: Journal of Indigenous Studies and First Nations and First Peoples' Culture,* vol. 2 no. 2 (2018): 8.

30 Amy Lonetree, "Review: Diba Jimooyung: Telling Our Story," *The Journal of American History,* vol. 95, no. 1 (2008): 158–63; Cottrell, *Competing Discourses*, 180, 188–90. On the important role of tribal sovereignty and Indigenous perspectives in North American museums, see also the contributions in Susan Sleeper-Smith, *Contesting Knowledge: Museums and Indigenous Perspectives* (Lincoln, NE: University of Nebraska Press, 2009).

31 On the problem of collaboration from Eurocentric perspectives see Cottrell, *Competing Discourses*, 25–6.

32 Pauline Wakeham, "Performing Reconciliation at the National Museum of the American Indian: Postcolonial Rapprochement and the Politics of Historical Closure," in Amy Lonetree and Amanda Cobb (eds), *The National Museum of the American Indian: Critical Conversations* (Lincoln, NE: University of Nebraska Press, 2008), 354. See also Cottrell, *Competing Discourses*, 3, 9.

33 Michael Bernhard and Jan Kubik, "A Theory of the Politics of Memory," in Michael Bernhard and Jan Kubik (eds), *Twenty Years After Communism: The Politics of Memory and Commemoration* (Oxford, UK: Oxford University Press: 2014), 17; Dovilė Budrytė, "Decolonization of Trauma and Memory Politics: Insights from Eastern Europe," *Humanities,* vol. 5, no. 7 (2016): 6.

34 Carrier, *Holocaust Monuments and National Memory*, 27, 164.

35 Rubinstein, *Members of the Tribe,* 165, 169; Elaine Heumann Gurian, "A Blurring of the Boundaries, 1994," in *Civilizing the Museum: The Collected Writings of Elaine Heumann Gurian* (New York: Routledge, 2006), 176.

36 See the discussions in Chapter 3.

37 Zuzanna Dziubian, "Introduction: Haunting in the Land of the Untraumatized," in Zuzanna Dziubian (ed.), *The "Spectral Turn": Jewish Ghosts in the Polish Post-Holocaust Imaginaire* (Berlin: Transcript-Verlag, 2019), 7–49; Marianne Hirsch and Leo Spitzer, *Ghosts of Home: The Afterlife of Czernowitz in Jewish Memory* (Berkeley, Los Angeles, and London: University of California Press, 2010), xx. According to Sendyka, Jewish descendants and allied researchers such as Hirsch and Spitzer thus become "screens for spectral existence . . . carrying within themselves the ghosts of the dead." See Roma Sendyka, "Sites that Haunt: Affects and Non-Sites of Memory," in *The "Spectral Turn"*, 85–107.

38 Tomasz Majewski, "Litzmannstadt Ghetto," in Tomasz Majewski and Anna Zeidler-Janiszewska (eds), *Pamiqc Shoah: Kulturowereprezentacje i praktyki upamiqtnienia [Memory of the Shoah: Cultural Representations and Practices of Commemoration*] (Lodz: Officyna, 2009), 117–18.

39 On the implications of Holocaust memory once the last of these survivors have passed away, see the important discussion in Nicholas Char, "Holocaust Memory in a Post-Survivor World: Bearing Last Witness," in S. Gigliotti and H. Earl (eds), *The Wiley Companion to the Holocaust* (London: Wiley-Blackwell, 2020), 519–36. See also the essays in Diana I. Popescu and Tanja Schult (eds), *Revisiting Holocaust Representation in the Post-Witness Era* (London: Springer, 2015); Esther Jilovsky, *Remembering the Holocaust: Generations, Witnessing and Place* (London and New York: Bloomsbury Academic, 2015).

40 Krmpotich and Peers, *This Is Our Life*, 42–3.

41 Gerald Vizenor, *Manifest Manners: Narratives on Postindian Survivance* (Lincoln, University of Nebraska Press, 1999), vii. See also Christine M. DeLucia, *Memory Lands: King Philip's War and the Place of Violence in the Northeast* (New Haven, CT: Yale University Press, 2018), 22; DeLucia, "Memory on the Move," 9, 90. Sonya Atalay makes similar arguments in her

important and ongoing work on public archaeology and Indigenous approaches. See Sonya Atalay, *Community-Based Archaeology: Research With, By and For Indigenous and Local Communities* (Berkeley: University of California Press, 2012); Amy Lonetree and Amanda J. Cobb, *The National Museum of the American Indian: Critical Conversations* (Lincoln, NE: University of Nebraska Press, 2008), 196.

42 The stumbling blocks were "designed not only to commemorate the past but also to encourage and provoke spectators to reflect on the process and tradition of commemoration itself." See Carrier, *Holocaust Monuments and National Memory: France and Germany since 1989*, 21.

43 "Stolpersteine & Andere Gedenksteine in Berlin," http://www.stolpersteine-berlin.de/berlinF.

44 James E. Young, *The Texture of Memory: Holocaust Memorials and Meaning* (New Haven, CT: Yale University Press, 1993), 90.

45 Ruth B. Phillips, "The Museum of Art-thropology: Twenty-First Century Imbroglios," *Res:Anthropology and Aesthetics*, vol. 52 (Autumn 2007): 13, 78.

46 Carrier, *Holocaust Monuments and National Memory: France and Germany since 1989*, 40.

## Conclusion

1 See Jerome Friedman, "Jewish Conversion, the Spanish Pure Blood Laws and Reformation: A Revisionist View of Racial and Religious Antisemitism," *The Sixteenth Century Journal*, vol. 18 no. 1 (1987): 3–30; Yosef Hayim Yerushalmi, *Assimilation and Racial Anti-Semitism: The Iberian and the German Models* (New York: Leo Baeck Institute, 1982); David Nirenberg, "Was There Race Before Modernity? The Example of 'Jewish' Blood in Late Medieval Spain," in Miriam Eliav-Feldon, Benjamin Isaac, Joseph Ziegler (eds), *The Origins of Racism in the West* (Cambridge, UK: Cambridge University Press, 2009); Robert Bonfil, "Aliens Within: the Jews and Anti-Judaism," in Thomas A. Brady, Heiko Augustinus Oberman, and James D. Tracy (eds), *Handbook of European History, 1400–1600: Late Middle Ages, Renaissance and Reformation*, (New York, Brill: 1994), 263–302; Henry Munson, "The Permeable Boundary between Christian Anti-Judaism and Secular Antisemitism," in *Explaining, Interpreting, and Theorizing Religion and Myth: Contributions in Honor of Robert A. Segal* (Leiden: Brill: 2020), 174–95.

2 On early modern memory see Judith Pollmann, *Memory in Early Modern Europe, 1500–1800* (New York: Oxford University Press, 2017); Judith Pollmann, Erika Kuijpers, Jasper Van Steen, and Johannes M. Müller (eds), *Memory Before Modernity Practices of Memory in Early Modern Europe* (Leiden: Brill, 2013); Anthony Grafton, *What Was History? The Art of History in Early Modern Europe* (Cambridge, UK: Cambridge University Press, 2005); Claire Richter Sherman, *Writing on Hands: Memory and Knowledge in Early Modern Europe* (Carlisle, PA: Folger Shakespeare Library, 2000). See also Jonathan Boyarin, *Jews, Indians, and the Identity of Christian Europe* (Chicago: University of Chicago Press, 2009); James Adair, *The History of the*

*American Indians Particularly Those Nations Adjoining to the Mississippi, East and West Florida, Georgia, South and North Carolina, and Virginia* (London, 1775).

3 See Winona LaDuke, *Last Standing Woman* (Stillwater, MN: Voyageur Press, 1997), 127–28; Jennifer Nez Denetdale, "'No Explanation, No Resolution, and No Answers': Border Town Violence and Navajo Resistance to Settler Colonialism," *Wicazo Sa Review*, vol. 31, no. 1, Special Issue: Essentializing Elizabeth Cook-Lynn (Spring 2016): 111–31.

4 Stanislaw Meducki, "The Pogrom in Kielce on Museum Ethnographers Group,4 July 1946," *Polin: Studies in Polish Jewry,* vol. 9 (1996): 158–69; Jan T. Gross, *Fear: Anti-Semitism in Poland After Auschwitz: An Essay in Historical Interpretation* (New York: Random House, 2006); Jan Grabowski, "Rewriting the History of Polish–Jewish Relations from a Nationalist Perspective: The Recent Publications of the Institute of National Remembrance," *Yad Vashem Studies,* vol. 36, no. 1 (2008): 268; Lukasz Kaminski and Jan Zaryn (eds), *Reflections on the Kielce Pogrom* (Warsaw: Institute of National Remembrance, 2006); Joanna Beata Michlic, "'At the Crossroads': Jedwabne and Polish Historiography of the Holocaust," *Dapim: Studies on the Holocaust,* vol. 31, no. 3 (2017): 297, 299. See also Diana Dumitru, *The State, Antisemitism, and Collaboration in the Holocaust: The Borderlands of Romania and the Soviet Union* (New York: Cambridge University Press, 2016); Shimon Redlich, *Together and Apart on Brzeżany, Poles, Jews and Ukrainians 1919–1945* (Bloomington: Indiana University Press, 2002); Anna Bikont, *The Crime and the Silence: Confronting the Massacre of Jews in Wartime Jedwabne* (New York: Farrar, Straus and Giroux, 2015); Christoph Mick, *Lemberg, Lwów, L'viv, 1914–1947: Violence and Ethnicity in a Contested City* (West Lafayette, IN: Purdue University Press, 2016); Christopher Browning, *Ordinary Men: Reserve Police Battalion 101 and the Final Solution in Poland* (New York: Harper-Perennial, 1998).

5 Lars Rensmann, "Guilt, Resentment, and Post-Holocaust Democracy: The Frankfurt School's Analysis of 'Secondary Antisemitism' in the Group Experiment and Beyond," *Antisemitism Studies,* vol. 1, no. 1 (2017): 4; Karen Auerbach, "Review Essay: Holocaust Memory in Polish Scholarship," *AJS Review*, vol. 35, no. 1 (April 2011): 138; Jan Gross, *Fear*; Anna Cichopek, "The Cracow Pogrom of August 1945: A Narrative Reconstruction," in Joshua Zimmerman (ed.), *Poles and Jews during the Holocaust and Its Aftermath*, (New Brunswick, NJ: Rutgers University Press, 2003), 221–38.

6 Winona LaDuke, *Last Standing Woman,* 127–8; Winona LaDuke, *Recovering the Sacred: The Power of Naming and Claiming* (Cambridge, MA: South End Press, 2005).

7 Deborah Lipstadt, "The Trump Administration's Flirtation with Holocaust Denial," *The Atlantic*, January 30, 2017; Deborah E. Lipstadt, *Antisemitism: Here and Now* (New York, Schocken Books: 2019).

8 Statement by former President Trump on International Holocaust Remembrance Day, January 27, 2017, https://www.whitehouse.gov/the-press-office/2017/01/27/statement-president-international-holocaust-remembrance-day; Statements by Hope Hicks to CNN, January 28, 2017, http://edition.cnn

.com/2017/01/28/politics/white-house-holocaust-memorial-day/,; "White House Admits They Intentionally Omitted Jews From Holocaust Statement," *Daily Stormer*, January 31, 2017, https://www.dailystormer.com/white-house-admits-they-intentionally-omitted-jews-from-holocaust-statement/; Lipstadt, *Antisemitism: Here and Now,* 125–211; Alvin H. Rosenfeld (ed.), *Deciphering the New Antisemitism* (Bloomington: Indiana University Press, 2015); Jonathan Judaken, "So What's New? Rethinking the 'New Antisemitism' in a Global Age," *Patterns of Prejudice*, vol. 42, no. 4–5 (Autumn 2008): 531–60.

9 See for example, Alvin H. Rosenfeld (ed.), *Deciphering the New Antisemitism*, or Gavriel D. Rosenfeld, *Hi Hitler! How the Nazi Past is Being Normalized in Contemporary Culture* (Cambridge, UK: Cambridge University Press, 2015); Deborah E. Lipstadt, *Antisemitism: Here and Now* (New York: Schocken Books: 2019).

10 On the trajectory of the Pocahontas stereotype see Jacquelyn Kilpatrick, *Celluloid Indians: Native Americans and Film* (Lincoln, NE: University of Nebraska Press, 1999), 150–3. For Indigenous responses to Trump's words, as well as Trump's attempts to frame them as a response to Warren's offense, see Gabrielle Bruney, "Trump and Don Jr. Seem to Think That the Genocide of Native Americans Is Funny," *Esquire*, Februay 10, 2019, https://www.esquire.com/news-politics/a26272910/trump-warren-native-americans-rob-low-trail-of-tears/; Mairead Mcardle, "Native Americans React to Warren's DNA Test," *National Review,* October 15, 2018, https://www.nationalreview.com/news/native-americans-react-to-warrens-dna-test/; Jennifer Bendery and Dana Liebelson, "Trump Keeps Being Racist To Native Americans and Getting Away with It," *Huffington Post*, February 15, 2019; "Native American Groups Slap Down Trump's 'Pocahontas' Comment," *Daily Beast*, October 27, 2017, https://www.thedailybeast.com/native-american-groups-slap-down-trumps-pocahontas-comment; Adrienne Keene, "How I Feel As a Native Woman When Trump Idolizes Andrew Jackson," *Teen Vogue*, April 19, 2017, https://www.teenvogue.com/story/andrew-jackson-native-woman-idolize-donald-trump; Simon Moya-Smith, "Trump's Disrespect for Native Americans Is Nothing New," *CNN Online*, November 30, 2017 : https://edition.cnn.com/2017/11/29/opinions/trump-native-americans-moya-smith-opinion/index.html; Nolan D. McCaskill, "Trump Taunts 'Pocahontas' During Native American event," *Politico Magazine*, November 27, 2017, https://www.politico.com/story/2017/11/27/trump-navajo-code-talkers-pocahontas-260989; Jason Lemon, "Trump Says He Has 'More' Native Blood Than Elizabeth Warren, But Thinks He'll Keep Calling Her Pocahontas," *Newsweek*, October 28, 2018, https://www.newsweek.com/trump-says-he-has-more-native-blood-elizabeth-warren-thinks-hell-keep-calling-1190789.

11 See Alyssa Mt. Pleasant's discussion of Warren and Indigenous identity: https://twitter.com/BettyRbl/status/1095067707773456385. See also Cecily Hilleary, "Native Americans Speak Out on Elizabeth Warren DNA Controversy," *Voice of America News*, October 16, 2018, https://www.voanews.com/usa/native-americans-speak-out-elizabeth-warren-dna-controversy; Rebecca Nagle, "Elizabeth Warren Has Spent Her Adult Life Repeating A Lie. I Want Her To Tell The Truth," *Huffington Post*, August 8, 2019, https://www.huffpost.com/

entry/elizabeth-warren-cherokee-apology_n_5d5ed7e6e4b0dfcbd48a1b01; Joseph Pierce, "Elizabeth Warren's Apology to Native Peoples Was Woefully Inadequate," *Protean Magazine*, August 21, 2019, https://proteanmag.com/2019/08/21/elizabeth-warrens-apology-to-native-peoples-was-woefully-inadequate/. See also the important bibliography on this phenomenon complied by Adrienne Keene, Rebecca Nagle, and Joseph M. Pierce at http://www.criticalethnicstudiesjournal.org/blog/2018/12/19/syllabus-elizabeth-warren-cherokee-citizenship-and-dna-testing.

**12** Masha Gessen, "Elizabeth Warren Falls for Trump's Trap—and Promotes Insidious Ideas About Race and DNA," *The New Yorker*, October 16, 2018: https://www.newyorker.com/news/our-columnists/elizabeth-warren-falls-for-trumps-trap-and-promotes-insidious-ideas-about-race-and-dna. See also Kim TallBear, *Native American DNA: Tribal Belonging and the False Promise of Genetic Science* (Minneapolis: University of Minnesota Press, 2013); Krystal Tsosie, "Elizabeth Warren's DNA Is Not Her Identity" *The Atlantic*. October 17, 2018, https://www.theatlantic.com/ideas/archive/2018/10/what-make-elizabeth-warrens-dna-test/573205/; Krystal Tsosie and Matthew Anderson. "Two Native Americans Geneticists Interpret Elizabeth Warren's DNA Test," *The Conversation*. October 22, 2018, https://theconversation.com/two-native-american-geneticists-interpret-elizabeth-warrens-dna-test-105274.

**13** See note 7 above.

**14** See, for example, Tom Lawson and Andy Pearce, "Preface," in Tom Lawson and Andy Pearce (eds), *The Palgrave Handbook of Britain and the Holocaust* (Basingstoke, UK: Palgrave Macmillan, 2021), x; Susan Neiman, *Learning from the Germans: Race and the Memory of Evil* (New York: Farrar, Straus and Giroux, 2019).

**15** AP Report: Over 600 bodies found at Indigenous school in Canada, June 24, 2021 https://apnews.com/article/canada-67da8a8af88efc91e6ffc64630796 ec9?; Rachel Bergen, "Mother figure or colonial oppressor? Examining Queen Victoria's legacy after Winnipeg statue toppled," *CBC News*, July 7, 2021: https://www.cbc.ca/news/canada/manitoba/queen-victoria-winnipeg-statues-residential-schools-colonialism-british-empire-1.6090322.

**16** TRC Canada, *Truth and Reconciliation Commission of Canada Final Report: Reconciliation,* vol. 6 (Montreal: McGill-Queens University Press, 2015), 212. See the discussion in David B. MacDonald, "Indigenous Genocide and Perceptions of the Holocaust in Canada," in S. Gigliotti and H. Earl (eds), *The Wiley Companion to the Holocaust* (London: Wiley-Blackwell, 2020), 588.

**17** "Toppled Civil War Statue at Colorado Capitol to Be Replaced by Sculpture of Native American Woman," *Denver Post*, November 22, 2020. https://www.denverpost.com/2020/11/22/colorado-capitol-civil-war-statue-replaced-native/.

**18** "Holocaust scrolls" are used in the synagogue of St. Thomas, US Virgin Islands. Rescued from Budyne nad Ohri in Czech Republic, the Torah scrolls are on "permanent loan" to the synagogue, one of 1,564 scrolls that were provided by the Westminster Synagogue Holocaust Scroll Memorial Trust to various temples. According to the synagogue, should "there ever be, once again, a living Jewish community in the town from which our scroll came we would, perhaps, receive a Tweet, or a Facebook message, saying: 'Can we have our scroll back?' Until such a time as that happens, we are honored with the sacred task of 'redemption.' We keep this scroll in use, as it was meant to be, as an ongoing response to those who would have it any other way." See https://synagogue.vi/our-historic-synagogue/.

# SELECT BIBLIOGRAPHY


Aarons, Victoria, and Alan L. Berger. *Third-Generation Holocaust Representation: Trauma, History, and Memory* (Evanston, IL: Northwestern University Press, 2017).

Abramson, Henry. "A Double Occlusion: Sephardim and the Holocaust," in Zion Zohar (ed.), *Sephardic and Mizrahi Jewry: From the Golden Age of Spain to Modern Times* (New York: New York University Press, 2005), 285–99.

Alba, Avril. *The Holocaust Memorial Museum: Sacred Secular Space* (Basingstoke, UK: Palgrave Macmillan, 2015).

Aldred, Lisa. "Plastic Shamans and Astroturf Sun Dances: New Age Commercialism of Native American Spirituality." *American Indian Quarterly,* vol. 24, no. 3. (2000): 329–52.

Aleksiun, Natalia. "On Humanizing Victims and Perpetrators of the Holocaust in Eastern Europe," *Journal of Genocide Research*, vol. 20, no. 4 (2018): 645–9.

Alexander, Jeffrey C. "On the Social Construction of Moral Universals: The "Holocaust" from Mass Murder to Trauma Drama," *European Journal of Social Theory*, vol. 5, no. 1 (2002): 5–86.

Alexie, Sherman. "Inside Dachau," *The Beloit Poetry Journal,* vol. 46, no. 4 (Summer 1996), https://warwick.ac.uk/fac/cross_fac/ehrc/events/sherman_alexie_-_inside_dachau.pdf.

Allwork, Larissa. *Holocaust Remembrance between the National and the Transnational: The Stockholm International Forum and the First Decade of the International Task Force* (London: Bloomsbury, 2015).

Allwork, Larissa. "Interrogating Europe's voids of memory: trauma theory and Holocaust Remembrance between the National and the Transnational," *Quest: Issues in Contemporary Jewish History,* vol. 10 (2016): 1–22.

Anderson, Kjell. "The Margins of Perpetration: Individual Roles in Genocide," in Alette Smeulers, Maartje Weerdesteijn, and Barbora Hola (eds), *Perpetrators of International Crimes: Methodology, Theory and Evidence* (Oxford, UK: Oxford University Press, 2019), 132–52.

Anderson, Tea Sindbæk. *Disputed Memory: Emotions and Memory Politics in Central, Eastern and South-Eastern Europe* (Berlin: De Gruyter, 2016).

Araujo, Ana Lucia. *Reparations for Slavery and the Slave Trade: A Transnational and Comparative History* (London: Bloomsbury, 2017).

Araujo, Ana Lucia. *Slavery in the Age of Memory: Engaging the Past* (London: Bloomsbury, 2020).

Archuleta, Elizabeth. "Gym Shoes, Maps, and Passports, Oh My!: Creating Community or Creating Chaos at the National Museum of the American Indian?," in Amy Lonetree and Amanda Cobb (eds), *The National Museum of the American Indian: Critical Conversations* (Lincoln, NE: University of Nebraska Press, 2008), 426–49.

Arigho, Bernie. "Getting a Handle on the Past: The Use of Objects in Reminiscence Work," in Helen Chatterjee (ed.), *Touch in Museums: Policy and Practice in Object Handling* (Oxford, UK: Berg, 2008), 205–12.

Assmann, Aleida. "The Holocaust—a Global Memory? Extensions and Limits of a New Memory Community," in Aleida Assmann and Sebastian Conrad (eds), *Memory in a Global Age: Discourses Practices and Trajectories* (London: Palgrave, 2010), 97–117.

Atalay, Sonya. *Community-Based Archaeology: Research with, by and for Indigenous and Local Communities* (Berkeley: University of California Press, 2012).

Atalay, Sonya. "No Sense of the Struggle: Creating a Context for Survivance at the NMAI," *American Indian Quarterly*, vol. 30, no. 3/4 (2006): 597–618.

Baer, Alejandro, and Nathan Sznaider. *Memory and Forgetting in the Post-Holocaust Era. The Ethics of Never Again* (Milton, UK: Routledge, 2017)

Ball, Karyn, and Per Anders Rudling. "The Underbelly of Canadian Multiculturalism: Holocaust Obfuscation and Envy in the Debate about the Canadian Museum for Human Rights," *Holocaust Studies: A Journal of Culture and History*, vol. 20, no. 3 (2014): 33–80.

Bardgett, Suzanne. "The Genesis and Development of the Imperial War Museum's Holocaust Exhibition Project," *Journal of Holocaust Education*, vol. 7, no. 3 (1998): 28–37.

Bardgett, Suzanne. "Witness Statements: Testimonies at the Holocaust Exhibition," *Museum Practice*, vol. 1, no. 1 (2004): 54–6.

Bardgett, Suzanne, and Annie Dodds. "Exploring the Common Threads of Genocide: The Crimes Against Humanity Exhibition at the Imperial War Museum," in Toby Haggith and Joanna Newman (eds), *Holocaust and the Moving Image: Representations in Film and Television since 1933* (London and New York: Wallflower, 2005), 280–7.

Bartmanski, Dominik, and Jeffrey C. Alexander. "Introduction: Materiality and Meaning in Social Life: Toward an Iconic Turn in Cultural Sociology," in Jeffrey C. Alexander, Dominik Bartmanski, and Bernhard Giesen (eds), *Iconic Power: Materiality and Meaning in Social Life* (New York: Palgrave Macmillan, 2012), 1–12.

Bartov, Omer et al. "An Open Letter to the Director of the US Holocaust Memorial Museum," *New York Review of Books*, July 1, 2019, https://www.nybooks.com/daily/2019/07/01/an-open-letter-to-the-director-of-the-holocaust-memorial-museum/.

Bartov, Omer. "Genocide and the Holocaust: Arguments over History and Politics," in Karl Schleunes and Hilary Earl (eds), *Lessons and Legacies*, vol. XI (Evanston: Northwestern University Press, 2014), 5–28.

Bartov, Omer. "The Holocaust as Genocide: Experiential Uniqueness and Integrated History," in Claudio Fogu, Wulf Kansteiner, Todd Presner (eds), *Probing the Ethics of Holocaust Culture* (Cambridge, MA: Harvard University Press, 2016), 319–31.

Bartov, Omer. "The Voice of your Brother's Blood: Reconstructing Genocide on the Local Level," in Norman J. W. Goda (ed.), *Jewish Histories of the Holocaust New Transnational Approaches* (New York and Oxford, UK: Berghahn, 2014), 105–13.

Bartov, Omer, and Eric D. Weitz, eds. *Shatterzone of Empires* (Bloomington: Indiana University Press, 2013).

Bataille, Gretchen M., ed. *Native American Representations: First Encounters, Distorted Images, and Literary Appropriations* (Lincoln, NE: University of Nebraska Press, 2001).

Bauer, Yehuda. "Against Mystification: The Holocaust as a Historical Phenomenon" (1978), in Michael R. Marrus (ed.), *The Nazi Holocaust: Perspectives on the Holocaust* (Berlin: De Gruyter, 1989), 98–117.

Bauer, Yehuda. "Reviewing the Holocaust Anew in Multiple Contexts," *Post-Holocaust and Anti-Semitism*, 80, May 1, 2009.

Beck, Paul N. *Columns of Vengeance: Soldiers, Sioux, and the Punitive Expeditions 1863–1864* (Norman: University of Oklahoma Press, 2013).

Beckles, Hilary. *Britain's Black Debt: Reparations for Caribbean Slavery and Native Genocide* (Barbados: University of West Indies Press, 2013).

Belich, James. "Riders of the Whirlwind: Tribal Peoples and European Settlement Booms, 1790s–1900s," in *Raupatu: The Confiscation of Maori Land* (Wellington, NZ: Victoria University Press, 2009).

Benvenuto, Jeff. "Revisiting Choctaw Ethnocide and Ethnogenesis: The Creative Destruction of Colonial Genocide," in Andrew Woolford, Jeff Benvenuto, and Alexander Laban Hinton (eds), *Colonial Genocide In Indigenous North America*, (Durham, NC: Duke University Press, 2014), 208–25.

Berenbaum, Michael, and Abraham J. Peck, *The Holocaust and History: The Known, the Unknown, the Disputed, and the Reexamined* (Bloomington and Indianapolis: Indiana University Press, 2nd ed., 2002).

Berg, Nicholas. *The Holocaust and the West German Historians: Historical Interpretation and Autobiographical Memory* (Madison: University of Wisconsin Press, 2015).

Berghahn, Volker. "German Colonialism and Imperialism from Bismarck to Hitler," *German Studies Review* 40, no. 1 (2017): 147–62.

Berkhofer, Jr., Robert F., *The White Man's Indian: Images of the American Indian from Columbus to the Present* (New York: Vintage Books, 1978).

Bernhard, Michael, and Jan Kubik. "A Theory of the Politics of Memory," in Michael Bernhard and Jan Kubik (eds), *Twenty Years After Communism: The Politics of Memory and Commemoration* (Oxford, UK: Oxford University Press: 2014), 7–36.

Bieder, Robert E. "Representations of Indian Bodies in Nineteenth-Century American Anthropology," in Devon Mihesuh (ed.), *Repatriation Reader: Who Owns American Indian Remains?* (Lincoln, NE: University of Nebraska Press, 2000), 19–36

Bilsky, Leora, and Rachel Klagsbrun. "The Return of Cultural Genocide?" *European Journal of International Law*, vol. 29, no. 2 (May 2018): 373–96.

Blackhawk, Ned. *Violence Over the Land: Indians and Empires in the Early American West* (Cambridge, MA: Harvard University Press, 2006)

Blatman, Daniel. "The Holocaust as Genocide: Milestones in the Historiographical Discourse," in *The Wiley Companion to the Holocaust*, 95–114.

Blee, Lisa. *Framing Chief Leschi: Narratives and the Politics of Historical Justice* (Chapel Hill: University of North Carolina Press, 2014), 123–28.

Blee, Lisa. "Struggles Over Memory: Indigenous People and Commemorative Culture," *Reviews in American History*, vol. 46, no. 4 (December 2018): 597–604

Blee, Lisa, and Jean M. O'Brien, *Monumental Mobility: The Memory Work of Massasoit* (Chapel Hill: University of North Carolina Press, 2019).

Bloxham, Donald "Exhibiting Racism: Cultural Imperialism and Representation," *Rethinking History,* vol. 2, no. 3 (1998): 349–58.

Bloxham, Donald. *Genocide, the World Wars and the Unweaving of Europe* (Oxford, UK: Oxford University Press, 2009).

Blue Spruce, D., ed. *Spirit of a Native Place: Building the National Museum of the American Indian* (Washington, D.C.: National Museum of the American Indian, 2004).

Blue Spruce, D., and T. Thrasher, eds. *The Land Has Memory: Indigenous Knowledge, Native Landscapes, and the National Museum of the American Indian* (Washington, D.C.: National Museum of the American Indian, 2008).

Bombay, Amy, Kim Matheson, and Hymie Anisman. "Intergenerational Trauma: Convergence of Multiple Processes among First Nations People in Canada," *Journal de la santé autochtone* (November 2009), 6–47.

Bond, Lucy, and Stef Craps. *Trauma* (Abingdon, UK: Routledge, 2020).

Bond, Lucy, Stef Craps, and Pieter Vermeulen, eds. *Memory Unbound: Tracing the Dynamics of Memory Studies* (New York: Berghahn Books, 2017).

Bowes, John P. *Land Too Good for Indians: Northern Indian Removal* (University of Oklahoma Press, 2016).

Boyarin, Jonathan. Greg Sarris, and Menahem Prywes. "Europe's Indian, America's Jew: Modiano and Vizenor," *Boundary* 2, vol. 19, no. 3, Special issue: *1492–1992: American Indian Persistence and Resurgence* (Autumn, 1992): 197-222

Boyarin, Jonathan. *The Unconverted Self: Jews, Indians, and the identity of Christian Europe* (Chicago: University of Chicago Press, 2009)

Brave Heart, M., J. Chase, J. Elkins, and D.B. Altschul. "Historical Trauma Among Indigenous Peoples of the Americas: Concepts, Research, and Clinical Considerations," *Journal of Psychoactive Drugs,* vol. 43, no.4 (2012): 282–90.

Brave Heart, Maria Yellow Horse. *Historical Trauma and Unresolved Grief: Implications for Clinical Research and Practice with Indigenous Peoples of the Americas* (Smith College School for Social Work, 2015), https://www.ihs.gov/telebehavioral/includes/themes/newihstheme/display_objects/documents/slides/education/historicaltrauma_100412.pdf.

Brooks, James. *Captives and Cousins Slavery, Kinship, and Community in the Southwest Borderlands* (Chapel Hill: University of North Carolina Press, 2002).

Brooks, Lisa. The *Common Pot: The Recovery of Native Space in the Northeast* (Minneapolis: University of Minnesota Press, 2008).

Brooks, Lisa. *Our Beloved Kin: A New History of King Philip's War* (New Haven, CT: Yale University Press, 2019).

Brown, Alison K., and Laura Peers. "The Blackfoot Shirts Project: "Our Ancestors Have Come to Visit," in Sharon Macdonald and Helen Leahy (eds), *The International Handbooks of Museum Studies* (Hoboken, NJ: John Wiley & Sons, 2014), 1–21.

Brown-Rice, Kathleen. "Examining the Theory of Historical Trauma Among Native Americans," *The Professional Counselor* vol. 3, no. 3 (2013): 117–30.

Browning, Christopher R. "Contextualizing the Holocaust: Modernization, Modernity, Colonialism, and Genocide," in Michael Meng and Adar R. Seipp (eds), *Modern Germany in Transatlantic Perspective* (New York, Berghahn Books, 2017), 73–95.

Bruyneel, Kevin M. *The Third Space of Sovereignty: The Postcolonial Politics of U.S.–Indigenous Relations* (Minneapolis, MN: University of Minnesota Press, Indigenous Americas Series, 2007).

Burnard, Trevor. "Empire Matters? The Historiography of Imperialism in Early America, 1492–1830," *History of European Ideas* 33 (2007): 87–107

Burzlaff, Jan. "The Holocaust and Slavery? Working Towards A Comparative History of Genocide and Mass Violence," *Journal of Genocide Research*, vol. 22, no. 3 (2020): 354–66.

Busby, Karen, Adam Muller, and Andrew Woolford, eds. *The Idea of a Human Rights Museum* (Winnipeg: University of Manitoba Press, 2015).

Butcher, Thomas M. "A 'Synchronized Attack': On Raphael Lemkin's Holistic Conception of Genocide," *Journal of Genocide Research,* vol. 15, no. 3 (2013): 253–71.

Byrd, Jodi A. "Introduction" to "Forum: Indigeneity's Difference: Methodology and the Structures of Sovereignty," *J19: The Journal of Nineteenth-Century Americanists,* vol. 2, no. 1 (Spring 2014): 131–61.

Byrd, Jodi. *The Transit of Empire: Indigenous Critiques of Colonialism* (Minneapolis: University of Minnesota Press, 2011).

Calliou, Brian. "Methodology for Recording Oral Histories in the Aboriginal Community." *Native Studies Review,* vol. 15, no. 1 (2004): 73–105.

Calloway, Colin G. *New Worlds for All: Indians, Europeans, and the Remaking of Early America* (Baltimore: Johns Hopkins University Press, 2013).

Cameron, Catherine M., Paul Kelton, and Alan C. Swedlund, eds. *Beyond Germs: Native Depopulation in North America* (Phoenix: University of Arizona Press, 2015).

Carmichael, Cathie. "Raphael Lemkin and Genocide before the Holocaust," in S. Gigliotti and H. Earl (eds), *The Wiley Companion to the Holocaust* (London: Wiley-Blackwell, 2020), 45–57.

Carr, Graham. "War, History and the Education of (Canadian) Memory," in Katherine Hodgkin and Susannah Radstone (eds), *Memory, History, Nation: Contested Pasts* (New Brunswick: Transaction, 2006), 67–8.

Carranco, Lynwood, and Estle Beard. *Genocide and Vendetta: The Round Valley Wars of Northern California* (Norman: University of Oklahoma Press, 1981).

Carrier, Peter. "Holocaust Memoriography and the Impact of Memory on the Historiography of the Holocaust," in Bill Niven and Stefan Berger (eds), *Writing the History of Memory* (London: Bloomsbury, 2014), 199–218.

Carrier, Peter. *Holocaust Monuments and National Memory Cultures in France and Germany since 1989: The Origins and Political Function of the Vél' d'Hiv' in Paris and the Holocaust Monument in Berlin* (New York: Berghahn Books, 2005).

Catlin, Jon. "How Jewish Was the Holocaust?" *Makom*, (2013), 24–34

Cave, Alfred A. *Lethal Encounters: Englishmen and Indians in Colonial Virginia* (Lincoln, NE: University of Nebraska Press, 2011).

Cave, Alfred A. *The Pequot War* (Amherst: University of Massachusetts Press, 1996).

Chalmers, Jason. "Canadianising the Holocaust: Debating Canada's National Holocaust Monument," *Canadian Jewish Studies,* vol. 24 (2016): 149–65.

Chalmers, Jason. "Settled Memories on Stolen Land: Settler Mythology at Canada's National Holocaust Monument," *American Indian Quarterly,* vol. 43, no. 4 (Fall 2019): 379–407.

Chandler, Michael, and Christopher Lalonde. "Cultural Continuity as a Moderator of Suicide Risk Among Canada's First Nations," in Laurence J. Kirmayer and Gail G. Valaskaskis (eds), *Healing Traditions: The Mental Health of Aboriginal Peoples in Canada* (Vancouver: University of British Columbia Press, 2008), 221–48.

Chang, David. *The Color of the Land: Race, Nation, and the Politics of Land Ownership in Oklahoma, 1832–1929* (Chapel Hill: University of North Carolina Press, 2010).

Chaplin, Joyce E. "Expansion and Exceptionalism in Early American History," *Journal of American History*, vol. 89, no. 4 (March 2003): 1431–55.

Char, Nicholas. "Holocaust Memory in a Post-Survivor World: Bearing Last Witness," in S. Gigliotti and H. Earl (eds), *The Wiley Companion to the Holocaust* (London: Wiley-Blackwell, 2020), 509–36.

Chatterjee, Helen, Sonjel Vreeland, and Guy Noble. "Museopathy: Exploring the Healing Potential of Handling Museum Objects," *Museum and Society,* vol. 7 (2009): 164–77.

Chatterley, Catherine D. "Canada's Struggle with Holocaust Memorialization: The War Museum Controversy, Ethnic Identity Politics, and the Canadian Museum for Human Rights," *Holocaust and Genocide Studies*, vol. 29, no. 2 (2015): 189–211.

Cherepinsky, Jacqueline. "Babi Yar: The Absence of the Babi Yar Massacre from Popular Memory," in Victoria Khiterer (ed.), *The Holocaust: Memories and History* (Newcastle, UK: Cambridge Scholars Publishing, 2014).

Chrisjohn, Roland, and Tanya Wasacase. "Half-truths and Whole Lies: Rhetoric in the 'Apology' and the Truth and Reconciliation Commission," in Gregory Younging, Jonathan Dewar, and Mike DeGagné (eds), *Response, Responsibility, and Renewal: Canada's Truth and Reconciliation Journey* (Ottawa: Aboriginal Healing Foundation, 2009), 217–29.

Churchill, Ward. *A Little Matter of Genocide: Holocaust and Denial in the Americus, 1492 to the Present* (San Francisco: City Lights. 1997).

Churchill, Ward. *Kill the Indian, Save the Man: The Genocidal Impact of American Indian Residential Schools* (San Francisco: City Lights, 2004).

Clifford, James. "Museums as Contact Zones," in James Clifford, *Routes: Travel and Translation in the Late Twentieth Century* (Cambridge, MA: Harvard University Press, 1997), 190–3.

Cobb, Amanda. "The National Museum of the American Indian as Cultural Sovereignty," *American Quarterly,* vol. 57, no. 2 (2005): 485–506.

Cobb, Daniel M. Native Activism in *Cold War America: The Struggle for Sovereignty* (Lawrence: University of Kansas Press, 2008).

Coffey, Wallace, and Rebecca Tsosie. "Rethinking the Tribal Sovereignty Doctrine: Cultural Sovereignty and the Collective Future of Indian Nations," *Stanford Law and Policy Review* vol. 12, no. 1, (2001): 191–210.

Cole, Douglas. *Captured Heritage: The Scramble for Northwest Coast Artifacts* (Vancouver: UBC Press, 1995).

Cole, Tim. *Images of the Holocaust: The Myth of the "Shoah Business"* (London: Duckworth, 1999).

Cole, Tim. "The United States Holocaust Memorial Museum, Washington, D.C.," in *Selling the Holocaust: From Auschwitz to Schindler: How History Is Bought, Packaged, and Sold* (New York: Routledge, 1999), 146–71.

Colls, Caroline Sturdy. *Holocaust Archaeologies: Approaches and Future Directions* (New York: Springer, 2015).

Colls, Caroline Sturdy, and M. Branthwaite. "This Is Proof"? Forensic Evidence and Ambiguous Material Culture at Treblinka Extermination Camp," *International Journal of Historical Archaeology,* vol. 22 (2018): 430–53.

Colwell, Chip. *Plundered Skulls and Stolen Spirits: Inside the Fight to Reclaim Native America's Culture* (Chicago, IL: University of Chicago Press, 2017).

Conaty, Gerald, and Clifford Crane Bear. "History, Connections, and Cultural Renewal" in S. Boehm (ed.), *Powerful Images: Portrayals of Native America* (Seattle: University of Washington Press, 1998), 63–74.

Confino, Alon. *A World without Jews: The Nazi Imagination from Persecution to Genocide* (New Haven, CT: Yale University Press, 2015).

Confino, Alon. *Foundational Pasts: The Holocaust as Historical Understanding* (Cambridge, UK: Cambridge University Press, 2012).

Conn, Steven. *Do Museums Still Need Objects?* (Philadelphia: University of Pennsylvania Press, 2010).

Conn, Steven. "Heritage vs. History at the National Museum of the American Indian," *The Public Historian,* vol. 28, no. 2 (2006): 69–73.

Cooke, Steven. "Negotiating Memory and Identity: The Hyde Park Holocaust Memorial, London," *Journal of Historical Geography,* vol. 26, no. 3 (July 2000): 449–65.

Cooper, John. *Raphael Lemkin and the Struggle for the Genocide Convention* (Basingstoke, UK: Palgrave Macmillan, 2008).

Cooper, Levi. "The Assimilation of Tikkun Olam," *Jewish Political Studies Review,* vol. 25, no. 3–4 (Fall 2013).

Corntassel, Jeff. "Indigenous Storytelling, Truth-telling, and Community Approaches to Reconciliation," *ESC: English Studies in Canada*, vol. 35, no. 1 (2009): 137–59.

Cothran, Boyd. *Remembering the Modoc War: Redemptive Violence and the Making of American Innocence* (Chapel Hill: University of North Carolina Press, 2014).

Cottrell, Courtney. "Competing Discourses, Developing Partnerships: Navigating Differences Between Ethnographic Museums and Tribal Museums," PhD diss., University of Michigan, 2017.

Coulthard, Glen. *Red Skin, White Masks: Rejecting the Colonial Politics of Recognition* (Minneapolis: University of Minnesota Press, 2014).

Coulthard, Glen. "Subjects of Empire: Indigenous Peoples and the 'Politics of Recognition' in Canada," *Contemporary Political Theory*, vol. 6, no. 4, (2007): 437–60.

Craps, Stef. "Holocaust Literature: Comparative Perspectives," in Jenni Adams (ed.), *The Bloomsbury Companion to Holocaust Literature* (London: Bloomsbury Academic, 2014), 199–218.

Craps, Stef. *Postcolonial Witness: Trauma Out of Bounds* (Basingstoke, UK: Palgrave Macmillan, 2013).

Craps, Stef, et al. "Decolonizing Trauma Studies Round-Table Discussion," *Humanities,* vol. 4 (2015): 909–10.

Craps, Stef, Rick Crownshaw, Jennifer Wenzel, Rosanne Kennedy, Claire Colebrook, and Vin Nardizzi. "Memory Studies and the Anthropocene: A Roundtable," *Memory Studies,* vol. 11, no. 4 (2018): 498–515.

Critchell, Kara. "Remembering and Forgetting: the Holocaust in 21st Century Britain," *Quest. Issues in Contemporary Jewish History. Journal of Fondazione CDEC,* vol. 10 (December 2016): 23–59.

Crownshaw, Richard. *The Afterlife of Holocaust Memory in Contemporary Literature and Culture* (Basingstoke, UK: Palgrave Macmillan, 2010).

Crownshaw, Richard, ed. *Transcultural Memory* (London and New York: Routledge, 2014).

Curtis, Neil G. W. "Repatriation from Scottish Museums: Learning from NAGPRA," *Museum Anthropology*, vol. 33, no. 2 (2010): 234–48.

Dalton, Derek. *Encountering Nazi Tourism Sites* (New York: Routledge, 2020).

Dean, Carolyn J. *The Fragility of Empathy after the Holocaust* (Ithaca, NY: Cornell University Press, 2004).

Dean, Carolyn J. "History and Holocaust Representation," *History and Theory,* vol. 41, no. 2 (2002): 239–49.

Debary, Octave, and Melanie Roustana. "A Journey to the Musée du Quai Branly: The Anthropology of a Visit," *Museum Anthropology*, vol. 40, no. 1 (2017): 5.

Brave Heart M. Y., and L. M. DeBruyn. "The American Indian Holocaust: Healing Historical Unresolved Grief," *American Indian and Alaska Native Mental Health Research*, vol. 8, no. 2 (1998): 56–78.

Deighton, Anne Deighton. "The Past in the Present: British Imperial Memories and the European Question," in Jan-Werner Müller (ed.), *Memory and Power in Post-War Europe: Studies in the Presence of the Past* (Cambridge, UK: Cambridge University Press, 2002), 100–20.

Dekel, Irit. "Jews and Other Others at the Holocaust Memorial in Berlin," *Anthropological Journal of European Cultures*, vol. 23, no. 2 (2014): 71–84.

Dekel, Irit. *Mediation at the Holocaust Memorial in Berlin* (New York: Palgrave, 2013).

Dekel, Irit. "Subjects of Memory? On Performing Holocaust Memory in Two German Historical Museums," *Dapim: Studies on the Holocaust*, vol. 30, no. 3 (2016): 296–314.

Deloria, Philip J. *Indians in Unexpected Places* (Lawrence: University Press of Kansas, 2004).

Deloria, Philip J. *Playing Indian* (New Haven: Yale University Press, 1998).

DeLucia, Christine M. "Continuing the Intervention: Past, Present, and Future Pathways for Native Studies and Early American History," *The American Historical Review*, vol. 125, no. 2 (April 2020): 528–32.

DeLucia, Christine M. *Memory Lands: King Philip's War and the Place of Violence in the Northeast* (New Haven, CT: Yale University Press, 2018).

DeLucia, Christine M. "Memory on the Move: Confronting Indigenous and Settler Colonial Commemorations in Stone and Bronze," *Reviews in American History*, vol. 48, no. 1 (March 2020): 82–97.

Denson, Andrew. "Memories of Western Violence, Lost and Found," *Reviews in American History,* vol. 42, no. 2 (2014): 273–8.

Denson, Andrew. *Monuments to Absence: Cherokee Removal and the Contest Over Southern Memory* (Chapel Hill: University of North Carolina Press, 2017).

Dewar, Jonathan. "'Where Are the Children?' And 'We Were So Far Away. . .': Exhibiting the Legacies of Residential Schools, Healing, and Reconciliation," in *The International Handbook of Museum Studies,* 85–111.

Dias, Nelia. "Double Erasures: Rewriting the Past at the Musée du Quai Branly," *Social Anthropology,* vol. 16 (2008): 300–11.

Diner, Dan. "The Destruction of Narrativity: The Holocaust in Historical Discourse," in Moishe Postone and Eric Santner (eds), *Catastrophe and Meaning: The Holocaust and the Twentieth Century* (Chicago: University of Chicago Press 2003), 67–80.

Diner, Dan. "The Irreconcilability of an Event: Integrating the Holocaust into the Narrative of the Century," in Dan Michman (ed.), *Remembering the Holocaust in Germany, 1945–2000* (New York and Oxford, UK: Berghahn Books, 2002).

Docker, John. "Are Settler-Colonies Inherently Genocidal? Re-reading Lemkin," in A. Dirk Moses (ed.), *Empire, Colony, Genocide*, 81–101.

Doerfler, Jill. "'Making Ourselves Whole with Words': A Short History of White Earth Anishinaabeg Tribal Citizenship Criteria," in Norbert Hill and Kathleen Ratteree (eds), *The Great Vanishing Act: Blood Quantum and the Future of Native Nations,* 189–209.

Doerfler, Jill. *Those Who Belong: Identity, Family, Blood, and Citizenship Among the White Earth Anishinaabeg* (East Lansing: Michigan State University Press, 2015).

Domanska, Ewa. "The Environmental History of Mass Graves," *Journal of Genocide Research*, vol. 22, no. 2 (2020): 241–55.

Donnelly, Mark. "'We Should Do Something for the Fiftieth': Remembering Auschwitz, Belsen and the Holocaust in Britain in 1995," in Caroline Sharples et al. (eds), *Britain and the Holocaust* (New York: Palgrave Macmillan, 2013), 171–89

Donnelly, Rachel. "Imperial War Museums: Reflecting and shaping Holocaust Memory," in Andy Pearce (ed.), *Remembering the Holocaust in Educational Settings* (London and New York: Routledge, 2018), chap. 7.

Doss, Erika. *Memorial Mania: Public Feeling in America* (Chicago: University of Chicago Press, 2010).

Dougherty, Matthew W. *Lost Tribes Found Israelite Indians and Religious Nationalism in Early America* (Norman, OK: University of Oklahoma Press, 2021).

Dreyfus, Jean-Marc, and Marcel Stoetzler. "Holocaust Memory in the Twenty-First Century: Between National Reshaping and Globalisation," *European Review of History—Revue européenne d'histoire,* vol. 18, no. 1 (2011): 69–78.

Drinnon, Richard. *Facing West: The Metaphysics of Indian-Hating and Empire Building* (Minneapolis: University of Minnesota Press, 1980).

Duthu, N. Bruce. "Commentary: Reconciling Our Memories in Order to Re-envision Our Future," in Catherine Bell and David Kahane (eds), *Intercultural Dispute Resolution in Aboriginal Contexts* (Vancouver: University of British Columbia Press, 2004), 232–7.

Duthu, N. Bruce. *Shadow Nations: Tribal Sovereignty and the Limits of Legal Pluralism* (New York and Oxford, UK: Oxford University Press, 2013).

Dziuban, Zuzanna, ed. *Mapping the "Forensic Turn": Engagements with Materialities of Mass Death in Holocaust Studies and Beyond* (Vienna: New Academic Press 2017).

Dziuban, Zuzanna. "The Politics of Human Remains at the Peripheries of the Holocaust," *Dapim—Studies on the Holocaust,* vol. 29 (2015): 154–72.

Dziuban, Zuzanna. "(Re)politicising the Dead in Post-Holocaust Poland: The Afterlives of the Human Remains at the Belzec Extermination Camp," in E. Anstett and J-M. Dreyfus (eds), *Human Remains in Society: Curation and Exhibition in the Aftermath of Genocide and Mass-Violence* (Manchester: Manchester University Press, 2016), 38–65.

Eckel, J., and C. Moisel, eds. *Universalisierung des Holocaust? Erinnerungskultur und Geschichtspolitik in internationaler Perspektive* (Göttingen: Wallstein, 2008).

Edkins, Jenny. "Remembering Relationality: Trauma Time and Politics," in Duncan Bell (ed.), *Memory, Trauma, and World Politics: Reflections on the Relationship between Past and Present* (New York: Palgrave Macmillan, 2006), 99–115.

Edwards, Elizabeth, Chris Gosden, and Ruth B. Phillips, eds. *Sensible Objects: Colonialism, Museums and Material Culture* (Oxford and New York: Berg Publishers, 2006).

Ehlers, Cindy L., Ian R. Gizer, David A. Gilder, Jarrod M. Ellingson, and Rachel Yehuda. "Measuring Historical Trauma in an American Indian Community Sample: Contributions of Substance Dependence, Affective Disorder, Conduct Disorder and PTSD," *Drug and Alcohol Dependence,* vol. 133, no. 1 (2013): 180–7.

Elliott, Michael A. "Not Over: The Nineteenth Century Indian Wars," *Reviews in American History,* vol. 44 (2016): 277–83.

Eltringham, Nigel, and Pam Maclean, eds. *Remembering Genocide* (London: Routledge, 2014).

Epstein, Julia, and Lori Lefkovitz. *Shaping Losses: Cultural Memory and the Holocaust* (University of Illinois Press, 2001).

Estes, Nick. *Our History Is the Future: Standing Rock Versus the Dakota Access Pipeline, and the Long Tradition of Indigenous Resistance* (New York: Verso, 2019).

Ethridge, Robbie, and Sherie M. Shuck-Hall, eds. *Mapping the Mississippian Shatter Zone: The Colonial Indian Slave Trade and Regional Instability in the American South* (Lincoln, NE: University of Nebraska Press, 2009).

Evans, Richard J. *The Third Reich in History and Memory* (New York: Oxford University Press, 2015).

Evans-Campbell, T. "Historical trauma in American Indian/Native Alaska communities: A multilevel framework for exploring impacts on individuals, families, and communities," *Journal of Interpersonal Violence,* vol 23, no. 3 (2008): 316–38.

Farmer, Sarah. *Martyred Village: Commemorating the 1944 Massacre at Oradour-sur-Glane* (Berkeley and Los Angeles: University of California Press, 1999).

Feest, Christian. "Germany's Indians in a European Perspective," in Colin G. Calloway, Gerd Gemuenden, and Susanne Zantop (eds), *Germans and Indians: Fantasies, Encounters, Projections* (Lincoln, NE: University of Nebraska Press, 2002), 29–31.

Felman, Shoshana. "The Return of the Voice: Claude Lanzmann's Shoah," in Shoshana Felman and Dori Laub, *Testimony: Crises of Witnessing in Literature, Psychoanalysis, and History* (New York: Routledge, 1992), 205.

Fenton, Elizabeth. *Old Canaan in a New World: Native Americans and the Lost Tribes of Israel* (New York: NYU Press, 2020).

Fienup-Riordan, Ann. *Ciuliamta akluit/Things of Our Ancestors: Yup'ik Elders Explore the Jacobsen Collection at the Ethnologisches Museum Berlin.* Trans. Marie Meade (Seattle: University of Washington Press, 2005).

Fienup-Riordan, Ann. "Yup'ik Elders in Museums: Fieldwork Turned on Its Head," in Alison K. Brown and Laura Peers (eds), *Museums and Source Communities: A Routledge Reader* (London and New York, Routledge: 2003), chap. 1.

Fine, Elizabeth. "The Absent Memory: The Act Of Writing in Post-Holocaust French Literature," in Berel Lang (ed.), *Writing and the Holocaust* (New York: Holmes and Meier, 1998), 41–57.

Fine-Dare, Kathleen. *Grave Injustice: The American Indian Repatriation Movement and NAGPRA* (Lincoln and London: University of Nebraska Press, 2002).

Finkielkraut, Alain. *The Future of a Negation: Reflections on the Question of Genocide* (Lincoln, NE: University of Nebraska Press, 1998).

Fischer, Klaus P. *Hitler and America* (Philadelphia: University of Pennsylvania Press, 2011).

Fitzpatrick, Matthew P. "The Pre-History of the Holocaust? The Sonderweg and Historikerstreit Debates and the Abject Colonial Past," *Central European History,* vol. 41, no. 3 (September 2008); 477–503.

Fixico, D. "Change Over Time: The National Museum of the American Indian," *The Public Historian,* vol. 28, no. 2 (2006): 81–4.

Flanzbaum, Hilene, ed. *The Americanization of the Holocaust* (Baltimore: Johns Hopkins University Press, 1999).

Flint, Kate. *The Transatlantic Indian, 1776–1930* (Princeton: Princeton University Press, 2009).

Ford, Lisa. *Settler Sovereignty: Jurisdiction and Indigenous People in America and Australia, 1788–1836* (Cambridge, MA: Harvard University Press, 2011).

Forde, Cressida, Jane Hubert, and Paul Turnbull, eds. *The Dead and Their Possessions: Repatriation in Principle, Policy in Practice* (New York and London: Routledge, 2004).

Foster, Stuart, Alice Pettigrew, Andy Pearce, Rebecca Hale, Adrian Burgess, Paul Salmons, and Ruth-Anne Lenga. *What Do Students Know and Understand about the Holocaust? Evidence from English Secondary Schools* (London: UCL IOE, 2016).

Freeman, Michael. "Puritans and Pequots: The Question of Genocide," *New England Quarterly,* vol. 68, no. 2 (1995): 278–93.

Freeman, Victoria Jane. "'Toronto Has No History!' Indigineity, Settler Colonialism and Historical Memory in Canada's Largest City," PhD diss., University of Toronto, 2010.

Friedberg, Edna. "Does the Holocaust Play an Outsized Role in Contemporary Jewish Identity?," 2019, http://www.jtsa.edu/stuff/contentmgr/files/1/271f91ea975bce4d8eed02ac2444f4fb/pdf/yomhashoah5779.pdf.

Friedberg, Lilian. "Dare to Compare: Americanizing the Holocaust," *The American Indian Quarterly,* vol. 24, no. 3 (Summer 2000): 353–80.

Friedländer, Saul. *Memory, History, and the Extermination of the Jews of Europe* (Bloomington & Indianapolis: Indiana University Press, 1993)

Friedländer, Saul. *Reflections of Nazism: An Essay on Kitsch and Death* (Bloomington and Indianapolis: Indiana University Press, 1984).

Galloway, Patricia K. *Choctaw Genesis: 1500–1700* (Lincoln, NE: University of Nebraska Press, 1995), 183–99.

Garroutte, Eva Marie. *Real Indians: Identity and the Survival of Native America* (Berkeley: University of California Press, 2003).

Gaudenzi, Bianca, and Astrid Swenson. "Looted Art and Restitution in the Twentieth Century—Towards a Global Perspective," *Journal of Contemporary History,* vol. 52, no. 3 (2017): 491–518.

Gerlach, Christian. *Extremely Violent Societies: Mass Violence in the Twentieth Century* (Cambridge, UK: Cambridge University Press, 2010).

Gerstenfeld, Manfred. *The Abuse of Holocaust Memory: Distortions and Responses* (Jerusalem: Jerusalem Center for Public Affairs / Anti-Defamation League, 2009).

Gigliotti, Simone. *The Memorialization of Genocide* (London: Routledge, 2016).

Gigliotti, Simone. "Review: History's Dark Sides: Writing Genocide and Post-Holocaust Obligations," *Journal of Contemporary History,* vol. 41, no. 4 (October 2006): 767–78.

Gilbert, Shirli, and Avril Alba, eds. *Holocaust Memory and Racism in the Postwar World* (Detroit, Michigan: Wayne State University Press, 2019).

Glowacka, Dorota. "'Never Forget': Intersecting Memories of the Holocaust and the Settler Colonial Genocide in Canada," in Shirli Gilbert and Avril Alba (eds), *Holocaust Memory and Racism in the Postwar World* (Detroit, Michigan: Wayne State University Press, 2019), 389–411.

Glowacka, Dorota. "Sexual Violence against Men and Boys during the Holocaust: A Genealogy of (Not-So-Silent) Silence," *German History*, vol. 38, no. 4 (December 2020): 8–9.

Gone, J. P. "A Community-Based Treatment for Native American Historical Trauma: Prospects for Evidence-Based Practice," *Journal of Counseling and Clinical Psychology,* vol. 77, no. 4 (2009): 751–62.

Gone, J. P., and C. Alcántara. "Identifying Effective Mental Health Interventions for American Indians and Alaska Natives: A Review of the Literature," *Cultural Diversity & Ethnic Minority Psychology,* vol. 13, no. 4 (2007): 356–63.

Gould, Eliga. "Independence and Interdependence: The American Revolution and the Problem of Postcolonial Nationhood, circa 1802," *William and Mary Quarterly,* vol. 74 (October 2017): 729–52.

Grabowski, Jan. "The Role of 'Bystanders' in the Implementation of the 'Final Solution' in Occupied Poland," *Yad Vashem Studies,* vol. 43, no. 1 (2015): 113–32.

Greene, Jerome A. *American Carnage: Wounded Knee, 1890* (Norman: University of Oklahoma Press, 2014).

Gross, Jan T. *Neighbors: The Destruction of the Jewish Community in Jedwabne, Poland* (Princeton, NJ: Princeton University Press, 2001).

Grover, Linda LeGarde. *Onigamiisin: Seasons of an Ojibwe Year* (Minneapolis: The University of Minnesota Press, 2017).

Grua, David W. *Surviving Wounded Knee: The Lakotas and the Politics of Memory* (New York: Oxford University Press, 2016).

Gruber, Ruth Ellen. *Virtually Jewish: Reinventing Jewish Culture in Europe* (Berkeley and Los Angeles: University of California Press, 2002).

Guettel, Jens-Uwe. *German Expansionism, Imperial Liberalism, and the United States, 1776–1945* (Cambridge, UK: Cambridge University Press, 2013).

Guettel, Jens-Uwe. "The US Frontier as Rationale for the Nazi East? Settler Colonialism and Genocide in Nazi-occupied Eastern Europe and the American West," *Journal of Genocide Research*, vol. 15, no. 4 (2013): 401–19.

Hancock, Ange-Marie. *Intersectionality: An Intellectual History* (New York: Oxford University Press, 2016).

Hansen-Glucklich, Jennifer. *Holocaust Memory Reframed: Museums and the Challenges of Representation* (New Brunswick, NJ: Rutgers University Press, 2014).

Harper, Rob. "Looking the Other Way: The Gnadenhütten Massacre and the Contextual Interpretation of Violence," in Philip G. Dwyer and Lyndall Ryan (eds), *Theatres of Violence: Massacre, Mass illing, and Atrocity Throughout History* (New York and Oxford, UK: Berghahn Books, 2012): 81–94.

Hartmann, William E., et al. "American Indian Historical Trauma: Anti-Colonial Prescriptions for Healing, Resilience, and Survivance," *American Psychology,* vol. 74, no. 1 (January 2019): 6–19.

Harvey, Sean P. *Native Tongues: Colonialism and Race from Encounter to the Reservation* (Cambridge, UK Harvard University Press, 2015).

Hatoum, Rainer. "'The First Real Indians That I Have Seen': Franz Boas and the Disentanglement of the Entangled," *ab-Original: Journal of Indigenous Studies and First Nations and First Peoples' Culture,* vol. 2. no. 2 (2018): 157–84.

Henderson, Jennifer, and Pauline Wakeham (eds), *Reconciling Canada: Critical Perspectives on the Culture of Redress* (Toronto: University of Toronto Press, 2013).

Heni, Clemens. "The Prague Declaration, Holocaust Obfuscation, and Anti-Semitism," 8: http://www.clemensheni.net/the-prague-declaration-holocaust-obfuscation-and-antisemitism/.

Hermansky, Martin. "War Bonnets and Calumets in the Heart of Europe: Native American Exhibition in Rosenheim, Germany," *Lidé města / Urban People,* vol. 13 (2011): 277–301.

Himka, John-Paul, and Joanna Beata Michlic. *Bringing the Dark Past to Light: The Reception of the Holocaust in Postcommunist Europe* (Lincoln, NE: University of Nebraska Press, 2013).

Hinton, Alex, and Devon Hinton, eds. *External Genocide and Mass Violence: Memory, Symptom, Recovery* (Cambridge, UK: Cambridge University Press, 2015).

Hinton, Alexander Laban, Andrew Woolford, and Jeff Benvenuto, eds. *Colonial Genocide in Indigenous North America* (Durham, NC: Duke University Press, 2014).

Hirsch, Marianne. *The Generation of Postmemory: Writing and Visual Culture After the Holocaust* (New York: Columbia University Press, 2012).

Hirsh, David. *Contemporary Left Antisemitism* (London: Routledge, 2017).

Hixson, Walter L. *American Settler Colonialism: A History* (New York: Palgrave Macmillan, 2013).

Holtschneider, K. Hannah. *The Holocaust and Representations of Jews: History and Identity in the Museum* (London and New York: Routledge, 2011).

Horowitz, Sara R. "'If He Knows to Make a Child. . .' Memories of Birth and Baby-Killing in Deferred Jewish Testimony Narratives," in Norman J. W. Goda (ed.), *Jewish Histories of the Holocaust New Transnational Approaches* (New York and Oxford, UK: Berghahn, 2014), 135–51.

Horsman, Reginald. *Race and Manifest Destiny: The Origins for American Racial Anglo-Saxonism* (Cambridge, MA: Harvard University Press, 1981).

Hoxie, Frederick E. *A Final Promise: The Campaign to Assimilate the Indians, 1880–1920* (Lincoln, NE: University of Nebraska Press, 2001).

Hoxie, Frederick E. "Retrieving the Red Continent: Settler Colonialism and the History of American Indians in the US," *Ethnic and Racial Studies*, vol. 31, no. 6 (2008): 1153–67.

Hoxie, Frederick E. "Sovereignty's Challenge to Native American (and United States) History," *J19: The Journal of Nineteenth-Century Americanists,* vol. 2, no. 1 (Spring 2014): 137–42.

Hubbard, Tasha. "'Kill, Skin, and Sell': Buffalo Genocide," in *Colonial Genocide in Indigenous North America,* in Andrew Woolford, Jeff Benvenuto, and Alexander Laban Hinton (eds), *Colonial Genocide in Indigenous North America* (Durham, NC: Duke University Press, 2014), 292–305.

Huener, Jonathan. *Auschwitz, Poland, and the Politics of Commemoration, 1945–1979* (Athens: Ohio University Press, 2003).

Hurvich, Marvin. "The Place of Annihilation Anxieties in Psychoanalytic Theory," *Journal of the American Psychoanalytic Association*, vol. 51, no. 2 (2003): 579–616.

Huyssen, A. "International Human Rights and the Politics of Memory: Limits and Challenges. *Criticism,* vol. 53, no. 4, (2011): 607–24.

Huyssen, A. "Monument and Memory in a Postmodern Age," in J. E. Young (ed.), *The Art of Memory: Holocaust Memorials in History* (New York: Prestel–Verlag/ The Jewish Museum New York, 1994), 1–13.

Huyssen, Andreas. *Twilight Memories: Marking Time in a Culture of Amnesia* (London: Routledge, 1995).

Irvin-Erickson, Douglas. *Raphael Lemkin and the Concept of Genocide* (Philadelphia: University of Pennsylvania Press, 2017).

Jacknis, Ira. "A New Thing? The NMAI in Historical and Institutional Perspective," *American Indian Quarterly,* vol. 30, no. 3/4 (2006): 511–42.

Jacobs, J. "The Cross-Generational Transmission of Trauma: Ritual and Emotion Among Survivors of the Holocaust," *Journal of Contemporary Ethnography*, vol. 40, no. 3 (2011): 342–61.

Jacobs, Margaret D. "Seeing Like a Settler Colonial State," *Modern American History*, vol. 1, no. 2 (July 2018): 257–70.

Jacobs, Margaret. *White Mother to a Dark Race: Settler Colonialism, Maternalism, and the Removal of Indigenous Children in the American West and Australia, 1880–1940* (Lincoln, NE: University of Nebraska Press, 2009).

Jacoby, Karl. "The Broad Platform of Extermination: Nature and Violence in the Nineteenth Century North American Borderlands," *Journal of Genocide Research*, vol. 10 (2008): 249–64.

Jacoby, Karl. *Shadows at Dawn: An Apache Massacre and the Violence of History* (New York: Penguin, 2008).

James, Kirstin. "Gifting Culture: Comparing Display Practice at the British Museum and the Pitt Rivers Museum," PhD diss., Leicester, 2015.

Jilovsky, Esther. *Remembering the Holocaust: Generations, Witnessing and Place* (London and New York: Bloomsbury Academic, 2015)

Jinks, Rebecca. "Holocaust Memory and Contemporary Atrocities: The Imperial War Museum's Holocaust Exhibition and Crimes Against Humanity Exhibition," in *Britain and the Holocaust*, 142–59.

Jinks, Rebecca. *Representing Genocide: The Holocaust as Paradigm?* (London and New York: Bloomsbury, 2016).

Joeden-Forgey, E. von. "Genocidal Masculinity," in Adam Jones (ed.), *New Directions in Genocide Research* (New York and London: Routledge, 2012), 76–94.

Jokusch, Laura. *Collect and Record: Jewish Holocaust Documentation in Early Postwar Europe* (Oxford, UK: Oxford University Press, 2012).

Jones, Adam. *Genocide: A Comprehensive Introduction* (New York: Routledge, 2006).

Jones, Adam. "The Great Lakes Genocides: Hidden Histories, Hidden Precedents," in Alexander Laban Hinton, Thomas La Pointe, and Douglas Irvin-Erickson (eds), *Hidden Genocides: Power, Knowledge, Memory* (New Brunswick, NJ: Rutgers University Press, 2014), 129–48.

Jones, David S. *Rationalizing Epidemics: Meanings and Uses of American Indian Mortality Since 1600* (Cambridge, MA: Harvard University Press, 2004), 21–8.

Jones, David S. "Virgin Soils Revisited," *William and Mary Quarterly,* vol. 60, no. 4 (2003): 740–2.

Jordan, Miriam, and Julian Halaydn. "Formations of 'Indian' Fantasies: European Museums and the Decontextualization of Native American Art and Artifacts," in Karsten Fitz (ed.), *Visual Representations of Native Americans: Transnational Contexts and Perspectives* (Heidelberg: Universitätsverlag Winter [American Studies Monograph Series], 2012), 179–93.

Judt, Tony. "The 'Problem of Evil' in Postwar Europe," *New York Review of Books*, vol. 5, no. 2 (Feb. 14, 2008).

Kakel, Carroll P., III. *The American West and the Nazi East: A Comparative and Interpretive Perspective* (New York: Palgrave Macmillan, 2011).

Kalshoven, Petra. *Crafting "the Indian": Knowledge, Desire & Play in Indianist Reenactment* (New York: Berghahn Books, 2012).

Kansteiner, Wulf. "Genealogy of a Category Mistake: A Critical Intellectual History of the Cultural Trauma Metaphor," *Rethinking History,* vol. 8, no. 2 (2004), 193–221.

Kansteiner, Wulf. "Losing the War, Winning the Memory Battle," in Claudio Fogu, Wulf Kansteiner, and Richard Lebow (eds), *The Politics of Memory in Postwar Europe* (Durham, NC: Duke University Press, 2006), 102–56.

Kansteiner, Wulf. "Testing the Limits of Trauma: The Long-Term Psychological Effects of the Holocaust on Individuals and Collectives," *History of the Human Sciences,* vol. 17, no. 2–3 (2004): 97–123.

Karlsson, Klas-Göran. "Public Uses of History in Contemporary Europe," in Harriet Jones, Kjell Östberg and Nico Randeraad (eds), *Contemporary History on Trial: Europe since 1989 and the Role of the Expert Historian* (Manchester: Manchester University Press, 2007), 27–45.

Kattago, Siobhan. *Ambiguous Memory: The Nazi Past and German National Identity* (Westport, CT: Praeger Press, 2001), 56–62.

Katz, Dovid. "Is Eastern European 'Double Genocide' Revisionism Reaching Museums?" in *Dapim: Studies on the Holocaust*, vol. 30, no. 3 (November 2016): 191–220.

Katz, Dovid. "The Extraordinary Recent History of Holocaust Studies in Lithuania," *Dapim: Studies on the Holocaust,*, vol. 31, no. 3 (December 2017): 285–95.

Katz, Dovid. "On Three Definitions: Genocide Holocaust Denial: Holocaust Obfuscation," in Leonidas Donskis (ed.), *A Litmus Test Case of Modernity: Examining Modern Sensibilities and the Public Domain in the Baltic States at the Turn of the Century* (New York: Peter Lang, 2009), 365–74

Katz, Steven T. "Comparing Causes of Death in the Holocaust with the Tragedy of the Indigenous Peoples of Spanish America: The View of David E. Stannard," *Journal of Genocide Research*, vol. 22, no. 3 (2020): 373–90.

Katz, Steven T. "The Depopulation of the New World in the Sixteenth Century," in *The Holocaust in Historical Context: vol. I: The Holocaust and Mass Death before the Modern Age* (New York: Oxford University Press, 1994), 87–91.

Katz, Steven T. *The Holocaust in Historical Context: vol. I: The Holocaust and Mass Death before the Modern Age* (New York: Oxford University Press, 1994).

Katz, Steven T. "The Pequot War Reconsidered," *New England Quarterly,* vol. 64, no. 2 (1991): 206–24.

Katz, Steven, T. "Pequots and the Question of Genocide: A Reply to Michael Freeman." *New England Quarterly,* vol. 68, no. 4 (1995): 641–9.

Katz, Steven T. "The 'Unique' Intentionality of the Holocaust," *Modern Judaism—A Journal of Jewish Ideas and Experience*, vol. 1, no. 2 (September 1981): 161–83.

Katz, Steven. "The Uniqueness of the Holocaust: The Historical Dimension," in Alan Rosenbaum (ed.), *Is the Holocaust Unique? Perspectives on Comparative Genocide* (Boulder, Co: Westview Press, 1996), 21.

Kelman, Ari. *A Misplaced Massacre: Struggling over the Memory of Sand Creek* (Cambridge, MA: Harvard University Press, 2013), 136–44.

Kelton, Paul. *Epidemics and Enslavement: Biological Catastrophe in the Native Southeast, 1492–1715* (Lincoln, NE: University of Nebraska Press, 2007).

Kerr, Whitney. "Giving up the 'I': How the National Museum of the American Indian Appropriated Tribal Voices," *American Indian Law Review,* vol. 29 (2004), 421–2.

Khiterer, Victoria. ed. *The Holocaust: Memories and History* (Newcastle: Cambridge Scholars Publishing, 2014).

Kiel, Doug. "Competing Visions of Empowerment: Oneida Progressive-Era Politics and Writing Tribal Histories," *Ethnohistory*, vol. 61, no. 3 (2014): 419–44.

King, Lisa Michelle. *Legible Sovereignties: Rhetoric, Representations, and Native American Museums* (Corvalis: Oregon State University Press, 2017).

King, Lisa Michelle. "Revisiting Winnetou: The Karl May Museum, Cultural Appropriation, and Indigenous Self-Representation," *Studies in American Indian Literatures*, vol. 28, no. 2, (Summer 2016): 25–55.

King, Thomas. *The Inconvenient Indian: A Curious Account of Native People in North America* (Minneapolis: University of Minnesota Press, 2013).

Kingston, Lindsey. "The Destruction of Identity: Cultural Genocide and Indigenous Peoples," *Journal of Human Rights,* vol. 14, no. 1 (2015): 63–83.

Kirchick, James. "The Holocaust Without Jews," *Tablet Magazine*, May 3, 2016, http://www.tabletmag.com/jewish- news-and-politics/201420/the-holocaust-without-jews.

Kirshenblatt-Gimblett, Barbara. *Destination Culture: Tourism, Museums, and Heritage* (Berkeley and Los Angeles: University of California Press, 1998).

Kirshenblatt-Gimblett, Barbara. "World Heritage and Cultural Economics," in I. Karp, Corinne A. Kratz, Lynn Szwaja, and Tomas Ybarra-Frausto (eds), *Museum Frictions. Public Cultures/Global Transformations* (Durham, NC: Duke University Press, 2006), 183–8.

Klein, E. *The Battle for Auschwitz: Catholic-Jewish Relations under Strain* (London: Vallentine Mitchell, 2001).

Knowles, Chantal. "Object Journeys: Outreach Work Between National Museums Scotland and the Tlicho," in A. Brown (ed.), *Material Histories: Proceedings of a Workshop Held At Marischal Museum, University of Aberdeen, 26–27 April 2007* (Aberdeen, Scotland: Marischal Museum, University of Aberdeen, 2008), 37–56.

Koffman, David S. *The Jews' Indian Colonialism, Pluralism, and Belonging in America* (Rutgers, NJ: Rutgers University Press, 2019), chap. 5.

Konkle, Maureen. *Writing Indian Nations: Native Intellectuals and the Politics of Historiography, 1827–1863* (Chapel Hill: University of North Carolina Press, 2004).

Kosslak, R. "The Native American Graves Protection And Repatriation Act: The Death Knell For Scientific Study?" *American Indian Law Review*, vol. 151 (2000): 130.

Kovács, Éva. "Limits of Universalization: The European Memory Sites of Genocide," *Journal of Genocide Research*," vol. 20, no. 4 (2018): 490–509.

Krmpotich, Cara, and Laura Peers, *This Is Our Life: Haida Material Heritage and Changing Museum Practice* (Vancouver: UBC Press, 2013).

Kühne, Thomas. "Colonialism and the Holocaust. Continuities, Causations, and Complexities," *Journal of Genocide Research*, vol. 15, no. 3 (2013): 347–52.

Kühne, Thomas. "Great Men and Large Numbers. Undertheorizing a History of Mass Killing," *Contemporary European History*, vol. 21, no. 2 (2012): 133–43.

Kushner, Tony. "Belsen for Beginners: The Holocaust in British Heritage," in Monica Riera and Gavin Schaffer (eds), *The Lasting War: Society and Identity in Britain, France and Germany after 1945* (Basingstoke, UK: Palgrave Macmillan, 2008), 226–47.

Kushner, Tony. "From 'This Belsen Business' to 'Shoah Business': History, Memory and Heritage, 1945–2005," *Holocaust Studies*, vol. 12, no. 1–2, (2006):189–216.

Kushner, Tony. *The Holocaust and the Liberal Imagination: A Social and Cultural History* (Oxford, UK: Berg, 1994).

Kushner, Tony. "Oral History at the Extremes of Human Experience: Holocaust Testimony in a Museum Setting," *Oral History*, vol. 29, no. 2 (2001): 83–94.

LaCapra, Dominick. *Representing the Holocaust: History, Theory, Trauma* (Ithaca, NY: Cornell University Press, 1996).

LaCapra, Dominick. "Trauma, History, Memory, Identity: What Remains?" *History and Theory*, vol. 5, no. 3 (October 2016): 375–400.

LaCapra, Dominick. *Writing History, Writing Trauma* (Baltimore: Johns Hopkins University Press, 2001).

Laczo, Ferenc. "The Europeanization of Holocaust remembrance," *Eurozine*, January 29, 2018, https://www.eurozine.com/the-europeanization-of-holocaust-remembrance/.

LaDuke, Winona. *Last Standing Woman* (Stillwater, MN: Voyageur Press, 1997).

LaDuke, Winona. *Recovering the Sacred: The Power of Naming and Claiming* (Cambridge, MA: South End Press, 2005).

Lal, V. "The Concentration Camp and Development: the Pasts and Futures of Genocide," in A. D. Moses and D. Stone (eds), *Colonialism and Genocide* (London: Routledge, 2007), 124–47.

Lang, Berel. *Genocide: The Act as Idea* (Philadelphia: University of Pennsylvania Press, 2016).

Lang, Berel. *Holocaust Representation: Art Within the Limits of History and Ethics* (Baltimore, MD: Johns Hopkins University Press, 1996)

Langenbacher, Eric, and Friederike Eigler. "Introduction: Memory Boom or *Memory Fatigue* in 21st Century Germany?" *German Politics and Society*, vol. 23, no. 3 (2005): 1–15.

Lawrence, Bonita. "Rewriting Histories of the Land: Colonization and Indigenous Resistance in Eastern Canada," in Sherene H. Razack (ed.), *Race, Space, and the Law: Unmapping a White Settler Society* (Toronto: Between the Lines, 2002), 21–47.

Lawson, Tom, and Andy Pearce, eds. *The Palgrave Handbook of Britain and the Holocaust* (Basingstoke, UK: Palgrave, 2021).

Lawson, Tom. "Britain's Promise to Forget: Some Historiographical Reflections on What do Students Know and Understand about the Holocaust?," *Holocaust Studies*, vol. 23, no. 3 (2017): 345–6.

Lawson, Tom. "Coming to Terms with the Past: Reading and Writing Colonial Genocide in the Shadow of the Holocaust," *Holocaust Studies: A Journal of Culture and History*, vol. 20, 1–2 (2014): 129–56.

Lawson, Tom. "Ideology in a Museum of Memory: A Review of the Holocaust Exhibition at the Imperial War Museum," *Totalitarian Movements and Political Religions*, vol. 4, no. 2 (2003): 173–83.

Lawson, Tom. "Memorializing Colonial Genocide in Britain: the case of Tasmania," *Journal of Genocide Research*, vol. 16, no. 4 (2014): 441–61.

Leeuw, Sara de, Margo Greenwood and Nicole Lindsay. "Troubling Good Intentions," *Settler Colonial Studies*, vol. 3, nos. 3–4, (2013), 381–94.

Lehrer, Erica. "Thinking through the Canadian Museum for Human Rights," *American Quarterly*, vol. 67, no. 4 (2015): 1195–1216.

Lemberg, Jennifer. "Transmitted Trauma and 'Absent Memory' in James Welch's *The Death of Jim Loney*," *Studies in American Indian Literatures*, vol. 18, no. 3 (2006): 67–81.

Lemkin, Raphael. *Axis Rule in Occupied Europe: Laws of Occupation, Analysis of Government, Proposals for Redress* (Washington, D.C.: Carnegie Endowment for International Peace, Division of International Law, 1944).

Lerner, P., and M. Micale. "Trauma, Psychiatry, and History: A Conceptual and Historiographical Introduction," in P. Lerner and M. Micale (ed.), *Traumatic Pasts: History, Psychiatry, and Trauma in the Modern Age, 1870–1930* (Cambridge: Cambridge University Press, 2001), chap. 1.

Levene, Mark. "Britain's Holocaust Memorial Day: A Case of Post-Cold War Wish-Fulfillment, or Brazen Hypocrisy?," *Human Rights Review*, vol. 7, no. 3 (2006): 26–59.

Levy, Daniel, and Natan Sznaider. *The Holocaust and Memory in the Global Age* (Philadelphia: Temple University Press, 2006).

Lindert, Jutta, and Armen T. Marsoobian, eds. *Multidisciplinary Perspectives on Genocide and Memory* (Basingstoke, UK: Palgrave Macmillan, 2018)

Linenthal, Edward Tabor. *Preserving Memory: The Struggle to Create America's Holocaust Museum* (New York: Columbia University Press, 2001).

Lipstadt, Deborah E. *Antisemitism: Here and Now* (New York, Schocken Books: 2019).

Lipstadt, Deborah E. *Holocaust: An American Understanding* (Rutgers University Press, 2016).

Littoz-Monnet, A. "Explaining Policy Conflict across Institutional Venues: European Union-level Struggles over the Memory of the Holocaust," *JCMS: Journal of Common Market Studies*, vol. 51 (2013), 489–504.

Logan, Tricia. "Memory, Erasure, and National Myth," in Andrew Woolford, Jeff Benvenuto, and Alexander Laban Hinton (eds), *Colonial Genocide in Indigenous North America* (Durham, NC: Duke University Press, 2014), 149–65.

Logan, Tricia. "National Memory and Museums: Remembering Settler Colonial Genocide of Indigenous Peoples in Canada," in Nigel Eltringham and Pam Maclean (eds), *Remembering Genocide* (London: Routledge, 2014), 112–30.

Logan, Tricia. "Settler Colonialism in Canada and the Métis," *Journal of Genocide Research*, vol. 17, no. 4 (2015), 433–452.

Lokensgard, Kenneth H. *Blackfoot Religion and the Consequences of Cultural Commoditization* (Burlington, VT: Ashgate, 2010).

Lonetree, Amy. "Continuing Dialogues: Evolving Views of the National Museum of the American Indian," *The Public Historian*, vol. 28, no. 2 (2006), 57–61.

Lonetree, Amy. *Decolonizing Museums: Representing Native America in National and Tribal Museums* (Chapel Hill: University of North Carolina Press, 2012).

Lonetree, Amy. "Missed Opportunities: Reflections on the NMAI," *American Indian Quarterly*, vol. 30, no. 3/4 (2006), 632–63.

Lonetree, Amy, and Amanda J. Cobb. *The National Museum of the American Indian: Critical Conversations* (Lincoln, NE: University of Nebraska Press, 2008).

Lowery, Malinda Maynor. *Lumbee Indians in the Jim Crow South: Race, Identity, and the Making of a Nation* (Chapel Hill: University of North Carolina Press, 2010).

Lukas, Richard C., ed. *Out of the Inferno: Poles Remember the Holocaust* (Lexington: University Press of Kentucky, 1989), 72.

Lutz, Harmut. "German Indianthusiam: A Socially Constructed German National(ist) Myth," in *Germans and Indians: Fantasies, Encounters*, 167–84.

Lyons, Claire. "Objects and Identities: Claiming and Reclaiming the Past" in Elazar Barkan and Ronald Bus (eds), *Claiming the Stones/Naming the Bones: Cultural Property and the Negotiation of National and Ethnic Identity* (Los Angeles: Getty Research Institute, 2002), 116–41.

Lyons, Scott Richard. "Rhetorical Sovereignty: What Do American Indians Want from Writing?" *College Composition and Communication*, vol. 51, no. 3 (February 2000): 447–68.

MacDonald, David B. "First Nations, Residential Schools, and the Americanization of the Holocaust: Rewriting Indigenous History in the United States and Canada," *Canadian Journal of Political Science/Revue canadienne de science politique*, vol. 40, no. 4 (December 2007): 1000.

MacDonald, David B. "Canada's History War: Indigenous Genocide and Public Memory in the United States, Australia, and Canada," *Journal of Genocide Research*, vol. 17, no. 4 (2015): 411–31.

MacDonald, David B. *Identity Politics in the Age of Genocide: The Holocaust and Historical Representation* (New York: Routledge, 2008).

MacDonald, David B. "Indigenous Genocide and Perceptions of the Holocaust in Canada," in S. Gigliotti and H. Earl (eds), *The Wiley Companion to the Holocaust* (London: Wiley-Blackwell, 2020), 577–97.

MacDonald, David B. *The Sleeping Giant Awakens: Genocide, Indian Residential Schools, and the Challenge of Conciliation* (Toronto: University of Toronto Press, 2019).

MacLachlan, Neillian. "Sacred and Secular: An Analysis of the Repatriation of Native American Sacred Items from European Museums," MA diss., University of Aberdeen, 2012.

Madley, Benjamin. *An American Genocide: The United States and the California Indian Catastrophe, 1846–1873* (New Haven, CT: Yale University Press, 2017).

Madley, Benjamin. "California's Yuki Indians: Defining Genocide in Native American History," *Western Historical Quarterly*, vol. 39 (Autumn 2008): 303–32.

Madley, Benjamin. "Reexamining the American Genocide Debate: Meaning, Historiography, and New Methods," *The American Historical Review*, vol. 120, no. 1 (February 2015): 98–139.

Madsen, Deborah. "Out of the Melting Pot, into the Nationalist Fires: Native American Literary Studies in Europe," *American Indian Quarterly*, vol. 35, no. 3 (Summer 2011): 353–71.

Magid, Shaul. "The American Jewish Holocaust 'Myth' and 'Negative Judaism': Jacob Neusner's Contribution to American Judaism," in A. Avery Peck, B. Chilton, W.S. Green and G.G. Porton (eds), *A Legacy of Learning: Essays in Honor of Jacob Neusner* (Leiden, Brill, 2014), 321–40.

Magid, Shaul. "Social Justice and the Future of Judaism," *Tablet Magazine*, June 13, 2018, https://www.tabletmag.com/jewish-arts-and-culture/264145/social-justice-and-the-future-of-judaism.

Magilow, Daniel H., and Lisa Silverman. *Holocaust Representations in History: An Introduction* (London: Bloomsbury Academic Press, 2015).

Magin, Michelle. "Toward a Globalised Memory of the Holocaust: An Exploration of the Exhibition Spaces and Educational Programmes at Four Sites of Remembrance in Post-Unification Berlin," PhD diss., University of Manchester, 2015.

Mailer, Gideon, and Nicola Hale. *Decolonizing the Diet: Nutrition, Immunity, and the Warning from Early America* (New York and London: Anthem Press, 2018).

Mann, Henrietta. "Foreword," in Kathleen Ratteree and Norbert S. Hill Jr. (eds), *The Great Vanishing Act: Blood Quantum and the Future of Native Nations* (Golden, CO: Fulcrum Publishing, 2017), xv.

Mann, Michael. *The Dark Side of Democracy: Explaining Ethnic Cleansing* (Cambridge, UK: Cambridge University Press, 2005).

Marcuse, Harold. "Holocaust Memorials: The Emergence of a Genre," *The American Historical Review*, vol. 115, no. 1 (February 2010): 53–89.

Marcuse, Harold. *Legacies of Dachau: The Uses and Abuses of a Concentration Camp, 1933–2001* (Cambridge, UK: Cambridge University Press, 2001).

Martini, Elspeth. "Borderlands, Indigenous Homelands and North American Settler Colonialism," *Reviews in American History*, vol. 45 (2017): 416–22.

Maurer, Evan. "Presenting the American Indian: From Europe to America," in W. Richard West Jr. (ed.), *The Changing Presentation of the American Indian* (Seattle: University of Washington Press, 2000).

Mazower, Mark. *Hitler's Empire: Nazi Rule in Occupied Europe* (London: Allen Lane, 2008).

McDonnell, Michael A., and A. Dirk Moses. "Raphael Lemkin as Historian of Genocide in the Americas," *Journal of Genocide Research*, vol. 7, no. 4 (2005): 501–29.

McGlothlin, Erin, Brad Prager, and Markus Zisselsberger, eds. *The Construction of Testimony: Claude Lanzmann's Shoah and Its Outtakes* (Detroit: Wayne State University Press, 2020).

McMaster, Gerald, Julia Lum, and Kaitlin McCormick. "The Entangled Gaze: Indigenous and European Views of Each Other," *ab-Original: Journal of Indigenous Studies and First Nations and First Peoples' Culture*, vol. 2. no. 2 (2018): 125–40.

McNally, Richard. *Remembering Trauma* (Cambridge, MA: Harvard University Press, 2005).

Meng, Michael. *Shattered Spaces: Encountering Jewish Ruins in Postwar Germany and Poland* (Cambridge, MA: Harvard University Press, 2011).

Mercer, Ben. "The Memory of Europe's Age of Catastrophe 1914–2014," in Nicholas Doumanis (ed.), *The Oxford Handbook of European History, 1914–1945* (Oxford University Press: Oxford, 2016), 625.

Meyer, Carter Jones, and Diana Royer, eds. *Selling the Indian: Commercializing & Appropriating American Indian Cultures* (Tucson, AZ: University of Arizona Press, 2001).

Michman, Dan. "Characteristics of Holocaust Historiography since 1990 and Their Contexts: Emphases, Perceptions, Developments, Debates," in Simone Gigliotti and Hilary Earl (eds), *The Wiley Blackwell Companion to Holocaust Studies* (London: Wiley Blackwell, 2020), 211–32.

Michman, Dan. "The Jewish Dimension of the Holocaust in Dire Straits? Current Challenges of Interpretation and Scope," in Norman Goda (ed.), *Jewish Histories of the Holocaust: New Transnational Approaches* (New York: Berghahn Books, 2014), 17–38.

Michman, Dan. "What is the Core of the Shoah—the 'Final Solution of the Jewish Question' or 'Total Removal of the Jews' and of Judaism?," in Emanuel Etkes, David Asaf and Yosef Kaplan (eds), *Milestones: Essays and Studies in Jewish History in honor of Zvi (Kuti) Yekutiel* (Jerusalem: Shazar Center, 2015), 397–409.

Mihesuah, Devon, ed. *Repatriation Reader: Who Owns American Indian Remains?* (Lincoln, NE: University of Nebraska Press, 2000).

Miller, Eric D. "The Double–Edged Sword of Remembering the Holocaust: The Case of Jewish Self–Identity," in Victoria Khiterer (ed.), *The Holocaust: Memories and History* (Newcastle, UK: Cambridge Scholars Publishing, 2014).

Millet, Kitty. *The Victims of Slavery, Colonization, and the Holocaust: A Comparative History of Persecution* (New York and London: Bloomsbury, 2017).

Mills, Charles. *The Racial Contract* (Ithaca, NY: Cornell University Press, 1997).

Milton, S. Jr. *Fitting Memory: The Art and politics of Holocaust Memorials* (Detroit: Wayne State University Press, 1991).

Morina, Christina, and Krijn Thijs, eds. *Probing the Limits of Categorization: The Bystander in Holocaust History* (New York: Berghahn Books, 2018).

Moses, A. Dirk. "An Antipodean Genocide? The Origins of the Genocidal Moment in the Colonization of Australia," *Journal of Genocide Research*, vol. 2 (2000): 89–106.

Moses, A. Dirk. "Anxieties in Holocaust and Genocide Studies," in Claudio Fogu, Wulf Kansteiner, and Todd Presner (eds), *Probing the Ethics of. Holocaust Culture* (Cambridge, MA: Harvard University Press, 2016), 340–5.

Moses, A. Dirk. "Conceptual Blockages and Definitional Dilemmas in the 'Racial Century': Genocides of Indigenous Peoples and the Holocaust," *Patterns of Prejudice*, vol. 36, no. 2 (2007): 7–36.

Moses, A. Dirk. "Das römische Gespräch in a New Key: Hannah Arendt, Genocide, and the Defense of Republican Civilization," *The Journal of Modern History*, vol. 85, no. 4 (December 2013): 901–06.

Moses, A. Dirk. "Does the Holocaust Reveal or Conceal Other Genocides? The Canadian Museum for Human Rights and Grievable Suffering," in Alexander Laban Hinton, Thomas La Pointe, and Douglas Irvin-Erickso (eds), *Hidden Genocides: Power, Knowledge, Memory* (New Brunswick, NJ: Rutgers University Press, 2014), 21–51.

Moses, A. Dirk. "Empire, Colony, Genocide: Keywords and the Philosophy of History," in A. D. Moses (eds), *Empire, Colony, Genocide: Conquest, Occupation, and Subaltern Resistance in World History* (New York: Berghahn Books, 2008), 3–54.

Moses, A. Dirk. "Genocide and Modernity," in Dan Stone (ed.), *The Historiography of Genocide* (Basingstoke, UK: Palgrave Macmillan 2008), 156–93.

Moses, A. Dirk. *Genocide and Settler Society: Frontier Violence and Stolen Indigenous Children in Australian History* (New York: Berghahn, 2004).

Moses, A. Dirk. "Genocide and the Terror of History," *Parallax*, vol. 17, no. 4 (2012): 90–108.

Moses, A. Dirk. "Genocide," *Australian Humanities Review*, 55 (November 2013): 26–40.

Moses, A. Dirk. "The Holocaust and Colonialism," in Peter Hayes and John Roth (eds), *The Oxford Handbook of Holocaust Studies* (Oxford, UK: Oxford University Press, 2010), 68–80.

Moses, A. Dirk. "The Holocaust and Genocide," in Dan Stone (ed.), *The Historiography of the Holocaust*, (Basingstoke, UK: Palgrave Macmillan, 2004), 533–55.

Moses, A. Dirk. "The Holocaust and World History: Raphael Lemkin and Comparative Methodology," in Dan Stone (ed.), *The Holocaust and Historical Methodology* (New York and Oxford, Berghahn Books, 2012), 272–89.

Moses, A. Dirk. "Lemkin, Culture, and the Concept of Genocide," in Donald Bloxham and A. Dirk Moses (eds), *The Oxford Handbook of Genocide Studies* (Oxford, UK: Oxford University Press, 2010), 19–41.

Moses, A. Dirk. "Paranoia and Partisanship: Genocide Studies, Holocaust Historiography, and the 'Apocalyptic Conjuncture,'" *The Historical Journal*, vol. 54, no. 2 (2011): 615–45.

Moses, A. Dirk. "Redemptive Antisemitism and the Imperialist Imaginary," in C. Wiese and P. Betts (eds), *Years of Persecution, Years of and Extermination: Saul Friedländer and the Future of Holocaust Studies* (London: Continuum, 2010), 233–54.

Moses, A. Dirk. "Revisiting a Founding Assumption of Genocide Studies," *Genocide Studies and Prevention*, vol. 6, no. 3 (December 2011): 289–302.

Mt. Pleasant, Alyssa, Caroline Wigginton, and Kelly Wisecup. "Materials and Methods in Native American and Indigenous Studies: Completing the Turn," *The William and Mary Quarterly*, vol. 75, no. 2 (2018): 207–36.

Myers, D.G. "Jews Without Memory: 'Sophie's Choice' and the Ideology of Liberal Anti-Judaism," *American Literary History*, vol. 13, no. 3 (Autumn 2001): 499–529.

Nagel, Joane. *American Indian Ethnic Renewal: Red Power and the Resurgence of Identity and Culture* (New York: Oxford University Press, 1997).

Nathans, Benjamin, and Gabriella Safran, eds. *Culture Front: Representing Jews in Eastern Europe* (Philadelphia: University of Pennsylvania Press, 2007).

Neiman, Susan. *Learning from the Germans: Race and the Memory of Evil* (New York: Farrar, Straus and Giroux, 2019).

Neu, Dean, and Richard Therrien. *Accounting for Genocide: Canada's Bureaucratic Assault on Aboriginal People* (Blackpoint, Nova Scotia: Fernwood Publishing, 2003).

Neumayer. L "Integrating the central European past into a common narrative: the mobilizations around the "crimes of communism" in the European Parliament," *Journal of Contemporary European Studies*, 23 (2015): 344–63.

Nirenberg, David. "Was There Race before Modernity? The Example of 'Jewish' Blood in Late Medieval Spain," in Miriam Eliav-Feldon, Benjamin Isaac, Joseph

Ziegler (eds), *The Origins of Racism in the West* (Cambridge, UK: Cambridge University Press, 2009), chap. 8.

Norton, Jack. *When Our Worlds Cried: Genocide in Northwestern California* (San Francisco: Indian Historian Press, 1979).

Novick, Peter. *The Holocaust and Collective Memory* (London: Bloomsbury, 1999).

Novick, Peter. *The Holocaust in American Life* (New York: Houghton Mifflin, 1999).

O'Brien, Jean M. *Firsting and Lasting: Writing Indians out of Existence in New England* (Minneapolis: University of Minnesota Press, 2010).

O'Brien, Jean M. "What Does Native American and Indigenous Studies (NAIS) Do?" *The American Historical Review*, vol. 125, no. 2 (April 2020): 542–5.

Onuf, Peter S. "Imperialism and Nationalism in the Early American Republic," in Ian Tyrrell and Jay Sexton (eds), *Empire's Twin: U.S. Anti-imperialism from the Founding Era to the Age of Terrorism* (Ithaca, NY: Cornell University Press, 2015), 21–40.

Ostler, Jeffrey. "'To Extirpate the Indians': An Indigenous Consciousness of Genocide in the Ohio Valley and Lower Great Lakes, 1750s–1810," *The William and Mary Quarterly*, vol. 72, no. 4 (October 2015): 587–622.

Ostler, Jeffrey. "Genocide and American Indian History," *Oxford Research Encyclopedia of American History*, 2015, http://oxfordre.com/americanhistory/view/10.1093/acrefore/9780199329175.001.0001/acrefore-780199329175- e-3.

Ostler, Jeffrey. "Locating Settler Colonialism in Early American History," *The William and Mary Quarterly*, vol. 76, no. 3 (July 2019): 443–50.

Ostler, Jeffrey. *Surviving Genocide: Native Nations and the United States from the American Revolution to Bleeding Kansas* (New Haven. CT: Yale University Press, 2019).

Otele, Olivette, Luisa Gandolfo, and Yoav Galai eds. *Post-Conflict Memorialization: Missing Memorials, Absent Bodies* (London: Palgrave Macmillan, 2021).

Owen, Suzanne. *The Appropriation of Native American Spirituality* (London: Bloomsbury, 2011).

Pagden, Anthony. *The Fall of Natural Man: The American Indian and the Origins of Comparative Ethnology* (Cambridge, UK: Cambridge University Press, 1986).

Pakier, Małgorzata, and Bo Stråth. *A European Memory?: Contested Histories and Politics of Remembrance* (New York, Berghahn Books, 2010).

Palmater, Pamela. *Indigenous Nationhood: Empowering Grassroots Citizens* (Halifax: Fernwood Press, 2015).

Parkin, David. "Mementoes as Transitional Objects in Human Displacement," *Journal of Material Culture* vol. 4 (1999), 303–20.

Parkinson, Robert G. *The Common Cause: Creating Race and Nation in the American Revolution* (Chapel Hill, NC: Omohundro Institute of Early American History and Culture and the University of North Carolina Press, 2016).

Paver, Chloe. *Exhibiting the Nazi Past: Museum Objects Between the Material and the Immaterial* (New York: Palgrave Macmillan, 2018).

Pearce, Andy. "The Anatomy of a Relationship: The Holocaust, Genocide and Britain," in *Remembering the Holocaust in Educational Settings*, 40–59.

Pearce, Andy. "Britain and the Formation of Contemporary Holocaust Consciousness: A Product of Europeanization, or Exercise in Triangulation?," in Lucy Bond and Jessica Rapson (eds), *The Transcultural Turn: Interrogating Memory Between and Beyond Borders* (Berlin: De Gruyter, 2014), 119–39.

Pearce, Andy. "Britain's Holocaust Memorial Day: Inculcating 'British' or 'European' Holocaust Consciousness?" in *Britain and the Holocaust*, 190–211.

Pearce, Andy. "An Emerging "Holocaust Memorial Problem?: The Condition of Holocaust Culture in Britain," *The Journal of Holocaust Research*, vol. 33, no. 2 (2019): 117–37.

Pearce, Andy. *Holocaust Consciousness in Contemporary Britain* (New York and London: Routledge, 2011).

Pearce, Andy. "Introduction: Education, remembrance, and the Holocaust: Towards pedagogic memory-work," in Andy Pearce (ed.), *Remembering the Holocaust in Educational Settings* (London and New York: Routledge, 2018), 8–11.

Peers, Laura. "Decolonization as a Permanent Process: PRM Relations with the Haida Nation, 1998–2018," in Laura Peers, *Decolonizing the Museum in Practice: Papers from Annual Conference of the Museum Ethnographers Group Held at the Pitt Rivers Museum 12–13 April 2018* (Museum Ethnographers Group, 2019).

Peers, Laura. "Museums and Source Communities: Reflections and implications," in W. Modest, N. Thomas, and C. Augustat (eds), *Matters of Belonging: Ethnographic Museums in a Changing Europe* (Leiden: Sidestone Press, 2019).

Penny, H. Glenn. *Objects of Culture: Ethnology and Ethnographic Museums in Imperial Germany* (Chapel Hill and London: University of North Carolina Press, 2002).

Penny, H. Glenn. "Elusive Authenticity: The Quest for the Authentic Indian in German Public Culture," *Comparative Studies in Society and History*, vol. 48, no. 4 (October 2006): 798–818.

Penny, H. Glenn. *Kindred by Choice: Germans and American Indians since 1800* (Chapel Hill: University of North Carolina Press, 2013).

Pergher, Roberta, et al. "The Holocaust: A Colonial Genocide? A Scholars' Forum," *Dapim: Studies on the Holocaust*, vol. 27, no. 1 (2013): 40–73.

Perry, Nicole. "Verwoben in "Indianthusiasm": A Uniquely German Entanglement," *ab-Original*, vol. 2, no. 2 (2018): 227–45.

Peterson, Nancy J. "'If I Were Jewish, How Would I Mourn the Dead?': Holocaust and Genocide in the Work of Sherman Alexie," *MELUS*, vol. 35, no. 3, Special Issue: Crime, Punishment, and Redemption (Fall 2010): 63–84.

Pettipas, Katherine. *Severing the Ties that Bind: Government Repression of Indigenous Religious Ceremonies on the Prairies* (Winnipeg: University of Manitoba Press, 1994).

Phillips, Katrina. *Staging Indigeneity: Salvage Tourism and the Performance of Native American History* (Chapel Hill: UNC Press, forthcoming).

Phillips, Ruth B. "Can National Museums be Postcolonial?: The Canadian Museum for Human Rights and the Obligation of Redress to First Nations," in Annie. E. Coombes and Ruth B. Phillips (eds), *The International Handbook of Museum Studies: Museum Transformations* (Hoboken, NJ: Wiley Blackwell, 2020), chap. 24.

Phillips, Ruth B. "The Museum of Art-thropology: Twenty-First Century Imbroglios," *Res: Anthropology and Aesthetics* 52 (Autumn 2007): 8–19.

Phillips, Ruth B. "A Proper Place for Art or the Proper Arts of Place? Native North American Objects and the Hierarchies of Art, Craft, and Souvenir," in Lynda Jessup (ed.), *On Aboriginal Representation in the Gallery* (Hull, Quebec: Canadian Museum of Civilization, 2002), 45–73.

Phillips, Ruth B., and Sherry Brydon. "'Arrow of Truth': The Indians of Canada Pavilion at Expo 67," in Ruth B. Phillips (ed.), *Museum Pieces: Toward the Indigenization of Canadian Museums* (Montreal: McGill-Queens University Press, 2011), 27–47.

Piercey, Mary. "Representations of Inuit Culture in the Cambridge Museum of Archaeology and Anthropology," *Material Culture Review*, vol. 65 (Spring 2007): 8–19.

Pinchvevski, Amit. "The Audiovisual Unconscious: Media and Trauma in the Video Archive for Holocaust Testimonies," *Critical Inquiry*, vol. 39, no.1 (Autumn 2012): 142–66.

Plessow, Oliver. "The Interplay of the European Commission, Researcher and Educator Networks and Transnational Agencies in the Promotion of a Pan-European Holocaust Memory," *Journal of Contemporary European Studies*, vol. 23 no. 3 (2015): 378–90.

Pollin-Galay, Hannah. *Ecologies of Witnessing: Language, Place, and Holocaust Testimony* (New Haven, CT: Yale University Press, 2018).

Poole, Ross. "Misremembering the Holocaust: Universal Symbol, Nationalist Icon or Moral Kitsch?," in Yifat Gutman, Adam Brown, and Amy Sodaro (eds), *Memory and the Future: Transnational Politics, Ethics and Society* (Basingstoke, UK: Palgrave MacMillan, 2010), 31–49.

Popescu, Diana I, and Tanja Schult, eds. *Revisiting Holocaust Representation in the Post-Witness Era* (London: Springer, 2015).

Powell, Christopher, and Julia Peristerakis. "Genocide in Canada: A Relational View," in Andrew Woolford, Jeff Benvenuto, and Alexander Laban Hinton (eds), *Colonial Genocide in Indigenous North America* (Durham, NC: Duke University Press, 2014), 71–5.

Preston, Jen. "Neoliberal Settler Colonialism, Canada and the Tar Sands," *Race and Class*, vol. 55, no. 2, (2013): 42–59.

Price, Sally. *Paris Primitive: Jacques Chirac's Museum on the Quai Branly* (Chicago: Chicago University Press, 2007).

Probst, Lothar Probst. "Founding Myths in Europe and the Role of the Holocaust," *New German Critique*, vol. 90 (2003): 45–58.

Prose, Francine. *Anne Frank: The Book, the Life, the Afterlife* (New York: HarperCollins, 2009).

Prucha, Francis Paul. *The Great Father The United States Government and the American Indians* (Lincoln, NE: University of Nebraska Press, 1984).

Quack, Sibylle. "The Holocaust Memorial in Berlin and Its Information Center: Concepts, Controversies, Reactions," in Annie E. Coombes and Ruth B. Phillips, *Museum Transformations: Decolonization and Democratization* (Hoboken NJ: Wiley, 2020), 3–28.

Radonić, Ljiljana. "From 'Double Genocide' to 'the New Jews': Holocaust, Genocide and Mass Violence in Post-Communist Memorial Museums," *Journal of Genocide Research*," vol. 20, no. 4 (2018): 510–29.

Radonić, Ljiljana. "Post-communist Invocation of Europe: Memorial Museums' Narratives and the Europeanization of Memory," *National Identities*, vol. 19, no. 2 (2017): 269–70.

Radonić, Ljiljana. "Introduction: The Holocaust/Genocide Template in Eastern Europe," *Journal of Genocide Research*," vol. 20, no. 4 (2018): 485–6.

Rana, Aziz. *The Two Faces of American Freedom* (Cambridge, MA: Harvard University Press, 2010).

Rand, Jacki Thompson. "Why I Can't Visit the National Museum of the American Indian," *Common-place.org,* vol. 7, no. 4 (July 2007).

Regan, Paulette. *Unsettling the Settler Within: Indian Residential Schools, Truth Telling, and Reconciliation in Canada* (Vancouver: UBC Press, 2010).

Reich, Walter. "Holocaust Museums and the Itch to Universalize," *Mosaic Magazine,* February 15, 2016, https://mosaicmagazine.com/response/2016/02/holocaust-museums-and-the-itch-to-universalize/.

Reich, Walter. "The Use and Abuse of Holocaust Memory," American Enterprise Institute Online, November 14, 2005, http://www.aei.org/print?pub:speech

Reid, Joshua L. "AHR Forum Introduction: Indigenous Agency and Colonial Law," *American Historical Review,* vol. 124, no. 1 (February 2019): 20–7.

Reid, Joshua L. *The Sea Is My Country: The Maritime World of the Makahs* (New Haven, CT: Yale University Press, 2015).

Rensink, Brenden. "Genocide of Native Americans: Historical Facts and Historiographic Debates," in Samuel Totten and Robert Hitchcock (eds), *Genocide of Indigenous Peoples, vol. 8 in Genocide: A Critical Bibliographic Series* (New Brunswick, New Jersey: Transaction Publishers, 2011), 1–25.

Rensink, Brenden. "The Sand Creek Phenomenon: The Complexity and Difficulty of Undertaking a Comparative Study of Genocide vis-à-vis the North American West," *Genocide Studies and Prevention: An International Journal,* vol. 4, no. 1 (Spring 2009): 9–27.

Reynolds, Daniel P. *Postcards from Auschwitz: Holocaust Tourism and the Meaning of Remembrance* (New York: NYU Press, 2018).

Rifkin, Mark. *Manifesting America: The Imperial Construction of U.S. National Space* (Oxford, UK: Oxford University Press, 2009).

Rigney, A. "Reconciliation and Remembering: (How) Does It Work? *Memory Studies,* vol. 5, no. 3 (2012): 251–8.

Rigney, A. "Transforming Memory and the European Project," *New Literary History,* vol. 43, no. 4 (2012): 607–28.

Rindfleisch, Bryan. "Native American History and the Explanatory Potential of Settler Colonialism," *Junto Blog,* February 10, 2016, https://earlyamericanists.com/2016/02/10/native-american-history-the-explanatory-potential-of-settler-colonialism/.

Robins, Nicholas A., and Adam Jones, eds. *Genocides by the Oppressed: Subaltern Genocide in Theory and Practice* (Bloomington, IN: Indiana University Press, 2009).

Ronan, Kristine. "Native Empowerment, the New Museology, and the National Museum of the American Indian," *Museum and Society,* vol. 12, no. 2 (2014): 132–47.

Rose, Wendy. "The Great Pretenders: Further Reflections on Whiteshamanism," in M. Annette. Jaimes, *The State of Native North America* (Boston: South End Press, 1992), 403–21.

Roseman, Mark. "Between Acceptance, Exceptionalism, and Continuity: German Jewry, Antisemitism and the Holocaust" *Contemporary European History,* vol. 19. no. 1 (2010): 55–74.

Roseman, Mark. "Beyond Conviction? Perpetrators, Ideas and Action in the Holocaust in Historiographical Perspective," in Frank Biess, Mark Roseman, and

Hanna Schissler (eds), *Conflict, Catastrophe and Continuity: Essays on Modern German History* (Oxford and New York: Berghahn Press, 2007), 81–103.

Roseman, Mark. "The Holocaust in European History," in Nicholas Doumanis (ed.), *Oxford Handbook of Modern Europe 1914–1945* (Oxford, UK: Oxford University Press, 2016), 518–36.

Roseman, Mark. "Racial Discourse, Nazi Violence, and the Limits of the "Racial State" Model," in Devin Pendas, Mark Roseman, and Richard Wetzel (eds), *Beyond the Racial State* (Cambridge, UK: Cambridge University Press, 2017), 31–57.

Rosenfeld, Alvin H. "The Americanization of the Holocaust," in Deborah Dash Moore (ed.), *American Jewish Identity Politics* (Ann Arbor: University of Michigan Press, 2008), 46–62.

Rosenfeld, Alvin H., ed. *Deciphering the New Antisemitism* (Bloomington: Indiana University Press, 2015).

Rosenfeld, Alvin H. *The End of the Holocaust* (Bloomington: Indiana University Press, 2013).

Rosenfeld, Gavriel D. *Hi Hitler! How the Nazi Past is Being Normalized in Contemporary Culture* (Cambridge, UK: Cambridge University Press, 2015).

Rosenfeld, Gavriel D. *Munich and Memory Architecture, Monuments, and the Legacy of the Third Reich* (Berkeley: University of California Press, 2000).

Rosenfeld, Gavriel D. "The Normalization of Memory: Saul Friedländer's Reflections of Nazism Twenty Years Later," in Dagmar Herzog (ed.), *Lessons and Legacies, vol. VII: The Holocaust in International Perspective* (Evanston, Il.: Northwestern University Press 2006), 400–10.

Rosenfeld, Gavriel D. "The Politics of Uniqueness: Reflections on the Recent Polemical Turn in Holocaust and Genocide Scholarship," *Holocaust and Genocide Studies*, vol. 13, no. 1 (Spring 1999): 28–61.

Rosenthal, Gilbert S. "Tikkun ha-Olam: The Metamorphosis of a Concept," *Journal of Religion,* vol. 85, no. 2 (2005): 214–40.

Roth, J., and E. Maxwell, eds. *Remembering for the Future: The Holocaust in an Age of Genocide*, 3 vols. (Basingstoke, UK: Palgrave Macmillan, 2001).

Rothberg, Michael. *Multidirectional Memory: Remembering the Holocaust in the Age of Decolonization* (Palo Alto, CA: Stanford University Press, 2009).

Rothstein, Edward. "The Problem with Jewish Museums," *Mosaic Magazine*, February 2016, https://mosaicmagazine.com/essay/2016/02/the-problem-with-jewish-museums/.

Rubinstein, Rachel. *Members of the Tribe: Native America in the Jewish Imagination* (Detroit, Michigan: Wayne State University Press, 2010).

Saler, Bethel. *The Settlers' Empire: Colonialism and State Formation in America's Old Northwest* (Philadelphia: University of Pennsylvania Press, 2014).

Salmons, Paul. "Universal Meaning or Historical Understanding: The Holocaust in History and History in the Classroom," *Teaching History*, vol. 141 (2010): 57–63.

Santiago, Mark. *Massacre at the Yuma Crossing: Spanish Relations with the Quechans, 1779–1782* (Tucson: University of Arizona Press, 1998).

Satia, Priya. *Time's Monster: History, Conscience and Britain's Empire* (New York: Penguin Allen Lane, 2020)

Saunt, Claudio. *Unworthy Republic: The Dispossession of Native Americans and the Road to Indian Territory* (New York: W.W. Norton, 2020).

Savage, Rowan. "The Political Uses of Death-as-Finality in Genocide Denial: The Stolen Generations and the Holocaust," *Borderlands*, vol. 12, no. 1 (2013): 1–22.

Savoy, Benedicte. "Plunder, Restitution, Emotion and the Weight of Archives: A Historical Approach," in Ines Rotermund-Reynard (ed.), *Echoes of Exile: Moscow Archives and the Arts in Paris 1933–1945* (Berlin and Boston: De Gruyter, 2015), 27–44.

Schaller, Dominik J. "From Conquest to Genocide: Colonial Rule in German Southwest Africa and German East Africa," in A. Dirk Moses (ed.), *Empire, Colony, Genocide: Conquest, Occupation, and Subaltern Resistance in World History* (New York: Berghahn Books, 2008), 296–324.

Schute, Ivar. "Collecting Artifacts on Holocaust Sites: A Critical review of Archaeological Research in Ybenheer, Westerbork, and Sobibor," *International Journal of Historical Archaeology*, vol. 22 (2018): 593–613.

Schwartz, Barry. "Rethinking the Concept of Collective Memory," in Anna Lisa Tota and Trever Hagen (eds), *Routledge International Handbook of Memory Studies* (London: Routledge, 2015), 9–21.

Schwarz, Maureen Trudelle. *Fighting Colonialism with Hegemonic Culture: Native American Appropriation of Indian Stereotypes* (Albany, NY: SUNY Press, 2013).

Semelin, Jacques. *Purify and Destroy: The Political Uses of Massacre and Genocide* (New York: Columbia University Press, 2007).

Sendyka, Roma. "Sites that Haunt: Affects and Non-Sites of Memory," in *The "Spectral Turn"*, 85–107.

Seymour, David M., and Mercedes Camino (eds,), *Holocaust Memory: Between Universal and Particular* (New York: Routledge, 2017)

Shafir, Michael. "The 'Comparative Trivialization' of the Holocaust," *East European Perspectives*, vol. 5, no. 2 (2003), http:/www.rferl.org/content/article11342472.html.

Shafir, Michael. "The Nature of Postcommunist Antisemitism in East Central Europe: Ideology's Backdoor Return," *Journal of Contemporary Antisemitism* (JCA), vol. 1, no. 2 (Fall 2018): 33–61.

Shallcross, Bozena. *The Holocaust Object in Polish and Polish-Jewish Culture* (Bloomington: Indiana University Press, 2011).

Shandler, Jeffrey. "From Diary to Book: Text, Object, Structure," in Barbara Kirshenblatt-Gimblett and Jeffrey Shandler (eds), *Anne Frank Unbound: Media, Imagination, Memory* (Bloomington: Indiana University Press, 2012), 25–58.

Shandler, Jeffrey. *While America Watches: Televising the Holocaust* (New York: Oxford University Press, 1999).

Sharples, Caroline. *Postwar Germany and the Holocaust* (London and New York: Bloomsbury, 2015).

Shaw, Martin. "Britain and Genocide: Historical and Contemporary Parameters of National Responsibility," *Review of International Studies*, vol. 37 no. 5 (2011): 2417–38.

Shear, Sarah B. "Cultural Genocide Masked as Education: U.S. History Textbooks' Coverage of Indigenous Education Policies," in Prentice T. Chandler (ed.), *Doing Race in Social Studies: Critical Perspectives* (Charlotte, NC: Information Age Publishing, 2015), 13–40.

Shear, Sarah B., Ryan T. Knowles, Gregory J. Soden, and Antonio J. Castro. "Manifesting Destiny: Re/Presentations of Indigenous Peoples in K–12 U.S.

History Standards," *Theory & Research in Social Education,* vol. 43, no. 1 (2015): 68–101.

Shelley, Lore, and Yehuda Bauer, eds. *Criminal Experiments on Human Beings in Auschwitz and War Research Laboratories* (New York: Edwin Mellen Press, 1991).

Shreve, Bradley G. *Red Power Rising: The National Indian Youth Council and the Origins of Native Activism* (Norman: University of Oklahoma Press, 2011).

Siebert, Monica. *Indians Playing Indian: Multiculturalism and Contemporary Indigenous Art in North America* (Tuscaloosa: University of Alabama Press, 2015), 22–7.

Sierp, A. *History, Memory, and Trans-European Identity: Unifying Divisions* (New York: Routledge, 2014).

Silverman, David J. *This Land Is Their Land: The Wampanoag Indians, Plymouth Colony, and the Troubled History of Thanksgiving* (London and New York: Bloomsbury, 2019).

Silverman, David J. *Thundersticks: Firearms and the Violent Transformation of Native America* (Cambridge, MA: Belknap Press of Harvard University Press, 2016).

Silverman, David. *Red Brethren: The Brothertown and Stockbridge Indians and the Problem of Race in Early America* (Ithaca, NY: Cornell University Press, 2010).

Silverman, Lisa. "Absent Jews and Invisible Antisemitism in Postwar Vienna: *Der Prozeß* (1948) and *The Third Man* (1949)," *Journal of Contemporary History,* vol. 52, no. 2 (2017): 211–28.

Silverman, Lisa. "Revealing Jews: Culture and Visibility in Modern Central Europe," *Shofar: An Interdisciplinary Journal of Jewish Studies,* vol. 36, no. 1 (2018), 134–60.

Simms, Brendan. *Hitler: Only the World Was Enough* (London and New York, Penguin, 2019).

Simpson, Audra. *Mohawk Interruptus: Political Life Across the Borders of Settler States* (Durham, NC: Duke University Press, 2014), 10–13.

Sinclair, James, and Warren Cariou, eds. *Manitowapow: Aboriginal Writings from the Land of Water* (Winnipeg: Highwater, 2011), 326–8.

Sleeper-Smith, Susan. *Contesting Knowledge: Museums and Indigenous Perspectives* (Lincoln, NE: University of Nebraska Press, 2009).

Smith, Paul Chaat. *Everything You Know About Indians in Wrong* (Minneapolis: University of Minnesota Press, 2009)

Smith-Rosenberg, Carroll. *This Violent Empire: The Birth of an American National Identity* (Chapel Hill: University of North Carolina Press (OIEAHC)) 2010).

Snyder, Christina. "Review of Monuments to Absence: Cherokee Removal and the Contest over Southern Memory by Andrew Denson," *Journal of the Civil War Era,* vol. 8, no. 1 (March 2018): 167–9.

Snyder, Timothy. *Black Earth: The Holocaust as History and Warning* (New York, NY: Penguin, 2015).

Stannard, David E. *American Holocaust: The Conquest of the New World* (New York: Oxford University Press, 1992).

Stannard, David E. "True Believer: The Uniqueness of Steven T. Katz," *Journal of Genocide Research,* vol. 22, no. 3 (2020): 391–409.

Stannard, David E. "Uniqueness as Denial: The Politics of Genocide Scholarship," in *Is The Holocaust Unique?: Perspectives on Comparative Genocide,* ed. Alan S. Rosenbaum (Boulder, CO: Westview Press, 1996), 89, 258–60.

Stier, Oren Baruch. *Committed to Memory: Cultural Mediations of the Holocaust* (Amherst: University of Massachusetts Press, 2003).

Stier, Oren Baruch. "Different Trains: Holocaust Artifacts and the Ideologies of Remembrance," *Holocaust and Genocide Studies* 19, no. 1 (2005): 81–106.

Stier, Oren Baruch. *Holocaust Icons: Symbolizing the Shoah in History and Memory* (New Brunswick, NJ: Rutgers University Press, 2015).

Stirrup, David. "Introduction," in James Mackay and David Stirrup (eds), *Tribal Fantasies: Native Americans in the European Imaginary, 1900–2010* (New York: Palgrave, 2010), 9.

Stone, Dan, ed. *The Historiography of Genocide* (Basingstoke, UK: Palgrave Macmillan, 2012).

Stone, Dan. "Beyond the 'Auschwitz Syndrome': Holocaust Historiography after the Cold War," *Journal Patterns of Prejudice,* vol. 44, no. 5 (2010): 454–68.

Stone, Dan. "From Stockholm to Stockton: The Holocaust and/as Heritage in Britain," in Caroline Sharples et al. (eds), *Britain and the Holocaust* (New York: Palgrave Macmillan, 2013), 212–29.

Stone, Dan. "Genocide and Memory," in *The Oxford Handbook of Genocide Studies*, 102–19.

Stone, Dan. "The Holocaust and its Historiography," in *The Historiography of Genocide*, 373–99.

Stone, Dan. "The Holocaust and 'the Human,' in Richard H. King and Dan Stone (eds), *Hannah Arendt and the Uses of History: Imperialism, Nation, Race, and Genocide* (New York: Berghahn Books, 2007), 236–9.

Stone, Dan. "Holocaust Historiography and Cultural History," in Dan Stone (ed.), *The Holocaust and Historical Methodology* (New York: Berghahn Books, 2012), 52–68.

Stone, Dan. "Introduction: The Holocaust and Historical Methodology," in Dan Stone (ed.), *The Holocaust and Historical Methodology* (New York: Berghahn Books, 2012), 9.

Stone, Dan. "Memory Wars in the 'New Europe,'" in Dan Stone (ed.), *The Oxford Handbook of Postwar European History* (Oxford, UK: Oxford University Press, 2012), 714–31.

Stone, Dan. "Memory, Memorials and Museums," in Dan Stone (ed.), *The Historiography of the Holocaust* (Basingstoke, UK: Palgrave Macmillan, 2004), 519.

Stromberg, Ernest. "Intergenerational Cultural Trauma and the National Museum of the American Indian," in Roger C. Aden (ed.), *US Public Memory, Rhetoric, and the National Mall* (New York: Lexington Books, 2018), 135–55.

Strzelecki, Andrzej. "The Plunder of Victims and Their Corpses," in Michael Berenbaum and Yisrael Gutman (eds), *Anatomy of the Auschwitz Death Camp* (Bloomington: Indiana University Press, 1998), 246–66, esp. 250–1.

Sturm, Circe. *Blood Politics: Race, Culture, and Identity in the Cherokee Nation of Oklahoma* (Berkeley: University of California Press, 2002).

Sturm, Circe. "Reflections on the Anthropology of Sovereignty and Settler Colonialism: Lessons from Native North America," *Cultural Anthropology,* vol. 32, no. 3 (2017): 340–8.

Sullam Calimani, Anna-Vera. "A Name for Extermination," *The Modern Language Review*, vol. 94, no. 4 (October 1999): 983.

Sundquist, Eric J. "Black Milk: A Holocaust Metaphor," in Victoria Aarons and Holli Levitsky (eds), *New Directions in Jewish American and Holocaust Literatures* (Albany, NY: SUNY Press, 2017), 31.

Swedish Government. *Holocaust Remembrance and Representation: Documentation from a Research Conference, Sweden, 2020* (Swedish Government Official Reports SOU 2020: 21, Elanders Sverige AB: Stockholm, 2020)

Taiaiake Alfred, Gerald. "Restitution Is the Real Pathway to Justice for Indigenous Peoples," in J. D. Younging and M. Degagné (eds), *Response, Responsibility and Renewal* (Ottawa, Canada: Aboriginal Healing Foundation, 2009), 179–90.

TallBear, Kim. *Native American DNA: Tribal Belonging and the False Promise of Genetic Science* (Minneapolis: University of Minnesota Press, 2013).

Tatz, Colin. "Genocide Studies: An Australian Perspective," *Genocide Studies and Prevention,* vol. 6, no. 3 (December 2011), 231–44.

Tatz, Colin, and Winton Higgins. *The Magnitude of Genocide* (Santa Barbara: Praeger Press, 2016).

Teeter, Don E. *Massacring Indians: From Horseshoe Bend to Wounded Knee* (Norman: University of Oklahoma Press, 2021).

Thobani, Sunera. *Exalted Subjects: Studies in the Making of Race and Nation in Canada* (Toronto: University of Toronto Press, 2007), 247–9.

Thornton, Russell. *American Indian Holocaust and Survival: A Population History since 1492* (Norman: University of Oklahoma, 1987).

Trachtenberg, Barry. *The United States and the Nazi Holocaust Race, Refuge, and Remembrance* (London and New York: Bloomsbury, 2018).

Trafzer, Clifford E., and Michelle Lorimer. "Silencing California Indian Genocide in Social Studies Texts," *American Behavioral Scientist,* vol. 58, no. 1 (2014): 64–82.

TRC Canada, *Truth and Reconciliation Commission of Canada Final Report: Reconciliation, vol.* 6 (Montreal: McGill- Queens University Press, 2015), 212.

Tsosie, Krystal, and Matthew Anderson. "Two Native Americans geneticists interpret Elizabeth Warren's DNA test," *The Conversation,* October 22, 2018, https://theconversation.com/two-native-american- geneticists-interpret-elizabeth-warrens-dna-test-105274.

Usbeck, Frank. *Fellow Tribesmen: The Image of Native Americans, National Identity, and Nazi Ideology in Germany* (New York: Berghahn Books, 2015).

Veracini, Lorenzo. "Introducing Settler Colonial Studies," *Settler Colonial Studies,* vol. 1, no. 1 (2011): 1–12.

Vicenti Carpio, Myla. "(Un)disturbing Exhibitions: Indigenous Historical Memory at the NMAI," *Indian Quarterly,* vol. 30, no. 3/4 (2006): 619–31.

Vigil, Kiara. *Indigenous Intellectuals: Sovereignty, Citizenship, and the American Imagination, 1880-1930* (Cambridge and New York, Cambridge University Press, 2015).

Vizenor, Gerald. *Fugitive Poses: Native American Indian Scenes of Absence and Presence* (Lincoln, NE: University of Nebraska Press, 1998).

Vizenor, Gerald. *Manifest Manners: Narrative on Postindian Survivance* (Lincoln, NE: University of Nebraska Press, 1994).

Wade Beorn, Waitman. "All the Other Neighbors: Communal Genocide in Eastern Europe," in Hilary Earl and Simone Gigliotti (eds), *The Wiley Blackwell Companion to the Holocaust* (Hoboken, MJ: Wiley and Sons, 2020), 153–72.

Wallace, David. *Education for Extinction: American Indians and the Boarding School Experience, 1875–1928* (Lawrence: University of Kansas Press, 1995).

Wake, Caroline. "Regarding the Recording: The Viewer of Video Testimony, the Complexity of Copresence and the Possibility of Tertiary Witnessing," *History and Memory,* vol. 25, no. 1 (Spring–Summer 2013): 111–44.

Wakeham, Pauline. "At the Intersection of Apology and Sovereignty: The Arctic Exile Monument Project," *Cultural Critique,* vol. 87, no. 1 (Spring 2014): 84–143.

Wakeham, Pauline. "Performing Reconciliation at the National Museum of the American Indian: Postcolonial Rapprochement and the Politics of Historical Closure," in Amy Lonetree and Amanda Cobb (eds), *The National Museum of the American Indian: Critical Conversations* (Lincoln, Nebraska: University of Nebraska Press, 2008), 354.

Wakeham, Pauline. "Reconciling 'Terror': Managing Indigenous Resistance in the Age of Apology," *American Indian Quarterly,* vol. 36, no. 1 (Winter 2012): 1–33.

Waldram, James, ed., *Aboriginal Healing in Canada: Studies in Therapeutic Meaning and Practice* (Ottawa: Aboriginal Healing Foundation, 2014).

Weaver, Jace. *The Red Atlantic: American Indigenes and the Making of the Modern World 1000–1927* (Chapel Hill: University of North Carolina Press, 2014), 254–7.

Weisman, Jonathan. *(((Semitism))), Being Jewish in America in the Age of Trump* (New York: St. Martin's Press, 2018).

Wernitznig, Dagmar. *Europe's Indians, Indians in Europe: European Perceptions and Appropriations of Native American Cultures from Pocahontas to the Present* (University Press of America, 2007).

Wesley-Esquimaux, Cynthia C., and Magdalena Smolewski. *Historic Trauma and Aboriginal Healing* (Ottowa, ON: Aboriginal Healing Foundation).

Westermann, Edward B. *Hitler's Ostkrieg and the Indian Wars Comparing Genocide and Conquest* (Norman OK: University of Oklahoma Press, 2016).

Whitman, James Q. *Hitler's American Model: The United States and the Making of Nazi Race Law*, (Princeton, NJ: Princeton University Press, 2018).

Whitt, Laurelyn. *Science, Colonialism and Indigenous Peoples: The Cultural Politics of Law and Knowledge* (Cambridge, UK: Cambridge University Press, 2009), chap. 1 and 2.

Whitt, Laurelyn, and Alan W. Clarke. *North American Genocides: Indigenous Nations, Settler Colonialism, and International Law* (Cambridge, UK: Cambridge University Press, 2019).

WilD.C.at, Matthew. "Fearing Social and Cultural Death: Genocide and Elimination in Settler Colonial Canada—an Indigenous Perspective," *Journal of Genocide Research,* vol. 17, no. 4 (2015): 391–409.

Williams, Paul. *Memorial Museums: The Global Rush to Commemorate Atrocities* (Oxford and New York: Berg, 2007).

Wilson, Angela Cavender. "Grandmother to Granddaughter: Generations of Oral History in a Dakota Family," *American Indian Quarterly,* vol. 20, no. 1 (Winter 1996): 7–13.

Wilson, Waziyatawin Angela. *In the Footsteps of Our Ancestors: The Dakota Commemorative Marches of the 21st Century* (St. Paul, MN: Living Justice Press, 2006).

Wilson, Waziyatawin Angela. *What Does Justice Look Like? The Struggle for Liberation in Dakota Homeland* (St. Paul, MN: Living Justice Press, 2008).

Witgen, Michael. *An Infinity of Nations: How the Native New World Shaped Early North America* (Philadelphia: University of Pennsylvania Press, 2012).

Wolfe, Patrick "Corpus Nullius: The Exception of Indians and Other Aliens in US Constitutional Discourse," *Postcolonial Studies,* vol. 10 (2007): 127–51.

Wolfe, Patrick. "Settler Colonialism and the Elimination of the Native," *Journal of Genocide Research*, vol. 8 (December 2006): 387–409.

Wolfe, Patrick. "Structure and Event: Settler Colonialism, Time, and the Question of Genocide," in A. D. Moses (ed.), *Empire, Colony, Genocide: Conquest, Occupation, and Subaltern Resistance in World History* (New York: Berghahn Books, 2008).

Woolford, Andrew. "Nodal Repair and Networks of Destruction: Residential Schools, Colonial Genocide, and Redress in Canada," *Settler Colonial Studies*, vol. 3, no. 1 (2013): 65–81.

Woolford, Andrew. "Ontological Destruction: Genocide and Canadian Aboriginal Peoples," *Genocide Studies & Prevention*, vol. 4 (2009): 81–97.

Woolford, Andrew. *This Benevolent Experiment: Indigenous Boarding Schools, Genocide, and Redress in Canada and the United States* (Winnipeg: University of Manitoba Press, 2015).

Woolford, Andrew. "Transition and Transposition: Genocide, Land, and the British Columbia Treaty Process," *New Proposals: Journal of Marxism and Interdisciplinary Inquiry*, vol. 4, no. 2 (2011), http://ojs.library.ubc.ca/index.php/newproposals/article/view/2010.

Woolford, Andrew. "Unsettling Genocide and Transforming Group Relations in Canada" ["Repenser le concept de genocide en dehors du colonialism et transformer let relations de groupe au Canada"] *Directions: Research and Policy on Race Relations in Canada*, Special issue on *The Power of Words* (Winter 2016): 44–57.

Woolford, Andrew, and Jeff Benvenuto, eds. *Canada and Colonial Genocide* (Milton, UK: Routledge, 2017).

Wulf, Karin. "Vast Early America: Thee Simple Words for a Complex Reality," *Humanities*, vol. 40, no. (Winter 2019).

Yair, Gad. "Neutrality, Objectivity, and Dissociation: Cultural Trauma and Educational Messages in German Holocaust Memorial Sites and Documentation Centers," *Holocaust and Genocide Studies* vol. 26, no. 3 (2014): 482–509.

Yerushalmi, Yosef Hayim. *Assimilation and Racial Anti-Semitism: The Iberian and the German models* (New York: Leo Baeck Institute, 1982).

Yirush, Craig. *Settlers, Liberty, and Empire: The Roots of Early American Political Theory, 1675–1775* (Cambridge, UK: Cambridge University Press, 2011).

Young, James E. *At Memory's Edge: After-Images of the Holocaust in Contemporary Art and Architecture* (New Haven, CT: Yale University Press, 2000).

Young, James E. *The Texture of Memory: Holocaust Memorials and Meaning* (New Haven, CT: Yale University Press, 1993).

Zalc, Claire, and Tal Bruttmann, eds. *Toward a Microhistory of the Holocaust* (New York and Oxford, UK: Berghahn Books, 2016), 1–8.

Zantop, Susanne. *Colonial Fantasies: Conquest, Family, and Nation in Precolonial Germany, 1770–1870* (Durham: Duke University Press, 1997).

Żbikowski, Andrzej. "The Dispute over the Status of a Witness to the Holocaust: Some Observations on How Research into the Destruction of the Polish Jews and into Polish–Jewish Relations during the Years of Nazi Occupation Has Changed since 1989," in *New Directions in the History of the Jews in the Polish Lands*, 402–22.

Zedeno, Mira. "Bundled Worlds: The Roles and Interactions of Complex Objects from the North American Plains," *Journal of Archaeological Method and Theory*, vol. 15 (2008): 362–78.

Zimmerer, Jürgen. "The Birth of the Ostland Out of the Spirit of Colonialism: A Postcolonial Perspective on the Nazi Policy Of Conquest and Extermination," in Moses and Stone (eds), *Colonialism and Genocide*, 101–23.

Zimmerer, Jürgen. "Colonialism and the Holocaust: Towards an Archaeology of Genocide," in A. D. Moses (ed.), *Genocide and Settler Society: Frontier Violence and Stolen Indigenous Children in Australian History* (New York: Berghahn Books, 2004).

Zimmerer, Jürgen, and Dominik Schaller, eds. *The Origins of Genocide: Raphael Lemkin as a Historian of Mass Violence* (London: Routledge, 2007).

Zubrzycki, Geneviève. "Nationalism, 'Philosemitism,' and Symbolic Boundary-Making in Contemporary Poland," *Comparative Studies in Society and History*, vol. 58, no. 1 (2016): 66–98.

# INDEX

*Note: Page numbers in italics indicate photographs.*


*8sâmeeqan*, the Sachem 71–3, 99–100

Abenaki 22
abolition 63
Aboriginal art 77
Aboriginal Healing Foundation (AHF) 78
Aboriginal people 41, 129
"absent memory" 10, 98
abstraction, memorialization and 88, 138
aestheticism, colonial power structures and 121–2
Africa
  European atrocities in 163
  German expansion in 47–8
African Americans
  civil rights of 73
  reparations for 130
Agamben, Giorgio 30
Alaska, decolonization in 147
Alaska Native communities 41, 147
Albania 23–4
Alcatraz 100
*Aleinu* 104
Alexie, Sherman 61–2, 63
Algonquin people 84
Alter, Robert 95
American expansionism
  European colonialism and 114
  European imperialism and 132
American Jews
  historical commemoration and 89–90
  vanishing 90–7
American liberalism, narrative of 62–3
American residential schools 41
American West, Nazi East and 46–51
Amherst, Jeffrey 27, 57
ancestral trauma, public memory and 89–90
Andean Great Rebellion 51
anti-colonial ideology
  imperial expansionism and 52–3
  settler-colonial paradigm and 56
anti-colonization movement, terminology of 159
anti-Semitism 46, 50, 51–2, 159
  as effect of Nazi policies toward Jews 48
  exterminationist 48
  imperialism and 54
  indigenous European 66
  nationalism and 67
  in Nazi-occupied populations 54–5
  non-Jewish resistance to 23–4, 26
Arapaho 27, 29, 75
archives of memory 6, 157
  alternative 99–100
  Indigenous 99–102
  integration into European public sites 13, 137–56
  public institutions and 9
Arendt, Hannah 47, 53–4
Assembly of First Nations 78
assimilation 3, 89–107
  fear of 90–7
  forced 41–2
  group history and 92–107
  historical commemoration and 89–92, 95–7
  Holocaust commemoration and 91–2, 95–7
  Indigenous suffering and 97–102

memory and 10
mourrnfulness and 92–3, 97–102
prevention of 12, 89–107
traumatic memory and 5
assimilationism 99
assimilationist policies 100, 150
"blood quantum" and 100–2
Auschwitz 3, 22, 29, 43, 66, 123, 126, 134, 140, 142
Catholic Poles at 67
invisibility of Jewish suffering at 117
Australasia, British violence in 129
Australia 41, 129

Balkans 130
Baltic 130
Baron, Salo 95
Bartov, Omer 8, 26, 49
Bastian, Adolf 112–13
Bauer, Yehuda 65, 68
Bauman, Zygmunt 42, 134
BBC 124–5, *125*
Bear River Massacre 27
Belarus 29
Belgium 26
belonging, Indigenous rituals of 100–2
benevolence, depictions of 77
Benin bronzes 115
Berenbaum, Michael 65
Bergen-Belsen 124–5, *125*, 126, 128
Berlin Ethnologisches Museum 114–16, 146–7
Berlin Royal Museum of Ethnology (Königliches Museum für Völkerkunde) 112
Beth Shalom Holocaust Memorial Centre 126
Big Head, Ramona 148–9, 150
biological determinism 18
breakdown of Indigenous–Jewish alliance and 18–20
critiques of 36–7
disease and 32
perpetrator intent and 17–44
biological immunity 17–44
Birenbaum, Halina 164–5
Birkenau 134
black dispossession, reparations for 130
Black Lives Matter movement 129, 162–3
Blackfeet Tribe 147–50, 151, 153, 154
Blackfoot Shirts Project 147–50, 153, 154
Blinder, Samuel *39*
"blood quantum" 100–2, 103
Blumenthal, W. Michael 87, 119–20
Boas, Franz 114
Bourdieu, Pierre 121–2
Britain 152, 158
counter-terrorism offensives and 128
Holocaust memory in 124–9, 155
Indigenous genocide and 128–9
memorials in 142–3
museums in 142
occlusion of Empire and, 124–9
slave trade and 129
British Empire 54, 124–9
British exceptionalism 128–9
British Holocaust Memorial Day (HMD) 126, 127
British House of Commons Select Committee Report 34
British Jews 152
British Museum 149
British North America Act 150
Bucharest Pogrom 29
Budyně nad Ohří, Czech Republic 165
Buffalo Bill's Wild West Show 133
Bulgaria 23–4
bystander intent 25–6, 138

Calgary Winter Olympic Games 77
California, Indigenous population decline in 28
Cameron, David 127, 128, 142
Canada 101, 158
exceptionalism of 111
expansionism and 159
Indian Residential Schools (IRS) in 41–2, *43*, 76–7
multicultural memory in 79–88
Canadian IRS system settler-colonial dynamics and 42–3
Canadian Jewish Congress 43, 86

Canadian Museum of Civilization 77
Canadian Museum of History 81
Canadian Museum for Human Rights (CMHR) 7, 12, 63–4, 69, 78, 81–5
Canadian museums, critiques of 81–2, 87
*see also specific museums*
Canadian Museums Association 78
Canadian Residential Schools 9, 41, 76–7, 78, 129, 163
empathetic engagement on 43–4
remains of children found at *43*
sexual abuse at 44
Canadian Tribute to Human Rights (CTHR) 84
Canadian Truth and Reconciliation Commission (TRC) 41–4
Carrier, Peter 5, 156
Carter, Jimmy 64, 65
causation, abstract/universalistic depictions of 17–44
Césaire, Aimé 47–8
Chambers of Commerce 74
chauvinism 32–3, 50, 162
perpetrator intent and 30
Cherokee 25, 74
Cherokee removal 75, 78
commemoration of 74
historical representation of 73–4
Cheyenne 27–8, 29, *29*, 75
children, removal from parents 41–2, 77
Chirac, Jacques 121, 122, *122*, 123–4
Chivington, John M. 29, 75, 164
Choctaw 25
Christological understandings of redemption and suffering 67–8, 133
Churchill, Ward 37
cigar store Indians 106–7
civic memorials 75–6, 80
*see also specific memorials*
civil rights 158
civil rights movements 62–3, 73, 75
Civil War 75
memorials to 163–4
civilizational motifs 73
civilizational narratives, European imperialism and 159
Cody, Iron Eyes *4*, 102
Cold War 73, 74, 116–17
Cole Hill, “National Day of Mourning” near 97–8
collaboration
definitions of 152
with Nazis 25–6, 160
collective memory 64, 99
colonial chauvinism 50
colonialism 17–44, 76
Indigenous genocide and 70
Indigenous objects and 133–4
Nazism and 46–51
structures exacerbating Indigenous population loss 36–7, 73
colonial power structures, aestheticism and 121–2
colonization, Indigenous mass death and 57
Colorado Capitol Building, toppling of statue at 163–4
Colorado Cavalry 29
Colorado militia 75
Columbus, Christopher 18, 46
Comanche, demographic success of 24–5
commemoration 9
abstraction and 138
alternative 97–8, 99–100
assimilation and 89–90
centralized vs. local initiatives 160
as competitive game 65
cultural renewal and 90, 150
as cultural ritual 102–3
vs. desire to avoid mournful paralysis 99
education and 154
historical education as 13
as impetus for group cohesion 89–90
of Indigenous genocide 99–101
Indigenous peoples and 89–90
of Indigenous suffering 97–102
Jews and 89–90
mournful 100–1
redefined as ongoing educational process 154

subjectivity and 138, 156
unifying role as cultural medium 9
*see also* public memory/memory work
Committee to Exonerate Chief Leschi 76
Communism 130
comparative discussions, future work and 160–1
comparative genocide, local and oral contexts for 21–6
comparative genocide analysis 105–6
comparative genocide studies 11–12, 17–44, 45–58, 64, 85
comparative genocide theorists 6
comparative history 5
"contact zones," museums as 151
contingency, toward consensus on 30–7
counter-memorials 154
counter-memory, Indigenous 13, 144–51
Croatia 130
"Crying Indian" motif 3, 102–4
cultural appropriation, universalized history and 102–3
cultural assimilation 3, 12, 89–107
"cultural chauvinism," settler-colonialism and 32–3
cultural cohesion, lachrymose memory and 95
cultural destruction, population loss and 10–11
cultural genocide 8–9, 37–44, 151
biological and demographical legacy of 40–1
conventions of biological genocide in Canada's TRC and 44
definitions of 41
language and 40–1
representations of 37–44
stolen objects *39*
toward consensus on representation of 37–44
cultural initiatives, centralized vs. local 160
cultural renewal 150
commemoration and 150
historical commemoration and 90
Holocaust commemoration and 96–7
traumatic memory and 12, 89–107
cultural ritual, historical commemoration as 101, 102–3
cultural sovereignty, practice of 79
"Culture of Redress" 84
curatorial methodologies 68, 77–9, 85, 112, 122, 131–2, 137, 138, 152
curatorial techniques, influence of Indigenous communites on 144–51, 155–6

Dachau 61–2, 117
Dakota 103
Dallin, Cyrus Edwin 71–3, 72
Dayksel, Shmuel, *Indianische dertseylungen* (*Indian Tales*) 92–3
Declaration of War Against Exploiters of Lakota Spirituality 103
decolonizaton 74, 128, 147, 150
Deer Island 100
Deloria, Philip J. 69–70, 71, 87
DeLucia, Christine M. 26, 100
demographic recovery 18–19, 37
Dershowitz, Alan 94, 101
*Diary of Anne Frank, The* 68
diasporic metaphor 153
Dimbleby, Richard 124–5, *125*
*Discover the Past for the Future* 138
disease
biological determinism and 32
colonial interventions exacerbating 36–7
demographic recovery and 18–19
during Holocaust 31–2
toward consensus on 30–7
weaponizaiton of 27
diversity 121, 126, 127
DNA analysis, Indigenous group identity and 100–3, 162
Double Genocide theory 85
Drinnon, Richard T. 53, 69–70, 71
Dzyatlava massacres 29

early American Studies 26
Eastern Europe

Christological understandings of redemption and suffering 67–8
de-Judaization of Holocaust in 67–8, 130–1
Holocaust denial in 67
memory cultures in 111
multiple victimhood narrative of Holocaust in 67–8, 130–1, 155
"philosemitism" in 106–7
pogroms in 2
*see also specific countries*
East Germany 117
education 138–44, 160
changes in approach to 142
as commemoration 13
commemoration and 154
educational curricula 6, 7, 48, 77, 80, 123, 126, 138, 160, 163
importance of 137
public memory and 142–4
Eisenman, Peter 119
eleven million motif 65
empathetic engagement, between Indigenous and Jewish communities 43–4
empathy 85
Empire, occlusion of 124–9
*see also* imperialism
equal protection, doctrine of 74, 76
Estonia 130
ethical universalism 106
"ethnic cleansing" 28
ethnographic museums 155–6
as "contact zones" 151
ethnography 158
influence of Indigenous communities on 144–51, 155–6
move away from Eurocentric approaches to 144–51
reconfiguration of 144–51
universalism and 112–21
ethno-national identities, in Nazi Germany 55–6
EU Agency for Fundamental Rights 135
European colonialism 2, 46
American expansionism and 114
Indigenous dispossession and 12–13, 111–35, 163
Indigenous genocide and 8, 46–51, 163
perpetrator intent and 158
European imperialism
American expansionism and 132
civilizational narratives and 159
Holocaust and 8
Indigenous dispossession and 158
Indigenous genocide and 8, 46–51, 135, 163
racism and 1–2
European integration 130–5
European Union (EU) 126
Agency for Fundamental Rights project 138
cultural institutions 111
enlargement of 130
instrumentalization of Holocaust in 160
memory work in 135
parliament 130
standards on Holocaust memory 138
supra-national cultural institutions of 12
Exodus liturgy, universalization of 104
expansionism
Canada and 159
United States and 114, 132, 159
Expo 67 77
exterminatory discourses, circulation of 27

Fackenheim, Emil 95–6
Farber, Bernie 43, 86
Far Right 161
fascism 83
Fenimore Cooper, James, *Last of the Mohicans* 91, 93
Fine, Ellen S. 10, 98
Finkielkraut, Alain 3, 5–6, 89, 94
Firsting/Lasting archetypes 69–71
First Nations (Canada) 10, 63, 84
boycott of *The Spirit Sings* exhibition 77–8
children removed from parents 41–2, 77
*see also specific groups*
First Nations Studies 17, 152

Fischer, Joschka 118
forensic archaeology 133
Forest County Potawatomi Museum 151
France 111, 152, 158
  Holocaust memory in 122–3, 155
  human rights discourse in 123–4
  ideal of diversity through universalism 121
  Indigenous dispossession and 121
  memorials in 143–4, *143*
  Republican universalism and abstraction of trauma in 121–4
  Vichy regime 122–3, 152
  "Vichy Syndrome" 122–3
Frank, Anne 3, *4*, 31, 32, 65, 68
Free-Soil liberalism 49
French Jews 143–4, *143*, 152
French Revolution, ideals of 123
Friedberg, Edna 96–7
Friedländer, Saul 66, 68

Galt Museum 148
Garroutte, Eva Marie 103
genocidal intent
  "cultural chauvinism" and 32–3
  representations of 26–30
  strict vs. loose definitions of 17–18, 24–5, 33–7
  structural vs. strict approaches 33–7
  *see also* perpetrator intent; structural intent
genocide 3
  definitions of 17, 19–20, 28, 34–6, 40, 41, 57
  described as inevitable 30
  imperial turn in historiography of 11–12, 45–58
  imperialism and 11–12, 45–58
  as intrinsically colonial technique of occupation 57
  Lemkin's definition of 34–6
  misrepresentation or erasure in public memory 30
  public treatment of histories of 3–5
  settler-colonial paradigm and 83
  shift in representation of from local to universal 4–5
  structural vs. strict approaches 33–5
  subaltern genocide 51–8
  UN Convention 34–6, 40, 41–2
  UN definition of 8, 27, 33, 40
  use of terminology to describe Indigenous history 21
  *see also* Holocaust; Indigenous genocide
Genocide Studies 85
Georgia 73–4
Gerlach, Christian 20
German Jewish organizations 118
German supranational power *56*
German *Volk* 54–5
Germans, as "indigenous people" in Nazi germany 55
Germany 111
  civic identity in 116–21
  contrition in 116–21
  ethnography and universalism in 112–21
  Holocaust memory in 112–21, 155
  human rights discourse and 118–19, 120
  Jews in 152
  museums in 138–40, *141*, 142–3
  public memory in 116–18
Ghost Dance Shirt 132–3, 144–6, *146*
Glenbow Museum 148
Gnadenhütten, Ohio, vote to destroy Native Americans in 27
Greek Jews 22, 23–4
group belonging 101
group cohesion, historical trauma and 90–107
group identity
  historical trauma and 89–90, 91, 101
  Holocaust memory and 91–7
group memory 3
  assimilation and 92–107
  vs. national/supra-national memory 157
  public memory and 9–11, 89–90, 92–107, 137–56
  role of 9
  trauma and 8
guilt 160

Habermas, Jürgen 117
Haida collaboration 149, 153, 154
Haida people 149
Haiti 51
Hart-Moxon, Kitty 124
Hasidic Jews 40
Heritage Cultural Centre 145
historical knowledge, replacement with shorthand icons 137
historical memory 101
  cultural assimilation and 90–107
historical trauma
  abstraction of 3–7
  appropriation of 102–4
  commemoration of 89–90
  commodification of 106–7
  definitions of 90
  group cohesion and 90–107
  group identity and 89–90, 91, 101
  healing from 99
  public representation of 3–6, 10, 12, 61–88, 111–12
  universalization of 10, 12, 89–107
  *see also specific traumas*
*Historikerstreit* (historians' dispute) 117
"History Wars" 129
Hitler, Adolf 30, 46, 48, 54, 56, 95
Holocaust 2–3, 5, 7, 11, 17–44, 111–12, 114–35
  as aberration 45, 135, 158
  abstraction of 9, 111, 116, 158
  Americanization/Canadianization of 78, 79
  Christological understandings of redemption and suffering and 133
  concerns about risks of relativizing 28
  definition of genocide and 35–6
  de-Judaization of 46, 63, 65, 66–7, 111, 116–21, 124–6, 130
  depicted as aberration in trajectory of European civilization 111
  disease during 31–2
  European imperialism and 8
  as Europe-wide project, not strictly German 56
  French representations of 122–4
  French role in 123
  generalizations of 117
  guilt and 160
  instrumentalization of in Europe 155
  local perpetrators and 129
  in the media 65–6, 84–5, 91, 102–7, 126
  minimization of 117–18, 161
  North Americanization of 61–88
  perpetrator intent and 158
  pluralistic approaches to 91
  relativization of 80, 84–5, 117–18
  representations of 6–7, 9, 17–44, 45, 65–7, 78–80, 84–5, 91, 102–7, 111, 116–18, 126, 129–30, 133–5, 137, 157–8
  representations of in Western Europe 111
  representations of material culture 133–4
  represented as aberration in European civilization 130
  silence about 124, 126
  specificity in representing 129
  universalization of 3–5, 7, 9, 46, 63, 65–7, 69, 85–7, 102–7, 111, 116–21, 123, 124–6, 130, 135, 157
  vision of multiple victimhood 65, 66–7
  *see also* Holocaust memory
*Holocaust* 126
*Holocaust* (TV series) 64
Holocaust artifacts
  display of 134
  as "sacred" 133
Holocaust Centre 126
Holocaust Commission 127
Holocaust denial 66–7
  "Softcore" 161, 162
Holocaust education 138–44
  assimilation and 96–7
Holocaust Educational Trust 142
  Lessons from Auschwitz Project (LFA) 142
Holocaust Education Trust 127
Holocaust historiography 30
"Holocaust icons" 6

Holocaust Memorial, London 142–3
Holocaust Memorial Day, Trump administration's 2017 statement on 161
Holocaust memory
  abstraction of 127, 161
  Americanization/Canadianization of 94–5
  assimilation and 91–2, 95–7, 103–7
  assimilation of Jewish spiritual culture and 103–7
  in Britain 124–9, 155
  British instrumentalization of 124, 127–8
  confrontation of 92
  as cultural identifier 95
  cultural renewal and 96–7
  de-Judaization of 161
  de-specification of 157, 158, 161
  dialectical turn in 137–43
  in Eastern Europe 66–8, 106–7, 111, 130–1, 155
  enters public sphere 126–7
  EU enlargement and 130
  EU standards on 138
  figurative use of 161
  fragile nature of public 9
  in France 122–3, 155
  generalizations of 94–5, 126
  German instrumentalization of 116–21, 124
  in Germany 112–21, 124, 155
  group identity and 91–2, 93–7
  Indigenous critiques of 78–9
  instrumentalization of 63–4, 116–21, 124, 126–9, 135, 152, 158, 163
  intentionalist approaches to 117
  multiple victimhood narrative of 160
  in national and international commissions 44
  normative use of to represent other histories of genocide 17
  particularism of 63–4
  politicization and distortion of 138
  redemptive narratives and 67–8, 83, 133
  relativization of 155
  ritualization of 91–2, 95
  scholars of 5–6
  in Soviet Union *131*
  subaltern genocide and 51–8
  universalization of 87, 94–5, 103–4, 116–21, 126
  values of 124–9
  victim-centered approaches 138, 142
  *see also specific institutions and monuments*
"Holocaust redemption," myth of 95
*Holocaust Remembrance and Representation* conference 138
Holocaust Studies 17, 20, 23, 85, 106, 152
  contingent nature of disease mortality and 31–2
  cultural genocide and 37
  methodological approaches in 25
Holocaust survivors 124, 127, 138, 153
  *see also specific survivors*
Holocaust terminology
  *tikkun olam* and 105
  ubiquity and banality of 66, 68
  used figuratively 85, 87
*Holodomor*, the 82
hopefulness, mournfulness and 99–100
House of European History, The 130
House of Wannsee Conference Memorial and Education Centre 118, 143
Hudson's Bay Company 148
human rights discourse 118–19, 120, 123–4, 126, 127
humanitarian interventions 36
humanitarianism 17–44
Humboldt Forum 115
Hungary 130
Hunkpapa Lakota 27–8

Iberian inquisitions 1–2
icons 157, 158
  *see also specific motifs*
immigration 128
imperial expansionism, anti-colonial ideology and 52–3
imperial power, problem of 45–58

Imperial War Museum (IWM) 140, 142, 153–4
  "Crimes against Humanity" section 129
  Holocaust exhibition at 129
imperialism 24, 124–9, 159
  anti-colonial ideology and 52–3
  anti-Semitism and 54
  genocide and 11–12, 45–58
  Indigenous objects and 133–4
  Nazism and 49–50
  *see also* British Empire; European imperialism
Improved Order of Red Men (IORM) 71
inclusivity 77, 160
Indian Act (Canada) 131
Indian Department 100
"Indian" identity, definitions of 100–3
Indian objects, repatriation of 131–2
Indian Residential Schools (IRS), *see* Canadian Residential Schools
Indian subcontinent, British violence in 129
"Indian Wars" 75
*Indianer Nordamerikas: Eine Spurensuche* (Native Cultures of North America: Following the Trail) 116
"Indians of Canada Pavilion," Expo 67 77
Indigenous activists 79, 97–8, 144–6
Indigenous agency 97
Indigenous autonomy 80, 84, 152
Indigenous belonging 100–2
Indigenous children, removed from parents 41–2
  *see also* Canadian Residential Schools
Indigenous counter-memory 99–100, 144–51
Indigenous culture
  authenticity and 100–3
  Indigenous commemorative rituals 99–101
  spiritual live-force of objects and 132–3
Indigenous dispossession 49, 50, 51–8, 70, 74–5, 80, 83, 159
  "blood quantum" and 100–2
  civic memorials and 75–6
  depicted in Europe as an American rather than a European phenomenon 111
  euphemistic descriptions of 90
  European imperialism and 12–13, 111–35, 158, 163
  France and 121
  German appropriation of 120–1
  guilt and 160
  in the media 111
  overlooked 63–4, 163–4
  reparations for 130–2
Indigenous genocide 2, 3, 5, 7, 80
  abstraction of 9
  as "American," not European 45
  British imperialism and 128–9
  British violence and 129
  erasure of 158, 161–2
  European colonialism and 45, 70, 135
  European imperialism and 8, 46–51, 135, 163
  local perpetrators and 129
  marginalization of 63–4
  misrepresentation of 69–79, 161–2
  public representation of 9, 157
  representations of 9, 69–79, 111, 137, 157, 161–2
  settler-colonial paradigm and 8, 46–51
  universalization of 3–5, 7, 9, 69
  white written records about 99
  *see also* Indigenous mass death; Indigenous population loss; Indigenous trauma
Indigenous genocide 111–35
Indigenous group identity, DNA analysis and 100–2
Indigenous groups, targeted elimination of 27
Indigenous history 130–5
  Euro-American representations of 6
  liberal ideology and 79
  public memory and 87
  rewriting of 69–79
  subaltern genocide and 51–8

three key aspects of memorializing 100
universalization of 87–8
Indigenous–Jewish alliance
breakdown of 18–20
empathetic engagement and 43–4
template for public memory work 152–6
Indigenous mass death 79
abstraction of 81
colonization and 57
distortion of 81
German appropriation of 120–1
as natural phenomenon 69–70
universalization of 81
*see also* Indigenous genocide; Indigenous population loss
Indigenous memory work 69–79, 99–100
Indigenous methodologies 6
Indigenous objects
colonialism and 133–4
in French museums 121–2, *122*
imbued with spiritual life-force 132–3
imperialism and 133–4
inter-state standards on display of 131–2
in museums 134, 144–51, more
repatriation of 144–6
in rituals of commemoration 144–6
Indigenous peoples 3
definitions of membership in tribes and nations 100–3
forced reliance on US state 49
historical commemoration and 89–90
land-based nationhood and 37
marginalization of 77
mortality rates of 22
narrative representations of in nineteenth century 69–70
naturalistic imagery in representation of 69–70
population loss among 3, 7, 11, 17–44
traumatic history and 97–102
*see also specific groups*
Indigenous population loss
abstraction of 32, 74, 116, 157–8
in California 28
colonial interventions exacerbating 36–7, 73
demographic recovery and 37
forced relocation and 33
nutritional degradation and 33
presented as abstract environmental occurrence 157–8
public memory and 18–19
slavery and 33
universalization of 116
Indigenous self-identification 103
Indigenous sovereignty 76, 147, 152, 153
Indigenous Studies 6, 24, 26, 106
cultural genocide and 37
methodological approaches in 25
Indigenous survival, representations of 79–80
Indigenous trauma
abstraction of 157
as American rather than European in origin 158
assimilation and 97–102
"lachrymose" approach to 97–102
marginalization of 63–4
media and 102–7, 111
misrepresentation of 69–79
overlooked in the United States and Canada 111
representations of 79–80
rituals of commemoration and 97–102
specificity of 116
universalization of 63–4
individual rights 74, 97–8
protection of 73, 75
insider intent 138
institutions
instrumentalization of Holocaust by 160
memory work and 137
representations of Holocaust by 157
representations of Indigenous genocide by 157
survivor groups and 9, 12, 13, 61–88, 137–56

use of metaphor by 7–8
*see also specific institutions*
intentionalist approaches 117
*see also* genocidal intent; perpetrator intent
international law 17–44
International Meeting on Nazi Gold 126
International Task Force (ITF) 126
Intergovernmental Conference on the Holocaust (2000) 126–7
intolerance, generalizations of 17–44, 68, 79, 86–7, 94, 126, 127
Inuit 81–2, 83
Iraq war 128
Island-Carib communities 165

Jackson, Andrew 73, 162
Jacksonian Indian Removal 71, 73–4
Jelgava massacres 29
Jewish Diaspora 95, 153
Jewish dispossession 129
reparations for 130
Jewish Enlightenment (*Haskala*) 105
Jewish "extinction," Nazi discussion of 30
Jewish historiography, "lachrymose" approach to 95
Jewish identity 3, 92
Jewish Museum, Berlin 119, 139–40, 143
"Memory Void" (Leerstelle des Gedenkens) in 140, *141*
"Jewish problem" 52
Jewish spirituality 95, 103–5, 133
Jewish Studies 20, 85
Jewish suffering, invisibility of 117
Jewish writers, use of Native American analogies 92–3
Jews 10
Ashkenazi 2–3, 22, 23
in Germany 152
Greek 22, 23–4; *see also* Salonikan Jews
historical commemoration and 89–90
liberal ideology and 86–7
mortality rates among subgroups during Holocaust 22–3
Nazi depiction of 30
North American 90–7, 101–2
Sephardic 1–2, 22–3, 40–1, 165
vanishing motifs and 90–7, 101–2
Jüdisches Museum Berlin 85, 87

Kamloops Indian Residential School, remains of children found at *43*
*Kanada* 134
*kanadziarze* 134
Karl May Museum 7, 114, *115*, 132
Katz, Stephen 20
"Keep America Beautiful" ad 102
Kelvingrove Museum 7, 132–3, 144–6
Kenya, British violence in 129
Khanan-Yakov, *Tsvishn Indianer* (Among the Indians) 91
"KinaGchiNishnaabegogamig" 34
Kindertransport 128
Kishinev, Bessarabia (Moldova), 1903 pogrom in 2
*Kitty: Return to Auschwitz* 126
Kohl, Helmut 118
*Kunstkammer* (Cabinets of Curiosity) 115

lachrymose memory, cultural cohesion and 95
LaDuke, Winona 160
Lakota 26, 70, 98, 99–100, 103, 133, 144–6
Lakota "Ghost Dance" ceremony 70
land autonomy, Indigenous claims to 84
land sovereignty 77
language
cultural genocide and 40–1
as "fossil poetry" 40
*see also specific languages*
Lanzmann, Claude 25
Las Casas, Bartolomé de 36–7
Latvia 29, 130
Legacy of Hope Foundation (LHF) 78
Leipciger, Nate 43–4
Lemkin, Raphael 9, 34–6, 105, 106
autobiographical reminiscences of 38
cultural genocide and 37–8

definitions of genocide and 34–9, 57
discussions of Indigenous population loss 36–7, 57
founding of genocide studies and 34–9
influence of *tikkun olam* on his approach 105–6
reading of Las Casas 36–7, 57
understanding of extent of Holocaust 35–6
universalism of his approach 106

Lenape 27
Leschi, Chief 75–6, 77
Levande Historia (Living History) project 126
Levi, Primo 22
Levinas, Emmanual 105
liberal ideology 75, 86–7, 92
Indigenous histories of dispossession and 79
Jews and 86–7, 104–5
narrative of progress 62–3
universalization of Holocaust and 62–3, 67

Libeskind, Daniel 82, 119, 139–40
*limpieza de sangre* (purity of blood) 1–2
Linenthal, Edward T. 69
Lipstadt, Deborah 161, 162
Lithuania 130, 160
local anti-Semitic violence, Nazism and 159
local memory, vs. national/supra-national memory 157
Lodz ghetto 153
Lonetree, Amy 79–80, 81
"Lucky Jew" figurines 106–7
Lummi Tribal Court 76
Lyons, Scott Richard 6

McLuhan, Marshall 49–50
Madison, James 52–3
Malamud, Bernard, *The Last Mohican* 93
Manitoba 84
MARKK (formerly Museum of Ethnology (Völkerkunde)) 116
Massachusetts, public memory in 99–100
Massasoit statues 71–3, *72*, 78, 97–100, 144
commodification of 106–7
counter-memorialization and 154

mass murder, described as natural and providential 30
May, Karl, *Winneou* 113, 114
media 3–4
Holocaust and 65–6, 84–5, 91, 102–7, 126
Indigenous trauma and 102–7, 111

mediation, memory work and 156
Melammed, Renée 40
memorial design 90
Memorial of German Resistance 143
"memorial texts" 6
Memorial to the Murdered Jews of Europe, The (Das Denkmal für die ermordeten Juden Europas) 118–19, *120*, 124, 138–9, *139*, 142–3, 154
Information Center at 138–9, 140, 153–4
Room of Families 138–9

memory 3, 152
"absent memory" 98
assimilation and 10
definitions of 10
lachrymose 95
lapses of 89
metaphors and 94
multicultural 79–88
national/supra-national memory vs. group memory 157
public 3–4
trauma and 89–107
*see also* commemoration; public memory/memory work

memory work, *see* commemoration; public memory/memory work
metaphor
diasporic 153
memory and 94
use of 6–8, 157, 161

Métis 81–2, 83, 84
Middle Passage 157
Mihesuah, Devon 132, 133

Millet, Kitty 11
Miniconjou Lakota 27–8, 70
Miniconjou Lakota Big Foot's band 70
Mitterrand, François 123
Modoc's War 74, 78
Mohawk, John C. 101
Mohican motifs 93
Monument de la rafle du Vél' d'Hiv' 16 et 17 Juillet 1942 123–4, 143–4, *143*, 152
monuments, subjectivity and 156
Moses, A. Dirk 5, 38, 49, 106
motifs 157
  *see also specific motifs*
Mt. Pleasant, Alyssa 161–2
mournful commemoration, rituals and 98, 100–1
mournfulness
  assimilation and 92–3, 97–102
  hopefulness and 99–100
mourning rituals 98
multiculturalism 74–5, 80, 83, 84, 160
  memory and 79–88
  public history and 87
multicultural memory, in Canada and the United States 79–88
Mumford, Lewis 89
Musée du quai Branly 121, 122, *122*, 123–4
museums 153
  as "contact zones" 151
  European 112
  foundation of 89
  in France 121–2, *122*
  Indigenous-led tribal 64
  Indigenous objects in 134, 144–51
  influence of Indigenous communities on 155–6
  memory museums 116
  memory work and 137
  *see also specific museums*
Museumsinsel 114–15

Nacotchtank 61
National Day of Remembrance of the Greek Jewish Witnesses and Holcaust Heroes *24*
National Holocaust Monument (NHM) (Canada) 78, 82–4, *83*, 86
National Holocaust Monument Act (NHMA) 82
national identity, in "diasporic" form 153
National Memorial for the Victims of War and Terror (proposed, in Germany) 118–19, *119*
"national metaphysics of Indian-hating" 53
National Museum of the American Indian (NMAI) 7, 12, 63, 64, 79–80, *80*, 81, 84, 154–5
  "conflict resolution" at 80
  critical Indigenous response to 79–81
  critiques of 79–81, 85, 87
  erasure of impact of settler-colonialism 79–80
  universalism at 84
National Park Service (NPS) 75
national/supra-national memory
  vs. group memory 157
  vs. local memory 157
nationalism, anti-Semitism and 66
Native American analogies, used by Jewish writers 92–3
Native American Graves Protection and Repatriation act (NAGPRA) 12, 78, 132, 133, 144–6
Native Americans (U.S) 10, 56
  *see also specific groups*
Native American Studies 17, 152
Nazi East, American West and 46–51
Nazi Germany
  ethno-national identities in 55–6
  United States and 46–51
Nazi-occupied populations, anti-Semitism in 54–5
Nazis 2–3, 8, 116, 130, 159
  collaboration with 160
  use of bureaucratic metaphors and euphemisms 42–3
  use of forms similar to imperial authority 46–51
Nazism 54–5, 115, 116–17
  colonialism and 46–51

de-humanization of Jews in 118, 134
depiction of Jews as vermin 30
imperialism and 49–50
improvised local violence and 56–7
local anti-Semitic violence and 159
Nazi expansionism 49, 50
Nazi totalitarianism 50
non-Jewish resistance to 23–4, 26
neo-Nazis 161
Netherlands 26, 160
Neue Wache Memorial to the Victims of War and Tyranny 118–19, *119*, 143
Neusner, Jacob 95–6
"New Antisemitism" 161, 162
New Echota, 1835 treaty at 73
Newfoundland 34
Nigeria 115
Nisqually 75–6
Nolte, Ernst 117
North American freedom 73, 74, 81
narratives of 45, 69
North American Jews, vanishing motifs and 90–7, 101–2
North American memory work, Indigenous responses to 144–51
Nuremberg Trials 34, 44

Obama, Barack *86*
O'Brien, Jean M. 69–70, 71, 98
Office for Democratic Institutions and Human Rights (ODIHR) 130
Oneida Nation 132
Oneida Nation Museum (ONM) 151
Oneida Nation Trust and Enrollment Committee 101
oral testimony 25–6
Oregon 74
Organization for Security and Cooperation in Europe (OSCE) 130
out-marriage 10
outsider intent 138

paddle ceremonies 100
"Pages of Testimony" 139
Pears Foundation 142
Peers, Laura 148, 150, 154
Pennsylvania Carlisle Indian School 41
Pequots 32, 33, 52, 53
Pequot Wars 52
perpetrator intent 20, 29, 30, 76, 79, 99, 116, 129, 159
biological determinism and 17–44
contingent effects of 36–7
disguising of 70, 157–8
European colonialism and 158
Holocaust and 158
occlusion of nature and scale of 157
overlooking of 159
racial chauvinism and 30
strict notions of 33
perpetrators 85
*see also* perpetrator intent; perpetrator sites
perpetrator sites 3–4
Pew Research Survey of Jews in the United States 96, 104
Phillips, Ruth B. 77, 155
"philosemitism," in Eastern Europe 106–7
Piikani 147
Pitt Rivers Museum, Oxford, England 147–50, *149*
"Plastic Shamanism" 102–3
pluralism 63, 73–5, 80, 83, 85, 87, 97–8, 127, 158
Plymouth, 1621 treaty at 71
Plymouth Rock "counter-memorial" 97–8, 144
Plymouth Rock tercentenary 97–8, 144
Pokanoket Wampanoag 71
Poland 138, 153, 160
population loss
caused by colonization, not lack of immunity 18–19
cultural destruction and 10–11
societal interventions exacerbating 18–19, 44
*see also* Indigenous population loss
Portland Museum of Art 151
Portugal, Jewish exile from 1–2
power, imperial frameworks of 45–58
Powhatan 33
Pratt, Richard Henry 41
President's Commission on the Holocaust 64, 65

"Proposal for International Commemoration of the Holocaust" 126–7
Prussian-Brandenburg Kingdom, 1794 Royal Cabinet 115
public history, *see* public memory/memory work
public memory/memory work 3–4, 9–10, 12, 45–58, 61–88, 154, 158
  ancestral trauma and 89–90
  critiques of 6, 51, 63–4, 69
  education and 142–4
  European 12–13, 111–35
  funding for 74
  in Germany 116–18
  group history and 92–107
  group memory and 9–11, 89–90, 137–56
  Indigenous critiques of 78–9
  Indigenous history and 18–19, 87
  an Indigenous-Jewish template for 152–6
  Indigenous responses to North American 144–51
  institutions and 137
  Jewish critiques of 79
  Jewish vs. German 116–17
  in Massachusetts 99–100
  mediation and 156
  misrepresentation or erasure of in public memory 30
  multiculturalism and 87
  museums and 137
  subjectivity of 138, 144, 154
  trauma and 162–3
  universalism and 69–79
Puget Sound War 75
Puritan settlers 32, 52
"purity of blood" (*limpieza de sangre*) 1, 159

Quack, Sybille 138
Quiemuth, Chief 76

Race Institute, Frankfurt, German *39*
racism 1–2, 30, 163
  *see also* chauvinism
reconciliation, displays of, as neocolonial politics 84
redemption 83, 95, 133
  narratives of 67–8, 83
"Red Man" 113
Red Power movement 79, 98
Reform Judaism 105
Reich, Walter 65, 87
relativization 88
"Reminiscence therapy" 151
reparations 13, 126, 130–1
  for black dispossession 130
  for Indigenous dispossession 130–2
  for Jewish dispossession 130
Report of the Royal Commission on Aboriginal People (RCAP) 78
Republican universalism 121–4
Reservation system 49
restitution 13, 126, 130
  *see also* reparations
Revolutionary war era 52
"rhetorical sovereignty" 6
rituals
  historical commemoration as 101, 102–3
  knowledge and practice of 10
  mournful commemoration and 100–1
Roma 61
Romania 29, 160
Romanticism 114
Rosenfeld, Alvin H. 68
Rosenfeld, Gavriel 117
Rothberg, Michael 18, 64
Rothstein, Edward 87
Rousso, Henry 122–4
Royal Commission on Aboriginal Peoples (RCAP) 41, 78
Rubinstein, Rachel 69, 93

Sacred Run and Paddle ceremony 100
Sagkeeng Ojibway First Nation 44
St. Thomas, US Virgin Islands 164–5
Salonikan Ladino 40–1
Salonikan Jews 22–3, 24, *24*, 40–1
"salvage anthropology" 114
Sand Creek Massacre 26, 27, 28, 29, *29*, 74–5, 164

Sand Creek National Historic Site *29*, *75*
San Francisco Contemporary Jewish Museum 85, 86–7
"Saphor Torahs" *39*
Sault St. Marie Tribe of Chippewa Indians 132
*Schindler's List* 68
Schröder, Gerhard 118
Sephardic Jews 1–2, 22–3, 40–1, 165
settler-colonial dynamics
  Canadian IRS system and 42–3
  continuation of 101
settler-colonial ideology 17–44, 51–2
  assimilationist legacies of 80
  "cultural chauvinism" and 32–3
  impact of 80
settler-colonial paradigm 8, 17–44, 76, 87, 112
  anti-colonial ideology and 56
  Indigenous genocide and 46–51, 83
settler-colonial studies 11–12, 17, 45–58, 133–4
  repudiation of biological determinism in 32–3
"shatter zones" 23, 32
shorthand, use of 6, 8, 137, 138
Shoshoni 27
Simon Wiesenthal Center 65
Skirball Cultural Center 85, 86
slavery 157, 163
  as an "American" problem 130–1
  memorialization of 130
slave trade 129, 157
smallpox
  smallpox blankets 27, 57
  spread of 32–3
social justice 87
"social-justice Judaism" 104–5
social loss 151
South Dakota State Historical Society Museum 145
sovereignty 74, 100
  cultural 79
  land 77
Soviet Union 73, 82, 158
  Holocaust memorial in *131*
Spain, Jewish exile from 1–2
*Spirit Sings, The*, exhibition, First Nations boycott of 77–8
Stannard, David 22
state-building 70, 75, 77, 80, 82, 158
statues, removal of 162–3
Stier, Oren Baruch 6, 68
Stockholm Declaration 127
Stolpersteine project 154, *155*
Stone, Dan 85
structural intent 19, 30–7
Sturm, Circe 103
Styron, William, *Sophie's Choice* 66–8
subaltern genocide 51–8
  definitions of 53–4
subjectivity, of public memory 138, 144, 154
survival 98, 99
  capacity for 99–100
Survival International 132
"survival syndrome" 99
"survivance" 9, 13, 100, 101, 144, 145, 150, 151, 164
survivor groups 9–11
  generations of 9–10
  institutions and 9, 12, 13, 61–88, 137–56
"survivor syndrome" 99
Sweden 138
"systemic genocide" 33

Tainos 165
Takini (Survivor) Network 99
Task Force on Museums and First Peoples 78
Tenenboym, Shia, "Among the Indians in Oklahoma" 93–4
Terms of Reference of the Holocaust Commission 128
"Thanksgiving" motif 71
Thessaloniki, Greece *24*
"third space" 74
*tikkun olam*
  assimilation of 103–5
  Holocaust terminology and 105
  influence on Lemkin's approach 105–6
Tlingit communities 151
Tlingit language 41
tolerance 26, 73, 120, 126, 127, 158

Topography of Terror 143
Torah scrolls, burial of 133
Traditional Hunkpapa Lakota Elders' Council 98
Trail of Tears 75
Trail of Tears National Historic Trail 74
traumatic history 133
abstraction of 88, 121–4
assimilation and 5
commemoration of 17
cultural assimilation and 12, 89–107
as cultural form 97–102
cultural renewal and 12, 89–107
group histories 5
group memory and 8
Indigenous peoples and 97–102
memory and 1, 12, 89–107
narratives of 67–8
public memory and 162–3
public representation of 5, 8
relativization of 88
representations of 8, 17, 63–4, 89–90, 97–102
universalization of 88
*see also* Holocaust; Indigenous genocide; Indigenous trauma
Treblinka 67
tribal autonomy 84, 158
tribal museums, Indigenous-led 64
tribal sovereignty 74, 77, 87, 100, 152, 153
Trouillot, Michel-Rolph 69
Trudeau, Justin 82
Trump, Donald
administration of 161
admiration for Andrew Jackson 162
use of "Pocahontas" to refer to Warren 161–2
Truth and Reconciliation Commission 9, 77, 163
*Two Millennia of German Jewish History* 119–20

UCL Centre for Holocaust Education 142
Ukraine 130, 160
Ukrainian-Canadians 82
Ukrainian famine 82
United American Indians of New England 97, 144
United Kingdom 111
United Nations
definition of genocide 8
Genocide Convention (UNGC) 9, 28, 34–6, 38, 40, 41–2
proclamation of genocide as international crime 36
United States 101, 158
exceptionalism of 111
expansionism and 114, 132, 159
multicultural memory in 79–88
Nazi Germany and 46–51
*see also* United States Holocaust Memorial Museum (USHMM)
United States Holocaust Memorial Museum (USHMM) 7, 12, 25, 61–2, 64–6, 68–9, 71, 79–81, 87, 96, 153
balance between specificity and universalism and 85
critiques of 85, 104
mission of 104
Obama and Wiesel at *86*
particularism at 84
universalism 80, 88
countering tendencies toward 142
critique of 63
ethical 106
ethnography and 112–21
French understanding of 121–4
Indigenous memory and 69–79
memory work and 69–79
performed through particularism 105–6
universalized history, cultural appropriation and 102–3
*Unto These Hills* 73
US Congress 28, 74
U.S. Seventh Cavalry 70, 99

"Vanishing Indian"
Euro-American notion of 30
narratives of 69–70
vanishing motifs 89–107, 114, 115, 152, 155–6
"blood quantum" and 101

North American Jews and 90–7, 101–2
"Vanishing Indian" 30, 69–71
Veracini, Lorenzo 34
*Vergangenheitsbewältingung* 117, 155
Vichy regime 122–3, 152
"Vichy Syndrome" 122–3
Victoria, Queen, statues of 129, 163
Virginia, high Indigenous mortality rates in 33
Virginia Company 33
Vitoria, Francisco de 36
Vizenor, Gerald 6, 100, 101, 144, 164

Wampanoag 71, 99–100
"War Hawks" 52–3
War of 1812 53
Warren, Elizabeth 161–2
Washington Conference on Holocaust-Era Assets (1998) 126–7
Washington Supreme Court 76
Washington Territory 75, 76
Weller, Governor John 28
West, J. Richard 81
West Germany 117, 118, 158
Wiesel, Elie *86*
Williams, Paul 116
Winnipeg 129, 163
Wolfe, Patrick 34
World War II 48, 116–17
memorialized in Germany 117–19
Soviet occupation compared to Nazism 67
Wounded Knee Creek 27
Wounded Knee Massacre 26, 27–8, 70, 75, 99–100, 132–3
public commemoration of 70–1
white written records about 99
Wounded Knee Survivors' Association 133, 144–6

Yad Vashem 139
Yellow Horse Brave Heart, Maria 98, 99
Yellow Old Woman, Herman 150
Yiddish-American writers 90–1, 93–4
Yiddish language 91–2, 93–4
Young, James E. 6, 90, 154
Yuki 28
Yup'ik 147

Ziibiwing Center of Anishinabe Culture and Lifeways 151, *151*

www.ingramcontent.com/pod-product-compliance
Lightning Source LLC
Chambersburg PA
CBHW071841270326
41929CB00013B/2067